Market Orientalism

Syracuse Studies in Geography
Don Mitchell, Tom Perreault, and Robert Wilson, *Series Advisers*

Syracuse University Press is pleased to announce the launch of our new series, Syracuse Studies in Geography, with the publication of Benjamin Smith's book *Market Orientalism: Cultural Economy and the Arab Gulf States*. This series is distinguished by works in historical geography, political economy, and environmental geography but also publishes theoretically informed books across the breadth of the discipline.

Market Orientalism

Cultural Economy and the Arab Gulf States

Benjamin Smith

Syracuse University Press

First Paperback Edition 2017

17   18   19   20   21   22   6   5   4   3   2   1

∞ The paper used in this publication meets the minimum requirements
of the American National Standard for Information Sciences—Permanence
of Paper for Printed Library Materials, ANSI Z39.48-1992.

For a listing of books published and distributed by Syracuse University Press,
visit www.SyracuseUniversityPress.syr.edu.

ISBN: 978-0-8156-3522-2 (paperback)   978-0-8156-3410-2 (hardcover)   978-0-8156-5344-8 (e-book)

Library of Congress has cataloged the hardcover edition as follows:

Smith, Benjamin (Associate professor)
    Market orientalism : cultural economy and the Arab Gulf States /
Benjamin Smith. — First edition.
        pages cm. — (Syracuse studies in geography)
    Includes bibliographical references and index.
    ISBN 978-0-8156-3410-2 (cloth : alk. paper) — ISBN 978-0-8156-5344-8 (e-book)
1. United Arab Emirates—Economic conditions.   2. Cultural property—United
Arab Emirates.   I. Title.
    HC415.36.S65 2015
    330.95357—dc23   2015015921

Manufactured in the United States of America

Contents

Illustrations

Acknowledgments

The research that led to this book began a decade ago while I was a graduate student in the Department of Geography at the University of Kentucky. It was a wonderful place of learning, with tremendous graduate student colleagues and faculty—in particular my adviser, Rich Schein, and my committee members, Anna Secor, Matt Zook, and Ellen Furlough. I thank both the department and the University Graduate School for the financial support they provided me over the years. To all my friends in Lexington: thank you for being kind, thoughtful, and fun. While at the University of Kentucky in 2005, I was awarded a Doctoral Dissertation Research Improvement Award from the National Science Foundation, which greatly lengthened the time I was able to stay in the Persian Gulf, making this work possible. I hope future generations of graduate students will be provided with the same generous opportunity.

I also thank the College of Arts and Sciences, the Department of International Relations, and the Department of Global and Sociocultural Studies at Florida International University for all the support they have provided me over the years, especially the time and space given to assistant professors to write. In particular, I thank department chairs John Clark, Rick Tardanico, and Rod Neumann; the director of the School of International and Public Affairs, John Stack; and the director of the Middle East Studies Center, Mohiaddin Mesbahi. My colleagues and students have made my job a great pleasure.

I am grateful to acquisitions editor Deanna McCay at Syracuse University Press for believing in the project and all the kind words and encouragement she provided throughout the process as well as to those at the press involved with the production and distribution of the book.

In particular, I thank freelance copyeditor Annie Barva for her efforts in streamlining and clarifying the text. I also thank the anonymous reviewers for their exceptionally detailed comments—they saw the best of what I wanted to do in this text and helped guide me toward achieving it. I hope to draw on their excellent examples when next called upon to review the work of others. I am also grateful to the consistently excellent *Middle East Report* for allowing me to include a revised version of my article "The Great Ports Panic of 2006," *Middle East Report*, no. 237 (2008): 40–44, as the section "Case Study: Culture and Economy in Dubai Ports World" in chapter 1.

I very much appreciate the many individuals in the Persian Gulf states—friends, colleagues, and informants—who were so generous with their time and opinions. I was initially attracted to the Gulf because of the spectacular buildings—it was my great fortunate to have subsequently met many wonderful people. I especially owe thanks to "Ivan from Macedonia," who gave more of his time, opinions, and friendship than anyone else. I am also grateful to the Dubai Chamber of Commerce Library for establishing an archive and allowing a place for people to sit, read, and write.

Finally, I thank my family for all their support and love over the years—my mother and stepfather, Mary Jo and Russ Motz, and the entire extended Fetter clan (as well as the Hudsons, Sheffields, Gaedas, Motzes)—as well as all my friends in Strasburg, Athens, Swansea, and Miami. But most of all I thank my partner, Vanessa Hudson, and our daughter, Ramona Smith, for coming to the Gulf with me and putting up with the huge amounts of time and messiness that writing this book entailed. Without Vanessa's insight, close readings, and suggested improvements for the past dozen years (starting even before my dissertation proposal and extending through the final manuscript), there never would have been a book. You both mean the world to me and are the reason I kept trying.

Market Orientalism

1

Between Hope and Chastity in the Gulf

The landscape of the Arab states of the Persian Gulf is overflowing with amazing structures ripe with metaphorical potential. Some have obvious and intended symbolic power, having been constructed with an eye toward grabbing attention. They include Dubai's Burj Khalifa, the world's tallest building, and the multiple artificial islands that dot the Gulf's shores—fashioned in shapes that include palm trees, waves, horse-shoes, and a world map. Another type of landscape, however, one that was meant to have low visibility, has nonetheless become equally symbolic of the Gulf's cultural economy: the mammoth labor camps (sometimes consisting of nothing more than repurposed cargo containers), crammed full of "bachelor" workers from other parts of Asia. Observers of many stripes, ranging from reporters and academics to many of my research informants in the Gulf, have made much of the intimate connection and contrast between the two: you cannot have the spectacular without the labor camps; you cannot have the high-living wealthy without the down-trodden poor. Or, to put it yet another way, the beauty and epicness of the great structures both obscure and naturalize the ugliness of the spaces of hard labor.

There is no doubt that the rich/poor dynamic highlighted by the con-trast between spectacular developments and labor camps is a part of the Gulf's story. It is part of many places' story. But it was another, seemingly mundane structure I personally found most telling about the situation of the Gulf: a malfunctioning billboard advertising perfume. It was situated near my apartment in Dubai, on a wide feeder street at the start of Sheikh

Zayed Road, which is that emirate's major axis of development. Its display rotated between three brands of perfume produced by local scent maker Rasasi. For me, the names of two of these brands stood out as particularly apt metaphors for the dual currents that define much of the discourse surrounding the Gulf: "Hope" and "Chastity."

The centrality of hope to the Gulf is obvious. When I saw this billboard in 2005, there was more acreage of planned construction in Dubai than built acreage, a situation that was soon repeated in Abu Dhabi and Doha. Since the oil booms of the 1970s (and even earlier in Saudi Arabia and Kuwait), the dominant Gulf model has been "if you build it, they will come," where ideas and money preceded the existence of various institutions and sectors. Indeed, if there has been one consistency about the Gulf since that first boom, it is that the construction sector has always been one of the most important nonoil sectors, literally laying the groundwork in hope for what was to come. Of course, this model makes Gulf cities very much like many previous investment-driven upstart cities, including Chicago in the nineteenth century (Cronon 1991), Las Vegas in the twentieth (Rothman 2002), and Astana (Koch 2010) in Central Asia today.

The focus of all this hopeful building has recently begun to shift, however. In the past, Gulf cities were focused primarily on rolling out a fully functional distributive infrastructure (including roads, sewers, schools, and a state bureaucracy) where previously there had been very little. The goal was to create a comfortable life for Gulf citizens (or at least for the rulers and the segments of society closest to them) while finding ways to recycle petrodollars both domestically and internationally. Even as late as the mid-1990s, my informants who worked or grew up in Dubai, which is now universally considered the excitement capital of the Gulf, described the time before the coming of the first megamall as "calm," "quiet," or even "sleepy" for the emirate.

But nowadays the focus has shifted. Gulf cities are seeking to be individually more appealing to those within and beyond their borders. They are doing so through spending some of their surplus on the building of tourist attractions, free zones, investible real estate, and media companies. The hope is that the Gulf will not just be comfortable but also increasingly visible and respected in regional and global imaginations. Although

1. and 2. Perfume billboards in Karama, Dubai, near Sheikh Zayed Road, 2005. Photographs by the author.

this shift is somewhat the story of urban development the world over since the late 1980s, such a move in the Gulf (coupled with several Gulf states' outsize ability to pay for visibility on multiple fronts) makes it a fascinating place to examine these dynamics.

However, since the arrival of the first foreign oil companies in the early twentieth century, the Arab states of the Gulf have been full of hope for another reason: the large number of people from elsewhere who come to reside in the region because it is imagined to possess opportunities unavailable to them at home. Of course, anyone's reasons for migrating are ultimately a complex mix of factors (such as having friends or family already in the Gulf or maybe wanting a change), but the majority of my foreign informants told me their version of a similar-sounding story: "I love Lebanon, but I make ten times the money here"; "In Sydney, I worked on maybe one tower a year, here I work on twenty"; or "South Africa is beautiful, but there is no future there for me." Some love the Gulf; others tolerate it for lack of other options; others (especially laborers and domestic servants) find themselves crushed; but all come hoping for something more.

The second archsymbolic current is chastity, which on the perfume billboard is given the tagline "The Essence of Purity." In many sectors of the Anglophone discourse, chastity (or at least enforced chastity) is what the often conflated combination of Saudi Arabia, Iran, the Persian Gulf, the Arab world, and the Muslim world is all about. This straw-man version of Islam comes across as a religion (and "Islamic lands" come across as a region) based on the denial of worldly things and the maintenance of purity. The common tropes include the following: Muslims cannot drink alcohol; Muslims cannot eat pork; Muslim women cannot express themselves through fashion; Muslim women cannot control their lives; Muslims dislike outsiders/infidels in their lands. In fact, I argue it is this outsider-driven perception that Muslims are overly concerned with being chaste that accounts for why in simplistic discourses of globalization Muslims largely became the refusing Other to the consumerist "West," which is a region typified by antidenial and a "prohibition to prohibit" (Virilio 2002, 25) instead of by chastity. This discourse of denial also extends to the realm of economic critique, where Gulf countries are seen as trying "foolishly" to resist the "inevitable" forces of globalization by reserving key

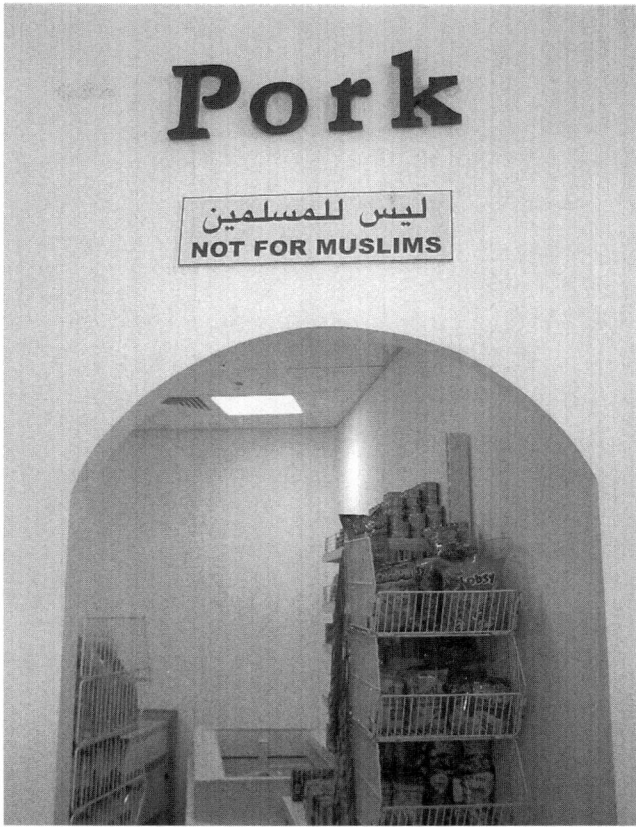

Pork

ليس للمسلمين
NOT FOR MUSLIMS

3. Sign at entrance to the pork section in a Dubai supermarket, 2005. Photograph by the author.

sectors such as land and business and migrant sponsorship for nationals while maintaining comparatively large state sectors and social services in an era of austerity.

That perceptions of chastity affect the way Gulf economies are imagined is no small thing. I contend here that there are very real international hierarchies of value that influence the way "markets," such as the Gulf states, are viewed and acted in and on. I further contend that hierarchies are not just determined by rankings of gross domestic product (GDP) per capita or potential purchasing power but also influenced by imaginations of good and bad economic practice. The Gulf states—owing to their foreigner-heavy workforces, perceived cultural differences, and general economic unorthodoxy—get scripted as Other (often inferior or strange) types of economic spaces.

In exploring these contentions, this book builds on arguments made earlier by Edward Said (1993, 1994), who popularized the critique of Orientalism (i.e., the imaginations, practices, and institutions through which "the East" was separated from "the West"). This book, however, shifts them to a more "economic" realm in order to bring them into conversation with ideas and terrains with which they have too infrequently been in contact. This maneuver allows a clearer view of how this othering of the Gulf is in part a strategy of defining "normal" economic behavior by painting a picture of where the "norm" is not (i.e., the Gulf). This distinction provides chances to produce and profit from "positional superiority" (Said 1994, 7) in cultural economic realms as well as the opportunity for non-Gulf individuals and societies to enjoy how much "better" their cultural economies are than those in the Gulf. All of the recent hopeful construction in the Gulf—the towers, malls, university branches, grass golf courses, and islands—can be seen as an effort to redress these imaginations.

For example, Dubai's rulers have attempted to convince multiple audiences from within and beyond the region (especially those hesitant to establish a presence in the Middle East) that their emirate has flown beyond a focus on denial and purity, that Dubai is not irretrievably Other. They let it be known, by hosting events and arranging tours for media members and key economic and geopolitical actors, that Dubai is tolerant of outsiders and their consumption habits, religious preferences, dress codes, and business practices. At the same time, they also position their city as one that still "speaks for" and remains in touch with the "values" of the Indian Ocean region, thus serving as its "natural" pinnacle. Alternatively, from Abu Dhabi and Doha, the discourse and urban production are less about bridge building and meeting on common ground and more about a highly civilized and "cultured" Islamic modernity with museums, solar energy, and universities in an atmosphere that is less raucous than Dubai's but still open to outside investment and skilled labor. These efforts speak more to the displacement of cultural and social cache of established Arab cities like Cairo, than to Dubai's attempt seemingly to replicate and surpass Singapore or some other trade center. Although both Dubai's entrepôt and Doha and Abu Dhabi's shining capital strategies are positive visions, each wrestles with multiple groups' imaginations of a supposedly chaste, backward, and slow-moving region.

Thus, it was a golden metaphorical moment to have a billboard that rotated between Hope and Chastity. Even better was the night that the billboard got stuck halfway between changing from "Hope" to "Chastity" and thus read "Hopetity." That is the Gulf: caught between hopes for future ascendance and perceptions of a region scripted as being primarily interested in saying "no" to new possibilities. Although the more common metaphorical contrast of high living and low-down dirty labor highlighted at the beginning of this introduction certainly speaks to an important facet of life in the Gulf, even the small Ohio town in which I grew up has both trailer parks with migrant workers and mansions (although on a far, far more limited scale). That is a common, albeit important, dynamic present throughout the world. However, only in the Gulf can Hopetity's broad impact on cultural economic imaginaries be seen so clearly.

Refocusing Cultural Economy through the Gulf

The Arab states of the Persian Gulf—Saudi Arabia, Kuwait, Bahrain, Qatar, the United Arab Emirates (UAE), and Oman—are widely considered winners in the global economy in terms of absolute wealth, with per capita GDP ranging from middle income to among the world's highest.[1] They have had a much harder time, however, becoming accepted in the

---

1. This book does not discuss Iraq and Iran (which share the Persian Gulf with the states listed) or Yemen (which shares the Arabian Peninsula with them) at great length, for a number of reasons. None of the three is in the Gulf Cooperation Council, which links the Gulf states institutionally. Iran is a much larger and older polity that has been a geopolitical rival of much of the rest of the Gulf for the past three decades. Iraq, although having roughly the same population as Saudi Arabia, has been republican for much of its brief history and torn apart by war. It also invaded Kuwait. Yemen is remote from the Persian Gulf and much poorer than any council state. All three are part of the story of the Gulf states, of course, but they are not the main focus here.

equally fractured and hierarchal realm of cultural economies, where practices, signs, and perceptions of propriety help to shape configurations of power. This book argues that the Gulf's widely covered, spectacular postmillennial development has been (at least in part) about addressing the gap between wealth and acceptance not just by the Global North, but also by other Arab and developing world states and their people. The comparatively wealthy Gulf's continuing awkward position in the realm of cultural economy allows us to see that there is more to competing—and succeeding—than just being at the center of flows of money. It requires grappling with and playing against ideas of good and bad (often arranged along classic lines of difference and utilizing well-worn justifications) and the enjoyment that comes to those who consider themselves to be performing economic culture correctly.

Besides trying to think about the Gulf differently, this book also aims to reinvigorate and refocus the study of cultural economies more broadly. But what are cultural economies? By *economies*, following on J. K. Gibson-Graham's (2006, 60) conceptualization, I refer to practices and imaginations around the production, transaction, distribution, appropriation, and consumption of goods, services, labor, and livelihoods. By *culture*, I mean both the powerful "idea of culture" that Don Mitchell (1995) argues does the work of division *and* (not following Mitchell) all those processes and practices purged as peripheral from purified categories such as politics, economy, and environment. Thus, by using the term *cultural economies*, I mean to highlight the notion that all that we call "economic" is always already inflected by that which we call "cultural"—a fact that both standard political economy and mainstream economics too often ignore.

In using this term, I am also referring to the "cultural economy" literature, which analyzes the intersection I have just described. Although the universe of what is considered either "cultural" or "economic" has been greatly expanded by this body of work, this literature is also in need of refocusing. Cultural economy as a field of study has developed into an umbrella of sorts as opposed to a unified perspective (C. Gibson 2012), under which there is variously a focus on cultural industries, calculation, clusters, practices, cultures of management, consumption, and affective embodiment. To deduce this, one need look no further than the fact that this literature is dominated by edited collections instead of by unified monographs (e.g., see Amin and Thrift 2004; Anheier and Isar 2008; du Gay and Pryke 2002; Pratt and Jeffcutt 2009). Even the excellent *Journal of Culture Economy* has little conceptual unity from issue to issue. In fact, as Trevor Barnes and Eric Sheppard (2010) argue, a similar lack of cohesion haunts economic geography in general, leaving the subdiscipline divided into a series of territorialized conversations that do not overlap and are often dismissive of one another.

This trend toward divergence represents a missed opportunity. There is so much more to explore at the intersection of culture and economy beyond the pigeon-holing of scholarship into the array of fields I have listed. There should instead be an emphasis not only on consolidating gains made in the various fields but also on adding to and borrowing from other contemporary literatures such as critical geopolitics, psychoanalysis, critical development studies, diverse economies, and postcolonial studies. Past scholarship, such as that produced by the Frankfurt School and early cultural studies, which had similar goals to cultural economy, does not need to fade into the background. In fact, as Joanne Entwistle and Don Slater put it, much cultural economy scholarship "does not do 'cultural economy' symmetrically: it has had a lot to say about economy but much less to say about culture" (2013, 162). Furthermore, we must acknowledge that cultural economies exist outside of the major Euro-American cities where much of the current research is situated.

The result of this book's attempt to read sympathetically across literatures (as opposed to adhering faithfully to one) is the development of an approach I term "market Orientalism." This approach shows the ways in which "emerging" markets are truly imaginative geographies in Edward Said's (1994) sense of the word: practiced spaces that are ranked, structured, theorized, assembled, and sometimes punished in ways inseparable from earlier forms of dealing with supposedly "backward" economies and peoples. Market Orientalism exists in thought, feeling, and practice and is not confined to the Global North or just to neoliberal believers. Nor is it directed only toward the Gulf. Instead, it functions anywhere questions of wealth (or lack of it) come down to cultural and economic differences between "our" place and "theirs." Whenever a new economic power rises—for example, Japan in the 1970s, China or India in the 1990s—there is often a period of alarmist discourse about the "unfair" advantages that new place seems to have. For some places, gradual acceptance comes as time passes, and the challenge that place represented becomes domesticated not as "unfair" but as inevitable and logical. But at other times the alarmist rhetoric can outlast a boom, so that alarm is often transformed into righteous condemnation. The term *market Orientalism* gives a name to, categorizes, and explains the power of the processes that produce the gap between the acknowledgment of a place's new status and the realization and incorporation or defeat of economic diversity that this new actor represents.

For example, in *Culture and Imperialism* Said points briefly to the gap between wealth and acceptance as it applied to the emergence of Japan during the 1980s:

> Although there was some prefiguring of this in the brief ascendency of Arab oil-producing states in the 1970s, Japanese international economic power was unparalleled, especially, as Miyoshi says, in being tied to an almost total absence of international cultural power. . . . Miyoshi diagnoses a new problematic for culture as a corollary to the country's staggering financial resources, an absolute disparity between the total novelty and global dominance in the economic sphere, and the impoverishing retreat and dependence on the West in cultural discourses. (1993, 330)

This statement aside, it is the culture of *imperial* as opposed to *contemporary* economies that receives most of Said's attention. As chapter 3 covers in more detail, Said demonstrates how newly emergent imperial economies marked as inferior all those associated with them, even the Europeans, despite the wealth these colonies (sometimes) generated. Indeed, scholars too numerous to name in this introduction have emphasized how the establishment of cultural hierarchy during the time of colonialism (as well as in the post–World War II development era) was necessary for the maintenance of political and economic dominance.

This is relevant today because some scholars, most notably David Harvey (2003), have argued that we live in a time of economic and military *neoimperialism,* where major powers once again seem to be willing to use military force (at least in part) to advance some of their economic interests. Recent examples include the US debacle in Iraq, Russian advances in the Ukraine, and Chinese encroachment on the South China Sea. Many have seen zero-sum neoliberal competition at work in such cases as well as the willingness to reduce Others to bare life through extralegal states of exception (Agamben 1998, 2005). Both of these dynamics are in play, of course, yet there still needs to be a wider focus on how "culture" does the work of creating positional superiority in today's economies. A focus on the broader ways economic hierarchies are struggled over is what a cultural economic perspective such as market Orientalism can provide. I spend much of my text critiquing imaginative geographies that circulate popularly beyond academia, but I also argue that otherwise incredibly useful political economy treatments should be taking more seriously the work done by these imaginative geographies of cultural economic hierarchy.

Even though market Orientalism is a generalized phenomenon, there is no better place to examine it than the Gulf. The Gulf offers one of the most vividly articulated laboratories for issues on which those who are interested in the intersection of culture and economy can focus and should be focusing. The case of the Gulf tells the story of the production of an imagined region, full of intraurban competition, that involves not only the usual projects, such as free zones and condo canyons, but also disputes regarding whether and where alcohol is allowed, what women can wear, what foreign nationalities (and their accompanying practices) are most valued, and what types of economic diversity are considered desirable. Furthermore, because of the large number of foreign residents in the Gulf, relations that are often kept distant within the global economy (between comparatively well-paid workers in the richer nations and poorly paid ones in developing-world factories and farms) become spatially proximate in the Gulf. In other words, an examination of the Gulf renders the effects of transnational wage gaps visible instead of allowing them to stay hidden away in a distant land. All of these issues are political economic in nature, for sure, but in the Gulf the cultural economic component is so foregrounded that it becomes hard to ignore.

The urgency of these issues is even greater because they are set against a backdrop where imaginative geographies developed from the time of Orientalism, concerning trust and propriety, continue to haunt the present. I argue that although the Gulf is very much a part of cultural economic trends seen elsewhere in the world (contra the ideas of Gulf "exceptionalism," so thoroughly and excellently critiqued by Robert Vitalis [2007]), nonetheless the confluence of wealth, the amplified drive to "get ahead," and the strong discourses surrounding issues of culture and economy in the Middle East render these trends much more clearly in the Gulf than perhaps in any other region on earth.

Even though this book is an intervention into theories of cultural economy via the Gulf, it also seeks to make a contribution to Middle East studies more broadly. In Middle East studies, economic and urban issues tend to take a back seat to politics, international relations, and history. The market Orientalism and cultural economy approach put forward here has the potential to provide new windows onto the region and its place in the world. And so with this approach I hope to add to the small but emerging field of critical studies of the Gulf (e.g., S. Ali 2010; Elsheshtawy 2010; Fuccaro 2009; Gardner 2010; Kamrava and Babar 2012; Kanna 2011; Mahdavi 2011; Vitalis 2007) and of the wider region's economy (e.g., Gran 1990; Elyachar 2005; Hanieh 2011; Hazbun 2008; Kamrava 2012a; T. Mitchell 1988, 2002b). But even among these excellent texts, what is needed is more sustained work that foregrounds the imaginations and practices that shape the region's economic place in the world.

The Dubai Ports World saga demonstrates the importance of such imaginations very clearly.

Case Study: Culture and Economy in Dubai Ports World

As later chapters show, one of the sustained critiques that those representing the transnational economic consensus levy against the Gulf holds that

Gulf Arabs in particular (but also Arabs in general) are not "producers" in the global economy. They are said, rather, to be consumers of government largess or silent investors who passively use their money to gain returns off the business strategies of others (see Friedman [1999] 2000). Never mind that the existence of companies such as SABIC, the huge Saudi chemical manufacturer, would call such a perspective into question. Just as Said has showed in the case of Orientalism, projecting a nuanced picture of the "lands and peoples" of the Gulf economies is not the point; rather, the consistency of the globalization discourse is what matters.

A few select quotes from the *Economist* "Survey of the Gulf" in 2002 demonstrates this dynamic well. The survey begins in a complimentary enough manner, noting that despite starting from a very low baseline, over the past fifty years, "by most measures, they [the Arab Gulf states] have done well" (Rodenbeck 2002, 2). It highlights in particular the very real and significant strides made in education, income levels, and infrastructure. This compliment is not surprising, given the survey's author, Max Rodenbeck: he grew up in Cairo and in other works he has authored shows that he possesses a more multilayered perspective on the region than the vast majority of English-language journalists. For example, in an essay that appeared in the *New York Review of Books*, Rodenbeck reviewed a series of mostly alarmist texts about Saudi Arabia published in the wake of the attacks of September 11, 2001. He noted that what such books demonstrate above all else is that Saudis "present an especially plump, slow-moving target" for too easy criticism, not just from the "West" but also from "urbane fellow Arabs [who] have long pilloried their desert cousins as a Tartuffishly hypocritical cross between Beverly Hillbillies and witch-burning Puritans" (2005). For Rodenbeck, this view leaves the actual realities of the kingdom mostly little understood.

However, even though the *Economist* survey begins by recognizing that the Gulf has had actual successes in terms of improvement of livelihoods (but also very real issues, such youth unemployment) and it was written by someone who in other venues has shown an appreciation for the specificity of the circumstances in the region, it soon commences to separate the Gulf from the cultural economic norm. It begins this process by bracketing off the Gulf's ability to make strides as a thing of the past:

> The period of nation-building is pretty much over. So, too, is the phase when oil wealth alone could make and keep the region prosperous, as well as insulate Gulf societies from the buffeting winds of globalisation. This survey will argue that the Arab states of the Gulf, with few exceptions, have been slow to gear up for the problems ahead. . . . Cradle-to-grave welfare systems will begin to come apart. With prospects for oil revenues flat for the indefinite future, diversification efforts must start now, while coffers are still fairly full. The chances of success would be much improved by an unconditional embrace of open markets and a big shift in government priorities, from planning and oil production to regulation and arbitration. (Rodenbeck 2002)

Having declared that the Gulf needs to change, the author continues: "Gulf Arabs are proud of their traditions, and have tended to cast them in stone. Resistance to change need not be a bad thing, but the inflexibility of some Gulf societies holds back their potential for growth and for general well-being." In other words, their clinging to a state-led model no longer in fashion—a paradigm that the pages of the *Economist* have long rallied against—and their failure to treat the coming age of austerity as inevitable mean that their future is threatened.

After referring to Kuwaitis as "coddled" because some of their massive oil wealth goes toward providing free electricity for national households, the final section of the survey, titled "Beyond Oil," goes on to note that the Gulf needs "diversification" away from oil and that "the prescription is one that most outside analysts agree on. Privatisation needs to make rapid headway, and not only because private firms are more efficient. It is the best way of attracting back at least some of the $700 billion that wealthy Saudis have salted away abroad." Even though this survey was written by someone who has had a lifetime of living in the wider region and who recognizes that many women and men in the Gulf are both worldly and savvy, it nonetheless falls back onto tropes about inevitable globalization and its Gulf Arab Other. Such images are reproduced by the vast majority of reporters for American and British media outlets called upon to write about the region, many of whom have spent no more than a few days in the Gulf. Even if the Gulf's success on different terms is briefly recognized, it is usually refolded into an imagination of failure.

However, by 2002, for every time these refrains about being "coddled" and "inefficient" were uttered, the proposed way forward for the Gulf as a whole was to become like Dubai. Already welcoming tourists in large numbers, Dubai's government and ruling family were also building corporate brands to compete outside Gulf markets through their sovereign wealth funds. These brands included Jumeirah Hotels, Emaar Properties, Emirates Airlines, and, most especially, Dubai Ports World (DP World), which had grown to be one of the world's largest maritime firms. Case in point, from the same *Economist* survey: "But the Gulf's most dynamic and diverse economy, and the model that its neighbors increasingly turn to, is the tiny city-state of Dubai. It is so far ahead that it threatens to vacuum up much of the Gulf's free-floating business" (Rodenbeck 2002).

I discuss this long-running phenomenon of elevating one place in the Gulf as the "good example" more fully later, but suffice it to say now that Dubai's rulers and high-ranking officials took the increased levels of attention they began to get in the 1990s and ran with it. They emphasized repeatedly in word and deed that they were on the "globalization" bandwagon. One would think that opinion leaders who were part of the Davos set (especially those from the post-2001 United States) would, like this *Economist* article, welcome Dubai's every effort to produce corporate power the way China, India, Korea, and Japan did before Dubai and to enter Thomas Friedman's "fast world" that embraces globalization. However, things are never so easy when dealing with the Gulf.

This became clear when in 2006 the government-funded DP World won a bidding war for control of the privately held British shipping firm Peninsular & Oriental (P&O). Among the several dozen port-management contracts DP World acquired in P&O's truly global portfolio were the operations at six ports in the United States: Baltimore, Miami, New Jersey, New Orleans, New York, and Philadelphia. It was this part of the acquisition that set off a firestorm in the United States and showed just how real market Orientalism is.

Although initially there were some shocked reactions to the deal in the US media, real coherent opposition emerged when major Democratic Party politicians began hammering away with a discourse centered on how "our" ports (which had been run by British P&O) were being sold to shadowy "foreign interests."[2] Indeed, what the DP World deal provided Democrats was an opportunity to turn the US-versus-them dynamic that the Bush administration had created after the attacks of September 11, 2001, against President Bush, who had green-lighted the deal. However, in the case of DP World, unlike the invasions of Iraq and Afghanistan, the victims of this polarization would not be average Afghans or Iraqis (who could be cast as innocent) but Gulf Arabs, who by virtue of their oil wealth and perceived "cultural difference" garnered far less sympathy. Even Republican Lindsey Graham (SC) was surprised by Bush's support for Dubai given the potential opening it gave the administration's critics, arguing that "it's unbelievably tone deaf politically at this point in our history. Most Americans are scratching their heads, wondering why this company from this region now" (quoted in *Wall Street Journal* 2006).

On usually opposed political blogs, there was rare agreement between the Left and Right that this purchase should be met with bombastic outrage, with DarkSyde of the popular liberal blog *Daily Kos* saying that "the average American loses nothing if a bunch of mega-wealthy oil-rich theocratic thugs have to put their money into a golf course or condos, instead of our ports" and that "this deal is a potential terrorist bonanza in many ways" (2006) and right-wing blogger Michelle Malkin pleading, "STOP THE PORT SELLOUT" (2006). Other media outlets joined in on the hysteria, often trying to insinuate Dubai's guilt by association with "Muslim terrorists" who may or may not have passed through Dubai, which of course is the Middle East's major air hub. One statement in a *New York*

---

2. The politicians referred to were most notably Senators Charles Schumer and Hillary Clinton of New York and Robert Menendez of New Jersey, whose ports would be impacted.

Sun editorial titled "Peril in Port" provides a typical example: "Entrusting information about key US ports—including, presumably, government-approved plans for securing them, to say nothing of the responsibility for controlling physical access to these facilities—to a country known to have been penetrated by terrorists is not just irresponsible. It is recklessly so" (Gaffney 2006).

By that logic, of course, considering that the hijackers who carried out the attacks of September 11, 2001, also lived in New Jersey and Florida, could companies from the United States be trusted with information about their own ports? Lest one think this suspect logic was confined to tabloids, another example comes from a *Washington Post* article based on an interview with Thomas King, former head of antiterrorism in the customs unit of the US Treasury Department:

> The official said a company the size of Dubai Ports World would be able to get hundreds of visas to relocate managers and other employees to the United States. Using appeals to Muslim solidarity or threats of violence, al-Qaeda operatives could force low-level managers to provide some of those visas to al-Qaeda sympathizers. . . . Dubai Ports World could also offer a simple conduit for wire transfers to terrorist operatives in the Middle East. Large wire transfers from individuals would quickly attract federal scrutiny, but such transfers, buried in the dozens of wire transfers a day from Dubai Ports World's operations in the United States to the Middle East would go undetected. (VandeHei and Weisman 2006)

This statement assumes a great deal. It assumes that DP World would not audit its own activity, despite the fact that much of Dubai's success was based on a culture of governance in key departments (such as the ports) that focused obsessively on self-auditing; that the US government would not audit DP World's activity; that Muslim/Arab workers are so morally weak they would compromise their jobs just because another Muslim/Arab asks them to; and that DP World is largely staffed by Arabs/Muslims. If one looked at the senior management of DP World at the time of the transaction, all the department heads (i.e., all of those in charge of operations) had names such as "Moore," "Smith," "Dalton," and "Narayan."

And it would be safe to guess that the rest of DP World's management and labor force includes a fair amount of Filipinos (prominent in both worldwide shipping and Dubai) and Indians (who by some estimations make up 50 percent of Dubai's population).

Ultimately, under all the pressure, DP World relented and agreed to sell its US operations to an American company, which turned out to be AIG Global Investment Group. AIG named its new subsidiary Ports America and gave it a logo that incorporated the US flag. Of course, this is the same AIG whose London-based Financial Products Group insured nearly every junk collateralized debt obligation created during the first decade of the 2000s and the very same AIG that became the largest recipient of post-2008 financial crisis US bailout funds. Not that Dubai's record on making oversize bets ended up much better (more on this later), but financial wholeness never entered into the debate about who should manage the ports. The only things that mattered were the imagination of cultural economic geographies of fear based on stereotypes of the nationality and ethnicity of the company in question and the enjoyment that came with rallying against it. In the United States, the Gulf Arabs are a rare group that fit easily into both Democrat and Republican polarization scripts: for Democrats, Gulf Arabs are wealthy ne'er-do-wells who put their own interests above those of average Americans; for Republicans, they are a culturally Other group that does not possess "American" values. In other words, Gulf Arabs can do work in both populist and racist imaginations, making them perhaps one of the most easily stereotyped groups in the context of the United States.

Here, Dubai's power brokers tried to do exactly what commentators said Arabs do not do often enough: participate in global corporate power. Despite their efforts, however, they were not allowed to do so owing to the conjuring of a shadowy imaginative geography. It seems, at least in this case, that Dubai proved more useful as a distant cultural economic Other than as a coequal cog in the global economy. I explain more about the particulars later, but this case of maintaining positional superiority through the separation of "their" wealth from "ours" is, in a nutshell, market Orientalism.

Methods and Impacts

Explaining the genesis of the book is the best way to explain the methods used to create it.

The concept of market Orientalism initially grew out of my doctoral research, which focused on how leaders in Dubai were using "landscape"—in all the senses geographers mean it (e.g., Cosgrove 1984; P. Lewis 1979; D. Mitchell 1996; G. Rose 1993; M. Rose 2006; Wylie 2005)—to shift Dubai's cultural and economic position. For this research on the various types of work that landscape does (B. Smith 2010, 2011) and for subsequent research on landscape that included much of the rest of the Gulf, I relied on an approach that drew data from four sources: a self-created archive of post-2000 news stories concerning the Gulf, archival research at the Dubai Chamber of Commerce Library, participant observation of landscape and economic practice in the Gulf, and semistructured interviews with a cross section of Gulf residents and visitors. In my conceptualization and organization of the data, no single source took the lead, and information found in one area, such as the archive, often led to investigations in another, such as landscape observation. I formulated the notion of market Orientalism—which produces the imaginative geographies that maintain the gap between the Gulf's wealth and the perceived poverty of its cultural economies—early in the writing process. Even though the notion of market Orientalism was not the driving force behind the landscape project, once it had a name, I increasingly came to rely on it as something that could go a long way toward explaining why those in the Gulf were building as they did. It provided a way to avoid considering the Gulf's recent construction boom solely as a local iteration of the global processes of neoliberalization (even if such processes were indeed part of the story). Since 2005, I have taken four research trips to the Gulf, totaling ten months.

But as I started to take my research about the Gulf into the world, the idea of market Orientalism—which I saw as so important to explaining what I witnessed in the region—proved to need more support. When I mentioned the gap at the heart of market Orientalism, many people familiar with the Gulf (including Gulf residents) instantly recognized it and the work it did, even if it did not have a name. However, others less familiar with the Gulf did not place much importance on the gap, sometimes dismissing it as tangential in comparison to the Gulf's geopolitical or geoeconomic role as a Muslim/Arab producer of oil. Sometimes I was told the Gulf monarchies were so unusual in terms of global processes that what happens there is of little import.

I understand where this dismissal came from: the Gulf states are mostly small and tend to be understood through relatively few lenses— usually oil, security, religion, and gender and class oppression—indicating that there are very entrenched but not extensively developed imaginations surrounding them. Thus, there was work to be done. It was not enough on my part to simply declare that market Orientalism existed beyond my contemporary research and to expect other people somehow to automatically sense its potential broader significance and long duration. Thus, this book represents a shift in my own research from examining the work that landscape does to documenting and analyzing the contours and effects of market Orientalism.

As I approached this shift, I was confronted by something at which my time in the archives had hinted—namely, that no matter from which decade the text I examined was, it was likely that many of the features of market Orientalism as I outline it in this book were at least partially present, either being parroted or argued against (except perhaps in the most banal of reports). It became obvious that the formation of market Orientalism predated my own and many of my informants' lifetimes. Thus, dealing with market Orientalism and the work it did would require tracing it back through time. I also realized that what I was dealing with was less the world itself—in this case, tangible, visible, lived-in Gulf landscapes—and more, to use Raymond Williams's (1977) concept, the "structures of feeling" surrounding cultural economic activity. I came to understand that it was in these structures of feeling that the imaginative geography of the Gulf played a startlingly large role.

Being a geographer, I quickly determined that market Orientalism was productive of imaginative geographies, but it took more reflection to parse exactly what its impacts were. For example, what type of work did it do? How did it accomplish this work? Who benefited and why? There is obviously a strong discourse of culture and economy out there in the world, one that circulates around a few key nodes (such as New York and London), institutions (such as the World Bank and the International Monetary Fund [IMF]), and publications (such as the *Wall Street Journal* and the *Economist*). It is easy enough to argue that what such actors say about the Gulf carries weight and that any deviation will be noted.

But market Orientalism is also something more than the bureaucratic and discursive sanctioning of Others' practices. It is not just *what* is being said about Gulf economies and why they are considered abnormal; it is also *how* everything is being said that is especially striking. Immense feelings of pleasure and righteousness seem to come from denouncing the Gulf and its people (who are more diverse than usually acknowledged, with histories and ties spanning not only the Middle East but also the entirety of the wider Indian Ocean region) as well as from making insinuations of the speaker's absolute separation from "them." Given all the emotions that circulate around the production of market Orientalism, happening upon the notion of "structures of feeling," which Williams developed in *Marxism and Literature* (1977), was a key moment for me in determining just where and how market Orientalism does its work.

According to Williams (1977), he developed the term *structure of feeling* as an alternative to *worldview* or *prevailing ideology* (or *discourse*, as used by most authors writing slightly after Williams coined his phrase) because of how explicit, laid-out, and fixed those terms seemed to him. For Williams, what others would call a "spirit of an age" is often as much felt and practical as already reflecting a dominant ideology. Shifts in the structure of feeling often first appear in the realm of "style" and aesthetics or in forms and conventions. It is in such arenas that new directions are articulated before some aspects of them are calcified into institutions and routines. As Williams puts it, "[Structure of feeling] is a kind of feeling and thinking which is indeed social and material, but each in an embryonic phase before it can become fully articulate and defined exchange. Its relations with the already articulate and defined are then exceptionally complex" (1977, 131). Thus, it has affinity with later concepts such as Pierre Bourdieu's (1984) "popular aesthetics" and Andrew Sayer's (2005)

"lay normativity"—both of which focus on the more ad hoc and practical imaginations that guide everyday behavior and preference, which in
turn are often determined by notions of right and wrong. Like Williams's
structures of feeling, these imaginations are not explicitly theorized by the
actors who rely on them.

As for why Williams chose this particular phrase over other available
options, he admits:

> The term is difficult, but "feeling" is chosen to emphasize a distinc-
> tion from more formal concepts of "world-view" or "ideology". . . . We
> are concerned with meanings and values as they are actively lived and
> felt. . . . We are then defining these elements as a "structure": as a set,
> with specific internal relations, at once interlocking and in tension. Yet
> we are also defining a social experience which is still in process, often
> indeed not yet recognized as social but taken to be private, idiosyncratic,
> and even isolating, but which in analysis (though rarely otherwise) has
> its emergent, connecting, dominant characteristics, indeed its specific
> hierarchies. These are often more recognizable at a later stage, when
> they have been (as often happens) formalized, classified, and in many
> cases built into institutions and formations. (1977, 132)

In some senses, Williams's "structures of feeling" are still-forming precur-
sors to what Luc Boltanski and Laurent Thévenot (2006) term "orders
of worth," which are interwoven sets of routinized justifications that are
called upon in order to value some things, practices, and people more
than others.

In addition, Williams also offers a methodology for trying to discern
these "cultural hypotheses." Although he considers structures of feeling to always be in the process of being remade, he asks his readers to
focus on "evidence of forms and conventions (semantic figures—which,
in art and literature, are often among the very first indications that such
a new structure is forming)" and to make "attempts to understand such
elements and their connections in a generation or a period, and needing always to be returned, interactively, to such evidence" (1977, 133).
In other words, he suggests a very typical method for those engaged in
analysis of representations or discourse, but now with an emphasis on

feeling, which sometimes gets missed. I also find it key throughout this book to look at what these structures of feeling actually make people do. Plus, I would emphasize looking for how structures of feeling not only form connections during a "period" of time but also attach themselves to particular geographies.

The term *structures of feeling* directly speaks to the terrain on which market Orientalism does much of its work. Although market Orientalism definitely produces imaginative geographies of cultural economic malfunction, it does not completely support any particular ideology and cannot be reduced to simply being a tool of one or another view. It helps pave the way for neoliberal processes by arguing that Gulf Arabs lack entrepreneurialism and are in need of reform, but that is hardly the only kind of work it does. Here I echo an idea put forward by Peter Gran concerning the inability to reduce Orientalism to the status of mere side effect of capitalism: "Capitalism has contributed to all modern thought, but capitalism, as Gramsci showed in his study of Italian fascism, can coexist with a number of political and cultural structures, some of which are not Orientalist. It therefore seems that Orientalism in the United States and the United Kingdom is an element, and a very important one, of the hegemonic cultures rather than a product of capitalism as an economic system" (1990, 229). As chapters 4 and 5 demonstrate, market Orientalism has persisted (albeit in mutated form) and remained productive across what most commentators would posit as multiple, distinct geoeconomic eras: the post–World War II Keynesian era that ended with the 1970s oil boom, the neoliberal era that began in the 1980s and continues to persist today, as well as the transition period of the 1970s. Market Orientalism also does not fit neatly into any particular style of international relations or geopolitical worldview; Egyptians can use it just as easily as Americans (just as those in the Gulf can make use of it when, for example, discussing India's increasing success). Market Orientalism provides direction and focus to feelings of disruption by fostering positional superiority over those who challenge established cultural economic hierarchies.

To be clear: even though the terrain on which market Orientalism works entails structures of feeling, those structures certainly affect practice as well. For example, market Orientalism helps create a climate where cultural economies such as those of the Gulf are thought of as so other yet so critical that the United States (and the United Kingdom before it) *simply must* be there to defend and shape them. It creates a "natural right" to oversee and judge that is flexible, can withstand many broader changes, and can be potentially lucrative. Indeed, one of the ways Sheikh Mohammed of Dubai has promoted his business-friendliness is by letting reporters know he has utilized consulting firms such as McKinsey to help him develop his vision for Dubai—in other words, that his plans have been endorsed by the "transnational" business elite (whom he certainly had to pay a considerable sum). The UAE and Saudi Arabia are the first- and third-biggest foreign-government spenders on lobbying efforts in the United States, respectively, each spending more than $10 million a year (Sunlight Foundation 2014). This shows an obvious asymmetry in who has to pay money to whom in order to argue their case for worthiness.

Such asymmetries are created, as chapter 3 demonstrates, because market Orientalism performs the work of what Bourdieu (1984) calls "distinction," making certain groups and the constellation of practices and preferences associated with their worldview seem righteous by comparison. It is in conjuring intense personal and group feelings of betterness and rightness that market Orientalism is often at its most productive.

Despite changes in both wider and narrower milieus (and the existence of multiply located structures of feeling at any one time) the "semantic figures" against which one can define one's cultural economic self are continually found in the Gulf. The actually diverse people of the region are often left tilting at windmills because structures of feeling are decidedly and repeatedly against them.

In developing this book, I sought to capture these forms and conventions as they are related to the Gulf—which was plainly visible to me in my contemporary qualitative research—and as they emerged across the decades. Barring a massive oral-history project, the best way to approach the task was through an analysis of texts—not just for what they said happened in the Gulf but also for the tone, the emotions, and condescension surrounding imaginations of the region in them.

The point of all this is not just to say, "Oh, the Gulf is talked about unfairly." Instead, it is to see how imaginations of and feelings about the

Gulf's relationships with the rest of the world have developed certain regularities, which have turned into calls for "change" or charges of economic unorthodoxy, causing some people to act certain ways toward the Gulf and the polities and people in the Gulf to act in certain ways in response or preemption. These imaginations help consolidate "normal" cultural economic behavior by making the Gulf the definition of what lies outside of "normal."

But which texts to turn to? In the end, I leaned most heavily on the *New York Times*, the *Wall Street Journal*, the *Washington Post*, the *Financial Times*, the (London) *Times*, and the *Economist*. I supplemented these newspapers with a smaller number of academic works, regional newspapers, magazines, and popular-culture texts.

There are a number of reasons for relying most heavily on these particular US and UK newspapers. First, all of them are widely read across their respective countries, with both national and local audiences. Second, they have greater depth of coverage than other newspapers and are comparatively free from the time and space constraints imposed on broadcast media. It is much easier to glean examples from longer pieces than from shorter ones. Third, where they are published and the composition of their readership make them attractive: they are the home newspapers and magazines of the business, cultural, media, and political elite of the United States and the United Kingdom—that is, those influence makers most likely to set foreign policy or do international business. They best reflect and are most likely to affect the structures of feeling concerning the Gulf that originate from such places because someone in a position of power is likely to read or to converse with someone who reads such publications. This was especially true in the pre-Internet days. Furthermore, no cities in the United States prior to the 1990s had greater levels of international connection (or power to shape international agendas) than New York and Washington; the same can be said for London. With respect to research on the past, what was said in such places better reflected and had a chance to impact structures of feeling beyond their borders. Fourth, as I found in my research, these sources have written much more about the Gulf's cultural economies than any other English-language news sources, apart from those based in the Gulf itself. They provide large numbers of examples, which makes them invaluable for tracing changes in imaginative nuances over time.

Because I am working with largely journalistic, post–World War II texts concerning the Middle East, I have borrowed heavily from the insights Edward Said develops in *Covering Islam* (1997), in which he works with similar source material. He clarifies three perspectives that I want to highlight here because they influenced how I analyzed the writings I had collected and complemented my market Orientalism perspective: (1) the reductionism of the media, (2) lack of knowledge leading to generic explanation, and (3) the politics of strange alliance.

Regarding the reductionism of the media, in *Covering Islam* Said focuses on how a straw-man version of Islam is used to explain practically everything that happens involving people from Muslim-majority countries. In many accounts, the religion functions in a manner that geographer James Duncan (1980) would call "superorganic" in that Islam is seen to exist outside of society but yet also to hold a singular, deterministic power over the lives of all Muslims. As Said argues, starting from such a position can only lead to partial and often farcical representations that nonetheless do the work of separation. What such a stance glosses over is that "'Islam' defines a relatively small proportion of what happens in the Islamic world, which includes dozens of societies, traditions, languages and of course an infinite number of different experiences. . . . What we expect from the serious study of Western societies, with its complex theories, enormously variegated analyses of social structures, histories, cultural formations, and sophisticated languages of investigation, we should also expect of the study of Islamic societies in the West" (1997, xvi). I similarly examine the ways journalistic texts reduce the Gulf region's cultural economy to make it fit a small number of possible framings, many of them connected to notions of oil wealth and repression.

Concerning lack of knowledge, Said notes the "immediacy" with which the Middle East in general and Gulf states in particular historically "passed in the general consciousness from the status of barely acknowledged existence to the status of news" (1997, 40). This meant there was "no significant segment of the population" ready to explain this new phenomenon, which led to its being placed within a generic "world-historical" framework of good versus evil. In such a framework, these new states were treated as if they have "no history of their own, or if a history is conceded to, that history will either seem irrelevant or it will essentially replicate itself—violence, fanaticism, despotism—over and over across the centuries" (42). This vacuum of information concerning the region—which was particularly acute in the United States compared to the United Kingdom, where there was at least a reservoir of (often dubious) colonial-era knowledge—was filled by promoting a climate of vilification, crisis, and separation. This climate was sometimes advanced by those with a political axe to grind. At other times, it was advanced by authors wanting to increase their own notoriety by writing in an attention-seeking, alarmist manner. Quite often the reporter merely reflected the "conventional wisdom." Once established, however, these tropes—recycled or misplaced as they might have been—became hard to displace.

On the third point, Said notes the strange alliance that forms among those who comment on the Middle East. Indeed, the tropes of market Orientalism that I outline in chapter 3 and demonstrate in detail in chapters 4 and 5 are commonly held by those who would usually have little in common with each other, given their political or class locations or both. On this phenomenon as it relates to Islam, Said comments: "Yet there is a consensus on 'Islam' as a kind of scapegoat for everything we do not happen to like about the world's new political, social and economic patterns. For the right, Islam represents barbarism; for the left, medieval theocracy; for the center, a kind of distasteful exoticism" (1997, lv). On the cultural economic front, it is hard to imagine an area with fewer supporters than the Gulf, as the Dubai Ports World case shows.

What my research ultimately demonstrates is that the opinions expressed in these media outlets—even sixty-year-old opinions—very much parallel in tone and distanciation (if not in all the details) what many of my informants in the Gulf, contemporary reporters who cover the Gulf, academics, students, and everyday citizens based in the United States and United Kingdom continue to write and say about the Gulf. The structures of feeling that I document and analyze in the historical sources eerily resemble the spirit of what I have observed to this day. So although much of what is written in the first two-thirds of this text rarely draws directly from what I witnessed in the Gulf or from the people I met there, my time there is always in the background, guiding my analysis. My research in the Gulf convinced me that market Orientalism is real, showed me its dimensions, and provided insight on what would prove most fruitful to investigate in the media archives. Even if the analysis of texts is the most prevalent method followed in this book, all of the research methods I used were equally important to my conceptualization of market Orientalism.

Plan of the Book

Each of the subsequent chapters approaches the task of understanding the effects of market Orientalism in a slightly different manner. Chapter 2 lays out the book's theoretical contribution, which, as stated earlier in this chapter, is to push ideas of cultural economy to new objects and into new zones of study while bringing them into conversation with potentially sympathetic literatures. Such a move allows cultural economy theories to take on some of the "bigger" economic imaginations out there in the world and to overcome the lack of cross-pollination that plagues the field. After highlighting the work of Edward Said, chapter 2 critiques the notion that there are parts of the economy that matter as objects of study and parts that do not and then reviews scholarly attempts to destabilize that binary. It also provides an overview and sympathetic critique of cultural economy literatures and sets the stage for the notion of market Orientalism.

Chapter 3 begins by examining the key terrain on which market Orientalism does its work: structures of feeling around cultural economic hierarchies. After establishing the importance of these hierarchies, the chapter presents an assortment of perspectives that are useful in analyzing them, including imaginative geographies of distinction, the perils of mimicry, and the importance of feelings of righteousness. To connect the literature to an actual case study, the chapter also critiques the use of the "rentier state" concept as the default frame through which Gulf cultural economies are imagined, showing how its primary impact has been in creating positional superiority rather than increasing knowledge about the area.

Having laid the theoretical groundwork, chapter 3 concludes by tracing the contours of the concept of market Orientalism. Building on

Said's critique of Orientalism, the chapter highlights four mechanisms through which market Orientalism shapes the imagination of emerging markets. First, it argues that assumptions about how emerging markets diverge from the global ideal are as much "cultural" as they are "economic" and thus reflect centuries of thought and practice about how to deal with others. Second, it posits that most mainstream economic imaginaries hold that the world can be transparently divided into identifiable and practicable fields of economic action, known as "regional markets" (e.g., the Gulf, Southeast Asia), which are just as leveling and reductive as the original concept of the Orient. Third, it shows that just as Arabs were often scripted in Orientalist discourses as lacking full contemporaneous modernity, so too are emerging markets castigated for their supposed lack of maturity. Finally, it explains how the imagining of emerging markets produces a field (as well as actors that sell a field) of impenetrability just as Orientalism produced the idea that the Middle East region was under a "veil" that only the most "skillful" (inevitably male) outsiders could "lift." Thus, more to the point, market Orientalism highlights the cultural assumptions about the maturity and impenetrability of emerging markets and how these assumptions affect the practice of and structures of feeling around global cultural economic hierarchies. It is my contention here that only by emphasizing this intersection between Orientalist and market imaginations can the current position of Gulf economies or of any newly wealthy places and peoples as well as actors' responses to them be understood.

Chapters 4 and 5 analyze the changing notions of economic "right and wrong" that have surrounded the Gulf city-states during the past half-century. By utilizing the critique of market Orientalism developed in chapter 3, these chapters produce a distinctly different type of historical economic geography of the Gulf, one that puts cultural economic imaginaries—and the work they do—front and center instead of in the service of politics or international relations. By drawing primarily on historical accounts, these overviews trace the reactions to and evolution of the Gulf's cultural economies across two formative stages. Chapter 4 examines the pre-1971 era, and chapter 5 covers the boom era from the 1970s to the mid-1980s. Together, they show how ideas shifted (sometimes organically, sometimes in response to more widely felt events and trends) concerning what was necessary for a Gulf state to be considered to have a "good" cultural economy. These chapters show how each era tended to produce both a hero and a villain city-state, which were used to bludgeon the other states and their policies. They also introduce a cast of characters that worked on the structure of feeling, keeping the Gulf safely Other even as the region's wealth increased—part and parcel of how these reporters were defining their own cultural economies as much as the cultural economies of those countries they visited. They also show how these imaginations were negotiated via other actors within the region, the wider Middle East, and the world.

Chapter 6 again takes up the critique of market Orientalism but this time in order to analyze one of the primary charges that leads to the imagination of the Gulf as an other type of cultural economic space: that it refuses to perform "regionality" "correctly" (a task that is seen as increasingly important for territories all over the world). In other words, it analyzes the "failure" to move forward with a more comprehensive version of the Gulf Cooperation Council. The council is currently a customs union and political forum, but it has long been touted as a potential vehicle to greatly expand integration and coordination in the military and economic realms of this collection of (mostly) small states. In other words, it is seen as a way to address accusations that the Gulf states are "naturally" unable to get along and to create the economies of scale that "normal" developed places actively seek out. After briefly reviewing the history of (and the history of the rationale for) the Gulf Cooperation Council, the chapter takes on the assumptions that underlie a drive toward integration: that what all places necessarily need is less friction, that objections to pro-regional policies by the various city-states leaders indicate stubbornness rather than astuteness of their differing situations, and that what works (or was once thought to work) for Europe should work in every postcolonial context, even a relatively prosperous one. Chapter 6 also brings to bear on the topic several authors not usually associated with the study of regional integration—such as Georges Bataille, Jean Baudrillard, and J. K. Gibson-Graham—all of whom emphasize that economies are about more than attempts to achieve ever-more efficient levels of production.

Chapter 7 focuses on how those in Gulf city-states attempt to position their polities (not always successfully) within competitive geopolitical hierarchies. Thus, this chapter meets the Gulf halfway to its most common ground of scholarly interpretation: geopolitics and international relations. It does so through the examination of three case studies: Dubai's growth as the region's "excitement" capital both before and during the post-2000 boom, Saudi alcohol tourism in Bahrain, and the awarding of the 2022 World Cup games to Qatar. What all these case studies have in common is a relation to embodied forms of geopolitics, which provides an opportunity to allow the dynamics highlighted by the market Orientalism perspective to speak to ideas developed in several strains of critical political geography, such as feminist geopolitics, popular geopolitics, and the everyday state. This chapter shows how, just as market Orientalism is a strong influence on international hierarchies of economic value, embodied cultural economic practices that matter to differently marked bodies (such as the production of comfort and consumption of alcohol) ultimately affect geopolitical hierarchies as well.

Chapter 8 focuses on the Gulf's economic diversity, highlighting the values and practices that market Orientalism often obscures or ignores. Thus, this chapter stands as an attempt to think in terms other than market Orientalism, to write positively and not just critically. In so doing, it also provides a cultural economic take on the issue that, perhaps behind only terrorism and security, has dominated studies of the Gulf: the impact of the region's large, noncitizen population. Although others have studied the impact of these foreign residents on questions of identity, belonging, and workers' rights, this chapter takes a different route. After explaining how the large communities of foreign residents feed into narratives of Gulf economic otherness, this chapter draws on ethnographic and landscape observations I conducted in Dubai to analyze how the array of cultural economic expectations present in the Gulf shape the practices of work and consumption. It highlights hotels and malls, highly functioning Gulf infrastructures, and the spatialities of Ramadan.

To conclude, chapter 9 turns to imaginations of the Gulf's future. Such predictions come in two varieties. The first posits that, whatever makes the Gulf stand out (be it internal economic inequality, the spectacular and high-end nature of much of its infrastructure, its environmental footprint or the abundance of foreign residents there) points to a dark future for all cities in the world economy (M. Davis 2005). The second, more common strain speculates about what will happen to the Gulf's unorthodox path to economic development when "the oil runs out." In other words, this strain fantasizes about how the Gulf will be made to pay for its unorthodoxy in the postoil future. In highlighting these prognostications, this chapter shows how even what has not yet happened attracts structures of feeling on which the ideas of market Orientalism play out. It also summarizes the analytical lenses developed in the earlier chapters.

Although the style and content of this book are primarily a result of my intellectual interests concerning the interaction of culture and economy, what I write here is truly a coproduction of what I read in the media and archives, what I observed in the landscape, and what my informants revealed in our conversations together. In other words, I am forever grateful for the time people in the Gulf gave me. That being said, what follows is ultimately a series of arguments about a theory of how the world works, which the Gulf and all I learned from people and practices there pointed me toward making. In the end, no one else but I bears responsibility for it.

2

Reconfiguring Cultural Economy

This book contends that something I call "market Orientalism" produces imaginative geographies that infect the structures of feeling around cultural economic activity and influences how people act and react when questions of otherness and wealth come together. Although this concept expands on the critique developed in Edward Said's book *Orientalism* (1994) and in other postcolonial writings, it also situates itself within the somewhat nebulous literature that has come to be called "cultural economy." Before I focus more specifically on market Orientalism and the Gulf, in this chapter I explain both Orientalism and cultural economy in more depth.

First, I briefly outline Edward Said's critique of Orientalism and his notion of "imaginative geographies" because of the influence these ideas had on the development of this book. The chapter then pivots to the market side of market Orientalism. I explain the pervasive and persistent notion that cultural economy has spent the past fifteen years trying to combat: that there are parts of the economy that matter as an object of analysis and parts that do not. After explaining the history of—and the history of the critique of—that notion, I focus on authors who emphasize that culture and economy are intimately connected, such as those who were part of the Frankfurt School, early cultural studies, and late-twentieth-century critical cultural geography. I demonstrate the centrality of two analytics to such studies: (1) the process variously described as obfuscation, naturalization, or reification and (2) the ability to utilize the idea of culture to authorize and sanction diversity.

Having explored the precursor influence of cultural economy, I then review the literature. In so doing, I expand on the proposition made in chapter 1: that cultural economy is a field that has the potential to provide new perspective on wider economic imaginations—especially in terms of the focus on the mechanisms through which economic activities happen—if it would be willing to explore new (often internal) connections. Finally, I examine a currently in-favor political economy trope—that we live in a time of neoimperialism—to show how that notion is primed for a cultural economy intervention. All of these literature reviews serve to set the stage for the notion of market Orientalism.

Edward Said's Critique of Orientalism

Given the title of this book, it should be unsurprising that much of my perspective on the imagination of Other spaces has its roots in Edward Said's original analysis of Orientialism.

Said argues that there are three interwoven definitions of Orientalism as it developed in the age of imperialism. The first is Orientalism as an academic tradition, whose central object of study is "the Orient": that is, the lands east of Europe that are not Europe (almost always including the Middle East, sometimes extending as far as eastern Asia). The second is Orientalism as an imaginative tradition, a "style of thought based upon an ontological and epistemological distinction between 'the Orient' and (most of the time) the 'Occident.'" It is a style whose fundamental separation between Europeans and Others acts as "a starting point for elaborate theories, epics, novels, social descriptions and political accounts concerning the Orient, its people, customs, 'mind,' destiny and so on." The third meaning is Orientalism as the "corporate institution for dealing with the Orient—dealing with it by making statements about it, authorizing views of it, describing it, by teaching it, settling it, ruling over it: in short, Orientalism as a Western style for dominating, restructuring, and having authority over the Orient" (1994, 2–3).

Furthermore, Said argues that Orientalism, like other institutionalized discourses, nurtures "imaginative geographies" (see also Gregory 1995). Said views these imaginative geographies as productive stagings that societies and institutions use to make sense of those outside of and beyond their group—and thus to make sense of themselves. These imaginative geographies often involve taking some aspect of the outsider's society or culture and comparing it to an aspect of one's own society or culture, albeit in a way that makes the Other seem derivative or inferior. In the case of the imaginative geography of Orientalism, Said argues that "the Orient is the stage on which the whole of the East is confined" (1994, 63). This confinement allowed Europe to act, as Said would say, not just as a "puppet master" but as a "creator" that named and then attempted to rule its newly staged world.

Therefore, Orientalism limits what could be said about the imagined territory of the Orient to utterances that would reinforce "positional superiority" and allow those who engage in it to act on this superiority (sometimes with force). Thus, drawing on Said's critique for inspiration, my notion of market Orientalism can be defined as a style of thought and set of practices and institutions whose purpose is to examine, imagine, and scrutinize "emerging markets" in order to reinforce the superiority of "normal" markets (usually those from the Global North) within structures of feeling. Market Orientalism is not the property of any one institution or country; instead, it is productive of imaginative geographies that are dispersed throughout the networks that help to conceptualize and shape the economies of other places. Just as what Said identifies as Orientalism had dire geopolitical consequences for the Middle East in the age of imperialism, market Orientalism has resulted in great cultural economic consequences for the Middle East (and other regions) as well. It is to these cultural economic consequences that subsequent chapters turn. However, just as Said had to go to great lengths to demonstrate why the literary and scholarly works he analyzed had political consequences, similar care needs be taken to explain why market Orientalism as it appears in text, word, and practice has had quite real cultural economic consequences.

The Economy That Matters?

Although almost everyone is willing to believe that economic activity is not purely, 100 percent rational, the argument that both the idea of culture and the practices that we deem "cultural" really, fully matter in economic realms still meets with some resistance. In the discipline of geography, this resistance can be felt even from some scholars who are otherwise unsympathetic to the tenets of orthodox economics. It is a resistance that can occasionally be active, outright dismissive of attempts to grapple with the more obviously cultural parts of economic activity. But more often than not it is passive: whereas dozens upon dozens of articles are written about certain (albeit very important) topics such as rent-gap-driven gentrification, clusters, financialization, and privatization every year across the range of geography journals, only a handful of articles mention other more interpersonal processes—such as sales, training, resource allocation, and inter- and intragroup communication, all of which ultimately sustains all of those more attention-grabbing topics.

Both active and passive resistances have the same root: the strong idea of a "real" economy of toil, sustenance, and power, which is opposed to a "fictitious" economy of flows, excess, enjoyment, and emotion. Although nearly everyone admits to some big exceptions to pure economic rationality—such as the role of racialization in the slave and colonial system and the impacts of race, gender, and class on wages and career trajectory—many still hold onto a categorical distinction between the economy that matters as an object of study and its Other. As the scholar-activists J. K. Gibson-Graham (i.e., Julie Graham and Katherine Gibson) say of negative reactions to their own and others' work on diverse economies, although they were used to those who argue that capitalism is the one and only "major force in contemporary life," what was "more destabilizing was the criticism that politically we were barking up the wrong tree—that while we might help a few people in a few communities, our interventions could not make a dent in corporate globalization. . . . Last there was judgment that looking for alternatives was escapist and irresponsible. We are not dealing with the emergencies of our time, with the 'people who are starving out there'" (2006, 2–3). Indeed, the resistance faced by scholars merely attempting to study diverse economies—resistance generated by another group of scholars who also want social change—is remarkable. It also shows that even critical scholars are not above the processes of "distinction."

So what is this powerful idea of what really matters that Gibson-Graham found themselves working against? David Harvey's book *The*

Limits to Capital (1982)—which brilliantly established the genre of spatially aware political economy—lays out the position clearly: "Capitalists behave like capitalists wherever they are. They pursue expansion of value through exploitation without regard to the social consequences. They overaccumulate capital and in the end create the conditions that lead to devaluation of individual capitals and labor power through crisis" (424). Although this passage was written thirty-three years ago, it still represents a mainstream political economy take on spatial economies to this day: the content and progress of capital formation in individual places varies (because space matters), but the goals of capitalist behavior are truly universal and are focused almost solely on maximizing value to the extreme detriment of all else. As Harvey says in the same text, "local alliances" may seem to be attached to particular places under capitalism, but they occur only because of mutually found value maximization, and they will eventually be victims of savage devaluation because there is no ultimate spatial fix to capital.

This is not to say that scholarship that shares Harvey's perspective is unvaried or unchanged with time. Indeed, Harvey himself offers a slightly more flexible version of this argument in *The New Imperialism* (2003), which focuses much more on the violence and theft involved in "accumulation by dispossession" and pays lip service to the importance of the collective force of more microeconomic decisions. In fact, in an essay in the journal *Historical Materialism*, Harvey expresses his frustration that Marx's laserlike focus on the "general laws of motion" involved in capitalist production led Marx (and perhaps, by extension, Harvey himself) to "exclude the 'accidental' and social particularities of distribution and exchange and even more so the chaotic singularities of consumption from his political economic enquiries" (2012, 10). But even as the net is beginning to be cast wider, this vision is still rooted in an ontology according to which capitalism is flexibly everywhere, its "logics" can be clearly represented, and its most obviously exploitative or damaging aspects and the struggle against them are the topics that deserve the most attention. Such a position is grounded in an ontology that seeks to fight what it considers to be *the* power that creates injustice, and, to the extent that this ontology is not aggressively exclusionary, it has obvious ethical appeal. Unfortunately, even among those who hold this ontology for all the right reasons, it can occasionally lead to a policing of ideas, dividing scholarship into what is considered worthy and what is not.

The result, to put it in the familiar political economy terms (which Harvey [2012] argues Marx inherited from bourgeois political economy), is a separation between the "base," which is important (namely, the capitalist claiming the surplus value of the laborer in industrial production or firms claiming monopoly power on some resource or practice), and the "superstructure," which is basically everything else (ranging from not important to important to the extent it reproduces the base). To be fair, it must be said that the content of the base has expanded over the years. Who would now not consider the expansion of value through finance, patents, and marketization (or large-scale mining or agribusiness) just as central to capitalism as the usurping of surplus industrial labor? However, activities where the sociocultural component is most apparent, such as advertising and marketing, which Sharron Zukin (1991) dubs "the critical infrastructure," are often still considered barely more than an opiate for the masses that supports the more important processes (such as international division of labor and realization of ground rent). Indeed, it is telling that in the *Historical Materialism* essay, Harvey describes consumption as defined by "chaotic singularities" (2012, 10), beyond law making. As economist Eiman Zein-Elabdin argues, "The possibility of a distinct postcolonial economic approach depends on transcending the superstructural concept of culture found throughout social science and humanities discourse, a conception still common despite abundant denunciations of reductionism and economism" (2011, 39).

Of course, neither this book nor Zein-Elabdin's article is the first to try to combat such a distinction. For example, Stephen Resnick and Richard Wolff argued in 1987 that the marginalization of what was considered superstructural resulted not necessarily from a commitment to combating the gravest injustices but from a commitment to misunderstanding Marx's "unproductive" labor as "unimportant" labor. As an alternative, Resnick and Wolff asked scholars to embrace the lens of overdetermination, in which nothing is reducible to another process. Even earlier, Louis Althusser similarly attempted in *For Marx* (1969) to dismiss the base/superstructure distinction by turning to Marx's contemporary, Friedrich Engels:

> Here, then are the two ends of the chain: the economy is determinant, but in the last instance, Engels is prepared to say, in the long run, the run of History. But History "asserts itself" through the multiform world of the superstructures. . . . We must carry this through to its conclusion and say that this overdetermination does not just refer to apparently unique and aberrant historical situations (Germany, for example), but is universal; the economic dialectic is never active in the pure state; in History, these instances, the superstructures, etc.—are never seen to step respectfully aside when their work is done or, when the Time comes, as his pure phenomena, to scatter before His Majesty the Economy as he strides along the royal road of the Dialectic. From the first moment to the last, the lonely hour of the "last instance" never comes. (112–13)

Despite Althusser's plea—that at any given time there are only ever impure superstructures and never the pure base of the Economy—the separation persisted. As mentioned earlier, searching the contents of journals such as *Economic Geography* and *Journal of Economic Geography* demonstrates the peripheral nature of what is considered superstructural to the subdiscipline. During the past fifteen years, the *Journal of Economic Geography* has published only around a dozen articles that deal significantly with advertising, sales, marketing, and branding. *Economic Geography* does much better, with around forty, although many of these articles deal with retail or fashion businesses, where the impact of these activities is obvious even to the skeptical. Certainly, compared to the *Journal of Cultural Economy*, neither devotes much attention to what many would consider superstructural matters.

I have seen similar reactions during my decade of presenting research on the Gulf. According to some geographers I have encountered, what is important about Dubai is this aspiring world city's role as a transport hub and its status as an outpost of the global/British financial system in the midst of a region awash in petrodollars. The goods, money, and labor that move through Dubai should be what define it and give it importance. What does not matter as much is that Dubai's rulers find it necessary to overturn (and sometimes play up) perceptions about what the Gulf is like and that they do so by trying to transform Dubai into the "fun" capital of the region by constructing shopping malls and nightclubs that tourists might like, performing stunts, and creating seemingly oversize projects to garner attention and shift their city's functioning landscape. Similarly, I have been told that it does not really make much difference that Dubai's ruler, Sheikh Mohammed, feels compelled to call himself Dubai's CEO and to use Twitter to release motivational quotations in Arabic and English while touting the emirate's efforts to improve "customer service" because at bottom he is "a dictator" and that it is only of mild interest (perhaps only to those with a focus on Middle East studies) that Dubai is a city where women can drive and non-Muslims can drink alcohol and eat pork. At best, Dubai's flash should be briefly noted only because it feeds into its "real" role as a money-seeking port of call and serves as a distraction from the exploitation of foreign labor in the quest to behave in an authoritarian, neoliberal manner. What matters, others have told me, is Dubai's involvement with the one and only capitalism and nothing else.

Yet when it comes to the Gulf, "capitalists" do not behave just like capitalists are thought to behave. That Dubai's ruling family, the al-Maktoums, felt compelled to build an attention-seeking (and costly) landscape to tell the story of fun openness and to embody corporate ideals—despite the fact that Dubai is already a city-state with no income tax and has many free zones that allow unfettered repatriation of profits—matters a great deal. It is not just trivia or a distraction from labor exploitation or the folly of eccentric despots or just another example of acultural neoliberalization.

Of course, asserting that both cultural perception and the so-called superstructural also actually matter is hardly staking a position on untrodden ground. Jean Baudrillard—in *The Mirror of Production* (1975) among other places—was one of the primary late-twentieth-century writers who addressed the unwillingness of political economy approaches to engage with the nonproductive. Within geography, the work of Paul Kingsbury (2005, 2007) and Nigel Thrift (2001, 2011) has been particularly important in highlighting this disparity, showing not only that there is a blind spot with respect to enjoyment and the supposedly "unproductive" but that enjoyment is both a profound factor in the way groups relate to one another and a major driver of cultural economic processes. Similarly, the work of Nicky Gregson and Louise Crewe (1998) on secondhand consumption and of Daniel Miller (1998) on everyday shopping has argued that the parts of the economy largely concerned with care and love do not get near the attention of buzzier subjects such as technology startups. Many economic geographers have emphasized how professional styles and class (McDowell 1997); prejudices of race, gender, and nation (Wright 2001, 2006); and tacit knowledge (Gertler 2005) matter. J. K. Gibson-Graham (1996, 2006) repeatedly note how in the practice of "economic development" the only economic process that often receives any attention is "production"—leaving other facets such as distribution and consumption completely neglected.

This list is hardly exhaustive, but it does demonstrate that many scholars have chafed at the suggestion that major processes related to the economy do not matter and as a result have sought to cast a wider net. Looking to expand imaginations concerning which parts of the economy matter is one of the goals of this book, just as it is a goal of the cultural economy literature. But before discussing cultural economy itself, I think it is important to highlight prior movements that also examined the intersection of culture and economy.

Cultural Economy's Foundations

Efforts to critically examine the intersection of culture and economy are long established and became particularly prominent around the early part of the twentieth century, coinciding with an increasing readership of Karl Marx's political economy work (such as *Grundrisse* [(1939) 1973]). In 1899, Theodor Veblen produced *Theory of the Leisure Class* ([1899] 1994), which argued that the wealthy had created a system of "pecuniary emulation" in their wake, in which the lower classes attempted to imitate the manner and consumption patterns of the strata above them lest they face shame and ridicule from peers. This system allowed the rich to exploit and maintain hierarchies not just in the realm of consumption but also in the realm of production. In 1905, Max Weber produced the foundational text of economic sociology, *The Protestant Ethic and the Spirit of*

Capitalism, which showed (contra Marx) that religion cannot be reduced to an effect of capitalism but should instead be seen as helping to shape its direction. In 1925, Marcel Mauss created one of the foundational texts for economic anthropology, *The Gift* ([1925] 1990), which argued that the significance of trade went well beyond what was widely considered to be a mere exchange of use values. Instead, exchange should be seen as the foundation of building and maintaining relationships.

All of these texts serve as the beginning of a timeline of ideas that travel forward and culminate in something called "cultural economy." However, because I am a geographer, I trace the path that most affected my discipline. Thus—drawing on Don Mitchell (2000)—my abbreviated timeline of geography's critical engagement with the intersection of culture and economy begins with the Frankfurt School in the 1930s, carries through Althusser, and continues on to cultural studies. It is the inspiration provided by cultural studies that eventually leads critical cultural geography to reexamine more seriously the intersection of culture and economy, a focus that came to be common among scholars of the cultural landscape in 1980s and 1990s. What all these approaches have in common, each coming out of or at least grappling with a Marxist legacy, is the attempt to understand the important role that culture has played in the functioning and legitimation of capitalism and of the powerful structures that surround it.

Let us begin with the Frankfurt School—which was more of a loose collection of authors with similar interests than a group of scholars resident in Frankfurt—and their critic of the "culture industry." Max Horkheimer and Theodor Adorno gave sustained attention to the term *culture industry* in their book *Dialectic of Enlightenment* ([1944] 1986). For these authors, the culture industry stood as an extension of the industrial system of mass production into the cultural realm. It was an extension that led to the rise of mass culture (associated in particular with music recordings, radio, and film) and mass politics. Together, these mass institutions sought to encompass every person by slotting him or her into slightly differentiated consumption segments. For Horkheimer and Adorno, it was almost as if the competitive (and ultimately diverse) capitalist market Marx wrote and theorized about had been supplanted. In its place rose decidedly anticompetitive "monopolies," all of which were large institutions that promoted centralized control and had the effect of squashing existing diversity. Thus, even in the 1930s and 1940s authors began to question the unchanging nature of capitalist imperatives. This emphasis on the leveling, commoditizing, and prelocating of all difference shaded most contemporaneous and future writing produced by members of the Frankfurt School (e.g., Benjamin [1936] 1988; Marcuse 1955, 1964).

The culture industry's tendency to require little differentiation and to co-opt anything that is slightly but not too new allowed Horkheimer and Adorno to hit on one of the major dynamics of what is considered proper in cultural economies—incremental originality. Here is how they described it:

> It is still possible to make one's way in entertainment, if one is not too obstinate about one's own concerns, and proves appropriately pliable. Anyone who resists can only survive by fitting in. Once his particular brand of deviation from the norm has been noted by the industry, he belongs to it as does the land-reformer to capitalism. Realistic dissidence is the trademark of anyone who has a new idea in business. . . . The more immeasurable the gap between chorus and leaders, the more certainly there is room at the top for everybody who demonstrates his superiority by well-planned originality. ([1944] 1986, 7)

For Horkheimer and Adorno, what is most successful is that which is just slightly "off" what is recognizable, that which provides a little—not a lot—of novelty. I turn to this tolerance for only a small amount of novelty in the next chapter and throughout the text.

However, although Horkheimer and Adorno saw the culture industry and its deployment of culture as control as part of this now mass capitalism, they still considered it to be subordinate to other more "classically" industrial sectors, such as "steel, petroleum, electricity, and chemicals" ([1944] 1986, 9). For them, these industries still compose the base, and culture industries are still part of the superstructure.

Certainly, the Frankfurt School moved cultural production closer to the heart of critical studies of the economy. They also highlighted the low tolerance some sectors of the culture industry have for wider differences. They also developed the notion that by labeling something "cultural," capitalism was able to expand its penetration into everyday life. But they were not quite ready to abandon the designated separation between what was defined as the more and less important sectors of the economy; in Horkheimer and Adorno's work, culture is still subservient to the "real economy" and reflects its interests.

That is just one of several aspects of the Frankfurt School's work with which later scholars would take issue. Another is the insistence that the culture industry seems to work by perpetuating "mass deception," basically stupefying people through constant enjoinders to consume—thus leaving very little possibility for agency or resistance. Furthermore, in attacking mass culture, Adorno in particular did so out of a sort of romantic and elitist attachment to old "high" or avant-garde culture. For example, in one essay he referred to fans of jazz as members of "the mass of the retarded who differentiate themselves by pseudo activity," whose "ecstasies" are "stylized like the ecstasies savages go into in beating the war drums" and who dance like "the reflexes of mutilated animals." In sum, he found jazz to be an "ecstatic ritual [that] betrays itself as pseudoactivity by the moment of mimicry" ([1947] 2006, 281).

We will get to charges of mimicry and how it functions in systems of distinction in the next chapter, but for now it is important to note the extremely racist and classist overtones in Adorno's writings (that go with the masculinist overtones found throughout his work). They are especially glaring because in other works Adorno decried the use of characters only as foils. As authors such as Gayatri Chakravorty Spivak (1996), Edward Said (1993), and Peter Gran (1990) have noted, so ingrained was the naturalness of imperialism to Western intellectual activity of the period in which Adorno was writing that it was put to "productive" use even in the most critical of theories.

All of this—the lack of agency; the lack of awareness of the value of Others' culture (and how they utilize it to produce distinction); the notion that culture is, in the end, just the servant of more important spheres; that argument that culture dupes by pacifying—will come under attack from subsequent movements.

Already during the latter stages of the Frankfurt School authors' careers, French theorist Louis Althusser was beginning to exert more influence on the direction of the study of culture and economy. Taking a tone more in line with Antonio Gramsci's idea of hegemony (that those who govern rule with the consent of the governed), Althusser argued that the institutions that create culture (e.g., media and schools, which he called "ideological state apparatuses") were not entirely under the thumb of other types of capitalism, even if they did make the ruled accept the conditions of their subjectiveness. These institutions also did not directly represent class interests except in an unconscious way. As already noted, Althusser also rejected the base/superstructure distinction in favor of the notion of overdetermination—that is, that most phenomenon are not reducible to a single causality.

Althusser's ideas become centrally important to the cultural studies movement, which was initially associated with the Center for Contemporary Cultural Studies at the University of Birmingham and with the journal *New Left Review*. In cultural studies as contrasted to the Frankfurt School, there was a de-emphasis on high culture and more of a focus on the impact and importance of popular cultures. But as with the Frankfurt School, cultural studies scholars such as Stuart Hall and Raymond Williams always had one foot in earlier theories of Marxism, much more so than later writers did. In particular, Williams was interested in how culture worked to shape class, politics, places, and ways of life, an interest perhaps best typified in his work *The Country and the City* (1973). Similarly, in the late 1970s Hall led the charge against Thatcher-era representations of the poor and racialized, which had been used to divide working people to achieve Conservative electoral success in the United Kingdom. Consumption—the end of the chain of production that theorists had long neglected—was also an early focus of authors such as Angela McRobbie and Celia Lury.

However, as time passed, the issues of class and economy began to take a back seat in cultural studies. Instead of just class power, power in all forms became central to the movement (as it should have been): how power was enacted on and resisted by racial and ethnic minorities, by women, by all manners of sexualities, and even by consumers themselves, who were now seen as having the power to make their own meanings (Fiske 1992).

When geography began reacting to cultural studies in the 1980s, one of the arenas in which the analysis of cultural power meeting economic power gained the most traction was the study of landscapes. One of the best summaries of this mixing of the production of space, culture, and economy can be found in Don Mitchell's book *Cultural Geography: A Critical Introduction* (2000). Mitchell spends much of the book looking at how power intersects both "the idea of culture" and the production of difference through space in the realms of race, class, sexuality, and gender.

The "idea of culture"—as opposed to culture itself, which Mitchell sees as a chaotic concept that eventually comes to mean everything and thus nothing (see also D. Mitchell 1995)—is central to Mitchell's work. As he sees it, the idea of culture has "more and more become a tool of surplus value extraction . . . a means of wringing profit out of new markets at home and abroad, and a means for channeling dissent in productive directions" (2000, 78; see also D. Mitchell 1995). Not only that, but the idea of culture naturalizes the notion that there are deep and meaningful differences between groups of people, which can be utilized in the creation of differential power relations. For Mitchell, the idea of culture becomes powerful through the operation of Sharon Zukin's "critical infrastructure," which, as Zukin explains, consists of "those who communicate information about new consumer goods and services" as well as the influential urban spaces they have claimed as their own" (1991, 202). Certainly, for cultures of international business, the reporters I focus on in chapters 4 and 5 do such work.

Besides being able to attach values to what is properly cultural and what is not, the "idea of culture" (drawing on the Marxist conception of the commodity fetish) can variously hide, naturalize, normalize, or reify the workings of power. When the value-added label *cultural* (or *pleasing* or *enjoyable*) is attached to something, the object or practice is seemingly taken out of the realm of what can be questioned. Other geographers, such as Gillian Rose (1993), Dennis Cosgrove (1984), Amy Mills (2006), Richard Schein (1997), and Stephen Daniels (1989), have looked at this phenomenon with respect to landscapes. They note that landscapes naturalize through their status both as an object of use and space of practice (for example, a mall that hides its inner labor and machinery of segregation in a banally likable but intensely designed package) and as an image (for example, in landscape paintings, which might centrally feature only the lord and his dog amid the landscape, thus erasing the work of laborers and his own family's social reproduction). Landscape, like culture in general, makes distinctions in society look unworked and permanent.

During this era of critical cultural geography scholarship, there is a repeated emphasis on the fact that producing cultural difference is part of a power–knowledge strategy and beneficial to certain people. I utilize many of these lessons in analyzing market Orientalism: if the Gulf is imagined as Other through market Orientalism, then the latter concept must be doing work for someone. Indeed, market Orientalism creates opportunities to advise the Gulf, translate the Gulf, and design specialty marketing for the Gulf while scaring off some competitors with tales of the Gulf's badness. Market Orientalism can also be seen to naturalize or reify many things, such as the US military-corporate presence and the idea that capitalism and "free" markets should be the only moral economy for the Gulf.

Despites its path-breaking nature, such work in critical cultural geography had the occasional tendency to represent the powerful as too intentional, almost too ultracompetent. As the Iraq War demonstrated, the powerful are quite capable of performing a weak, confused, co-optable, and ignorable reification (which can nonetheless be devastating in its consequences). The powerful also act out of loyalty, righteousness, habit, and just plain meanness or stupidity in ways that do not advance any obvious larger material agenda—other than to make themselves feel powerful. They also quite often succeed in spite of themselves or owing to blind luck. Thus, although market Orientalism works to reproduce material positional superiority, it also works to produce positional superiority in structures of feeling, where the primary rewards are psychic.

These studies thus have a unifying focus on the workings of power and on how culture obscures, categorizes, reifies, and numbs people. Many of the authors writing since the era of the Frankfurt School also believe that the idea of culture does not take a back seat to economy and that most workings of economic power are at least somewhat overdetermined. With this background in mind, we can turn to cultural economy.

Cultural Economies and Their Neighborhoods

So far this chapter has highlighted the persistent idea that there are parts of the economy that matter as objects of study and parts that do not. It has also examined earlier attempts to more rigorously analyze the "cultural" aspects of the economy that are too often ignored. All of this sets the stage for the theory of cultural economy, which has the potential to leave behind the base/superstructure distinction and to open up the analysis of both culture and economy.

However, much of cultural economy's potential remains thwarted. In one of the more recent reviews of the subject, Chris Gibson bemoans the fact that even though work on the "cultural economy" is nearly two decades old, it remains a "mishmash of approaches" rather than a unified perspective (2012, 283). This tendency probably has to do with cultural economy's origin at the intersection of two broad ideas.

The first idea is that the economic is not divorced from other spheres of life, an idea that (as the previous section showed) has a half-century of lineage. However, the championing of the connection between culture and economy acquired greater urgency in the midst of an academy-wide "cultural turn" in the 1990s. Thus, bringing the two together once again became a rallying cry, especially within the subdiscipline of economic geography. Indeed, this is one of the differences between cultural economy and earlier cultural studies and critical cultural geography: cultural economy was initiated (mostly) by people already in economic subdisciplines such as economic geography, regional planning, and economic sociology; cultural studies and related work on landscape were initiated by people in the humanities, cultural geography, and mainline critical sociology.

The second of the broad ideas that define cultural economy is a stronger emphasis on qualitative research than in standard economic and political economic analysis, which relies more on abstract theory or masses of quantitative data or both. In addition, cultural economy work is most often situated closer to the ground in neighborhoods, cities, or regions. It also focuses as much on performance and practice as it does on spoken and written utterances. Thus, it stands as a response to both political economy work (which is often large in scope) and quantitative, model-based spatial science. *I would also argue that cultural economy has been more interested in the mechanisms that produce particular economic activities than in searching for broader patterns.* As the main promoters of the cultural economy perspective in geography, Ash Amin and Nigel Thrift, put it, cultural economy "stays close to economic trajectories and their connections as they are made and sustained, and seeks to decipher their ordering logic experimentally and pragmatically with the help of loose coalitions of metaphors, concepts, and ideas" (2007, 147). Again, this practice is in direct opposition to neoclassical economics (and even to some strains of economic geography), where potentially generalizable, quantitative research or explanation of structure is strongly preferred.

The emphasis on these two simple ideas—that culture and economy are not separate *and* that economies can be understood qualitatively— forms the heart of cultural economy's appeal because they held the promise of being able to take the study of economies in new directions. However, these broad points of emphasis also seem to be at the root of cultural economy's shortcomings. With few specifics tying the approach together, it should not be surprising that several disparate areas of scholarship emerged in and around cultural economy.

The first area involves both studies of cultural industries (Anheier and Isar 2008; Scott 2000)—such as media production, fashion, and food— and the examination of new trends in business cultures (McRobbie 2002; Boltanski and Chiapello 2005), with an eye to including both as important fields in need of analysis. This area of research sometimes has the same critical-of-capitalism edge in work by scholars such as Zukin, but not necessarily. The second area of scholarship further develops Michel Callon's science studies approach to the economy (Callon 1998b; Callon, Méadel, and Rabeharisoa 2002; Mackenzie, Muniesa, and Siu 2007). This approach involves examining the ways in which values and priorities become calculable and frameable in the laws, structures, and routines of business, financial, and market practice. It is from this particular area of scholarship that cultural economy's emphasis on the mechanisms that drive economic activity arises. Indeed, one of the most sustained attempts to bring theory that would fall under the cultural economy banner to Middle East studies drew from this subliterature: Timothy Mitchell's *Rule of Experts* (2002b), which combines Bruno Latour's emphasis on nonhuman actors with Callon's focus on how market relations are far from natural but instead produced through a series of framings to examine the long and patchy process of trying to craft a "market" and an "economy" in Egypt.

A third area of cultural economy scholarship analyzes the effects of embeddedness (Granovetter 1985) and networking to understand how they lead to growth clusters (Porter 1998) and creative neighborhoods (Vinodrai 2006) and how they enable everyday economic practice and tacit knowledge (Gertler 2005). A fourth area broadly focuses on consumption (Jackson 2000; Lury 2011; Miller 1998; Pike 2011), examining both how retailers influence consumers and how consumers enjoy and make meaningful relationships through the act of shopping. A fifth emphasis focuses on performative and "affective zones" around economic activity, which Amin and Thrift say include "passion, moral values, soft knowledge, trust and cultural metaphor" (2007, 143).

The result of the existence of several areas of focus in cultural economy is a rather fragmented perspective. Each area has a sort of champion theorist—Granovetter or Callon, for example—whose dominant ideas and the literatures around them have led to the foreclosure of other possible sources of theory, contra the spirit that initially drove the movement. Thus, literatures that have potential usefulness—such as postcolonialism, critical development studies, feminist or critical geopolitics, and diverse-economies approaches as well as perspectives developed by the likes of Pierre Bourdieu as well as Luc Boltanski, Eve Chiapello, and Laurent Thévenot—go mostly ignored. Such a meet-up is not impossible within the field itself: in Paul du Gay and Michael Pryke's (2002) edited collection on cultural economy (which contains work by several cultural studies luminaries, such as Angela McRobbie), Keith Negus's contribution stands as a positive counterexample. His chapter examines how industries can be structured by "factors such as class, gender relations, sexual codes, ethnicity, racial labels, age political allegiances, regional conflicts, family genealogy, religious affiliation and language" (2002, 118). But such efforts ultimately have proved to be the exception instead of the rule.

Further splintering the cultural economy perspective, as Chris Gibson and Lily Kong (2005) point out, is the fact that not all branches have the same agenda. Some branches, such as research on growth clusters, are fully embraced by those making urban policy, whereas others are primarily critical, and yet others are nonrepresentational, where what is rarely or barely perceptible is emphasized (see, e.g., Thrift 2005). Most of the cultural economy studies by geographers have been situated in the Global North (a trend borne out by an examination of the table of contents of most issues of the *Journal of Cultural Economy*). Relatively little work has been done to see how cultural economies matter across multiple spatial configurations (e.g., the multistate region), especially when the product is not a material good but an idea such as value or trust (for an exception, see Hall et al. 2009).

Nor has there been much effort to come up with a "wider" cultural economy theory that can travel across topics and take on broadly held imaginations. For example, Callon, probably one of the most widely cited scholars by those within the literature, provided welcome innovation to the study of market formation; however, his rather narrow focus on that topic makes his ideas somewhat harder to transpose into broader realms. Although Amin and Thrift see this absence of a wider theory as a feature, not a flaw, of this school of thought, for me it seems to limit others' ability to apply cultural economy ideas to their work. Thus, cultural economy often ends up being more of a feeling or style of scholarship than a particular lens through which to analyze the world. Again, this is not necessarily bad—without the field's initial open-endedness, many new and unexpected dimensions of cultural economic processes would have remained unnoted. However, this splitting into smaller and smaller fields with no connection in sight certainly makes conversations harder. I am all for allowing investigations to take their own trajectory into unexplored territory, but it would also be nice if there were efforts to build linkages as well.

This situation has led to a number of unnecessary disconnects. One of the biggest is that there has been little effort to read any aspect of cultural economy perspectives together with the diverse-economies perspective of J. K. Gibson-Graham (1996, 2006). By building on the insights of critical feminist theory and Stephen Resnick and Richard Wolff (1987) concerning the overdetermined nature of class and all other economic processes, Gibson-Graham have crafted a critique of the standard left critique of capitalism. More precisely, Gibson-Graham argue that authors who make capitalism seem all powerful (including those critical of it) are losing the battle before it starts. Indeed, if capitalism is both everywhere and unlimitedly flexible, what chance can any alternative stand? Gibson-Graham contend that such a stance devalues the many noncapitalist economic activities (especially those carried out by minorities, women, and the poor) as well as those activities outside the area of production that remain present and vibrant in economies all over the world. In this sense, these authors have much in common with scholars and activists who are critical of the development process and how it forecloses on the possibility of other knowledges and experiences (Escobar 1995, 2008; Ferguson 1994, 1998)—another arena that cultural economy tends to have limited overlap with, even though the potential for connection exists.

Gibson-Graham and their collaborators have also put these ideas about diverse economies into practice through qualitative, group, and participatory-oriented research, often in struggling economic communities. By emphasizing description (with a rich, new terminology for diverse economies) over analysis, Gibson-Graham have attempted to build what they call a "weak theory" of community economies to provide a counterpoint to both individual-centric theories of the economy and those theories that deem small in scope those activities considered either inconsequential or too specific to draw any wider examples from. Through such a stance, they signal a willingness to remain open to the new and previously unexamined rather than to discount ideas out of hand because they do not fit a particular theorization.

The similarities between the two movements are many. Both cultural economy and diverse economies are broadly qualitative. Both resulted from dissatisfaction with neoclassical and standard political economy takes on the economy. Both do not consider the construction of markets, the behavior of capitalists, and the contours economic space to be natural or inevitable, and each highlights the importance of processes that other perspectives have previously ignored. Both eschew "big" theory in favor of more specific interventions while utilizing authors not previously drawn upon in the study of the economy. Nor are they diametrically opposed: it is fully possible to believe much of what Gibson-Graham say about the economy being more than capitalist and much of what Amin and Thrift say about it being more than representational. Reading them together seems to make sense: these perspectives examine relatively similar processes in potentially complementary ways.

So why does the disconnect exist when there is so much common ground? I suspect three reasons for this lack of cross-pollination. The first concerns the institutional location of the scholars involved. Most people who have contributed to cultural economy perspectives are based in the United Kingdom or continental Europe, whereas Gibson-Graham and their primary collaborators have been based in the United States, Australia, and the Pacific. Second, as mentioned earlier, most cultural economy studies are extremely urban and deal with functioning parts of the global economy; diverse-economies theory, in contrast, tends to favor places that have undergone divestment, have seen large amounts of out-migration, or struggle in some way. Third, there is a critical but hopeful edge to almost all diverse-economy work; cultural economy seems instead to focus more on exploration of mechanisms.

Whatever the reasons, the cultural economy perspective could utilize much more of the "culture" in the diverse-economies perspective. Plus, the diverse-economies perspective does have a central, driving, analytical purpose that unites all those who contribute to it. Even though it favors "weak" theory, it is nonetheless highly focused on fighting ideas of an all-powerful capitalism through highlighting the diversity of economic activity. Thus, common ground exists between the two perspectives, especially around the areas of qualitative research, seeing diversity and specificity in the various processes normally just labeled "capitalism" and recognizing that emotions, security, and livelihoods matter. All of these similarities are woven into this book—especially in chapters 6 and 8, which combine aspects of both the cultural economy view and the diverse-economies view to argue against compulsory regionality and to highlight cultural economic processes that standard economic and political economic takes on the Gulf do not investigate.

So although cultural economy has opened up the process of economic analysis, further work must be done if cultural economy is to matter more. There needs to be—although this may be breaking Amin and Thrift's rules—if not "the" big theory of cultural economy, then some slightly wider theories that can travel and take on broadly influential economic discourses, practices, and feelings out there in the world. Such theories should also speak to places beyond major, developed-world, urban areas and the situations in which they are embedded.

Developing a slightly wider theory and seeing the work it does are exactly what I seek to accomplish with my critique of market Orientalism. In fact, part of this theory's potential broader connection stems from the fact that mainstream critical political economists have recently provided a new description of capitalist power that a more wide-ranging cultural economy theory can shed light on: neoimperialism.

Neoimperialism

In the wake of Operation Desert Storm in 1991, the "police action" by the North Atlantic Treaty Organization (NATO) in Bosnia, and the US response to the attacks of September 11, 2001, some scholars have proposed that the process referred to as "globalization" in the 1990s should more accurately be viewed as a new form of either empire or imperialism. The continued involvement of the United States and some allies in "security" in Mesopotamia and Afghanistan, its drone strikes in multiple countries, Russia's military presence in Ukraine, and China's attempt to extend its territorial waters in the South China Sea have only exacerbated these concerns.

The idea that we now live in a time of empire is associated in particular with the work of Michael Hardt and Antonio Negri, especially their book *Empire* (2000) but also their follow-up texts *Multitude* (2005) and *Commonwealth* (2009). In these texts, Hardt and Negri argue that new forms of sovereignty have emerged, which they deem "Empire." Empire is not to be confused with the old order of imperial nation-states. Unlike that order, Empire is unlimited. Instead of war between powers, Empire involves (nonetheless violent) policing of those who are seen not to conform to the global ideal (a process that is at once economic, political, and juridical). Just as Marx argued that capitalism secreted the proletariat whom it depended on and who could ultimately defeat it, so, too, Hardt and Negri argue that Empire creates the multitude, a singularity that is also multiple and emergent, on which Empire depends and that can generate potential waves of alternatives.

The related (but not equivalent) idea of neoimperialism had many proponents following the US invasions of Afghanistan and Iraq, but within many social science disciplines the most influential formulation was David Harvey's aforementioned book *The New Imperialism* (2003). There, Harvey details what he sees as an emergent "capitalist imperialism" that combines the "politics of state and Empire" and "the molecular processes of accumulation in space in time"—two logics that he argues can work together but are not necessarily congruent. This is because the former (political power) wants to hold territory, whereas the latter (the drive to accumulate) wants to be able to transcend boundaries to find the highest rate of profit. Although he does mention the importance of those "molecular" processes of capitalism (the sum effects of countless small-scale decisions) a few times and similarly notes that it is often easiest to thrust the devaluing effects of capitalism onto Others through a politics of racism and righteousness, these more dispersed and culturally inflected processes get far less attention in *The New Imperialism* than his presentation of an updated version of the arguments he first laid out in *Limits to Capital* (1982). In other words, in Harvey's "capitalist imperialism," Rosa Luxemburg's "stern laws of economic process" ([1913] 2003, 432, quoted in Harvey 2003, 137, 149)—which are universal in operation but diverse in implementation and outcomes—continue to have primacy, just as they did in Harvey's earlier texts. Although *The New Imperialism* bears resemblance to *Limits to Capital*, it is nonetheless an important text with genuinely new points of emphasis. For example, Harvey more richly theorizes ideas concerning primitive accumulation and accumulation by dispossession, wherein capitalism either finds existing spaces and practices currently outside its grasp into which to expand or creates "new" outsides through theft. His highlighting of Hannah Arendt's assertion that "the original sin of robbery" (Arendt 1968, 28) is constantly repeated in the course of capitalist expansion seems especially prescient, given what happened in the wake of the 2008 financial crisis. He also notes that the muscle of this capitalist imperialism amounts to police action, although often in the more narrow interests of the United States—thus making it new imperialism, not Empire. Harvey also he argues that the United States has often acted in ways that benefit the interests of "propertied" classes worldwide, most especially in all the work it has done to transform private property into a universal human right (2003, 40).

However, just as Said added a more robust vision of the importance of all sorts of not obviously political and economic productions to the study of power's functioning under imperialism, so too do these more recent formulations of Empire/imperialism leave themselves open for new interpretations of how authority works more broadly. For example, both perspectives might say much more about how the idea of culture works to create and enact power around distinctions in geoeconomic and geopolitical realms. Both might examine a larger number of narrower economic practices as well as processes that feed back into wider notions of what is properly imperial or not. *It is into this space that market Orientalism steps over the course of the next seven chapters—with the intention that analysis should not be an "either political economy or cultural economy" situation but instead a "both political economy and cultural economy" one.*

3

Market Orientalism

Chapter 1 outlined the book's broader goals and briefly introduced market Orientalism, explaining how it has produced imaginative geographies that maintain the gap between the emergent wealth and its acceptance within structures of feeling that surround cultural economic activity. Chapter 2 argued for the crucial importance of the cultural economy perspective, which is the theoretical umbrella under which my critique of market Orientalism stands. This importance arises from both the continued prejudice against scholarly work on the supposedly superstructural elements of the economy and cultural economy's ability to add new dimensions to more widely traveled political economy theories. This chapter focuses on a more complete explication of the book's key concept, market Orientalism, while highlighting its wider applicability to any case where cultural economic hierarchies are being upended (within and beyond Gulf).

But what are these cultural economic hierarchies, and how do we understand them? This chapter endeavors to answer these questions. The first section highlights the importance of the idea of hierarchy to both formal and popular imaginations of the economy. The subsequent section demonstrates how the amazing unity of hierarchical imaginations within the broader economic and business communities is maintained through three key processes: fashion, distinction, and feelings of righteousness. All of these processes produce consensus and help to determine which practices and imaginations come to be regarded as acceptably new and which ones get dismissed as being out of bounds.

The penultimate section examines what happens when consensus is challenged by those outside the normal networks of circulation. To do so, I call upon the key postcolonial concept of mimicry, which shows how (1) the desire for fidelity leads to misrecognition; (2) copies that are slightly off the norm are ridiculed and perceived as discomforting; and (3) new imaginations have the potential to upend existing formulations. The last point in particular is important because it shows that market Orientalism is not a closed circle of never-ending disdain but a process that can be moved around or even disturbed. The final section offers a fuller explanation of market Orientalism and a critique of the "rentier state" concept.

Economic Hierarchies Are Cultural Hierarchies

As has been stated numerous times, market Orientalism produces imaginative geographies of the gap between the wealth of and the acceptance experienced by emerging markets in the structures of feeling surrounding cultural economic activity. But if we take the idea of a gap as a given, that means there must also be scales of value—perhaps ad hoc and informal—that attach differing levels of relative desirability to places, people, practices, and institutions. In other words, there are hierarchies.

Indeed, if there is one thing on which those who study economies might actually agree, it is that hierarchies, comparisons, and rankings pervade the topic. Examining the economic often involves a ceaseless calculation of how actors, ranging from individual workers and departments to companies and states, are positioned and performing in comparison to their peers, both contemporary and historical. Of course, as Michel Foucault showed during the course of his career, categorizing and knowing the proper place for everything are at the center of the production of power knowledge in the economy just as much as in other spheres of life.

Although what those hierarchies can and should mean is an area for real debate, there is no doubt that tiering takes place, both explicitly and implicitly. As Michel Callon, Cécile Méadel, and Vololona Rabeharisoa put it, in the case of market positioning "economic agents devote a large share of their resources to positioning the products they design, produce, distribute or consume, in relation to others. . . . How could we describe, in practice and theory, the structures of competition within the same market, or between related markets, if relations of similitude or dissimilitude between the goods that circulate could not be established" (2002, 196). Or alternatively, as Luc Boltanski and Laurent Thévenot argue, making the world meaningful and actionable necessitates forms of "social coordination" that require "a continuous effort of comparison, agreement on common terms, and identification" (2006, 1).

When comparing polities, some choose to rank them by quantitative measures such as GDP per capita, Human Development Index scores, or even categories of world cities (devised by enumerating political, cultural, and producer service firms and institutions). Alternatively, world-systems theory imagines a planet divided into core, periphery, and semiperiphery states or areas by virtue of how they are positioned via transnational flows of trade and power. Marx, too, created a typology of historical modes of production, each dominant in different places and eras, differentiated by their notions of property, ruling classes, and dominant forms of economic production, all of which would eventually fall into capitalism and then socialism.

More to the point here, beginning in the 1980s the World Bank–associated International Finance Corporation developed a database ranking of relatively safe "emerging markets" and smaller, riskier "frontier markets" to aid investors. These compilations were based on capital-market formation, transparency, and security of investments (a product whose rights were eventually sold to Standard and Poor in 1999). The list of countries given was not equivalent to the total population of the "developing-world" states because some states were seen as so "undeveloped" that they could not even be considered "investible." This database is one of dozens of similar products that transform the Global South into an "actionable" field of investment through hierarchicalization, which, as James Sidaway and Michael Pryke argue, moves away from an imagination of coequal processes of development and back toward the "rhetoric of exploration-opportunity, [which] has closer affinities to classic colonial discourses" (2000, 195). Indeed, since Sidaway and Pryke wrote those words, increasing attention has been paid to how to turn the world's poorest individuals into profit opportunity through "more inclusive" paths of access to impermanent consumer goods (Prahalad 2005) and transform their informally titled (but often securely held) land into alienateable capital (De Soto 2000; but see also Elyachar 2005 and T. Mitchell 2007 for critiques of this emergent effort to transform the poor into consumer capitalists). Alternatively, scholars utilizing the relational economic geography and diverse-economies perspectives would argue against seeing comparative units as fixed structures and reducing people and places to these divisions alone, but these scholars also understand the power of the idea of hierarchy. Similarly, urban studies scholars increasingly have been calling into question how comparison of and modeling between cities unfold (Bunnell 2013; McFarlane 2010; Roy and Ong 2011) and what may or may not be appropriate about the desire to model in the first place. Both stances recognize the power of the practice. Thus, regardless of approach, there is a strong belief (or at least an acknowledgment of the power of the belief) that the economy produces winners and losers, the good and the bad, and that (rightly or wrongly) comparative measure is often how the separation between the two gets done.

It is my argument that the perception of these economic hierarchies is influenced in significant ways by hierarchies of cultural value. Thus, the processes that create, separate, and position cultural value impact economic value as well. To think this way takes seriously the notion that companies, persons, states, nongovernmental organizations, and other actors decide to "invest" their money, time, and lives based not just on "hard" numbers but on ideas of what they consider good and bad, intriguing or not, comforting or exotic. Not surprisingly, these ideas are strongly influenced by classical cultural axes of difference such as gender, class, race, sexuality, and nation, which are always multidirectional and emotional/affective in their impacts.

Again, the Gulf provides a vivid example of the effect that this creation of hierarchy through structures of feeling can have. If "value" in the global economy is defined purely by something such as GDP per capita, then Qatar should be considered one of the most admired countries in the world for the standard of living it provides. Although it has cachet among large numbers of people in the wider Indian Ocean region who appreciate its combination of world-class infrastructure and projection of a certain type of economic and religious values, those feelings are not shared globally. They are especially absent in the United States and Europe, where Qatar's "visible" Arab/Muslim identity—as seen in the style of national dress, architecture, and the news channel it sponsors, al-Jazeera—and the source of its wealth causes unease for some. Alternatively, if one measures importance and potential by participation in major trade flows, then should not Saudi Arabia's oil and large, young population and status as the "swing" oil producer earn it a letter in some trendy acronym for emerging economies, like BRIC (Brazil, Russia, India, China) and MINT (Mexico, Indonesia, Nigeria, Turkey)? Even though Saudi Arabia is among the world's largest oil exporters, a major consumer of media and technology products, and a much more functional state than Nigeria (which *is* included in an acronym), the policies of its extremely culturally conservative state (especially those concerning gender) leave it excluded from stories of the globalizing economy.

In fact, it is Saudi Arabia's poor cultural economic reputation that partially explains why Dubai's rulers believe it expedient to stage tennis matches on helipads and to create shaped islands. They primarily do these things not to hide or distract from some of the ugly aspects of Dubai's economy or because they are eccentric. Instead, such actions are an attempt at lighthearted intervention within structures of feeling that rarely view the Gulf favorably. Although it would be easy to dismiss Dubai's efforts as an exceptional example, having to show fidelity to consensus in order to be well placed in hierarchies is actually the norm.

Economic Consensus

Dealing with the standards of comparison that drive cultural economic hierarchies has been a challenge for the Gulf states, as it has been for all people and places that upset established economic orders. But what can be done to understand more about how this process unfolds? Lucky for us, there are many theoretical perspectives concerning the construction of consensus and the policing of the boundaries between "us" and "them"— theories that highlight processes such as fashion, distinction, justification, and moralization.

I begin here with the notion of economic consensus. To state the obvious: the field of "economics" and its more practical cousin "business" are incredibly limited discourses in terms of the variety of ideas they allow to be taken seriously at any one time. This is not to say that economics lacks debate (far from it), nor is it to claim that two competing businesses cannot adopt opposing strategies. My point is that such debates occur along surprisingly small number of quantitative and "rational/common sense/competition-driven" axes.

Thus, despite there being great diversity in the transnational economy, thousands of economics departments around the world, and even more government ministries charged with the task of improving and monitoring economies, there is widespread policy agreement centered on a few foci at any given time (Ferguson 1994; T. Mitchell 2005). This agreement is not just confined to academic and institution-based economists but also extends to what Callon and Rabeharisoa (2003) would call economists "in the wild." The latter group includes individuals working in business-media platforms with global influence (such as the *Economist*) as well as those low-level bureaucrats and managers who actually make the practical economy function every day through the establishment of routines and rules. Although import-substitution industrialization and other ideas have originated from postcolonial contexts, and the Internet is facilitating more South-to-North and South-to-South idea flow, especially in urban policy, as Timothy Mitchell (2005) points out, only a handful of major universities in the United States and the European Union tend to set a global agenda in concert with English-language journals and periodicals. This dominance is due in part to the fact that old, colonial world-order legacies still influence decisions concerning where key institutions such as the IMF and World Bank should be located, but it is also due in part to what Jamie Peck (2002) calls "fast policy transfer" through highly visible outlets.

Across all of these arenas, the way economies are practiced, written, and thought about (both in scholarly and in trade and popular business media) shows surprisingly little diversity. You could read the UAE-based magazine *Arabian Business*, the business pages of general readership newspapers such as *Gulf Daily News* or the *National*, or interview officials of the UAE Ministry of Economy and witness remarkable (but not total) similarity of opinion concerning policy and the status of the global economy to *Forbes* and the *Financial Times* and the *New York Times*. Historian Ussama Makdisi (2002) describes a similar situation in her examination of the phenomenon of Orientalism carried out by the Ottomans: although the nationality of the investigator changed and the goals were different (showing the need to modernize versus the will to dominate an Other), the practices of power knowledge were very similar whether carried out by an Ottoman or by a European Orientalist. Even among flows of expertise that do not originate from traditional power centers and are critical of their theories, agreement likewise tends to coalesce around a few select practices. Over the years, the Gulf states have originated many policies that have become part of the region's "common sense"—most concern either favored types of infrastructure projects or ways to increase citizen participation in the private-sector workforce.

Given the aesthetic unity and collective power of the structures of feeling produced by economics and business, what is said in these outlets that shape structures of feeling matters a great deal. It is on this terrain—not necessarily of policy or theory but of all of the human practice, prejudice, and feeling that surround policy and theory—that the imaginative work of market Orientalism happens. Even though powerful actors in the Gulf take economic action to satisfy citizens in a calculating way to maintain their support (and sometimes out of a sense of obligation and fairness), they also have to keep an eye on how their performances might be viewed by the wider economic-business consensus behemoth, which consists of real humans with real prejudices, some of whom are familiar with the circumstances in the Gulf and some of whom have no clue. These powerful Gulf actors, of course, do things for entirely noneconomic reasons as well (just as those whom they often try to appease do too).

Thus, the question is what on earth might appease this behemoth? Obviously, numbers are indeed important because the whole economic-business collective is underlined by neoclassicism and a devotion to accounting (not without good reason). But numbers and their effects are only ever understood in a context of what Callon (1998a) refers to as framing. Such frames are always shifting (for reasons that I outline later), so the particular numbers that matter change over time. This is by necessity, because to be useful and actionable, any frame has to be a severe reduction of the universe of all available information. In part, this explains why the variety of assumptions at any one time tends to be quite small.

However, it is important to note that for those who set or enact economic agendas, there is always something enticing about a place whose numbers can potentially lead to mammoth growth or that has a compelling "story" that resembles those of past "successes"—provided enough market structures can be put into place. In other words, there is something "beyond" the numbers that is quite appealing. Perhaps this is the answer to the appeasement question: these economic-business structures of feeling are like any other in that they are susceptible to cycles of fashion and fantasies of success as well as to the policing of boundaries through the idea of taste. That is why, if we are ever to understand the structures of feeling around cultural economic activity, we have to consider how value attaches to certain groups, ideas, and practices.

One of the ways change occurs is undoubtedly through shifting fashion—which is basically equivalent to the normal cyclical churn that occurs within any system. Although subsequent sections highlight how powerful institutions and groups can actively push, shape, and reject imaginations in pursuit of their own material and psychic benefit, it is important to note that change in value sometimes happens for change's sake. As Georg Simmel notes, "The essence of fashion consists in the fact that it should always be exercised by only a part of a given group, the great majority of whom are merely on the road to adopting it. As soon as a fashion has been universally adopted, that is, as soon as anything that was originally done only by a few has really come to be practiced by all . . . we are to no longer characterize it as fashion. Every growth of a fashion drives it to its doom" (1997, 192).

In business, economics, and development, it is crucially important to be seen to be innovative—at least within a certain set of parameters. In others words, it is necessary to be on the right side of the adoption curve for whatever paradigm is coming next—if for no other reason that experience has shown that being first mover often has its advantages. In the Gulf, changing fashion is at least partially responsible for why Kuwait and its welfare state were seen as shining models in the early 1970s and, more recently, Dubai's openness to foreign investment was considered the pinnacle of "good Gulfness." Of course, such changes in fashion can often easily enough be tied to institutional shifts and changes in wider processes. For example, welfare stateism in general came under attack during the Reagan–Thatcher era in part to benefit these leaders' antitax supporters and in part to separate the worthy from the unworthy poor for political and psychic gain.

However, such shifts cannot be reduced entirely to purposeful planning, either. Changes in value are also the result of a new generation's desire to make its mark and find its niche; in other words, they are part of a quest to distinguish the way things are done now from the ways things were done before. Doing so requires a new idea and a critique of an old idea, a shift that is reflected in changing structures of feeling. Explaining this type of change forms the heart of the arguments presented by Luc Boltanski and Laurent Thévenot in *On Justification* (2006)—namely, that any "economy of worth" will constantly be tested by critiques that both judge it on its own terms and challenge it from value systems external to it.

Scholars who have examined international or urban development easily recognize this phenomenon: aid priorities jump from one topic to another in spite of what grantees might want, just as urban best practice shifts from downtown offices and highways to speed workers in and out to downtown entertainment and then to walkable living and working and "resilience" to climate change and hazards. Each new paradigm materially critiques the previous one, despite (or possibly because of) the fact that what is new often promises nothing more than the potential for future returns.

Thus, being considered behind and hopeless sometimes only means being one year too late in implementing an idea that has no guarantee or track record of success. There is no end point, and even the strictest adherence to that which is up to date does not guarantee any advancement. Furthermore, in business and economics, changes in fashion are also driven by fickle investors (who seem to predominate over those who focus on the long term). Thus, the quest to cash-out gains and find the next big thing (and potential megareturns) tends to take precedence over more of the same, even if what is currently being done is working.

To be clear: what goes in or out a fashion almost always represents a material or symbolic gain for one group and a loss for another. There are consequences to changing fashion; it is not just a game. Thus, styles and practices are often defended and policed quite vigorously—sometimes consciously, sometimes unconsciously. It is in such realms of defense that Pierre Bourdieu's (1984) concept of "distinction" operates.

What drives Bourdieu is the attempt to understand how one comes to have interest in certain activities, how certain groupings of practices and objects (which he terms "fields") come to have accepted, circulateable value, and how these fields lead to hierarchies, both within themselves and between each other. Although the concept of social, educational, and cultural capital, as opposed to just economic capital, looms large in Bourdieu's theories, of particular interest here is the way objects or practices from seemingly unrelated fields (e.g., education, residence, food, music, sport, clothes, occupation) come together as the *constellations* of related preferences through what Bourdieu terms "habitus," which is "[out of] necessity internalized and converted into a disposition that generates meaningful practices and meaning-giving perceptions" (1984, 170). These constellations, which Bourdieu also refers to as "lifestyles," are both unconsciously formed and changeable with time. Immersion in the constellations that compose and reflect habitus serve as a method for unconsciously policing deserving insiders from undeserving outsiders based on the up-to-datedness and completeness of their information. Thus, for Bourdieu, status is not just about the cost of what you own but also about the quality of what you select to consume, the context in which it is used, and what you are able to see in it.

The problem for the Gulf—the problem for most emerging markets in general—is that its various constellations of practices rarely conform to the "ideal." This nonconformity negatively influences its hierarchical positioning. Again, if relative economic desirability were solely a result of quantitative measures such as per capita income or life expectancy (or even the percentage of women earning a college degree), much of the Gulf would be seen as performing admirably. Instead, the Gulf loses value because it lacks certain aspects of the "proper" constellation, aspects that are seemingly unrelated to traditional core economic issues. For example, because alcohol is less available in much of the Gulf than in other areas (or perhaps because of different sartorial norms), the whole region loses value as a business or leisure destination. Lacking key elements of the "proper" constellation leads to a seemingly odd situation: being seen as mostly unsuccessful even while finding some success. Emerging markets have long had to deal with this charge, which sustains imaginative geographies of positional superiority wherein *their* high GDP per capita is not the same thing as *our* high GDP per capita.

Although presented as "pragmatic" critiques of Bourdieu—in that they claim to pay attention to what is actually said as opposed to what is internalized and unconscious—the mechanisms of justification, as explained by Boltanski and Eve Chiapello (2005) as well as by Boltanski and Thévenot (2006), are far from incompatible with what Bourdieu argues in *Distinction* about the production of separation. These authors' research on justification argues that most constellations of value circulate around one of seven orders of worth (at least in the context of France)—the inspirational order (the realm of art and religion), domestic order (tradition and hierarchy), market (competition and monetary value), the civic order (collective and statist), the fame-centered order (celebrity and the approval of others), the industrial order (efficient and rational), and the projective order (connection and limited but intense interactions). In addition to having ideals of the common good, exemplars of good behavior, periods of time and places when more or less in ascendance, and tests to determine worthiness, each of these orders—which people can maneuver between and call upon selectively, depending on context—also has routinized critiques of the other orders of worth. For example, the "domestic" order critiques the "fame" order for making a spectacle of oneself; the "civic" critiques the "domestic" for supporting "old-boy networks"; the "market" critiques the "civic" for slowness of collective action; the "industrial" critiques the "market" for the wasteful allocation of resources and inflated prices associated with high-margin luxury products, and so on (see chapter 8 of Boltanski and Thévenot 2006 for an exhaustive description of how each order of worth critiques each of the other orders). *In other words, these orders of worth contain a deep well of charges to level against those policies and people from which you wish to distinguish yourself.* Reading the work of Boltanski, Chiapello, and Thévenot after I had already conducted my analysis of historical reports concerning the Gulf (which are presented in chapters 4 and 5), I was amazed how many of the patterns of critique I saw in the articles I analyzed were laid out in *On Justification* (Boltanski and Thévenot 2006) and *The New Spirit of Capitalism* (Boltanski and Chiapello 2005). Although I am not a fan of their downplaying of unconscious action and lack of attention to how "tests" play out between very different societies, I nonetheless think that Boltanski, Chiapello, and Thévenot's framework can shed light on the toolbox used to distinguish one's own constellation of practices from those of others—the very type of distinction that is at the heart of market Orientalism.

That being said, Bourdieu emphasizes one important point that Boltanski, Chiapello, and Thévenot do not: that differing notions of proper practice and taste can be quite visceral (and something that rarely leads to compromise and consensus, as the "pragmatic" authors would have it). According to Bourdieu, "tastes (i.e. manifested preferences) are the practical affirmation of an inevitable difference. . . . In matters of taste, more than anywhere else, all determination is negation, and tastes are perhaps first and foremost distastes, disgust provoked by horror or visceral intolerance ('sick-making') of the tastes of others. . . . [This] amounts to rejecting others as unnatural and therefore vicious. Aesthetic intolerance can be terribly violent" (1984, 49). Thus, an emotional payoff, not just the satisfaction of passing a test of worth, is at stake in these processes. To build on this point, I would also add that there is pleasure—*righteousness* is truly the best word for it—attached to feeling that you are on the side that is correct, just, and proper and that some other side is wrong. Righteousness is a powerful force within structures of feeling: it can cause people to act against their seeming material interests, lead them to forgo negotiation, and push them past the limits of their particular sense of decency if they are convinced they are truly in the right.

Perhaps there is no finer examination of the pleasures of moralizing righteousness than Roland Barthes's book *Mythologies* (1972). For Barthes, no genre portrays the operations of righteousness more clearly than professional wrestling. As he puts it, "But what wrestling is above all meant to portray is a purely moral concept: that of justice. The idea of 'paying' is essential to wrestling, and the crowd's 'Give it to him' means above all else 'Make him pay'" (21), even if it means bending the rules. Thus, professional wrestling is a form of popular, ongoing drama—much like a soap opera or a Punch and Judy show—that brings people back week after week to what is an endless repetition of the perpetration of injustice being met with "deserved punishment." Although the particular configuration of stylized characters changes over time—this year the "bastard" might be a Russian, the next year a Turk—the roles and script of the drama remain unchanged. Thus, it is not always fashion or lack of a full constellation of practices that drives the condemnation of Others—sometimes someone just needs to be put in his or her place or made to pay.

Barthes shows that such a process is not just confined to professional wrestling: in the law, he notes, there is a long tradition of prescripting the fate of certain Others who are marked by poverty, lack of education, or race. For Barthes, the categories of the law "are none other than those of classical comedy or treatises of graphology: boastful, irascible, selfish, cunning, lecherous, harsh, man exists in their [the legal establishment's] eyes only through the 'character traits' which label him for society as the object of a more or less easy absorption, the subject of a more or less respectful submission" (1972, 45). Again, as in wrestling, here we see the reduction of life and other beings to a morality play full of not well-rounded characters who deserve punishment and engender feelings of superiority. As in fashion, these plays of righteousness involve a never-ending churn: the particulars change (new defendants, new ethnic bad-guy wrestlers, new transgressions), but the script remains (mostly) the same and is consistently productive of feelings of superiority.

Not all cases of righteousness need to occur in such formalized settings; occasions for it also arise during the course of everyday life in our encounters with other people and what they enjoy. According to Slavoj Žižek, "what 'bothers' us in the 'other' (Jew, Japanese, African, Turk) is that they appear to entertain a privileged relationship to the object—the other either possesses the object treasure, having snatched it away from us (which is why we don't have it), or poses a threat to our possession of the object" (1999, xc). Paul Kingsbury (2007, 2011) translates this notion in his studies of mocking political bumper stickers and World Cup fandom, in which he notes nothing is more upsetting in polarized situations than the Other's enjoyment or at least the possibility that the Other can steal one's enjoyment (or position).

In the cultural economic realm, this possibility is the curse of being an upstart, such as the United States around the turn of the twentieth century, Japan in the 1970s, China and India since the 1990s, and the Gulf both in the 1970s and the 2000s. From different angles, these newly rich players are met with equal parts fascination about why their success is coming and anxiety, fear, and condemnation concerning the economic displacement they represent. In other words, economic disruption is often registered within structures of feeling. It is a rupture that brings out a profound sense of injustice and righteousness—as in "How dare they take what rightfully belong to us?" It also gives rise to a sense of annoyance because—à la Bourdieu—those who do not share all of "our" values and practices should not be given access to the rewards of success; they cannot possibly appreciate them properly.

Feelings of righteousness can attach not only to the performance of justice but also—as in the work of the French pragmatists—to the notion of duty and obligation. In *Culture and Imperialism*, Said highlights how during the age of imperialism the power of such feelings could sometimes even override the desire for material gain. "In the expansion of the great Western empires, profit and hope of further profit were obviously tremendously important. . . . So also was inertia, the investment in already going enterprises, tradition and the market or institutional forces that kept the enterprises going" (1993, 10). In other words, tradition and doing what needs to be done—even if ultimately economically unhelpful—were potentially psychically rewarding.

Part of this sense of obligation that comes with positional superiority arises from the enjoyment of just how inferior others can be. This dynamic is abundantly present throughout chapters 4 and 5 and is also the focus of Syed Hussein Alatas's book *The Myth of the Lazy Native* (1977). In that text, Alatas repeatedly demonstrates the entwining of development and pleasure that came with belittling colonized others, "playing down the capacities" of such societies, and affirming the superiority of Western culture. According to Alatas,

Every conceivable item was invoked to denigrate the Southeast Asian, including his size and physiognomy. Thus Geoffrey Gorer, an anthropologist specializing in the study of national character, a discipline intended to correct prejudices and arrive at true understanding, early in his career observed of the Javanese: "I did not personally find the Javanese very sympathetic; despite their fertility they give somehow the impression of being a race of old and exhausted people, only half alive. . . . A purely personal point which prevented me enjoying their company was the question of size; I do not like being among people who appear smaller and weaker than I am, unless they have corresponding superiority elsewhere; I dislike the company of those I feel to be my inferiors. (1977, 16)

Here, it is obvious that the right to rule is not only established in the colonizer's mind but also fixed there in the smuggest manner possible—which makes it all the more dangerous and entrenched. Yes, colonization made some people money through access to labor and consumer markets, thus also increasing their capacities for political power and violence. However, it also provided them with a sense of self-superiority and sources of enjoyment that they held equally as dear—a dynamic that chapters 4 and 5 make abundantly clear.

If hierarchies are policed by fashion, distinction, and righteousness, and economics or business is a relatively narrow practice with fairly limited imaginations of good or bad practice, there is enormous potential for sanctioning those who fall on the wrong side of consensus (as well as an enormous pool of denunciations from which to choose). Such sanctioning serves both to lessen competition and to produce righteous feelings about having taken the "correct" path. This dynamic is surely an active system *within* societies, easily turned against those who are similar but less advantaged by life's circumstances. However, such processes become even more charged when they interact with what is beyond their borders—an encounter that both consolidates and challenges established authority. It is to the challenge presented by these external Others that the chapter now turns.

Mimicry

Mimicry is an incredibly complex concept that is central to market Orientalism as well as to postcolonial studies more generally. It deserves particular attention because it takes the processes of distinction, taste making, and consensus and brings them into the unstable realm where differences meet (such as when emerging markets enter into imaginations of cultural economic value). Mimicry is also a charge affixed to Others in order to produce feelings of separation and righteousness.

One of the most widely cited views of mimicry comes from Franz Fanon (1962). According to Fanon, for those who are marked (especially those marked racially), "inferiority comes into being through the other" (112) so that their culture is seen as merely a poor reflection of the dominant culture. It is a situation that compels those so marked to attempt to adopt—or mimic—aspects of the dominant culture because they see this adoption as "the key that can open doors that were closed" (39). However, such attempts often leave individuals trapped between worlds as objects of ridicule who are at home nowhere. Thus, for Fanon, mimicry is all too often a humiliating requirement.

However, Fanon's is not the only view on the topic. For scholars such as Homi Bhabha (examined more fully later in this chapter), it is the uncertainty surrounding new encounters—in which Others are drawn near but also apart—and the hybridizing that ensues that make attempts at mimicry a site of potential novelty and the possible destabilization of the dominant culture itself.

Thus, this section highlights three areas where mimicry drives changes in the structures of feelings surrounding cultural economic value: (1) the desire for Others' fidelity that leads to missed recognition, (2) the ridiculing of the just slightly off copy, and (3) the potential to disturb existing imaginations and come to a new type of understanding. Besides helping me gain additional purchase in my critique of market Orientalism, this application of the notion of mimicry and of a postcolonial lens to economic issues is an endeavor that remains comparatively rare—despite the fact that postcolonialism was a massive, academy-wide movement and there are no shortage of scholars who study the economy (for some of the relatively few works in geography that have done so, see Bunnell 2002; Cook and Harrison 2003; Pollard, McEwen, and Hughes 2011; Sidaway and Pryke 2000). The first area where the charges of mimicry are particularly common is with respect to the desire for fidelity. Given the narrow nature of economic policy conventional wisdom, there is a tendency to compare everything to what is accepted as best practice—which is almost always considered to be whatever currently successful places or persons are doing. When an attempt to apply best practice comes from an "emerging economy," issues of fidelity to current policy tastes are usually not far behind. In other words, once a policy leaves its heartland, there are always queries surrounding those about to implement it and their ability to carry it out properly. Thus, charges of mimicry follow.

Fidelity is a problem faced by all sorts of authority: one wants to be able to order Others to act in one's image, but compelling others to act means they do act, but their action may not turn out as intended. Giving Others instructions means giving them agency, something that may (but not necessarily) deconsolidate one's authority over time. For those on the receiving end of charges of lack of fidelity, it is a maddening situation, especially in the economic realm. As Ian Cook and Michelle Harrison (2003) show in their study of postcolonial Jamaican food manufacturers, and as Rey Chow (2002) demonstrates through her concept of "coercive mimeticism," the choice is often between trying to embody "first-world" values in the third world or to portray (while hopefully subverting) third-worldness in order to capitalize on a desire in first-world markets for the unknown or exotic.

Issues of fidelity also speak to a key point of the diverse-economies literatures: that many people refuse to see in the economy anything but the influence of the one-and-only, all-powerful Capitalism. In such renderings, there is nothing truly different in other economies—only small, meaningless flailings that are ultimately co-optable. Making light of others' cultural economies is one way to obscure their uniqueness or to naturalize their inadequacy or both. It is a situation that causes the missed recognition of actual diversity as more of the same. As Gibson-Graham note,

> Here the diversity of market exchanges (for example, in local farmers' markets, international commodity markets, niche markets) is condensed into a single unity of "market exchange" that is in turn conflated with capitalist economy. At the same time, the diversity of economic behaviors (for example, of solidarity, beneficence, stewardship, obligation) is

interpreted through the lens of individual calculative rationality, displacing the significance and meaning of these behaviors by making them contiguous with a singular logic of self-interest or competition. Our economic language becomes impoverished (yet paradoxically more powerful) through the processes of condensation and displacement. (2006, 56–57)

A good example from the Gulf of the role that charges of mimicry can play in the economic realm comes from an article titled "A Financial Mirage in the Desert" (Sorkin 2009). It appeared in the *New York Times* and concerned the end of the early 2000s property bubble in Dubai. In discussing his interactions with a banker, the reporter noted: "He shared tips about various ways to create 'structured products' that would pass muster with Muslim investors. (To me, the investments looked like bonds, walked like bonds and talked like bonds—but he never called them that.) Some of the bonds that Dubai World is in jeopardy of defaulting on, by the way, are Shariah-compliant sukuk. Just don't call them bonds."

Here one can easily see the accusations of mimicry in action: according to the author, the Gulf tried to float debt and call it something else, but it was *really* bonds as we know them, just with a different name. To this author, the debt could not possibly or actually be a different product with a different moral economy—just the same old normal "junk" asset. However, as Jane Pollard and Michael Samers point out, Islamic banking and finance "involve[] a series of prohibitions on *riba* (translated as 'interest' or 'usury'), *maysir* or *qimar* (gambling and speculation), *gharar* (excessive uncertainty), and a number of other activities deemed *haram* (including the consumption of alcohol, pork, and prostitution). More broadly, *Shari'a* law places a strong emphasis on justice, the sharing of risks and rewards, and fairness and transparency in financial contracts and proceedings" (2011, 711). All of these things, for Pollard and Samers, show Islamic banking and finance to be productive of what they term "cosmopolitan financial geographies" (710) typical of the growing importance of South-to-South transfers. Of course, if you jokingly declare that *sukuk* are just like "our" bonds, except perhaps even fishier, and move on, you would miss all of that.

Which leads to the second point about how mimicry drives changes in the structures of feelings through producing slightly off copies. Although the dominant consensus often seems to want fidelity, it also profits psychically from creating distinction around attempts that seemingly just miss the mark. During the era of imperial economies, the situation was particularly acute. It was not just the colonized subjects who were marked as laughable or marginal during this era but also all the Europeans who made their money in the colonies as well. As Said notes, those people who were considered to be shining examples of European-ness were not involved in the business of empire. Imperialism was instead associated "with eccentric or unacceptable human beings, with fortune enhancing or fantasized activities like emigration, money-making, and sexual adventure. Disgraced younger sons are sent off to the colonies, shabby older relatives go there to try to recoup lost fortunes (as in Balzac's *La Cousine Bette*), enterprising young travelers go there to sow wild oats and to collect exotica" (1993, 64). Thus, Europeans who went to the colonies were tainted by association even if they were white and wealthy. They could be successful in monetary terms, but they were always somehow marked. In fact, the derogatory term *nabob* emerged in eighteenth-century Britain to signify those who had gained fabulous wealth through the British East India Company but were said in popular imaginations to have returned with peculiar manners and a tendency to display their earnings conspicuously—and thus to have become like the Easterners (Smylitopoulos 2008).

Though not in the postcolonial canon in even the most liberal interpretation, Slavoj Žižek's work speaks to how anyone associated with an undesirable space or identity can always be made to miss the point. As is typical of Žižek's work, he illustrates this point through the example of a film, *The Duelists*, a 1979 Ridley Scott picture. That film tells the story of the competition between an upper-class military officer and another officer born into the middle class who aspires to the upper class. As Žižek notes,

> What keeps them forever apart is the difference in the way each of them relates to the upper-class code of honour: the aspiring middle class officer doggedly follows this code, and for that very reason generates

the lasting impression of awkward ridicule, while his counterpart, the nobleman, constantly violates the explicit rules of the official code; and thereby asserts his true upper-classness. The problem of the aspiring lower-middle classes is that they misperceive the true cause of their failure. They think they are missing something, some golden rule, so that they have to learn to follow even more closely all the rules. (1999, 100)

To those who are guardians of taste, there is always something more—as Žižek calls it, some "mysterious X" (i.e., the Lacanian *l'objet petit a*)—beyond the practical knowledge of the formal elements. It is a permanently elusive element that those outside the guardians' group will inevitably miss because it is, after all, impossible to hold. Thus, for Žižek, it is a certain type of distance from constellations of fields, not fidelity, that marks one as a powerful actor with the ability to ridicule.

Žižek's emphasis is different from the positive content Bourdieu catalogs (and attempts to match to various types of capital). For Bourdieu, the social structure can be sensed, divided, and reproduced in every consumable element; in Žižek's psychoanalysis, it is the lack, the unobtainable, the indefinable content (which is nonetheless desired) that produces the separation. As with Simmel's fashion or Barthes's professional wrestling, the actual content of the current formulation is often of minor importance. This is because every attempt will *always* be viewed as "off" and because fashion can always be changed if necessary. This becomes clear in the critiques of Gulf Arabs I catalog in chapters 4 and 5. Although many of the structures of feeling I document resemble the critiques of orders of worth highlighted by Boltanski and Thévenot, what is amazing is that Gulf Arabs can be criticized from nearly every one of Boltanski and Thévenot's orders. There is no stability to the assault at all. Sometimes Gulf states are critiqued for being too traditional (i.e., too grounded in the domestic order); other times they are critiqued for being insufficiently traditional (too uncouth to understand important transnational customs yet also too alienated and modern to appreciate traditions of their own). From the market perspective, sometimes they are said to be at fault for valuing money too much; other times they are at fault for not being "proper capitalists." One gets the picture. Which particular critiques get selected drifts largely without direction because it is the distance between "us" and "them" that is most important, not consistency of argumentation.

In addition to the application of these imaginative geographies of just-off copies and the accompanying ridicule to less-gentile parts and classes of Europe during colonial times (as well as to the colonies themselves), Said in particular notes how such labels also were affixed to the former colonies not long after their independence. As he argues, despite a brief period after World War II when many on the US and European left actively supported third-world independence, the lack of success and stability that often followed the founding of a new state led to "a prevailing Western consensus that has come to regard the Third World as an atrocious nuisance, a culturally and politically inferior place. . . . No longer a noble poor, but a beggar to be zoned out of mind. It was also a place of revenge" (1993, 28). Thus, former colonies were like "modern" states, but not quite—and thus worthy of contempt, dismissal, or even violence.

Trying to compete on economic or cultural terms is therefore quite fraught, especially as every attempt provides a chance for others to feel righteous. Yet many do act, and not all efforts to engage are met with failure. Which raises the third point about how mimicry drives changes in the structures of feelings: encounters and attempts to fit in have the potential to disturb existing imaginations. The anxiety and potential that surround a new encounter and the coming of a new understanding are of particular interest to Homi Bhabha. According to Bhabha,

> such contradictory articulations of reality and desire—seen in racist stereotypes, statements, jokes, myths—are not caught in the doubtful circle of the return of the repressed. They are the effects of a disavowal that denies differences of the Other but produces in its stead forms of authority and multiple belief that alienate the assumptions of "civil" discourse. . . . The ambivalence of colonial authority repeatedly turns from *mimicry*—a difference that is almost nothing but not quite—to *menace*—a difference that is almost total but not quite. And in that other scene of colonial power, where history turns to farce and presence "to a part," can be seen the twin figures of narcissism and paranoia that repeat furiously, uncontrollably. (1994, 91)

Here, Bhabha explains that much of the ridicule and concerns about fidelity result not just from the enjoyment of one's own position but also from fear of that position being taken away.

The longer such interactions go on, the more unsure situations seem. Whereas Said (1994) turns to Christianity's interaction with Islam to understand mimicry, Bhabha prefers to examine its meet-up with Hinduism. Here, Hinduism (unlike Islam) was not treated as a "bad copy" of Christianity (because even Orientalists recognized Hinduism's almost total structural difference) but instead as something on which the "Truth" seemed to have no impact. Hindus were willing to believe in Jesus *along with* their existing belief and to note that they already believed in certain Christian ideas but in their own way, such as being born again many more times over. Thus, in trying to force fidelity, the official colonial discourse was hybridized, making the Word no longer enough in itself. As Bhabha notes, "Native catechists therefore had to be found, who brought with them their own cultural and political ambivalences and contradictions" (1994, 34).

In other words, encounters with other cultural economies require the work of translation, yet economic practice always feels surest where there is less translation. Economic expansion wants both to draw other social formations in (in order to profit) but also to push them away lest they become competitors. This relates to one of Harvey's key points in *Limits to Capital*: as capital expands to new markets (either to sell at high margins or to produce with low wages), it must make the society capital ready, thus planting seeds for competitors. So, even in that proud moment of capitalist expansion (e.g., into the Gulf, into China), there is the moment of doubt that this triumph can lead to downfall. The Gulf, as we will see, provided a case where the Economic Word itself was no longer sufficient because the region elided categories of easy economic understanding and found success by following a different set of rules (especially in the 1970s).

The menace and anxiety brought about by mimicry connects to another point: the fact that mimicry necessitates a mimic, someone on the other end pushing back (or at least maneuvering) against imaginations of fidelity. An emphasis on this fact in subsequent chapters keeps market Orientalism from becoming an inescapable, closed circle. Charges of mimicry mean *something* is being done, something that may be a reaction to ill-intentioned structures of feeling but that also may be directed toward completely different terrains of distinction. Commentators, even those critical of colonialism, great-power politics, and globalization, too often ignore this potential to push back or move otherwise. According to Said (1993), even the ultimate novel of imperial ambivalence, Joseph Conrad's *Heart of Darkness*, ends up making imperialism seem all powerful and unopposable.

Frederick Cooper and Ann Laura Stoler echo this sentiment, arguing against the notion that every move made by major powers during and after colonialism was "inherently disempowering," even if these moves were often aggressive and insensitive. As they note, development was often critiqued as disempowering,

> yet there is more to the idea of development in its historical context; like other concepts, this one can be seized, turned around from a structure of de-politicization into a claim for entitlements. . . . The "Third World" (deployed as a radical term at the Bandung Conference in the spirit of the "third estate") asserted itself around the idea that a decent standard of living was a fundamental human right. Within postcolonial states, governments legitimized their rule as leading the "battle for development," while opposition groups asserted that developed had been hijacked and that only they provide a genuine commitment to it. (1997, 35)

Even inherently unfair processes and imaginations (such as market Orientalism) that constrain the actors in emerging markets certainly do not doom them. Nor do they prevent them from producing their own imaginative geographies in order to maneuver or perhaps conjure positional superiority over different groups of Others. As chapters 6, 7, and 8 show, Gulf states are in many ways still developmentalist states focused on the idea of a "decent standard of living" (and its absence for some groups in Bahrain is a rallying point for political opposition). They have not fully bought into the "reality" that austerity is inevitable or desirable. Dubai likewise routinely plays up perceptions of Gulf otherness to its advantage in order to stand as an alternative; Doha and Abu Dhabi try to find other types of audiences and to facilitate new South-to-South imaginations.

To summarize, the deployment of a broadly defined cultural economy framework enables an analysis that bypasses the perniciousness of the base–superstructure distinction and provides a number of specific lenses for viewing how "culture" meaningfully influences the perceptions of economic value that surround "emerging markets." One of these lenses is paying attention to how the showing and measuring of fidelity to widespread, "accepted" policies are, as Bourdieu would have it, part of a power–knowledge strategy of hierarchical positioning that tends to level or deny actually existing difference. But such expectations for fidelity are also, as postcolonial theory shows, somewhat of a trap for those attempting to follow the norm—a trap that causes them to be critiqued and even ridiculed for missing the unspoken rules. Such traps also reinforce the material and physic positional superiority of those already considered to be part of the consensus. But these slightly off copies, which bring heated accusations and conceptual dissonance, are also openings for the disruption of standard practices. These menacing heresies imply actors remaking the deed through the doing and point toward new trajectories in the future. Furthermore, one has to recognize that, even in the deadly serious practices of business and development, not everything is purely rational or full of meaning and that enjoyment and fashion are factors in them as well. This type of enjoyment is a locus of power and prejudice, but it is also one of potential.

For the rest of this chapter (and this book), I bring these ideas under one conceptual umbrella: the imaginative geographies of market Orientalism.

Market Orientalism

Many commentators, including geographer Derek Gregory in his book *The Colonial Present: Afghanistan, Iraq, and Palestine* (2004), have documented the continued, stubborn persistence of colonial-era conceptualizations of the culture and religion of Arabs and Muslims as being universally backward, unchanging, violent, sneaky, and misogynist. In particular, gender relations in the region receive special attention from outside commentators, who often deny the agency of women in the region (Mernissi 1987) while fantasizing about what the practice of veiling signifies. Apart from leading to negative portrayals found in countless films (Semmerling 2006)—including Disney's *Aladdin*, where the most "Arab-looking" characters are the most sinister (Shaheen 2001)—these legacies, as Gregory so deftly shows, have had major geopolitical consequences for the region in that they have been used to justify aggression against Palestinians and Iraqis.

However, whereas the cultural and geopolitical repercussions of Orientalism have been commented on often—for example, by Edward Said (1993, 1994, 1997) and Timothy Mitchell (1988)—the effects of these ideas on "economic" discourses about the region have been focused on less. This lack of attention to economics is in part a result of the most Middle East specialists' disciplinary training—critical or otherwise—in history, literary studies, and political science. Yet it has been my argument in this book that especially since the oil windfall of the 1970s the idea of the Middle East as economically exceptional has been just as palpable as the idea of the region as a cultural Other. The region is seen at best to mimic (and sometimes to mock) but never to reach the level of economic best practice.

As already stated, market Orientalism produces imaginative geographies of cultural economic value, which work on the structures of feeling and systems of distinction concerning what is considered valuable or not. Although the particular content of these geographies shifts over time (as do the structures of feeling), market Orientalism is remarkably persistent in separating the Gulf and emerging markets more generally from what is considered normal and preferable. Although I address the particular contours (or aspects) of market Orientalism later in this section, for now note that its effects include: providing an opportunity to enjoy feelings of superiority and righteousness; compelling emerging markets to take seemingly extreme measures to react to, negotiate with, and occasionally undermine such imaginative geographies; and obscuring the diversity and different values present in such economies.

Who benefits from market Orientalism? Obviously no one person owns an imaginative geography or structure of feeling, even if people have differential ability to shape them. Some enjoy righteousness just for enjoyment's sake; some take comfort in the work that market Orientalism does to suture over inconsistencies in their favorite theories; others benefit from the fact that this separation of emerging markets from the "normal" and "preferred" makes them money (through creating extra profit owing to perceived "risk" or opportunities to offer advice on how to deal with such Other places).

One of the best demonstrations of this cultural economic othering, especially with respect to the Gulf, is the emergence of a new term, *rentier state*, that came primarily to describe Middle Eastern economies (although it later comes to be applied to other places). Although Hossein Mahdavy (1970) first introduced the term *rentier state*, and many have deployed and critiqued it since then (see Hertog 2010b), Egyptian economist Hazem Beblawi (1987) gave the most widely known explication of the concept. Beblawi, among other things, was interim prime minister of Egypt in 2013–14 and a former government official in Kuwait. Versions of his essay "The Rentier State in the Arab World" appeared in several places, including *Arab Studies Quarterly* (1987), as well as in two books that he coedited with Giacomo Luciani, *The Rentier State* (1987) and *The Arab State* (1990).

The rentier state, as described by Beblawi, has become the de facto analytic through which journalists and the policy community understand the Gulf. Its fingerprints are everywhere. Indeed, Beblawi's essay functions as a key vehicle of translation in the encounter between the mainline economic consensus and the upstart Gulf.

Unlike many who commented on the 1970s oil boom, Beblawi actually can explain what is happening in the Gulf economically in terms of the various channels through which states distribute funds. The sections of the essay concerning the distribution of wealth through land buying, the collapse of the Kuwaiti alternative stock market, and the sponsorship system are clearly laid-out and well-argued descriptions of key processes. The essay also has a sense of urgency, fanned by the ills Beblawi saw in the wider Arab world. Despite its clear descriptions and the passion behind his quasi-internal critique, in how it is framed "The Rentier State in the Arab World" nonetheless does the work of market Orientalism.

Beblawi's central idea is that rent (which can roughly be understood as money earned owing to monopoly control over some asset) is "more of a social function than [an] economic category" (Beblawi 1990, 86). Thus, in societies where the state dominates the economy through its collection of rent (a.k.a. a "rentier state"), a "rentier mentality" has developed that "distinguishes it[self] from conventional economic behavior" in that it "breaks the work–reward causation" (1990, 88). To put it in Bourdieu's terms, rentierism supplies the rewards of economic success without the accepted constellation of work practices supposedly associated with them. Beblawi states that "the contradiction between production and rentier ethics is, thus, glaring" and that the rentier is the "antithesis" of the entre-preneur, who is "dynamic, innovative, and risk bearing" (86). He also argues that this rentier ethic has infected the entire Arab world—even states without oil—through second-order rentierism. In other words, the Gulf rentier states have become the moral and functional Other of "nor-mal" economies, which actually work and innovate to produce things. Furthermore, these wrongly incentivized Gulf economies are so noxious that they are dragging down everyone around them. They have trans-formed from mimics of proper cultural economic behavior to menaces to its continued existence.

In fact, what seems to animate Beblawi's ire the most is that under rentierism as he sees it, social relations have almost completely evacu-ated the "usual" economic relations from society. Near the beginning of the essay, Beblawi notes that social scientists have long seen "a difference between 'earned' income and effortless 'accrued' rent" and that there is "a deep rooted mistrust of the economic profession against rent and rent-iers" (1990, 86). Although the descriptive sections of "The Rentier State in the Arab World" demonstrate that Beblawi does not fully believe rent is "effortless," he nonetheless seems to share the classic mistrust of rent, see-ing it as a productively and morally inferior form of human organization.

Again, Beblawi is most certainly not bigoted against Arabs (although one can detect the slightest bit of resentment that some people from more established Arab capitals feel for the upstart Gulf), and he identifies a number of real issues in Gulf and wider "Arab" economies. However, what his text ends up doing is providing "proof" that even Arabs think Arab economies are completely Other and backward and that this backwardness is the Gulf's fault. Putting aside the fact that there is actual diversity in Gulf economies beyond the accruement of rent (and beyond those few sectors often mentioned in calls for "diversification"), he solidifies the notions that Arab economies are unnaturally cultural and even amoral compared to the norm and that they badly mimic (or perhaps baldly mock) how things should function. So even though Beblawi offers actual descriptions of what was going on in the Gulf in the late 1980s, his contribution is remembered primarily for its shaping of the structures of feeling surrounding Gulf cultural economies.

The irony, in hindsight, is that many political economists, including David Harvey, have argued that the contemporary US economy no longer relies on manufactured goods for export income but instead on rents generated from producing and defending exclusive use of intellectual property in fields such as technology, cultural production, and medicine. The fruits of these rents are then passed on to shareholders or highly paid executives, which leaves much of the domestic workforce in the low-wage service sector. In fact, one of the criticisms leveled at the Arabic-speaking world in a United Nations–sponsored series of Arab Human Development Reports (United Nations Development Program 2002, 2003, 2004, 2005) is that the number of patents produced in that region is comparatively low. In other words, around thirty years after the publication of "The Rentier State," the region is chastised for not collecting enough rent, which is now considered the ultimate reward of innovation! If nothing else, this irony demonstrates the churn of economic fashion—the collection of rent, which was considered morally inferior a few decades ago, is now in a slightly modified form considered a legitimate path to national wealth accumulation. Of course, patent rents are collected by private entities and individuals, who are under no obligation to do anything but horde them; the Gulf monarchies—although very far from perfect—could not have kept all the oil money for themselves.

Nor did postcolonial states invent rentierism sometime in the 1950s as some "natural" extension of their oil wealth. As Cooper and Stoler argue,

Particular interests certainly profited from the restrictions of colonial economies, such as less competitive metropolitan industries, banks, and settlers given below market labor costs. There is no question that economic motivations played a large part in colonization. But numerous efforts to calculate benefits to metropolitan capitalism do not suggest a strong case that colonial rule made a substantial long-term difference to accumulation in France or Great Britain; the "imperialism of free trade" may well have been the better bargain. In fact, the very ability of colonial firms to get help from the state in extracting cheap labor or low-cost commodities from indigenous communities led to what some metropolitan leaders themselves perceived (by the 1920s or 1930s at least) to be a colonial sclerosis, an inability to generate innovation, increase productivity, or build a more integrated and differentiated regional economy. (1997, 19)

Here, Cooper and Stoler demonstrate that the prejudice against rent is indeed old—as Beblawi claims. However, in this light, perhaps the idea of the rentier state came about because colonies themselves were in fact run by their colonizers as "rentier states" where narrowly held returns were guaranteed both by law and by forced extraction from the majority.

In the end, Beblawi's story traveled well because, although he is "Arab," he writes and thinks like a "classical" political economist, and thus his story was easily relatable to the large audience trained in this same pattern of thought. He provided the moment of translation. I would also argue that the tone of what he wrote more than its content made the piece widely influential. The audience who wanted and continues to want to understand how land purchases serve as a wealth-distribution mechanism in the Gulf is rather small; the audience who wanted and continues to want to hear why the Gulf is morally suspect and to feel righteously superior to the Gulf is far larger. Indeed, there is little foreign reporters like more than a "native" informant who can appear as a character in their story to confirm what they think is wrong with the informant's country.

Beblawi's piece also demonstrates a major feeling present within some sectors of economic theory and practice: the fantasy of a perfect market, where there is perfect information and where there is no luck or human quality. The perfect market is of course a fantasy—so much in life is actually luck or beyond the individual's control—but it is a fantasy charged with certain types of enjoyment. It is also very seductive. Some of this love of the perfect market is the enjoyment of "fair play," of a justice that real life rarely displays (Boltanski and Thévenot 2006). For now, I just note their importance, but I return to the topics of fantasy and seduction in chapter 6.

But that old sense of righteousness also plays a role here: if perfect markets actually came to exist in a broad forms (as opposed to in the limited forms, such as flower auctions, that currently exist), "rational" thinkers such as economists would likely prevail in them, and all others would lose (including many of those who currently excel socially). There would be a triumph of people who think like economists, which is not a "fair" economy either, only a differently arranged one, where injustice gets distributed through countless mechanisms (e.g., school funding, standardized tests, financial deregulation) instead of being embedded in personal relationships. In much of the Gulf, taking care of citizens' basic needs and (more problematically) knowing the right people determine large sectors of the economy, at least for nationals; it is a return to the type of fuzzy society that neoclassic economics and economists have tried to erase.

Timothy Mitchell notes a long history of this type of disgust at other ways of distributing resources: "To Europeans, actions like these [the Pasha giving away land to acquaintances] expressed everything that was wrong with the East. They exemplified the shortcoming for which colonial officials liked to criticize native systems of rule: their arbitrariness. Compared to the universal rules of a modern system of law, native government proceeded by personal decision and the caprice of power. . . . This language belongs to an earlier century. But the views it expresses remain current" (2002b, 34).

Such cultural economic othering that is part and parcel of market Orientalism has only been strengthened since the 1990s and the emergence of imaginations of "globalization." Whereas East Asia's economic rise and supposed openness placed it at the center of globalist discourses (and in many ways sparked the development of these discourses) and Africa's weak connection to the world economy in anything but primary production basically relegates it to somewhere outside the discourse (see

Ferguson 2006), the Middle East is positioned as the supposed Other—and thus the constitutive outside—of globalization. The Middle East is the slow olive tree to the fast Lexus of globalization (Friedman [1999] 2000), the insular jihad to the flowing McWorld (Barber 1996). Just as the Orient helped define Europe, the Middle East allowed the discourse of globalization to be uttered—that is, globalization is whatever the Middle East is not. The combined effects of the antiglobalization imagination and the policeable-by-force status the wider region has been subject to for the past twenty years under what Harvey calls "new imperialism" are quite stark. Thus, the effects of market Orientalism need to be highlighted now more than ever.

As stated in chapter 1, I wish to focus on four aspects of market Orientalism, which bring together the literatures outlined so far: (1) assumptions about emerging markets' lack of fidelity to global ideals, which are imbued with centuries of thought and practice about how to deal with Others; (2) the mainstream economic imaginaries that hold that the world can be transparently divided into identifiable and practicable fields of economic action, known as "regional markets," which are imaginative geographies just as leveling and reductive as the original concept of the Orient; (3) the ways emerging markets are castigated for their supposed lack of maturity, which is a classic colonial trope used to establish positional superiority; and (4) the process through which the imagining of emerging markets produces a field of impenetrability (as well as actors that sell the existence of such a field) in a manner similar to how Orientalism produced the idea that the Middle East was a "veiled" woman that needed to be "uncovered" by "disciplined" (male, Western) knowledge. It is my contention that only by emphasizing this intersection between Orientalist and market imaginaries can the current position of Middle East cultural economies and the Gulf's various responses to them be understood.

Cultural Assumptions about Others

Despite imaginations to the contrary, "doing business" is not simply a mathematically driven phenomenon but also a thoroughly social one, with all of the attendant biases and preferences that go with sociality.

"Doing international business," as subsequent chapters demonstrate, clearly involves not just knowledge of markets but also the performance of lifestyle (or set of lifestyles). These lifestyles involve playing expected roles, embodying confidence, building relationships, practicing techniques of persuasion, indulging in niceties, traveling to desirable locales, and curating aspirational spaces (Nevarez 2003; Pryke and Lee 1995).

Whatever niceties (or necessities) are required for a place to be viewed as a good market "to do business in," the Middle East is often imagined not to have them. To begin with, "the culture" in the Middle East (always spoken of in the singular) is assumed to be violent, thus leading members of the "transnational capitalist class" (Sklair 2001) to avoid the region as much as possible—perhaps setting foot only in ultrasafe Dubai or Doha. Furthermore, as chapter 1 showed, the "Middle East culture" is also seen (however wrongly or partially) as being overly focused on chastity, denial of pleasure, and maintenance of purity. In this view, this "culture" does everything from denying women (and thus businesswomen) the right to drive and dress how they choose to curtailing all the "fringe benefits" associated with the masculinized performance of high transnational business, such as decadent meals and spirits (McDowell 2001). This perception persists despite the fact that parts of many actual places in the region, such as Cairo and Beirut, offer all of these things.

However, this script has a wrinkle. Within the "Middle East" and indeed in the rest of the world, no countries occupy quite the same unusual cultural economic position via imaginations of globalization as the Gulf oil monarchies.

As standard—and often quite partial—accounts go, Gulf citizens (or at least royals) are enjoying a fair amount of what are supposed to be the ultimate rewards of economic globalization: material wealth, freedom from want, and the ability to freely travel the world. In these scripts, Gulf Arabs possess these rewards but, as rentiers, have not done any of the right things to earn them. For example, some hold that the Gulf states' wealth seemingly stems only from an accident of geography, which granted them a winning ticket in the petroleum-resource lottery (as if luck were a factor nowhere else). Their public sectors are simultaneously imagined as well funded, gigantic, and ineffective. Squandering their supposedly great fortune, Gulf Arabs frequent hotels, boutiques, and jewelers in the toniest parts of the toniest cities that were built to serve celebrities and corporate elites, all the while wearing "traditional" dress. They can afford Lexuses, yet they do not allow women to drive them (which is true only in Saudi Arabia as of late). Once again, they are seen to break Bourdieu's constellation of practices. The result is that unlike poor Others such as Palestinians, Afghani villagers, Iraqi civilians, and the proletarian "Arab Street," the citizens of Gulf monarchies' fail to elicit a sympathetic response from either the tolerant Left or the militant Right. It seems all are free to righteously denounce the Gulf.

Imaginations of the Gulf paint a confusing picture. The Gulf is not a "typical" developing-world, "hardship pay" destination because the infrastructure largely functions. Nor is it seen as exactly like the rest of the "real" Middle East. It seemingly has many "normal" things but appears intent on utilizing them in odd ways. This ambiguous position leads to a great deal of consternated writing about how and sometimes even whether one should do business in the "exceptional" Gulf as well as to many efforts by those within the Gulf to address or go around such perceptions.

The Regional Market

Market is one of the most spatially (and generally) nebulous words in the English language. Despite this fact, the creation of "markets" has been *the* object of much IMF and World Bank policy since at least the 1980s. For these institutions, the creation of markets seemed to involve both the clearing of space (market as a space of noninterference) and the building of a legal architecture (market as a space of rules)—as in Jamie Peck and Adam Tickell's (2002) "roll-back" and "roll-out" neoliberalism. Timothy Mitchell (2002b) and Julia Elyachar (2005) show how in Egypt the conjuring of markets involved the creation of new rules, terrains, and privileges.

However, these rule- and architecture-centric views are but one type of understanding of the term *market*. For the purposes of going forward, I think it is also important to understand how markets are viewed by businesses that "market" goods and services. One of the most complete accounts of this corporate sense of the word *market* can be found in Marianne Lien's book *Marketing and Modernity* (1997, 89–98). In this ethnographic study of the marketing department of a major Norwegian food manufacturer, inspired by actor network theory, Lien identifies four metaphorical extensions that her research subjects often use when talking about the market. (1) Market as "territorial space": The market is something transparently identifiable that exists outside of any given seller, which a seller is able to enter and leave. It may form around a certain product (the upscale tourist market) or around a territory (East Asia). (2) Market as "battlefield": Connected to the idea of a limited, bounded territory is the notion that sellers must battle each other for a share of that territory and must compete with others by being faster, smarter, and/or leaner than other sellers. (3) Market as natural selection: Life-cycle metaphors are ever present in discussions of the market. The idea is that offerings have limited shelf life; those that don't innovate or keep costs down stagnate and die; those that do thrive. The market is also seen as having a carrying capacity: too many sellers will destroy the commons and cause the weakest to die off quickly. (4) Market as fastidious child: In this vein, the market is anthropomorphized as a child that inevitably grows, has ever-maturing sensibilities, yet remains fickle, demanding, and highly selective.

In this conception, markets are more than just the erasure of one legal and regulatory framework and its replacement with another à la Peck and Tickell (2002). Rather than being architectures, they are identifiable arenas in which business can be done, forming a socialized assemblage of potential competitors, distributors, retailers, and customers who are neither captive nor unlimited. It is this sense of a market that Elyachar captures so nicely in her recent ethnographic writing on Egypt, which seeks to unravel "the myth of a monolithic 'public sector'" through an examination of how officials call on tacit knowledge to create an action space defined by affective "street smarts" and collectively held "secrets of the trade" (2012, 89).

With what Lien discovered about markets in mind, we can now ask the following questions: What exactly might the "Middle East market" entail, and how would a "Gulf market" fit into that picture? And what effects does imagining such markets have? First, a "Middle East market" would have to possess a territorial space equivalent to the Middle

East. But defining the Middle East for any purpose has always been a tricky proposition. There seems to be consensus, at least from the outside, that something called the Middle East must exist and that something about it must be coherent—but what exactly? What is often considered the Middle East contains great diversity. Large countries such as Turkey and Iran do not speak Arabic; even Arabic speakers from different areas do not speak the language in the same way. Multiple localized and transnational Islamic belief systems interact with governments that possess a variety of attitudes toward the relationship between state and religion. These states in turn govern citizens with countless combinations of belief and behavior. Some areas of the region have strong connections to France and Germany, others to Britain and the United States. The Gulf has very strong ties to South Asia. No one characteristic defines a region that spans three continents. If markets are supposed to be visible, identifiable, and understandable, the "general perception" of the Middle East market would be of a market that is difficult to imagine indeed. And if it cannot be easily delineated, how can its demands be heard and directed? There is a difference between treating the idea of region as a shorthand, arbitrary construct (as I do here) and trying to animate and bound a region through practice.

Second, the Middle East market would have to be seen as contestable battlefield where the strongest survive and natural selection is allowed to take its course. Given the comparatively active state sectors in the region that often limit free-roaming foreign activity in the economy and give special privileges to citizen-actors, would such a battle be considered "fair" by those who are used to being able to act at a distance? Even though the Gulf scores very well on a number of economic-openness indexes, imaginations of it signal the opposite.

So not only does the stereotypical version of the Middle East not meet the cultural criteria many businesses need to feel comfortable enough to operate, but it does not seem to provide a readily visible, knowable, identifiable market arena in which to compete. It is seen not just as different, but as behind other areas of the world in terms of market formation. As mentioned elsewhere in the text, that is why many corporations ran and some still run their Middle East operations from Europe: they are reluctant to put resources on the ground given that the contours of its market seemingly remain unclear.

Maturity

"Maturity" or perceived lack thereof is the third aspect of my market Orientalism formulation. Postcolonial theorists as diverse as Franz Fanon (1967), Stuart Hall (1992), Gayatri Chakravorty Spivak (1996), Anne McClintock (1995), and Edward Said (1993, 1994) time and again have emphasized the work done through colonial texts and practices to depict the non-Western Other as somehow more childlike (or often less "manlike") than their "virile" colonial masters. More specifically, non-Westerners were seen as being simultaneously lazy and ruled by uncontrollable passions, which supposedly made them unsuitable to do things that require "discipline," such as establish and run a nontyrannical government or produce "high art." Thus, it was the "white man's burden" to rule those who "could not yet" be trusted to rule themselves. In this view, non-Westerners become just slightly off copies of Westerners—and therefore worthy of being shaped and disciplined.

So why mention this well-trodden ground concerning colonial perceptions of a lack of maturity in the Other? Because *maturity* is such a commonly used word in economic-business circles and, as suggested earlier, because the Middle East market—or anywhere labeled "emerging" for that matter—is notably considered to lack it. There is a constant transformation of milieus that are indeed different (and likely very well established and intricate) into spaces that are seen as lacking, undeveloped, and behind. As subsequent chapters show, Gulf Arabs are depicted as a perpetually youthlike and petulant leisure class that has everything without the usual responsibilities that come from having earned it. In other words, they need the paternalistic guidance of more mature others, or perhaps they need to be kicked out into the harsh realities of the world and its markets. This depiction also fits in with a highly gendered trope, noted in *Orientalism* (Said 1994), that Arabs can only be passive, not active, agents in global economic processes.

An odd result follows from these depictions: time and again calls are made for Gulf Arabs and those in emerging markets in general to be more open to global and American pop culture, norms, and investment within their own spaces (which they generally are already). However, whenever Gulf Arabs attempt to invest directly in "Western" economies, they are rarely met with open arms. Their motives are often considered suspicious, even when they simply travel to the United States or the United Kingdom for vacation (as documented in chapter 5). They are rarely regarded as serious economic actors despite serious achievements such as building what has become some of the world's most functional cities in only three decades (not to mention the large cities they have been building for the past few millennia). They are so fated because of the "original sin" of how they got their money, which some still see as a theft of well-earned power and prestige by a group of upstarts—a source of injustice to rail righteously against. If anything, this perception of the Gulf states highlights that even a wealthy market is not automatically seen as a mature one.

Impenetrability

As Said (1994) demonstrates, one of the major gestures of Orientalism was to declare the Middle East a veil, behind which only the especially attuned could see. All "emerging markets" are "shrouded" initially in fuzziness, of course, but the situation is particularly acute when it comes to the Middle East. Under this logic, everything "interesting" in the region is supposedly done in private; the people will say one thing but think and do another (often sinister) thing; government—in the form of an absolute ruler—is not transparent. Furthermore, this old formulation has seeped its way into the realm of the economy, where the region is imagined not only as being hard to understand from the outside but also as not letting outsiders in without conditions—whether the outsiders be products, capital, or people. For example, in the Gulf foreign companies have to hire local agents to be their exclusive distributors. Consumer boycotts originating in the region (such as those of Danish dairy products and American colas) get attention disproportionate to their actual effects.

The Middle East's supposedly "uniquely" malfunctive and reluctant engagement with the global economy has been a subject of much attention since before September 11, 2001, with a special focus on the Gulf states. It is often charged that the lack of openness is the cause of the region's comparatively high levels of unemployment. In fact, this supposed closedness of the Gulf states—despite generous tax and profit-repatriation policies—is often posited as the reason why youth there are "highly susceptible" to radical Islam (see Gregory's [2004] discussion of Fareed Zakaria's work as a case in point).

One interesting symptom of this assumption of opaqueness is the existence of a whole series of books that help English-language speakers do business (and live) in the Gulf, including *The Arab Way: How to Work More Effectively with Arab Cultures* (J. al-Omari 2003), *Serve Them Right: A Practical Guide to Multicultural Customer Care* (Dickens 1999), and *Don't They Know It's Friday? Cross-Cultural Considerations for Business and Life in the Gulf* (Williams 1998). Unlike many similar guidebooks for other destinations, which contain mostly practical information, these texts also have to work hard to convince English speakers to get over their fears and realize that it is actually OK to do business in the Gulf. For example, *Don't They Know It's Friday* (written by the founder of Handshaikh consultancy) largely concerns changing home-office perceptions of how the region works and preaches the adjustment of one's expectations. However, despite their practicality (including tips about dealing with hierarchy and differing ideas of timeliness) and their generally supportive-of-the-Gulf tone, these guides nonetheless act to reinforce the idea of a fundamental difference—a culture that does not appreciate or understand business as it is "normally" done. These works also posit a Gulf that is so impenetrable that it cannot be understood without some expert help. That a large part of the business culture in the Gulf in fact runs in English but yet is still seen as needing translation shows just how opaque it is thought to be.

If those are the contours of the imaginative geographies of market Orientalism, let me close by reemphasizing the major points made in this chapter. I set out in this book primarily to make an original contribution—to articulate a wider cultural economy theory. In the name of accomplishing that goal, this chapter highlighted one such "wider process": imaginations of economic hierarchy. I argued that these imaginations are heavily influenced by the ability to demonstrate fidelity to the preferences of a rather narrow economic consensus. In turn, these "economic" preferences—which lead to labels such as *rentier state*—are shaped by processes that would usually be deemed "cultural": fashion, distinction, justification, righteousness, and mimicry. It is those processes that come together in market Orientalism, which produces imaginative geographies that influence structures of cultural economic feeling about the maturity, unity, and impenetrability of emerging markets such as Gulf.

As subsequent chapters show, what is interesting about the otherness produced by market Orientalism is the ways it has shifted over the years. In the 1990s, Arab countries received demerits from the Friedmans of the world for their lack of engagement with the global economy. However, in the mid-1970s and early 1980s Arabs were condemned for their supposed *overengagement* in the world economy, to the point that they were portrayed as stupidly reckless, cold-hearted financial puppet masters whose "oil weapon" had unleashed a worldwide crisis when they staged an embargo against the United States for its support of Israel (see Licklider 1988; Maull 1975). That depiction, in turn, could be contrasted with the earlier Orientalist image of the Arab trade who was too clever by half and would without remorse prey on customers' lack of knowledge to get the maximum profit. In chapters 4 and 5, we will see these images repeated ad nauseam.

But before I go on, let me be clear about something: I am not writing this book because I feel the Gulf is free of problems. Indeed, there are many. Nor am I doing so because I think Gulf citizens and residents are above fault—especially its leaders (in fact, it is part of a leader's job to be questioned). Rather, I view the diversity of people in the Gulf as people who are mixtures of good and bad, altruism and unthought routine, like people everywhere (including the reporters whom I critique here). People in the Gulf should be judged on their own deeds, not prejudged as a collective; their institutions should be judged as institutions in context. They certainly do not need me to speak for them or to represent their "true" existence. This is a book about their places in economic imaginaries and how these imaginaries reflect long-standing prejudices and affect the present. I do not seek to shield the Gulf (or anywhere else) from well-documented criticism. Instead, I do want to reveal how the Gulf and many other places dubbed "emerging markets" are subjected to repeated and often far from accurate accusations that result from a quest, conscious or not, for economic self-definition through the use of Others (in fact, chapters 4 and 5 catalog dozens upon dozens of such instances). All too often, as Barthes notes, writing about other cultural economies is not much more than a morality play productive of righteousness. It is a play where certain places and people come to fill prescribed roles to play out the well-worn story of economic good and bad, reinforcing the notion of who has the authority or distinction to decide and act and who does not. These too easy mappings are what I want to combat while highlighting the work that they do.

4

A Historical, Cultural Economic Geography of the Gulf

Part One (1932–1972)

If I had to pinpoint a particular moment when the Gulf's encounter with market Orientalism became fully formed, I would choose December 30, 1959. On this day, no major oil discoveries were made, and no treaties were signed. Indeed, no event of particular geopolitical or geoeconomic importance occurred. Instead, it was the date the article "Saudis Struggle with Modern Era: They Fear Ridicule of Their Efforts to Adapt Ancient Society to 20th Century" (Schmidt 1959) appeared in the *New York Times*. The very first line reads, "Like a school boy who turns up in shorts at a school where all the boys wear long pants, the Saudis fear ridicule." On the surface, this simile seems an odd choice to lead the story that follows because the rest of the story presents very little evidence that the Saudis feel ashamed. The story is mostly a travelogue about a trip the author, Dana Adams Schmidt (a longtime Middle East correspondent for the *New York Times*), took to Saudi Arabia. However, as this chapter and the next show, this labeling of Saudis as "ashamed" was not a random flourish—it was the beginning of a long-running imagination of the Gulf as a place that may be wealthy (like the presumed readers of the *New York Times*) but is ultimately unhappy (unlike those readers). The Gulf would also come to be imagined as a place to feel and act superior toward.

Like the many writers following in the Orientalist tradition that preceded him, Schmidt says some things that make Saudis appear not too alien to his (assumed) American readers, such as their tendency to "smother him with hospitality," the fact that "education is catching hold at a tremendous rate" among the "middle classes," and that their 1958 budget crisis was not caused by the "lavish spending" of princes on "Cadillacs and palaces" but by huge monetary commitments to infrastructure. But once these exceptions are out of the way, he precedes to draw lines of separation.

Schmidt notes (rather casually) that "in spite of official prohibition, slaves can still be bought"; that "thieves' hands are chopped off time to time, on Fridays"; and that most Saudis are "too new to their roles [as workers and employees] to have much time for political thinking." Having met the king, Schmidt relays the following about him: King Saud "sought greatness in building palaces and giving away great sums of money"; his new palace is pink (of all colors!); he is "so short sighted that he must hold whatever he reads within inches of his eyes"; watching a school basketball match made him "rock back and forth in excitement"; and he "only spoke three times during dinner." Near the end of the article, Schmidt floats the following: "Whether this kingdom of paradoxes, contradictions and anachronisms can live long in the 20th century is a question debated by Arabists."

Although this news story does not address the regional question, the remaining aspects of market Orientalism make an appearance in the article. Schmidt's story is clearly one of what turns out to be many articles written about Saudi Arabia and the Gulf that deal with the contradiction between their "anachronisms" (mostly their cultural practices) and their modernity, which one can read as their wealth. In fact, Saudi money and culture are rarely ever spoken of separately; that the vastness of the former and the "backwardness" of the latter coincide is deemed something of an "embarrassment." This violation of cultural assumptions is the first aspect of market Orientalism. In reference to the third aspect, lack of maturity, the article begins by calling Saudis "school boys in shorts" (presumably in a world where big boys wear trousers). It states that the middle classes are "too new" for the advanced thinking that politics requires and that the king and the princes spend money foolishly (much like teenagers) on pink palaces and Cadillacs, while not knowing to speak during meals and getting too excited about basketball. Finally, with respect to the fourth tenet of market Orientalism, opaqueness, the kingdom is full of "contradiction." In fact, this article begins a fifty-year love affair of pairing Saudi Arabia with the word *paradox*. The author also brags elsewhere in the article about how hard it is for journalists to get to Saudi Arabia, before concluding that it is a wonder such a place can continue to exist at all. To Schmidt, Saudi Arabia is almost an impossible place, and he is exceedingly proud of having broken through its impenetrability.

Indeed, Schmidt's article is in many ways remarkable. Numerous articles comment on the purchases of palaces and cars, but no other article goes so far as to call the Saudis "school boys in shorts." The time spent making King Saud appear awkward is also noteworthy. Yet although this article does stand out, the general sentiments it expresses were widely held at the time it was published. Although some of Schmidt's article seems rather petty—especially the parts about not talking while eating and watching basketball wrongly—as I argued in chapter 3, even seemingly petty descriptions do important work. According to Hisham Sharabi, this text is typical of what "was prevalent in the final stages of imperialism and a type of writing that is anchored in the hegemonic self, directly and frankly contemptuous of the non-Western Other. It is paternalistic in its approach, with no self-doubt about its scholarly legitimacy or the integrity of its interpretation" (1990, 6). Peter Gran similarly notes that such racialized feeling is useful to "maintain loyalty" to a particular power structure despite the fact it "spawns guilt feelings and rationalizations of its persistence." The result is that a "moral scrutiny of behavior [is] imposed on the rest of humanity" that rarely gets applied to one's own group (1990, 229)—especially when it comes to how they watch basketball.

Although tone and focus shifted somewhat over time, many of the imaginative geographies outlined in this chapter remain present today. Saudis (and, to a lesser extent, other Gulf citizens) are still called anachronistic and paradoxical despite the fact that the overwhelming majority of Saudi citizens have never lived in a time before oil. The opaqueness label is even slapped on current regional "openness" star, Dubai, with surprising frequency. Certainly, the lack of maturity and the "unearned" nature of Gulf wealth remain staples of an image that never seems to fade completely away.

Like Schmidt, most mainstream commentators do say something nice out of some effort to appear even-handed, but then they proceed directly with the othering. Derek Gregory (2005) notes the same tendencies in the commentary that emerged after the attacks on September 11, 2001, in which writers such as Fareed Zakaria would proclaim Islam a religion of peace and then one sentence later declare it "has a problem" in that it "produces violent terrorists." One must remember, that is how Orientalism (and by extension market Orientalism) works: whether the author is complimentary or cutting, the important thing is the creation of a distance between "normal" and whatever Others are doing so that the writer can enjoy and enact positional superiority.

Although there has been great consistency over the decades, there have also been subtle differences in emphasis and structure of feeling over time. Indeed, the Gulf has experienced, reacted to, and reshaped market Orientalism in four distinct eras.

The first era, which is the focus of this chapter, begins with the initial oil strike in Bahrain in the early 1930s and lasts until the early 1970s. This is the "introductory" era, when the giant oil finds are made in Saudi Arabia, Kuwait, and Abu Dhabi. In addition, this era sees the initial rollout of "modern" infrastructures and garners the first set of reactions to the phenomenon of the "rich" tribal person. The second is the boom era, which begins with the "oil weapon" and price spike of 1973. That era, which is the subject of chapter 5, includes the broadening of mega-oil revenues to more Gulf states and the deepening engagement of outside economic actors in the Gulf. These actors imagine it as a lucrative consumer market, a source of investment funds, and perhaps even an emerging world power. It is also the era that includes the fateful year 1979. As Hamit Bozarslan (2012) points out, this year saw the culmination of revolution in Iran, a siege in Mecca during the Hajj pilgrimage, an invasion of Afghanistan, and the signing of the Camp David Accords. Combined, these events led to the end of leftism as the most powerful Arab oppositional stance and the rise of various brands of Islamism. The third era, which lasts from the mid-1980s to 2001, is the moralization and condemnation era, which coincides with lower oil prices and the invasion of Kuwait. This era is filled with pronouncements about the Gulf states paying for their unorthodoxy and is discussed briefly at the end of chapter 5 and then again in chapter 9. The final era, from 2001 to the present, is the "new boom" era following a recovery of oil and gas prices, which is dominated first by the rise of Dubai as Other to this region of Others and then by the emergence of Abu Dhabi and Qatar. Chapters 6, 7, and 8 address the production of cultural economic imaginations and structures of feeling during this contemporary era.

Again, it is important to understand that this chapter and the next are not meant to be the single, "true" history of the Gulf, its cultural economies, and its many different peoples during the eras covered. Although I contextualize my source material with events in the Gulf, I favor material with longer quotes in which structures of feeling can be most clearly discerned. Thus, in the selection of my sources I have aimed for representativeness of feeling instead of for the development of a prioritized historical narrative. Fortunately, many other fine efforts have been made to provide parts of this historical narrative, such as Robert Vitalis's book *America's Kingdom* (2007) and biographies produced by early migrants to the various states (e.g., al-Fahim 1998).

Furthermore, in no way do I imagine that all reporters covering the Gulf have loathed it personally (although some clearly do). However, as Said notes of Orientalism, these authors—no matter what they feel about the Gulf in their hearts—perform the work of dividing "their" cultural economies from "ours." Thus, they produce positional superiority simply by virtue of having the ability to travel and publish in these widely read outlets with influential audiences. So the point of these chapters is not to say that all reporters were and are racist, classist, or nationally chauvinistic. Instead, these chapters seek to trace both the evolution and amazing consistency of the geographic imaginary I call "market Orientalism," which has arisen from the combined effects of their work and is very real in its practical and emotional consequences.

Era One, 1932–1972: Getting to Know Our Distance

To begin, it is important to reiterate that the Gulf's primary challenge to established cultural economic imaginaries, both before and after the

Cold War, is the fact that people in the Gulf are not only "clearly" Other but also (unlike most Others) seemingly rich. In terms of economic epistemologies, there was almost no way to make sense of this contradiction, especially in the mid–twentieth century. The modernization process was thought to occur in a series of established steps, as laid out in works such as Walter Rostow's book *The Stages of Economic Growth: A Non-Communist Manifesto* (1960). However, the Gulf seemed to defy the expected pattern, engaging in very few of the constellations of practices that were considered a precondition for having an "advanced" society. This deviance from the expected led to a need to explain and then to dismiss its sudden emergence.

In the structures of feeling around development at the time, Europeans and North Americans were considered well off, having passed through the stages of growth (from agriculture to mass industrialization) in what was consider a "normal" sort of way. The Soviet Union was also considered developed but morally and politically inferior, according to theories such as Rostow's. It was also accepted that some non-Western people who were subjects of large, long-running empires or their successor states (e.g., Taiwan, India, Turkey, Iran, and Japan), as well as citizens of large Latin American countries, could also be rich as individuals. However, it was thought that these individuals could not generate broadly wealthy societies on their own (at least not yet). Their societies might show signs of progress, but they were still behind. Thus, these "great" developing world states—although never considered on par with the highest echelon of NATO-aligned states (at least not until Japan in the 1970s)—were not total pariahs in terms of cultural economic power.

However, "tribal" people, as people in the Gulf were and are still so often called, were never supposed to be rich because of the unadvanced stage their societies were thought to be at. By the 1970s, the contradiction that they were wealthy even though they weren't supposed to be was sutured by saying "they didn't earn their money" and "they have spent it all the wrong ways." But it must be appreciated that in the 1950s the fact that rich, non-empire-based "brown" people with seemingly exotic cultural practices came into being (seemingly overnight) was genuinely shocking and something of a curiosity. In some senses, the Gulf states were a successful case of development on many of development's own terms (much longer life expectancies, better health care, more education, and very valuable exports), but they also caused an uncomfortable cognitive dissonance because they did not follow the steps of the stipulated program of progress fully or in any particular order.

To be clear, it was not just Europeans and Americans who held a pessimistic view of these "tribal" people. The fact that the Gulf was now economically visible was also a novelty to people in places such as Cairo, Beirut, Baghdad, and Damascus, which were the early-twentieth-century urban heights of the Arabic-speaking world. Although the subtle and not so subtle racism was less present in these places than in US and British treatments of the Gulf states, the former's reaction was akin to the one the British had when Americans became wealthy beginning in the late nineteenth century. The Gulf's visibility was a major disruption to the way distinction functioned in the Arabic-speaking world. Cairo and Beirut were far more than Europeans' favorite places in the Middle East; they were the centers of intraregional intellectual, cultural, and economic production. During this time, Beirut was still a flourishing (but highly inequitable) urban space—or, as several British accounts put it, "a laissez-faire success" with an unfortunate number of "shantytowns." It was the unquestioned banking and possibly education center of the Arabic-speaking world. Certainly, Beirut and Cairo were the entertainment capitals.

At the same time, Egypt was home to Gamal Nasser, undoubtedly the most prominent Middle Eastern political figure of the post–World War II era, who sought not just cultural leadership through promotion of icons such as singer Umm Kulthum but geopolitical leadership as well. Sometimes Nasser was against the Gulf monarchies: Egypt and Saudi Arabia basically fought a proxy war in Yemen. Sometimes he was for them: Nasser supported Kuwait against General Qasim of Iraq, who was making claims on that state. So although Gulf Arabs during this era were the central focus of market Orientalism, it must be remembered they were working in and against multiple realms of distinction and structures of feeling (such as Beirut's economic clout and Nasser's geopolitical stature). This remains true throughout all eras. For example, as Relli Shechter (2009) documents, during the late 1970s, just as Anwar Sadat's reforms were hitting the traditional Egyptian intellectual class hard, waves of newly rich (but less-well-educated) migrants were returning from the Gulf, which set off waves of resentment among the established intelligentsia. Similar in tone was a supposedly clandestine audio recording that was circulated on social media in early 2015 and eventually reported about in global news outlets (e.g., Daragahi 2015), which claimed to consist of conversations between Egyptian president Abdel Fattah el-Sisi and his inner circle. In this recording, the voice that is purported to be el-Sisi's states that Egypt should not have to make compromises with the "half-states" of the Gulf, which "have money like rice."

However, the Gulf is not always a negative example. Especially today, places in the Gulf often serve as positive, comparative models for other cities in Muslim-majority countries in terms of both culture and economy. For example, Sarah Moser (2012) notes that Malaysia has recently turned away from utilizing locally traditional styles of mosque architecture and toward the Arabian Peninsula style because the latter signifies a purer, Islamic modernity among some powerful Muslim Malays. Indeed, for better or worse, voices from Saudi Arabia have had a major influence on the direction of Islamic theology globally, just as Dubai has become a desirable and emulateable business capital for many African and Asian traders and elites.

With that background in mind, I want to highlight several dimensions of the economic imaginations of this early era. The second section in the chapter focuses on the astonishment concerning just how much oil was in the Arab Gulf and the fantasies that accompanied the finds—fantasies that imagined the Gulf as a tantalizing colonial frontier that offered one last chance to utilize those well-worn methods of control and extraction. The third section deals with the process of state invention. In particular, it highlights the reactions to the mammoth amount of infrastructure building being undertaken in Kuwait and Saudi Arabia during this time. Such building elicited feelings not only of wonder and possibility but also of condemnation surrounding its supposedly improper use. The fourth section analyzes the phenomenon of conspicuous male consumption, which came to be one of the major ways residents of the region were marked as Other. Together, these tropes began to shape market Orientalism by solidifying the idea that there is a distinct, identifiable and somewhat actionable Gulf cultural region that is definitely different from "normal." Furthermore, the notion formed that it was a region governed by opaque ruling families (and populated by a number of classically "Oriental" characters), but in such a way that full modernity eluded the population despite all the trappings of it. Thus, the region had (and still has) to deal with charges of mimicry—of being developed, but not properly.

Dreams of Controllable Riches

One of the themes of chapter 6 is how the Gulf regional economic eco-system functions by cities and states taking advantage of opportunities created by their neighbors' policies. In 1951, one such opportunity presented itself, and it led to Arab Gulf states rising out of obscurity in the US and British press for the first time. This rise led to air of anticipation that in turn led the *Times* of London to produce articles about Gulf oil strikes with subtitles such as "No One Knows Where the Shower of Gold May Fall Next" (1955).

Prior to 1951, Gulf oil exportation was dominated by the United Kingdom's Anglo-Iranian Oil Company and the American, French, and Dutch companies that had subsequently taken a stake in Turkish Petroleum (which eventually became Iraqi Petroleum). In fact, it was various combinations of the European and North American oil companies involved in Anglo-Iranian Oil and Turkish Petroleum that began most Arab Gulf state oil companies. The first strike on the peninsular side of the Gulf was in Bahrain in 1932. By 1950, the fact that there were huge reserves in Kuwait and Saudi Arabia was already well established, even though those states were not exporting very much at that time. Certainly, notions of what those really huge amounts of oil might mean for the global economy had yet to fully sink in for many economic actors.

What changed in 1951 was that Iran's prime minister, Mohammed Mossadegh, attempted to nationalize Iran's petroleum resources. This was a major blow to Anglo-Iranian Oil (soon to be renamed British Petroleum), which at the time was Britain's most important overseas firm. Iran's fields were the center of the company's livelihood. In that very same year,

Kuwait increased its production by 70 percent—a direct result of the space in markets left by the Iranian nationalization. By the end of the year, J. H. Carmical could publish an article in the *New York Times* that plainly stated what oil companies and diplomats had already figured out: "Mideast Oil a Vital Factor in World Economy" (1951). Carmical listed several points he considered noteworthy about this development: "It is important for two reasons: first, because it [the Gulf] contains about half of the world's proved oil reserves; and second, because it is one of the two major oil exporting regions (the other is the Caribbean). Sparsely populated and having no big industries of its own to supply, the Mideast uses little of the 1,800,000 barrels it produces daily. Hence, nearly all of this production is available for export."

Several important ideas appeared even in this early account. First, although these new players had vast amounts of oil, they were effectively blank slates in international cultural economic hierarchies—references to them as "patches of sand" abound (e.g., *New York Times* 1961). In addition, they were thought to have so little use for oil that it seemed they should be happy to be rid of it! But very soon this blank slate was filled with two types of images: controllable and medieval. Both did the work of preparing the region for the well-established types of imperial and frontier practice.

The oft-promoted notion that these producers were controllable must have seemed reassuring at the time, especially considering that the United Kingdom and United States had to go as far as to orchestrate a last-ditch coup against Iran's democratically elected government to salvage their interests there (Kinzer 2003). Iran was a large, well-established state with thousands of years of history and its own agenda. In the post–World War II era, such places were becoming increasingly hard for Europeans (and Americans) to control. In fact, it was somewhat lucky that the US and British plan to reinstate the shah actually worked.

The colonized world was rapidly deteriorating into today's array of small or lightly populated territories—the very type of places the Gulf sheikdoms turned out to be. The potential of a Mossadegh figure arising in the Gulf who would be difficult to overcome seemed very remote at the time (even if oil produced great wealth). Plus, countries of such small size (and "tribal" nature) were thought to be unable to handle the complexities of distributing and marketing nationalized oil and thus were unlikely to strike out on their own.

Both the US and UK press repeatedly mentioned the length of the new leases that would guarantee decades of access to oil, the "American-controlled" oil in Saudi Arabia, and the presence of British military bases at Juffair in Bahrain and at Sharjah in the future UAE. Here is a good example of a reporter reassuring his audience of controllability: "The Saudi government is extremely contented with the American development here and entertains very friendly feelings toward the United States, especially on the ground that it is not an imperialistic power. They say that although King ibn Saud has been irritated with the question, the King told one Aramco executive that rumors that he might withdraw the oil concession because of American support of the Zionists were 'hot wind'" (Sulzberger 1946). The king's comment foreshadowed an increasingly important source of potential tension in the relationship between the United States and the Gulf. As time went on, US foreign policy increasingly came to see the Middle East through the dual lenses of supporting Israel and keeping oil supplies from the Soviet Union. There was always a worry that there might be a time when the United States might have to choose one over the other, that the "tribal" people might dictate to the United States what its policy on Israel should be. But at the beginning of this era, this possibility seemed remote.

Furthermore, the British and the Americans let it be known that they were willing to push for a change in rulers, as happened in the cases of King Saud of Saudi Arabia, Sheikh Shakbut of Abu Dhabi, and Sultan Said of Oman. The replacement rulers did not have to be empty robes. By the end of this period, many of the leaders in the region (especially King Faisal of Saudi Arabia and Sheikh Rashid of Dubai) were described as "shrewd," that classic Orientalist description of Arab traders, in their dealings in the international arena and with oil companies. But they had to be willing to engage in frontier developmentalism, and rulers who did not were pushed aside.

What also fed into the image of controllability was that in this early period in the rise of the Gulf states much emphasis was placed on how far from modernity most of the Gulf was perceived to be. American reporters in the 1940s and 1950s tended to put the region somewhere in "biblical" times or, if they were generous, the times of the Prophet Mohammed. The British, who drew upon a wider range of colonial knowledge, referred to Gulf Arabs as "tribal" or "Bedouin" if they were being specific, but the adjective *medieval* tended to dominate in their descriptions of the Gulf. This difference in language reflects the fact that in the era immediately after World War II there were still some differences between British and American Orientalism—the former's was defined by their colonizing experience, the latter's by the idea of their exceptionalism from all other nations, including European ones (Nayak and Malone 2009). Over time, the imaginations of the Gulf circulating in media on both sides of the Atlantic began to resemble each other more and more.

In the mid–twentieth century, both the Americans and the British, despite some differences, came to the consensus that a great leap was being made overnight from no modernity whatsoever to material abundance in the Gulf. Many reporters tried to paint a picture of how jumbled the Gulf's "natural" development trajectory had become. As the author of "US Oil Towns Dot Saudi Arabian Soil" put it, "Outside of a few Sheikhs' carts no wheels existed here until the airplane and automobile arrived. Even now a majority of the few cars to be seen are mounted on autowheels. Aircraft preceded the railway. Radio anticipated the telephone. And curiously enough the Arab accepted these with calm and little curiosity" (Sulzberger 1946). The author's implication seems to be that the "Arab character" is rather dull. Perhaps a better explanation of the situation he described is that many midcentury Gulf Arabs were aware of at least some of the tools of "modernity"—rifles come immediately to mind—even if they did not yet possess a large variety of such tools themselves.

As Anne McClintock (1995) demonstrates, believing that Others live in an anachronistic, isolated time and space is a common colonial trope. These Others are not just considered different; they also are thought to be behind. Gran (1990) similarly points to a belief that twentieth-century American scholars, even those in a political economy tradition, often clung to: that feudalism in the Arab world is an unchangeable, ahistoric "heritage." This belief had the effect of blinding scholars and writers to the many peasant struggles that actually happened in the region. Thus, instead of conceiving of the idea that the Arab world could (and actually did) change from within, chroniclers often "emphasized 'the coming of the West' as a necessary condition of the coming of capitalism or modern times" (Gran 1990, 235) to the exclusion of all other possible explanations.

By the 1960s, when oil was discovered in what were then called the Trucial States (now UAE), the following was written about the inevitability of "Western-driven progress" as it was being mapped onto a Gulf of widely divergent lifestyles: "But their apparently dissimilar ways of life have in fact a common pattern, for the states in which they live are at different stages of evolution, from primitive and simple societies to ones as sophisticated as are found anywhere in the Middle East. The east Arabian states are like archaeological strata with pre-oil, early-oil and later oil periods" (Belgrave 1966).

But this article was employing the general sorts of colonial tropes about a lack of modernity; the particularly Orientalist tropes "special" to the Middle East tended to be applied to the rulers and the landscape. In the 1950s and 1960s, there were frequent reports concerning how ill equipped that first generation of rulers was, who either did not see the wisdom in accepting the oil "gift" or who did not accept it "wisely." Regarding King Saud, one author stated that although the king shared the Bedouins' "pride in their archaic way of life, and he also shared their limitations[,] he never understood, or seemed to understand, the world outside the desert. . . . Saad continued to try to live in Arabia's past, maintaining a vast harem and pretentious palaces, and distributing limitless bounty. He and many of his brothers, sons and nephews became laughing-stocks for their extravagance, and victims of every dishonest salesman" (Howarth 1967). The author also declared that King Abdulaziz Ibn Saud (King Saud's father) "died an unhappy, bewildered old man, because he could not imagine what to do with so much money, and feared it would corrupt the strict principles on which he founded his kingdom." This is one of the earlier examples in the English-language press of turning a Gulf Arab ruler or state into a cautionary tale or moralistic fable about the corrupting power of riches. Although the Gulf was of course useful as a source of NATO-aligned oil and of Arab allies against Nasser and the Baathists, its role as a foil in cultural economic imaginaries was becoming increasingly prominent. The narrative around these early Gulf rulers quickly devolved into a morality play, wherein those who receive undeserved wealth find themselves doomed by it.

The then recently deceased sheikh of Kuwait, Ahmad al-Jaber al-Sabah, received a similar treatment. After claiming that the sheikh asked that his first oil royalty payment be given as a pile of money rather than as a line in a balance book, one article went on to state that "he belongs to a part of the world in which royal treasure is still kept in vaults or spent upon splendor. Here, in microcosm, is the special problem created whenever immense wealth suddenly accrues to an eastern despot. . . . How are the oil companies, or the western governments concerned, to explain to such people the folly of aristocratic hoarding and the advantages to be received from investing these new millions in improving the lot of the common?" (*Economist* 1950).

But not all rulers were displaced because they spent too much; others were displaced because they did not spend enough. Here is a description of the parsimonious Sheikh Shakbut of Abu Dhabi: "Fearing the envy of his neighbors, Shaikh Shakbut refused to spend—and therefore display—his sudden fabulous wealth, but is believed to have kept it in trunks stuffed with banknotes under his bed—where according to a probably apocryphal pendant to the main story—the rats were later discovered to have consumed a large part of the state's finances" (Rendel 1969). This story gets repeated dozens of times in the English press over the next two decades, losing only the "probably apocryphal" clause. For example, in a *National Geographic* article published six years later it was stated that the money was eaten by insects (Putnam 1975). But Sheikh Shakbut was not the only ruler to receive attention for not spending; Sultan Said of Oman was said to have an "eccentric and repressive rule" that caused Oman to be "like Rip van Winkle, who slumbered as the rest of the world moved on" (Pace 1976a). Even though these stories of miser sheikhs are diametrically opposed to stories of the more spendthrift rulers, it was the Gulf that supplied the ill-equipped protagonist in all cases.

Although these men, who were scripted as doomed by the combination of "limitless" capital and changing times, passed without mourning from the Anglo-American media, media coverage of the Gulf was not all realpolitik callousness from members of the press. Some writers missed the beauty of the unspoiled desert (that old Orientalist romance), as did the anonymous correspondent who produced an article about the Northern Desert near the Aden Protectorate, titled "Wilderness without Charm."

> I think of them [the oil explorers] sometimes now when I fill the petrol tank of my car, and reflect on what man must endure in his search for the beastly stuff. One can but wish them well. . . . [But] success will mean the end of the Northern desert as we saw it. The tribesmen will abandon their camels to become truck drivers, the tents will give way to ugly structures made of tin, and the women will wear beads from Birmingham instead of their traditional silvers, and a new way of life will replace the old. Only the sand will remain, blowing ceaselessly from dawn to dusk, and the sun will continue to beat down as remorselessly as ever. It will remain a wilderness, but it will be a wilderness without charm. (*Times* [London] 1964)

However, the author concluded by noting that because he or she "loves" the Bedouin, he or she won't "begrudge" the Bedouin the fact that they will soon have year-round access to clean water. This was also a common enough sentiment: this person cared about the Bedouin, but mostly to the extent that they populated his or her vision of a charming desert.

In this first era, a number of tropes were established. One is of a nearly empty desert frontier soon to vanish, harsh but beautiful, ruled by sometimes overwhelmed Oriental despots but increasingly by shrewd men, and ready for shaping by major powers in exchange for *Arabian Nights*–style riches to come. Although this era began with oil finds in Bahrain, Kuwait, and Saudi Arabia, it concluded with Abu Dhabi, Dubai, Qatar, and Oman making strikes. These strikes furthered the idea that an identifiable Gulf market, which shared many cultural economic characteristics, actually existed. It also began to provide characters for the righteous morality play that discussions of Gulf cultural economic production were to become. All these oil strikes also meant that there were political and economic structures to build.

The Long but Inevitable Road?

In his 1946 *New York Times* article on Saudi Arabia, C. L. Sulzberger wrote: "Little by little, the land is slowly assuming its role in the modern world with foreign legations, representation at the United Nations, the establishment of airlines, sewers and schools. It is a long but inevitable road rendered difficult by the need to overcome the conservatism and religious traditions of the inhabitants." This statement demonstrates just how foregrounded imaginations of automatic modernization were in the mid–twentieth century. In some senses, the Gulf would serve as a perfect laboratory for proving the validity of these visions—unlike places without recourse to permanent revenue streams, most of the Gulf would eventually be able to afford the full complement of modern items and institutions on offer.

These mainstream newspapers gave frequent, sometimes breathless, updates concerning the construction of Gulf state apparatuses and infrastructure, even though the Gulf was thousands of miles away. For example, one article printed in the *New York Times* on January 10, 1964, "Saudis Preparing Projects to Remake the Face of the Nation," stated, "Saudi Arabian economic development is coming out of the talking and into the doing stage. . . . They [development projects] now include roads, ports, airports, telecommunications and sewerage, as well as steel and petrochemicals. Vast geological and seismic surveys are meanwhile probing future mineralogical resources." It also mentioned the involvement of the following government departments and companies: Robert Ray of Houston, the US Geologic Survey, the airline KLM, the Ford Foundation, Arabian-American Oil Company, Kellogg Company of the United States, "American, Italian and German companies," and other "foreign concerns." Such roll calls helped readers to imagine Saudi Arabia as a land of corporate colonial frontier possibility; indeed, the article managed to mention all of these companies and projects despite being only half a column long. Yet it did not mention other simultaneous developments of particular interest to Saudis (but perhaps of less interest to American engineering firms), such as universities—Riyadh University (later renamed King Saud University), Princess Nora bint Abdulrahman University for women (also in Riyadh), College of Petroleum and Minerals in Dhahran (eventually renamed for King Fahd), and Islamic University of Madinah—countless primary, intermediate, and secondary schools (including those for women), as well as hospitals.

Especially in the early part of this period, it was thought that an American-style middle class would inevitably be born from all of this building. As one article on Kuwait put it, "Physically the place has the impertinent air of a fairground, here-today and gone-tomorrow, as if five years from now there will be little left of new roads and splendid schools as there was of the mud-walled Arab town that stood here ten years ago. After physical rebuilding comes social change" (*Times* [London] 1959a).

For example, in an article surveying the newly rich people of the Gulf, the Isa Town housing development under construction in Bahrain was declared to be "not merely a rehousing scheme but also an exciting social experiment which is likely to change the way of life of many Bahrainis" (Belgrave 1966). The article went on to argue that this anticipated middle class, who lived in neighborhoods such as Isa Town, "sets the pattern of local thinking; commercially it provides the main markets for manufactured goods; economically it provides local investment for the industrial projects and light industrial that follow upon the development of oil industries. Socially also this class creates new needs, for restaurants, cinemas, club and for other innovations which make for a fuller social life." Indeed, it would really be something if some American-style houses were to give birth to light industry and cinemas by their mere presence. Unfortunately, this type of thinking was not atypical regarding development in the era; there was little exploration of causality beyond the assumption that if a place had the same collection of stuff as America, it would become more like America.

However, the main stumbling block foreseen in the forthcoming pleasant suburbanization of the Gulf was the oft-mentioned "inherent conservatism." As the 1950s became the 1960s, there was less feeling that this inevitable middle class would actually emerge and that perhaps the Gulf might turn out to be a new type of cultural economy with different priorities. As Sharabi puts it, there was increasing fear in US foreign-policy circles by the latter part of this era that modernizers in the Middle East would follow "their 'own way,' by taking 'new routes' and risky 'by-passes' and by allowing 'xenophobic nationalism,' 'hatred created by anti-colonialism', and rejection of 'foreign tutelage' to guide their action" (1990, 11).

By the time Abu Dhabi struck oil in the mid-1960s and Sheikh Zayed had displaced his brother Sheikh Shakbut, building infrastructure no longer seemed quite enough to ensure full modernity: "Abu Dhabi is gradually assuming the proportions, if hardly the spirit, of a modern town" (Herbert 1969). That advanced infrastructure (which no one who traveled to major cities in the oil-rich parts of the Gulf could deny they had) and modernity were becoming delinked in many accounts was a major sign that the Gulf would soon become something other than expected.

This period would see the beginning of the division of the Gulf into "good" states and "bad" states based on how reporters rated their cultural economies. In other words, the inevitable creation of hierarchies within structures of feeling had begun. What is interesting (but probably not surprising) is that throughout the subsequent fifty years, the primary example of the bad cultural economic state nearly always remained the same: Saudi Arabia. One particularly scathing assessment in an overall scathing article titled "Riches Changing Saudi Life" was typical: "While [neighboring] Yemen is still, as a wit once put it, plunging forward into the twelfth century, Saudi Arabia has been catapulted into the twentieth; amid its material evidence of vulgar modernity one continually hopes to discover some functional efficiency, if only to compensate for the loss of the romantic charm it must once have possessed. But the efficiency is not there. . . . [All the modern infrastructure is] as yet only a costly icing on the same old cake" (*Times* [London] 1958). On top of Saudi Arabia's loss of charm and lack of efficiency, the article also managed to bring up its ability to overspend despite huge revenues and a small population; its tendency to administer severe punishments; its lack of opportunities for women; and its general lack of what the author considered fun. Indeed, here we can see the reporter's astonishment at the fact that despite a thick frosting of new stuff, Saudi Arabia remained "the same old cake" of Arab misogyny and despotism, which meant development was not succeeding as it should.

But, if Saudi Arabia was the bad example, Kuwait was considered good by comparison during most of this period. In the same article that claimed Abu Dhabi had the infrastructure but not "the spirit" of a modern town, that sheikhdom was compared with Kuwait: "In any circumstances an influx [of new, foreign residents] of this magnitude would be difficult to manage. Kuwait has done so somehow, but its situation remains awkward and it had a head start over Abu Dhabi" (Belgrave 1966).

There was general consensus that "Kuwait is fantastically rich, and to be a Kuwaiti is to be a member of a privileged caste" (*Times* [London] 1959b). But that privilege was thought to be not just born of a large amount of funds. The emir, Sheikh Abdullah III, was constantly praised for how "unostentatious" he is and how well "the people have been taken care of." Kuwait also received high marks for possessing "a welfare state in education, medicine, housing and material amenity generally, which is virtually unlimited by budgetary considerations: and [for] building up an infrastructure of commerce, industry, and overseas investment against the still distant time when oil resources, and the revenues that go with them, begin to dry up" (Marlowe 1966). In other words, Kuwait was thought to spend wisely and broadly, not just on royal plenty but on the collective consumption of society.

Other authors speculated that Kuwaitis were more historically worldly than Saudis, proposing that this worldliness might be the reason for their "superior" state. For example, one author argued that "no country could be more intensely Arab than Kuwait," stating that there were millionaires in Kuwait even before the coming of oil and that even though it was now filled with refineries that resembled "post-human science fiction cities," the country still contained "a solid human core of Kuwaiti individualism" (*Times* [London] 1971b). Even in later eras, Kuwait was singled out for what one author called its "unassuming face of capitalism": "Anyone who comes to this Arabian Texas and expects the streets to be paved with petro-dollars will be sorely mistaken. Hard-headedness, not ostentation, are the hallmark of Kuwaitis. No gold-plated Cadillacs will be found on the street, and men who could buy out the Bank of England tomorrow look little different from anyone else in their traditional dress, the flowing dishdash" (Hopkirk 1975b). As the Gulf region came to be defined, Kuwait was often presented as the semipositive example of good, merchantlike (but tribally loyal) Arabs that was used to bludgeon the other Gulf states.

For similar reasons, Bahrain—with far less oil—also received occasional praise: "Bahrain is reasonably confident in its future as an entrepôt for the Gulf. It is excellently administered in a colonial way, with a relatively large number of British officials" (*Times* [London] 1959b). Indeed, it is clear in this era that most reporters decided that the colonial way was the most "excellent" way. Even by the early 1970s, Bahrain was praised for using its "modest" oil income and for being "a jump ahead of its neighbors in terms of its attitude towards development" (*Times* [London] 1974). In fact, a common pattern emerged: whenever a Gulf citizen (or entire nation) was praised economically, it was often for his (or its) "trader" or "merchant" sensibility. Of all the Arab caricatures that populate Orientalism, the merchant is the one considered to be most like (or perhaps even a "medieval" model for) the keen-eyed capitalist (the hero of the Global North) in that he is viewed as willing to go after every cent. In fact, the imaginings of Gulf "merchants" that appear in these accounts very much followed the tropes of what Boltanski and Thévenot (2006) call the world of "market" values, wherein worth is judged by the negotiation of price and the competition for wealth and luxury becomes the most important social marker. Indeed, praising those who are "merchantlike" becomes practically the only trope of justification that US and UK writers ever called on in a noncritical matter in relation to the Gulf according to Boltanski and Thévenot's tableau. As chapter 7 shows, Dubai and its rulers have become particularly associated with the merchant ideal and have learned to manipulate it (mostly) to their advantage.

However, if there is one aspect of market Orientalism for which even Kuwait got demerits for embodying, it is impenetrability. One article claimed that the ruling family was "as closed to the outside world as a clenched fist," noting that in Kuwait there existed "no public documents" and "no budget" (*Times* [London] 1961). Such lack of openness made even the "best" Gulf state stand apart from the normal standard. This same article continued: "To its Arab sister States, Kuwait is a fabulous anomaly, enviably wealthy and politically backward. . . . Neither individual wealth nor Kuwait's welfare state with its free education and medical treatment can compensate the educated youth of Kuwait for the humiliation of submitting to archaic customs in a rapidly changing world." Once again, an author informs us that deep down, despite fabulous material prosperity, Gulf Arabs feel humiliated instead of happy. This imagined feeling became a key difference used to demarcate our wealth from theirs.[1]

This supposed gap between their wealth and full modernity connects to the notion that even if Gulf Arabs are rich and perhaps "merchantlike," they are rarely imagined as fully capitalist or productive. One factor driving this notion was how important "land" was in comparison to manufacturing in Gulf economies of this era. One description of this importance comes from the same 1961 *Times* article quoted earlier and matches that quotation's mixture of fact and harsh judgment: "If one asks how do these men [the rulers] live and fulfill their princely obligations, the answer is a slight shrug. . . . As regards to internal finances, a little polite probing soon brings up the key words 'land sales.' . . . This is the source of the ruling oligarchy's means and the method of distributing the wealth. . . . A sum of 50m a year spread among the landowners in a population which, including foreigners, is only about 250,000 soon creates new commercial moguls."

The centrality of land to wealth was also noted in Saudi Arabia (and criticized): "And some at least of the princes may find a solution for themselves by going into business. Some have already done so, but in a negative sort of way, by acquiring land and buildings in Riyadh (as well as apartment buildings in Beirut). But the more adventurous are beginning to think in brisker terms than being merely rentiers and landlords" (*Economist* 1961a). In the 1950s, the standard narrative was that those buying land were lesser capitalists than those who produced things. Indeed, Beblawi (1987) echoes this narrative three decades later in his critique of the rentier state (see chapter 3).

Even though land is obviously not an oil sector, what was (and is) always suggested to be good for the Gulf in the long term was economic "diversification," which in this era essentially meant industrialization. As Gran puts it, political economy perspectives of the mid–twentieth century

---

1. Within two years of this article being written, Kuwait convened a National Assembly, which, despite multiple dissolutions, allegations of frequent interference by the ruling al-Sabahs, and periods of more and less ability to influence policy, still exists.

equated the third world with agriculture, malnutrition, and poverty and led to the championing of "industrialization as a solution, so that [industrial] development was seen as a precondition for social and political change" (1990, 236). So it is unsurprising that industrialization was preselected as the path forward also for the Gulf. Little mind was paid to the fact that the Arab Gulf states were never overly agricultural and thus could not transition out of it. Nor was much heed paid to the rapid settlement of formerly seminomadic Bedouin in towns and cities, which meant that developing industry as a source of urban attraction was superfluous. Nor was such advice particularly concerned that mass industrialization might not be the best course of action in a relatively high-cost, small-market location such as the Gulf.

A good example of the importance placed on diversification comes from an *Economist* survey of the Arabian Peninsula in a section titled "Oil Is Not Enough": "The future of perils of economies based solely on oil revenues have, to a great extent, been realized. Minds are being turned to the possibilities of diversification, of using the oil and natural gas, not just for paying for welfare services and consumer goods and services, but as a source of energy and a raw material for other industries" (Wall 1970).

One must keep in mind that developed economies that manufactured things were still in vogue during this era. However, it was and is still a rather narrow interpretation (though hardly unprecedented for *Economist* reporters) to declare that Gulf economies were defined solely by oil and gas even when service sectors, both private and public, most definitely existed in these places. Although oil and gas did generate most of the foreign revenues, those foreign revenues did get respent in the domestic economy. In chapter 6, I touch more on the tendency to view export earnings as the only economically important category.

Besides being inaccurate, this stance is also spatially blind. A number of countries with total populations similar to Saudi Arabia's produced robust export earnings in an array of sectors during this era, but most of them were in Europe, where industrialization started. All of the other Gulf states had populations similar to those of midsize to large American urban areas. Cities or urban areas of 1.5 to 2 million persons generally produce fewer varieties of "exports" than countries of more than 20 million persons. Furthermore, the Gulf states, by emphasizing welfare and infrastructure, were behaving in a very typical postcolonial way; the only difference was that they had the funds to vastly increase their probability of success. Yes, they did not experience the same manufacturing-led export growth that Taiwan, Singapore, and South Korea enjoyed by the end of the twentieth century, but that is also true of almost every country on earth that was not Taiwan, Singapore, or South Korea.

This is a key point: beginning in the 1960s, there were countless calls for the Gulf to engage in diversification but always into one or another arena in which the United States or United Kingdom was more successful (be it industry, banking, high tech, or tourism) and that also happened to currently be in fashion. These calls had little to do with what was actually going on in Gulf economies and much more to do with commentators thinking that Gulf oil wealth was morally unproductive compared to wealth produced by the currently favored industrial sector. It does not matter if the calls for this or that sector were poorly thought out; indeed, by the 1980s, if the Gulf had actually managed to produce a major manufacturing sector, it likely would have been staffed by low-wage foreign workers in order to compete with the emerging low-wage manufacturers in East Asia.

Even though the Gulf eventually did get aluminum smelters, petrochemical industries, tourism enterprises, major banks, satellite TV networks, vertically integrated petroleum firms and the like, no amount of actual economic diversity would ever bring an end to the calls for diversification. Do not misunderstand: economic diversity is not a bad thing. Focusing on a lack of a certain type of diversity in order to use that lack as a weapon to reinforce positional superiority, however, is problematic. Thus, it is important to understand that the calls for "diversification" like the ones issued in the *Economist* are not equivalent to my stance concerning the value of the diverse economies in which all Gulf residents find themselves embedded.

That being said, a few more nuanced news pieces tended to hold up lightly industrialized and comparatively small Lebanon as a more appropriate state for decision makers in the Gulf to emulate. During this era, Beirut was the most important Arab link with the world economy. Its business community coordinated trade within Southwest Asia, produced all forms of media, trained many of the region's doctors, and provided a diverse array of banking services suited to the particular preferences of their newly wealthy Gulf clients. At this early stage, two places in the Gulf were singled out for being the most like "laissez-faire" Lebanon: Bahrain and Dubai. Even within much maligned Saudi Arabia, Jeddah—the long-established landing port for the holy cities of Mecca and Medina, with diversity typical of many port cities—was praised for being the commercial capital and contrasted with the unreality of Riyadh.

Although some Gulf Arabs and places were considered comparatively worldly, it was the presence of a large number of foreigners that was considered to truly represent cosmopolitanism (or, in this era, modernity) in the Gulf. An article published soon after Abu Dhabi's first major oil strike offered one such account of foreigners' role:

> It takes people to lay concrete and a tribal population largely used to pearling, fishing or traipsing around with camels is ill-equipped to do it for itself. The result, inevitably, is an influx of foreign "experts" whose credentials are often not necessarily what they seem to be and whose interests, political or otherwise, outside working hours are as different as possible from those of their hosts. The Lebanese businessman, sipping his dry Martini in the air-conditioned al-Ain Hotel, and the native Abu Dhabian brewing up his bitter coffee on a fire of camel dung beneath a stunted thorn tree are as different as chalk and Camembert. (Herbert 1969)

What is striking here (this piece is one of the most "striking") is that most of the big tropes are condensed into a single paragraph. Foreigners drink alcohol, whereas locals drink "bitter" coffee. Foreigners need air conditioning; locals are associated with the "stunted thorn tree" (which, one supposes, is the botanical cousin of Thomas Friedman's olive tree). Foreigners keep to a forty-hour, Monday–Friday workweek; the locals keep to something else. The reporter (also a foreigner) appreciates fine French cheese; that same reporter finds that the locals are too attached to their camels as both traipsing partners and sources of fuel. Just these few things, such as alcohol consumption and different conceptions of time, along with women's participation in the workforce and insider decision making, were often pointed to with consistency as to what separates "our" working world from "theirs." Yet these differences came to constitute an enormous chasm. Such distinctions were even flimsier by 1969, when this article was published, because fewer people seriously attempted to accuse those in the Gulf of preferring "bitter coffee" to "modern goods."

Even the seemingly negative mention of the foreigners' suspect "credentials" was in reality another poor reflection on the Gulf Arabs, who were represented as too naïve to know better. This was a fairly common trope in this era. Although some foreigners, especially British and American, were scripted as well intentioned (not surprisingly, given my source material), not all guest workers received such treatment. Here is some further description of those foreigners: "Most are Palestinian and Lebanese or workers from across the Gulf, who have come to make money. There is no shame in that and many of them are honest, well-intentioned men, but there are inevitably the sharks" (Herbert 1969).

To conclude, many of the tropes that remain associated with the Gulf states and economies to this day emerged during the first few decades of oil extraction there. They include the notion that the Gulf is an Other type of region with a dependency on a single sector, a situation that brings unhappiness and ruin. Although initially some proposed that the building of modern infrastructures would automatically bring generic American-style prosperity to the Gulf, commentators soon decided that would not happen. They chalked up much of this failure to the inhabitants' "inherent conservatism" and the ruling families' "secretive" nature—thus, the combination of a lack of maturity and impenetrability was holding these states back. However, some states and economies were thought of as better than others, mostly depending on how "merchantlike" they were—which, in itself, is an Orientalist trope. Kuwait was usually considered the best example, and Saudi Arabia the worst. However, in all cases there was too much of an emphasis on land and not enough on the best type of industrial capitalist behavior. Another looming issue will be the presence of foreigners—some of whom were apparently sharks seeking treasure from the supposed cultural economic minnows that inhabit the Gulf. I turn to the subject of the distribution and spending of treasure in the next section, but suffice it to say now that instead of seeing the Gulf for what it was becoming, the primary view of the region reveled in what the Gulf was considered to lack in comparison to "superior" cultural economies.

They Don't Like to Work

This chapter has already chronicled reactions to an oil strike of unimaginable wealth in a land sparsely populated enough to relive the dream of colonial days, where lines of demarcation between the modern and the supposedly premodern seemed clear and potentially lucrative. This oil-rich land was viewed as a backward place, but in a mysterious, frontier-possibility kind of way. The chapter has also highlighted what this strike produced in its wake: freshly built states and economies with "modern" infrastructures that increasingly ended many signs of poverty but did not bring what was considered "normal" middle-class modernity, as many thought such constructions should. In fact, what was created was considered a less than optimally allocated use of such wealth and thought to be overly reliant on foreigners, not all of whom were the right kind. In other words, a soon to be entrenched imaginative geography of malfunction was emerging—one that felt like both opportunity and inferiority.

The final element that came to define the structures of feeling around the Gulf in the early era was the emergence of the conspicuous, Gulf male consumer.

In the United States and particularly in Great Britain during this era, one was supposed to be against conspicuous displays of wealth. This is not to say people were supposed to refrain from consuming. Indeed, the 1950s and 1960s saw the rise of an unprecedented consumer society. However, there was a prohibition against consuming in obvious and theatrical ways, given that the scarcity of the Great Depression and World War II was still fresh on people's minds. Teenagers were given some leeway, but overtly following trends was considered a sign of immaturity. Furthermore, there was a gender aspect to this consumption: men in particular were supposed be restrained in appearance (favoring subtle, classic, fashionable touches), outside the cycles of style, and against the thrall of shopping as a hobby. If any gender must be adorned, it was—as the script went—women.

By the end of this era, chroniclers decided to notice (briefly) that they did not see Gulf national women much, or if they did, they saw only their "simple" black cloaks (which were imagined to be oppressively hot because black). For example, a *New York Times* notes simply: "Most women are only seen behind black veils" (Schmidt 1968). Over time, the discourse about women in the Gulf transformed into a kind of free-floating signifier that was increasingly separated from the (not necessarily rosy) complexities of reality. This signification was helped along by the fact that reporters spoke to amazingly few Gulf women during this era. However, as Said argues, the goal of these imaginations is not accuracy; it is separation.

Because the usual subjects of consumption, women, were unavailable to the largely male chroniclers of the Gulf, the Gulf male was placed in the void. There are two facets to the way male consumption was covered: the penchant for luxury goods (a sign of gross affluence) and the lack of production. Both of these facets in particular work on structures of feeling because they connect to ideas of values, aesthetics, and style. This emphasis on male consumption aided in the imagination of the Gulf as a backward place.

Let us first discuss luxury goods, or at least what were considered luxuries for "developing" people. One of the main items writers took note of was the preponderance of nice new cars, in particular Cadillacs. Indeed, Dana Adams Schmidt, looking back at Saudi Arabia in the 1950s, referred to that time as "the decade of the Cadillac," when "the great King's weak-willed son [Saud] had squandered its [the country's] first oil wealth" (1968). The consumption of watches also drew a disproportionate amount of attention, as did the fact that all such products were "duty free," which especially amazed British correspondents, who were used to paying high consumption taxes on luxury goods, under the pre-value-added tax "purchase tax" system. A description from 1980 is pertinent here because it shows the enduring fascination reporters had with men wearing watches in the Gulf: "The UAE imported two watches in 1979 for every man, woman and child living in the country. That sort of statistic is indicative of the taste for consumer goods and luxury items being developed by a nation which in 1979 had one of the highest per capita incomes in the world" (Whelan 1980b).

Also singled out for special attention were the "palaces," which were never referred to as "mansions" (as they would have been if they were in America) and rarely even as "villas," which is the term used in the region (the term *palace* tends to be reserved for the residences of royal families). For example, we see *palace* used as a descriptor in this passage: "Where herds of camels once grazed, wealthy Qataris have built their country houses, each with its own little garden carefully irrigated from the meager water supplies, like miniature versions of the Omayyad palaces that dot the Jordan countryside" (*Economist* 1966). A depiction of King Saud's new abode can be found an article titled "Riches Changing Saudi Life" under the subhead "Extravagant Palace." It is said to have "replaced an almost new" palace and to contain "four separate palaces for the reigning wives, 32 mansions for other ladies and their retinue and 37 villas for various princes, as well as schools, a hospital, a museum, a zoo, and the world's largest air conditioning plant" (*Times* [London] 1958).

Not only do these male consumers have expensive things, but they are also portrayed as never having enough. One of the very first articles to appear in the *New York Times* on the effects of oil in the Gulf stated under the subhead "Sheikh Dreams of Wealth" that "the Sheikh of Bahrain keeps begging 'BAPCO' [Bahrain Petroleum Company] officials to extract petroleum more rapidly regardless of the eventual non-economy of such a move because oil to him means motor cars and race horses and gold. He says time and again: 'I cannot sleep at night as I hear oil groaning and crying beneath the earth trying to get out'" (Sulzberger 1946). Notice how the sheikh is said to "beg" like a child, not to "ask" or to "decree," and how the ones who hold the real authority (and have the proper perspective) are the foreign oil executives.

What made all this spending particularly galling to reporters in this era was how men in the Gulf did not seem to have to work for it. We already have seen how Gulf Arabs were considered to have gone into business in a "negative sort of way," as rentiers rather than as producers or entrepreneurs. Although those rentiers were frowned upon, they were nowhere near as disdained as the average Gulf government employee. A rather lengthy quotation from a 1970 *Economist* survey of the Arabian Peninsula demonstrates this disdain:

> But a depressing factor is the general attitude of the peninsular Arabs to sustained work. They dislike it. They consider manual work, even that requiring a degree of technical knowledge and skill, beneath their dignity. In Saudi Arabia, Bahrain and Kuwait there are nationals, both from the ruling families and commoners, who are able, as forward-thinking and industrious as any of the hired brains—but they are the exceptions. . . . They may well ask, if education and health services are free, if there are generous unemployment and welfare benefits, if power, fuel, public transport and telephone services are free or heavily subsidised, if there are soft jobs running messages or behind desks going for the asking, why on Earth they should exert themselves to learn the trades of carpenters, plumbers, mechanics or radio and television engineers—especially as there are foreigners enough willing to fill these posts. . . . Such a labour force is an uncertain base for economic development. (Wall 1970)

The last part of this quotation, in particular, has been a running feature of the *Economist*'s surveys of the Gulf since the 1960s—nearly fifty years of it. The *Economist* has generally been as against the state being involved in the economy as any major publication in the world, but these sentiments about a lack of work ethic were widely felt by reporters for other outlets, if not as boldly stated. There was a tendency to both wonder at and find reasons to resent Kuwait in particular for all of the benefits accrued to its citizens (and during this era to its foreign residents as well). This is because welfare—even before the Reagan–Thatcher era—was something rarely supported in the United States or the United Kingdom unless it somehow went only to the "truly needy." The lines about Arabs not liking "work that dirties their hands" and not seeing the link between material benefits and productivity (which marked them as unworthy of support) should ring true to those familiar with US and British debates around welfare reform in the 1990s. However, in Kuwait (unlike in the United States, where the fantasy of the luxury-car-driving,

food-stamp-receiving masses originated) some "welfare" recipients actually did own new Cadillacs.

The judgment against these consumer-workers was harsh. Perhaps the
most sustained assault on the Gulf Arab came in the *New York Times*
from Jan Morris, who—even in this early point in her career—had already
written several books about the region. These books told the stories of the
more romantically cast and "classically" Arab sheikhs of Jordan and pre-oil
Oman, for whom Morris had great affection and admiration. The usually
subtly witty Morris felt far less sanguine about royals from elsewhere in the
Gulf and so described the oil sheikh as

> the stock comic figure of the Arab countries. He is gilded but uncouth,
> who lords it in dissolute grandeur among the night clubs of Europe and
> Levant, and who moves among his inferiors in a cloud of opulent hypoc-
> risy. . . . He has jumped direct from the camel to the Cadillac. In the last
> thirty or forty years he has been violently projected, heavy with wealth
> and dubious prestige, into a Western world whose true sophistications
> he does not begin to master, and whose laborious development means
> nothing to him. He is quite ignorant of the complicated processes and
> undercurrents of our material civilization . . . that [have] led, for exam-
> ple, to the delivery of his spanking new convertible. He knows only that
> he is very rich, that the world seems to be his oyster, that the chorus
> girls are extremely obliging. . . . Faith in Allah has been replaced by an
> unquestioning trust in unearned moneys. (1959)

Morris concluded this discussion by noting (just in case the previous
section did not leave the right impression) that "the oil sheikh can be a
winning figure. But bear in mind that he is probably very ignorant, shame-
fully lascivious, petty, childish and conceited—and the attentive servants
behind him are, in all but name, very likely slaves."[2]

2. Given the style and themes of Morris's later work, one reviewer of my book wondered whether this quote was satirical. Although her essay is full of hyperbole, it is not
satirical. She treats the "oil sheikhs" with much less nuance and affection than she treats
the other sheikhs she profiles elsewhere.

In *Culture and Imperialism* (1993), Said addresses such representations in a discussion of Hussein Alatas's book *The Myth of the Lazy Native* (1977). After asking why the myth of Arab laziness held for so long, Said notes "how[,] in Eric William's words quoted earlier, 'an outward interest, whose bankruptcy smells to heaven in historical perspective, can exercise an obstructionist and disruptive effect which can only be explained by the powerful services it had previously rendered and the entrenchment previous gained.' The myth of the lazy native is synonymous with domination, and domination is at the bottom, power" (254).

This is the crux of market Orientalism as it pertains to the citizens of the Gulf. Given the general hopefulness of independence movements and feel-good developmentalism, by the mid–twentieth century most places in the former colonial world were scripted as having good, potentially hard-working economic subjects, often trapped or crushed by the bad political economic infrastructure in which they lived. The Gulf, in contrast, was scripted as being full of bad economic subjects who get away with it. This is an almost unique formulation. For example, in the course of US history, various immigrant and minority groups were associated with a lack of work ethic, dirtiness, or some other undesirable trait. But such people were almost always seen to be "punished" for it by living in ghettos or poverty or some other ill situation. If late capitalism is the spatialization of class, then in many scripts the Gulf is the spatialization of the unproductive leisure class into postcolonial imaginaries. Perhaps the success of the Gulf was so unnerving because it seemed to lay bare the old capitalist myth that Marx mocked in volume 2 of *Capital*: that the capitalist is wealthy because he has worked hard and earned it. Maybe some capitalists do work hard (and hard work is certainly unlikely to hurt one's chances of success), but instead of fortune favoring the bold, many times wealth favors the fortunate.

Without a doubt, the 1932–72 era represented a major change in circumstance for the Gulf states. Although these states were not the "medieval" and completely unconnected places that the first wave of articles about them claimed they were (because the British and other European powers had already been active in the region for decades before the coming of oil, the Ottomans and Persians had been there even longer than that, and the marvel of human diversity that is the Hajj pilgrimage had been going on for centuries)—they were definitely peripheral to the emerging global economy of the time. Some places were more peripheral, some a bit less. By the standards of that emerging global economy, these societies were initially far from wealthy. Once the oil wealth came, and as more people became settled in bigger, more permanent houses connected to thick infrastructures, it is certain they quickly acquired many items that they had not previously possessed or had much personal exposure to. Some of the items were bought purely to be consumed in enjoyment; some people probably spent foolishly. I am sure that for many people the rhythms of life shifted dramatically and, at least at first, in a disorienting manner.

But by the end of this era, the people of Bahrain, Kuwait, and Saudi Arabia certainly had by and large adjusted to the notion of "shared" oil wealth—but not by becoming clones of members of other previous wealthy societies (for better or for worse). Although Gulf residents adjusted, the imaginative geographies produced by market Orientalism continued to plague them. Indeed, efforts to demean and separate the Gulf proved an excellent way to maintain the self-definitional Anglophone myth (which is especially common in the less class-rigid United States) that people who work hard and create are rewarded and those who do not work hard will be punished in due time. Creating all these infrastructures, transactions in land, changes of routine, and establishment of institutions in the Gulf was work, of course, but the reports produced about the Gulf never really recognized it as such.

In fact, one of the major reasons why the charges of the lack of diversity in their economies, of the lack of hard work, and of overconsumption have persisted is that (to observers based in the United States and the United Kingdom) events in the Gulf occurred in the wrong order. The Gulf received right up front what were supposed to be the final rewards of economic development, and in a teleological era such a breach of cultural economic hierarchy was hard to stomach. These economies seemed to have all the material rewards despite being immature, impenetrable, and very Other. As their wealth drew them nearer to notions of cultural economic normalcy, the structures of feeling seemed to work harder to push Gulf citizens and places away from those notions.

The amount of wealth generated in this era, however, was a mere drop in the bucket compared to what was to come.

5

A Historical, Cultural Economic Geography of the Gulf

Part Two, Peak Gulf (1973–1982)

The early oil era detailed in chapter 4 established many of the tropes that define market Orientalism's encounter with the Gulf. It established the idea of an identifiable Gulf regional market, which was both new because of the impacts of oil wealth and old because it was still a society full of "classic" Arab characters. Thus, the Gulf was considered a region and market that could be effectively controlled by skilled outsiders, even if the local rulers seemed somewhat impenetrable. It was also a place that quickly built an up-to-date infrastructure but was still seen as lacking full, modern maturity. The Gulf was additionally said to need further economic "diversification" because it eschewed the constellation of processes through which development was supposed to unfold. It was also viewed as possessing a seemingly unfashionable emphasis on consumption over production. Thus, it was seen to only mimic, not match, successful cultural economic practice. Such views transformed the Gulf into a yardstick to righteously measure one's own cultural economy against.

The boom era, which began in 1973 and is the focus of this chapter, saw a continuation of many of the tropes from the previous era. However, there would be some differences, particularly in the structures of feeling around the Gulf. One of the biggest differences was a shift in tone. Although many authors continued to talk down to the Gulf in a condescending or moralistic manner concerning the organization of their societies, there were not as many over-the-top, aggressively racist instances of prose. In other words, there were fewer references to "school boys in shorts," "traipsing around with camels," and "clouds of opulent hypocrisy." Bombastic language can still be found in the writing about the Gulf in this period, but it is much less prevalent. One can produce a list of reasons why this change might have occurred: a knock-off effect of civil rights movements; a younger generation of writers for whom the colonial world and its blatantly expressed hierarchies were more distant; or perhaps increased clout for the Gulf. Whatever the combination of reasons, the shift in tone is noticeable even if the desire to create positional superiority remained firmly in place.

Indeed, this increased clout is a major difference between these two eras. The idea that the Gulf was an empty, controllable land was mostly put to rest by the 1970s, for reasons I outline in this chapter. The result was that some people in the Gulf were treated, practically for the first time, as *both* Other and highly capable. Sometimes this capability was seen as a good thing; other times it was viewed as potentially menacing to the cultural economic heartlands from which these chroniclers largely came. This shift speaks to a point Frederick Cooper and Ann Laura Stoler make about colonialism in general but can just as easily be applied to market Orientalism: "The most basic tension of empire lies in what has become a central, if now obvious, point of recent colonial scholarship: namely, that the otherness of colonized person was neither inherent nor stable; his or her difference had to be defined and maintained" (1997, 6).

With all that in mind, in this chapter I focus on four additional tropes concerning the Gulf's encounter with the structures of feeling produced by market Orientalism that emerged beginning in the 1970s. Some are new tropes; others are refinements or updates of tropes discussed in the previous chapter. The first section focuses on the effects of the Gulf's increased geopolitical clout, which certainly shifted the Gulf's reputation from curio to potential competitor or from mimicry to more threatening menace. The second section focuses on the notion of "unsuccessful" success. This trope can be summed up by the comment, "The Gulf seems to have it all, but. . . ." In other words, it is a continuation of the idea that the Gulf has managed to separate high-end infrastructure and consumption from the "modern norms" that demonstrate "true" achievement in the imagination of cultural economic hierarchies. Even more than maintaining the previously established idea of the Gulf's supposed neediness, this trope reinforces "our" continuing cultural superiority in the face of "their" success, thus tempering the Gulf's newfound cachet. The trope covered in the third section—the lack of positive urban identity in the Gulf—is in some ways a subcategory of the previous trope. However, the idea that Gulf cities—Riyadh most of all—are generally stifling, unhappy places that fail to enrich their residents' inner lives in any way appeared with such frequency in writing about the Gulf in this era that I felt compelled to deal with it in its own section. The fourth section addresses something that is less a trope than a trend—namely, a growing recognition that the cast of characters in the Gulf is wider than the "traditional" Orientalist one and includes all manner of people from throughout the world.

Although the individual states' fortunes rose and fell in this era (and low oil prices in the mid-1980s and late 1990s caused some shared falls that brought about a series of condemnations), most of these major tropes about the Gulf still remained in place, even if slightly modified. Unlike for other newly wealthy places that fell under the sign of market Orientalism but eventually found some level of acceptance, these ill feelings about the Gulf states have mostly defied displacement.

The Gulf Weaponized?

All it took was one major event to change the perception that the Gulf was an easily controllable area that could be cajoled into obedience. This event was the deployment of the so-called oil weapon in response to the upping (and then reupping) of US military support for Israel during the Yom Kippur War in 1973. Or, more specifically, after Saudi Arabia and other Arab oil producers declared a price rise and reduced production levels in response to Richard Nixon's coming out strongly on the side of the Israelis, escalation of the conflict eventually led the oil producers to refuse to sell crude oil *directly* to the United States and some of its allies. Although this refusal did little to stop the flow of oil to the United States—more Gulf oil went to Europe, and more non-Gulf sources (or Gulf oil resold from Europe) went to the United States—it did lead to a new era of high prices. Saudi crude prices before the boycott were at $1.30 a barrel in 1970 and rose to a little higher than $2.00 by the end of 1971. In 1973, following the boycott, they quickly reached $5.60 per barrel and then $11.30 later that year. This tenfold rise from the 1970 price allowed the Gulf countries to begin to buy out the major oil companies that had previously done the exploration and pumping in their territories. Such an impact on prices was possible because the Organization of the Petroleum Exporting Countries (OPEC), to which most Gulf producers belonged, represented 80 percent of world oil production at the time and supplied western Europe and Japan with almost all of their oil.

The "oil weapon" accomplished a number of objectives. Perhaps most obviously, Arab oil producers wanted to send a message to the US government concerning its support of Israel. The producing states were also attempting to slow down skyrocketing oil-extraction rates (which were being driven by skyrocketing demand) because slower production meant reserves would last longer. The move additionally led to higher prices, which led to more robust government coffers. Some of the anticolonial undertones of the move even managed to leak into the reporting of it in the United States and Britain—including the shah of Iran's oft-quoted 1973 declaration that "they [the developed world] will have to realize that the era of their terrific progress and even more terrific income and wealth based on cheap oil is finished."

This successful maneuver vastly increased the size of Gulf economies. Imports are a good measure of this increase: the Gulf as a whole imported around $6 billion worth of goods in 1972 (before the "oil weapon" was used) and $38 billion worth in 1976 (Baily 1977). Reporters also expressed this phenomenon qualitatively. For example, just before the big rise, one such description concerned already wealthy Kuwait: "No visitor can miss the less subtle evidence of prosperity. Kuwait City is a place of concrete blocks, of wide streets filled with cars, of shops filled with every glittering— and mostly foreign—goody ever devised to tempt the consumers' dinar. As well as the highest income a head in the world, Kuwait enjoys the highest level of imports a head" (Roeber 1971). Another article "pithily" remarked,

"For countries like Japan and Britain, the basis for economic survival has been 'export or die'; the slogan [for the Gulf] might be 'import and live'" (Fenelon 1974).

Images of hapless, rich despots were soon replaced with images of secretive, somewhat shadowy, suddenly empowered rich despots. One article was headlined "Oil Is Mightier Than the Sword in the Arab World: Nothing Is Able to Stop Petrodollars" and argued that, "as a capital city, Riyadh is anything but impressive. Its palaces, citadel-like ministries, modest skyscrapers, and monotonous villas and housing estates look as though they rose out of the desert sand on which they are built. The multilane highways that snake through the city on their way to nowhere add to the dust-laden bleakness. . . . However, the fact is this has become one of the world's power centres. It is from here that Saudi Arabia exerts an ever-growing influence on a scale that not so long ago, would have been considered impossible" (Martin 1977).

So powerful was oil wealth thought to be that in the immediate aftermath of the Iranian Revolution it was reported that "Iranians never took the threat of European trade sanctions very seriously. . . . The shopping streets north of Ferdowsi are packed every morning, the shelves of the supermarkets crammed with every luxury except alcohol. You can buy anything from a new colour television set, a toaster or a washing machine to a box of British made chocolates" (Fisk 1980). Of course, the drain of the Iran–Iraq War (1980–88) and the weight of sanctions against Iran would eventually alter the situation. However, it is worth noting that at the time oil was thought to be so powerful that it could triumph over international isolation even though by the end of the 1970s some of the initial hysteria about the power of oil had subsided. A global recession, an increasing emphasis on fuel economy and energy conservation, and new oil finds meant the "wilder projections" about the scope of the Gulf states' surpluses did not come true.

As mentioned at the beginning of chapter 4, the events of the year 1979 also helped to shift the structures of feeling surrounding the Middle East (Bozarslan 2012). The Camp David Accords between Israel and Egypt represented an acceptance of Israel's continued existence by the country that had long been at the center of Arab republicanism. Along with Egyptian president Anwar Sadat's economic reforms, the accords signaled an end to leftist Nasserism and the loss of the Soviet Union's greatest ally in the region. The US foreign-policy apparatus would gradually cease to treat Egypt as the most threatening country in the Middle East. Almost immediately into this vacuum, however, stepped the specter of political Islam. Early in 1979, Ayatollah Ruhollah Khomeini came to power in Iran, replacing the shah, one of the key US allies in the region. The tensions between the United States and Iran eventually culminated in the takeover of the American embassy in Tehran in November. Later in that same month, militants seized the Grand Mosque in Mecca during the Hajj pilgrimage, which led to hundreds of deaths during the two-week siege. Feeling pressured, Saudi Arabia's royal family took the policing of domestic affairs in a more sharply religiously conservative direction. At the same time, with the Soviet invasion of Afghanistan, the United States began to support religious fighters from the Middle East (similar to those who had seized the Grand Mosque) who were willing to travel to the front against the Soviet Union. Whereas prior to 1979 many negative feelings in the United States and the United Kingdom surrounded the term *Arab,* more and more of those feelings get displaced onto the term *Muslim* after that point.

Even though the Gulf states' clout increased and the structures of feelings shifted, market Orientalism continued to do the work of dividing these states into good ones and bad ones. The leader of the good-state pack remained Kuwait. For instance, an article titled "The 'Smart Operators' of the Gulf" praised the Kuwaitis:

> With characteristic finesse the Kuwaitis have succeeded in establishing themselves as respected advisors to the Arab world. . . . Kuwaitis delight in describing themselves as the "smart operators" of the Gulf and they see nothing strange in having so readily accepted the dual role they have been assigned, that of financial provider to much of the Arab and Third World and of political counselor to their Gulf and other Arab neighbors. It was probably inevitable that Kuwait, occupying a position so geographically central to the Gulf, should have become adept at political balance and in helping others to keep theirs. (Grainge 1980)

In fact, Kuwaitis were considered to have become such "smart operators" that Westerners looking for a few quick bucks could not pull the wool over their eyes any more. The same article continued: "However, the Kuwaitis are among the shrewdest of Semites. . . . [Their] attitude to investment and value for money tends to be down to earth. When a highly-priced painting of a horse by Stubbs was offered for sale in Kuwait recently, one wealthy sheikh looked at it and remarked: 'Why, for that money I could buy a stable full of thoroughbreds'" (Grainge 1980).

Of course, it must be remembered that writers only considered these "shrewdest of Semites" to be running the best *Gulf* state, not an actually good state. This approach was admittedly a harder row to hoe during this era, given that the Gulf states were undoubtedly wealthier than before (something that in standard development scripts was considered to increase happiness). During this era, the effort put into convincing readers that the Gulf Arabs' situation was really still less than ideal seemed only to increase. For example, one reporter, after quoting a "local banker" complaining that Kuwaitis want "everything [done] yesterday," went on to write that "people who defend Kuwait's performance point out that it has been calm and restrained by comparison with down the Gulf. . . . That is rather like saying that someone with an aching tooth has no pain because another person has two aching teeth" (Caminada 1978b). The author had more to say about what Kuwait lacked: "Who or what generated this rush to spend? It is not a phenomenon reflected otherwise in ordinary daily life; only the huge cars, numbering somewhere between 300,000 and 500,000 and tearing along the highways on petrol at 15p a gallon, are symptomatic of rush. Service in hotels, banks or shops is no more headlong than it was in the Gulf 15 years ago." Therefore, at least according to this author, Kuwait was only slightly less like the experience of dental pain than the rest of the Gulf states. In addition, Kuwait managed to offer an unsatisfactory retail experience, having achieved no real progress in the field during the previous fifteen years.

Perhaps the biggest change during this period was that Saudi Arabia's rulers were not always the villains of the cultural economic morality play, at least in the realm of international relations. By 1974, oil minister Sheikh Ahmed Yamani and King Faisal of Saudi Arabia, in most journalistic accounts from the United States and the United Kingdom, were widely viewed as voices of moderation. They were touted as the OPEC "doves," who used Saudi Arabia's megareserves to apply the brakes when other producers wanted to cut production or raise prices or both: "Non-oil giants like Egypt and Syria and others who live on the breadline need money, and Saudi Arabia is in a position to give it to them—at a price. And this has been expulsion of communist influence, renunciation of radicalism and adherence to Saudi Arabia's policy of moderation" (Martin 1977). This praise was given even though the Saudis still "show their usual extreme discretion about their domestic affairs" and in response to the siege in Mecca "cut off all telephone and telex links between Saudi Arabia and the rest of the world" (*Times* [London] 1979). In fact, Yamani and Faisal basically were credited with preventing an "economic disaster" in the West by keeping prices from rising any higher than they did.

Following the assassination of Faisal by his nephew and the seizure of the Grand Mosque in Mecca in 1979, newspapers were openly worried what would happen if the Saudi regime fell, friend as it was to world stability and the West. An article covering the first OPEC meeting after the Iranian Revolution was even titled "Has Shaikh Yamani Saved OPEC and the West?" (Hirst 1979).

This era represents the high-water mark of the Gulf's perceived power in international political economies. Even in the early 2000s, when much of the Gulf was once again booming, the region was not perceived as "powerful"; it was merely thought of as rich. Unlike in the 1970s, when OPEC produced 80 percent of the world's oil, this oil cartel accounts for only 40 percent of production today. How various Gulf polities maneuver the gap between their wealth and geopolitical reputations is the subject of chapter 7. So although the label *powerful* proved impermanent, the 1973–82 era did at least do away forever with the widely held notion that the local leaders would automatically do the US or British bidding (even though they all remained closely aligned to either the United States or the United Kingdom). Once and for all, the old colonial ways would no longer work in the Gulf. But with new clout did not come acceptance, and new routes of separation moved to the forefront. Many of these routes of separation focused on the status of the Gulf's cultural economies.

The Unsuccessful Success of Gulf Cultural Economies

Although the Gulf states (Saudi Arabia in particular) gained some credibility and power in geopolitical realms during this era, the situation remained less than rosy for them in the realm of cultural economy. The Gulf states were *much* wealthier than during the previous era, which resulted in even more infrastructure expansion and increased consumption opportunities for more of its residents, both citizen and foreign. Yet it was still considered to be inferior or on the wrong path or both, despite an even better appearance on the balance sheets.

Examples of this sentiment abound. For instance: "Critics no doubt would say that they are no longer so much concerned with Saudi Arabia's foreign policy as with its internal policies. They point disapprovingly to the strict social restrictions on men as well as on women, to bureaucratic delays and to the lack of a constitution or the rudiments of self-government" (*Times* [London] 1971a). Even though by the mid-1970s Saudi Arabia had experienced almost thirty years of oil development, another article argued that "many governments elsewhere in the Third World undoubtedly cast envious glances in its direction. Most are eager to see what a country with, until recently, a backward economy can make of the opportunity" (Wilson 1976). The same author also considered Saudi Arabia "possibly the most enigmatic country in the Middle East." This sentiment was expressed despite the fact that by 1976 the majority of Saudis had been born after the coming of oil. By this logic, during the 1950s and 1960s Saudi Arabia was still backward and unknowable and had not yet been given an opportunity.

Other Gulf polities were also viewed as not quite right. One article described the UAE's newfound prosperity as both "a boon and a potential danger. On the credit side it permits the Emirates, which a decade ago were a group of poor states based on the traditional activities of fishing and agriculture, to fund the extensive developments needed to bring them speedily into the second half of the twentieth century. On the debit side, it shields them to a large extent from the consequences of their own mistakes, which in the long run could be dangerous" (M. Brown 1976).

Perhaps as some form of reassurance to readers, given the tremendous wealth these states had, the word *dependency* was increasingly applied to them. In dealing with Oman, one article stated: "Dependence on oil revenue is a characteristic which means, in turn, dependence on the western buyers of the sultanate's oil. The other dependence is on the east for expatriate workers, predominantly from the Indian sub-continent, who account for more than two thirds of the non-agricultural private sector labour forces and for one third of civilian government employees. Oman is dependent on imports for most of its food consumption and almost all manufactured products, apart from construction materials" (Whelan 1980a). However, it must be remembered that Oman during this time was a country with 1.2 million people, so it would be quite surprising if it managed to produce the full complement of raw materials, foods, and manufactured goods available to consumers at the dawn of the 1980s.

Another idea that emerged in this era (as somewhat of an extension of the Gulf male consumer trope) was that the Gulf had become too comfortable for its own good. Perhaps the strangest comment along these lines concerned Kuwait: "So welcoming is the network of modern schools, with their free meals, transport, books and medical services, that it is blamed for the high proportion of students who repeat classes" (Blake 1977). This is just one example of how the people of the Gulf were seen to *suffer* (as opposed to feel pride, happiness, or contentment) from having the government provide them (and in some cases their foreign residents) with much of what they need. The term *suffer* is not just a rhetorical flourish on my part: one 1981 article concerning Abu Dhabi in the *Times* of London was actually titled "Still Suffering from a Booming Economy" (Fyfe 1981).

In these articles, a common theme emerged: the idea that, despite appearances, Gulf Arabs really did not have it so good. It proved impossible to suture in widely circulated imaginations concerning cultural economies that these tribal people might have actually succeeded, so it had to be pointed out that their cities were terrible or full of foreigners or that their politics or restrictions made them deeply unhappy or that even though they could buy things, they did not have the joy of producing them. This view led to headlines such as the following, which appeared in the *New York Times* in 1976: "Saudis Having Second Thoughts about Their Oil-Boom Growth" (Pace 1976b). That title implies that the Saudis wanted to return to a time before oil, whereas the actual article shows that Saudis (unsurprisingly for a group of people experiencing rapid change) felt ambivalent and conflicted about the shifts in their society, which is hardly the same as wanting the boom to vanish. I would have chalked up the implication to poor word choice by the page editor, but the feeling that wealth actually made the Gulf unhappy was so often expressed that this instance could not have been a one-off editorial accident. Again, by my objection I do not mean to say that the lives of all Gulf residents were free of problems during the 1970s: they most certainly were not. Furthermore, the type of problems residents faced varied by their location in the Gulf, nationality, nearness to their royal family, personal networks, religion, and gender. However, for most of the history of development economics, money was the only measuring stick: I have become quite convinced that it was specifically the rise of the Gulf that precipitated the more widespread acceptance by the development industry of the idea that countries need more than money to be happy.

In addition to trying to prove the Gulf's underlying unhappiness, fretting about the "long term" also became a common focus in these articles, basically another way of saying that the Gulf's luck would run out. Once again calls for diversification took center stage. However, what is interesting is that in the 1960s a large number of the calls for diversification argued that Gulf states should buy out or replace oil companies in some parts of the production process and that they should also move into petrochemicals. These suggested changes actually were implemented by most of the Gulf states during the 1970s. For example, Saudi Arabia nationalized the formerly American-owned Aramco and expanded the small settlements of Jubail and Yanbu to serve as clean-slate industrial sites. These attempts at diversification were not half-hearted:

> Inhabitants of the sleepy fishing port of Jubayl on Arabia's east coast awoke one morning in 1975 and found themselves on the edge of one of the world's biggest construction sites. Now two huge new harbours are taking shape in an area of about 40sq km which has been wrested from

the open sea by a system of breakwaters. An armada of construction vessels owned by multinational contracting groups stretches far over the horizon. . . . The Jubayl industrial complex, at a cost put at £25,000m for want of a more accurate figure, is the biggest single project in the Saudis' efforts to assure the country's future based on the hydrocarbon and energy-intensive industry. (K. Brown 1978)

Not that the reporter would enjoy living in such production-oriented places: "But in this [eastern] province of Saudi Arabia, where most of the exciting industrial development is concentrated, living conditions take second place to the challenge and rewards of work."

In addition to the new Saudi industrial cities, there were aluminum smelters, dry docks, and new ports in both Bahrain and Dubai. Dubai built an exhibition center and gold souk (market) to attract visitors. Commercial fishing and greenhouse agriculture enterprises formed throughout the Gulf. The Gulf states and entrepreneurs within these states basically did exactly what they had been told to do in the 1960s by moving into fields related to what they already knew (hotels and energy-intensive industries). This does not even include the growing ranks of construction firms, which somehow have never been counted when measures of diversification are reckoned.

Unsurprisingly, these attempts at diversification did not protect the Gulf from being called "undiversified," nor did they halt calls for more diversification. During this era, there was one sector in particular into which the Gulf states—especially Kuwait—were supposed to move: banking. This call for greater Gulf involvement in banking was likely made because money was the other thing (besides oil) that outsiders thought there was an abundance of in the Gulf.

By this logic, Gulf states were to buy more international banks and internationalize their own banks, while also allowing more international banks to operate within their borders. One article from this period is titled "Curing Financial Xenophobia," which implies that Kuwaitis were closed-minded for limiting foreign banks in Kuwait: "Kuwait's wealth has long suggested that it could have a major role to play as a financial centre in the Middle East. But its achievements in this respect have yet to match up to its promise. It is not the latter day Beirut that many outsiders expected it to become, and shows few signs of being so. At the heart of the problem is a fervent belief by the state's rulers that Kuwait assets should be owned by Kuwait nationals. . . . What the country needs are banks and other financial institutions from abroad which are equipped to capitalize on its advantages" (Morison 1972).

The implication was that it was short-sighted of Kuwait not to take money from foreign financial investors—even though it had no need for more money, as shown by the vast sums its sovereign wealth funds invested abroad every year. Nonetheless, by 1974 the potential power the Gulf could wield in banking was perceived to be mammoth. For example, in an interview for a feature story about his career, the head of Banque de Paris estimated that by 1980 Arab countries would have "a capitalization five eighths of Wall Street, three times that of the City, 10 times that of Paris. . . . How will this mass be reduced and brought under control? How will we persuade the Arabs to invest?" (Hargrove 1974). This rather high projection was given even though by the time it was made in 1974 the estimation of Gulf states' wealth had declined considerably because not as much oil was being sold owing to recession in many other parts of the globe.

This constant insistence on the need to diversify into banking is rather odd because there was no actual shortage of local or foreign banks in the Gulf as a whole. One article noted that by 1976 the UAE had perhaps the highest bank office per capita rate in the world owing to its liberal bank-licensing policy, which saw more than fifty different banks operating in a country of around 2 million people (*Times* [London] 1977). Furthermore, banking is hard and risky, and without rigorous regulation it can be dangerous to one's economy, as the Great Recession of 2008 demonstrated to many places. Why commentators argued that people they otherwise thought so little of should move into a notoriously perilous industry seems strange on the surface. But if you put their argument in the market Orientalist frame, it makes more sense. Their advice was not really meant to help but to demonstrate that Gulf economies *lacked* something even in times of abundance. No one writer needed to consciously think this; there was no conspiratorial overlord forcing writers to say such things. The argument was simply shuffling in a new fashion of economic thinking (banking instead of industry) with respect to the same lack in the structures of feeling (that tribal people cannot be wealthy without "hard work" and "modern" ideals).

Of course, parts of the region did actually move into banking. Bahrain began offering off-shoring options and was praised for it. A few wealth funds and wealthy individuals from the Gulf made some small US bank purchases (and were met with intense scrutiny for their trouble). As the years passed, Gulf actors and institutions took many equity (as opposed to ownership) positions in some of the largest European and American banks—something the world learned of when banking stocks fell precipitously in 2008, causing a crisis in places such as Dubai. By the 2000s, the Gulf was in fact heavily involved in banking worldwide, yet the calls for diversification still did not go away.

It was not just in terms of their own development that the goalposts were moved for the Gulf states. In fact, in 1973 much ink was devoted to noting how the Gulf states needed to share more of their newfound revenues with other Arabs as well as with people in the developing world more broadly to prove their modernity. By the mid-1970s, they were doing just that, standing as some of the most generous donors on earth on a per capita basis (which many of them remain to this day). The UAE was giving around 10 percent of its gross national product at one point, and almost every Gulf state launched its own development bank.

However, even these flows of aid were deemed unsatisfactory, and multiple articles tried to demonstrate why aid from the Gulf (even though seemingly generous) was not the same sign of high-mindedness and modernity that aid from the West supposedly was. A common theme, which cropped up in an otherwise sympathetic article about aid from the Gulf, revolved around the idea that Gulf states were not *really* like other rich countries. "Despite their enormous wealth and rapid modernization, rich Arab states still identify with poorer developing nations. Not only do they share many of their traditions and some of their economic strains but also their future. Oil, their main wealth, is a depleted resource and at the current export rate Arab-proved deposits cannot last more than a few decades" (Sultan 1980). So instead of showing the Gulf states' modernity, giving aid demonstrated their continuing link to backwardness. (As an aside, I am personally curious what "traditions" the Gulf shared with far away developing states such as Bolivia, Vietnam, and Jamaica.)

Various other problems were pointed to whenever Gulf aid was discussed. Authors declared that much of the aid was "political," that it was used to shame the West by its size, and that it was mainly bilateral aid going to Arab states fighting Israel or to "poorer Islamic" lands (as opposed to the "truly" needy poor). One article titled "Altruism Overlaid by Other Considerations" even floated the idea that "these figures are not particularly remarkable nor even remarkable enough" because "many still hold OPEC to blame for the plight of the Third World since the 1973–74 oil price explosion" (Field 1978). Such claims held the Gulf to an otherwise nonexistent standard. For example, much US aid *was and is* political in nature and shared with allies (which some of the more even-handed treatments of Gulf aid actually pointed out). As for the plight of the "third world," certainly the lack of money to pay for oil was not the Gulf's fault; more likely than not it could be attributed to legacies of colonialism. But pointing out those colonial connections made it harder to use the Gulf as a depository for all manner of ills.

The idea that anyone but citizens of the Gulf might be responsible for the supposedly ill state of the Gulf or of the wider world economy was rarely uttered. The following statement comes the closest: "The spending headiness can be traced not simply to the intoxication of money—for the Kuwaitis are now used to money—but to the British advisers and entrepreneurs who beckoned them down the road of expansion 20 or 30 years ago, when Britain was the guiding power. In a well-meaning way these men did their job too well. Spread the new wealth for the people, was the insistent cry" (Blake 1977). The article almost reaches the point of placing some responsibility on a non-Gulf person but quickly brushes that thought away by arguing that mistakes only resulted from the British advisers being too good at their work in the face of "insistent cries." All the culpability for what was wrong with the Gulf remained firmly situated in the Gulf.

As the Gulf became wealthier and more powerful, it became harder for market Orientalism to easily position "us" over "them" in structures of feeling in the same old way. In the earlier era, the notions of "inherent conservatism" and "medievalism" did much of the work because it could be argued that people in the Gulf (such as the first generation of monarchs) did not "understand" how to properly use all the new goods and institutions they possessed. But as time went on, people in the Gulf did not stay at the same level; they became active in an ever-increasing number of realms. If the separation between "us" and "them" were to be maintained, the emphasis had to shift away from being centered on "not knowing" to "knowing what should be done but choosing to do it wrong" in areas such as aid, diversity, and reliance on foreign markets. In particular, these charges of unsuccessful success were applied to the makeup of Gulf cities.

Building without Soul

In this second era, not just the presence but also the quality of infrastructure in the Gulf began to garner more remarks. No longer were reporters simply chronicling ports, refineries, and basic services being rolled out on the new oil frontier under the supervision of foreign advisers (although Oman was seen as playing catch-up in these areas during the early years of this era). Perhaps the best summary of the attitude the press took toward Gulf building in the 1970s is given in the title of one article: "Designers Freed from Cost Shackles" (Wilson 1977).

The phenomenon of anticipatory building—which also dominated early 2000s coverage of the Gulf until the Dubai property crash—was a major fixture of the discourse in the 1970s. One comment was particularly evocative: "The visitor to Abu Dhabi today can almost watch it growing, like one of those exotic plants which open before your eyes. In the great open spaces just back from the dual carriageways, huge roundabouts and futuristic architecture, it is one vast construction site. Out of the sand, as far as the eye can see, rise half-completed buildings. This year alone more than 50 are due to be finished" (Hopkirk 1974). A similar description of Kuwait was given in the article "Building a Future on Oil and Money." After proclaiming that Kuwait's "second major resource is money," the article went on to note (by deploying a slightly different horticultural metaphor): "Giant empty dual carriageways carry the potential of urban development through virgin desert. But this is planning. Where the roads lead, the city cannot be far behind. And the villas of the new middle classes and newly stabilized Bedu, aided by massive government subsidies, sprout like mushrooms. It all rests on Kuwait's astonishing oil production" (Roeber 1971).

In this era, there was a sense (much like in the early 2000s) that money had the power to will most things into being. "One of the striking things about the modern city and the suburbs is the way thousands of trees have been coaxed to grow by constant irrigation, with grassy stretches soften-ing gardens and parks despite desiccating sun through much of the year" (Harris 1977). Even the obviously fantastical was worthy of comment in these largely staid papers: "Apart from a few buildings worthy of Brasilia, the architecture of this Arab world El Dorado is unassuming. . . . [But] inevitably, legends have begun to spring up around Kuwait and its riches. One of the most bizarre concerned a vast air-conditioned plastic dome which was going to cover the entire city, shielding its inhabitants from the crushing heat and humidity. Although quite untrue, this story gained wide currency at one time. But almost anything can be possible when money is no object" (Hopkirk 1975b). Although the possibility of making the fan-tastical into a reality might have enticed architects and engineers, in other arenas the rumors of the Gulf's unreal landscapes only further distanced it from "normal."

Despite the wonder at the funds available, another very clear theme emerged in this period: the Gulf was a place that lacked both identity and soul. Undoubtedly, this view was driven somewhat by conversations Gulf nationals had among themselves and in their newspapers about the direc-tions of their societies and by the fact that many Gulf nationals started to become minorities in their own major cities. But this domestic conversa-tion was seized upon by the more widely circulated reporters and came to be presented as a flaw of the Gulf instead of a debate in the Gulf. For example, one article compared Doha's landscape favorably to what could be found in the rest of the Gulf: "Although much of the large-scale build-ing of the past 15 years, particularly the commercial, is banal and badly detailed, Doha has so far avoided the western style concentration of high towers and slabs that are already a feature of the Abu Dhabi skyline. . . . It has also avoided the creation of a congested and cavernous central area, a feature of Dubai's business district" (A. Davis 1976). So just like Kuwait was considered a good state only in the context of the Gulf, Doha was considered a good city only when compared to other cities in the Gulf, such as Abu Dhabi or Dubai.

But no place in the Gulf was as universally despised by reporters as Riyadh. Articles that had little to do otherwise with the built environment would go out of their way to express their displeasure with the place. For example, the previously cited article about growing Saudi geopolitical power took time to describe Riyadh as "anything but impressive" and trapped in "dust laden bleakness" (Martin 1977). There are many entries in the genre, but one of the most emphatic in its critique was the article titled "Life without a Heart":

> It is the conservative heart of the Nejd in one the world's most religious and closed societies. . . . Riyadh is a place without character, not because it is has been built that way, but because it has almost cast off its past and is about to plunge into its future. For the moment near chaos appears to reign and it lives in a vacuum, its heart ripped out and no visible prospect of a transplant. For want of anything more noticeable the main focal point is an elegant watertower. . . . There is little physical evidence that Riyadh has a past. Traditional Nejdi decoration was used on the walls of the Ministry of Petroleum and Mineral Resources, but elsewhere there is an overwhelming desire to live in the greatest comfort and erase memories of less affluent times. It is easy for an outsider to forget that many Saudis still remember poverty. (Weston 1977)

The distaste reporters had for Riyadh—and I say this in all seriousness—bordered on the pathological in that there was no one thing that upset them all, but they all recoiled at the mention of it. The only common thread is that they all were really, really, bothered by it, which turned the city into a sort of urban boogeyman. This oft-professed unpleasantness of Riyadh added an aesthetic element to the catalog of Saudi Arabia's many failings (not all of which were quite as overblown as a dislike for the looks of the capital). Thus, even the style of buildings could be utilized as a terrain that enabled the creation of positional superiority over the Gulf states.

In all likelihood, most reporters assigned to the Gulf did not spend much time dwelling in Gulf cities, especially in those neighborhoods of uniform houses they disliked so much. They did, however, spend time in one of the iconic buildings of Gulf cultural economic landscapes: the hotel. Even the hotels were often found wanting, though. The commentary in an article about the growth of Abu Dhabi is typical for this period:

> Today this former fishing village is the El Dorado of the lower Gulf. It is besieged by foreign bankers and businessmen, expatriate advisers, and armies of skilled workers from neighboring countries, all hoping to win a stake in the Abu Dhabi miracle. Because of this invasion, the hotel crisis in this Arabian boom town is so acute that visitors have to double up, sometimes three executives sharing a room. But no one complains—not even at the harrowing prices charged—for all eyes are on the crock of gold. Moreover, everyone is anxious to be clear of the Gulf before the crushing summer heat starts. (Hopkirk 1974)

But the most colorful complaint about hotels can be found in a story on Saudi Arabia titled "Luxury Class for Camp Beds and Pubs with No Beer" (Crew 1976). It noted that Saudi Arabia had such a hotel and accommodation shortage that "businessmen are so desperate for somewhere to stay after investing much time and money in negotiating for a big contract that they have even been known to sleep on makeshift campbeds in a spare room or corridor rather than turn round and go home empty handed."

This crowding apparently would have been fine to the author if the hotels represented a good value. However, he determined that most of the kingdom's hotels were "poor by western standards, but not any the less expensive for that," costing the same as some of London, Paris, and Hong Kong's fanciest properties. Yet for that money the traveler had to deal with "a much smaller and less exotic hotel in which service and food is [sic] incapable of comparison and there is no alcohol to be had in the restaurant or anywhere else for that matter." Besides seeming surprised that more highly in demand locations cost more to stay in (i.e., the concept of ground rent), the author was also flabbergasted that a new Sheraton would have a replica English pub *without beer* and that the Intercontinental in Mecca was "built by Westerners" using closed-circuit TV because non-Muslims were not allowed to go into that city. So even the hotel, the quintessential visitors' retreat, could not be fully trusted in boom-time Gulf, although in places such as the UAE they actually became the primary place to buy alcohol and a major site where foreigner residents socialized.

The overpriced hotels, highways to nowhere, and lack of identity were some of the many things considered amiss with Gulf urban landscapes, despite the great amounts of money spent on them. Indeed, it was a further sign of their immaturity that they had the money to build the stuff of a world-class city but never could attain that status. That a unique sense of Gulfness could not be easily read from the landscape also provided further fuel to charges concerning the region's impenetrability and unworthiness. But buildings are only a part of market Orientalism, so it is to people I turn in the last section in this chapter.

Gulf People

One of the side effects of this time of enormous increase in prosperity was that more people from the Gulf become known persons in the realm of global business and economy, whereas in the past only monarchs were ever called by name. We have already seen how the Saudi oil minister, Sheikh Yamani, became a regular character of the discourse. There were attempts at raising others to this level. Unsurprisingly, if a Gulf Arab were deemed worthy of being highlighted owing to his (or very occasionally her) outstanding achievements, the time was also usually taken to show how exceptional that person was compared to his brethren (unless he or she was doing something unsavory, in which case he or she was considered typical).

One such attempt is a profile of Kuwaiti minister of planning Ali Mousa (Caminada 1978a). Apart from praising its subject, the article provided a vehicle for othering the remainder of the Kuwaiti national workforce by making Ali Mousa (who had started working at the ministry eight years before the article was written) seem exceptional from his type. The author argued that "in a small nation whose strong point, as even its friends admit, is not planning, he is the man, if any, who has to try to coordinate some 300 continuous government projects. I saw Ali Mousa in his office in a typically uninspiring government building at 5:30 in the afternoon. That seemingly trivial detail demonstrates that the planning director is a hard worker. In the Kuwait summer most government offices and embassies, after an early start, close at one o'clock for the day."

It is amazing what the reporter managed to pack into those few lines: the notion that Kuwait does not plan well, that Kuwait lacks oversight, that someone with only eight years experience can head the planning ministry for an entire country, that the city is ugly, and that in Kuwait almost everyone leaves work early. Although the reporter considered Mousa outstanding in many ways, he also saw Mousa as representative of his type. This "slight" man wears a dishdasha, which "makes Arab men of the same build indistinguishable, until one sees their faces," and has an expression that is "sharp and alive." Thus, although Ali Mousa is the lone hard worker and planner in his country, he still wears clothes that make him indistinguishable from other Arabs (apparently unlike the suits worn by bankers in London and New York). Of course, he is slight of build and has a "sharp" expression, like the merchants of old.

Whereas Mousa was a veritable merchant in government, the older idea of the free-spending prince began to migrate to the private sector. No one was more associated with this emerging image than Adnan Khashoggi, the globe-trotting, playboy deal maker. Khashoggi, who made much of his fortune as an intermediary on Saudi defense contracts, plowed much of his money into Triad International Marketing Corporation, which invested in an array of speculative projects all over the globe, including Sudan, Malaysia, South Korea, and the United States. Although not a prince himself, he was the son of the royal physician and a childhood companion of Crown Prince Fahd. He was described as the only Saudi "entrepreneur . . . whose business and colorful private life are no secret in the West. Indeed, Mr. Khashoggi's frequent appearances in the gossip columns of the Western press, his women, his private aeroplane, equipped with a 40ft sitting room and, above all, his unabashed involvement in the Lockheed bribery scandal have put him much in the public eye" (*Times* [London] 1978).

Khashoggi became the blueprint for the caricature of a Gulf businessman in place of actual knowledge about most rich people from the region.

He was seen as confident, contradictory (a Muslim but far from modest), charming, shrewd, and, above all, more than a little bit shady, as demonstrated by his involvement in a bribery scandal and later in the Iran–Contra Affair. He even allowed longtime Washington, DC, insider-reporter Ronald Kessler to follow him for an extended period of time to write the book *The Richest Man in the World: The Story of Adnan Khashoggi* (1986). Khashoggi was genuinely renowned in the United States and Europe by the 1980s, only to a slightly lesser extent than attention-seeking business moguls such as Donald Trump and Richard Branson are today.

The imagery that surrounded Khashoggi seemed to pull from deep within the social memory of rich Arabs coming to Europe, such as Knidive Ismail of Egypt, whose grand vision for urban Cairo and all of Egypt plunged his country into foreign-held debt. It was a vision formed following Ismail's (and his entire court's) much publicized and exoticized trip to the 1867 Universal Exhibition in Paris as well as his rounds of Europe's royal courts in 1869 to invite other monarchs to the opening of the Suez Canal (Said 1993)—trips that went heavy on pageantry and spending. Through his notoriety, Ismail set the standard for the "typical rich Arab" for decades to come. Khashoggi similarly became the extreme example taken as a type—a very common practice in market Orientalism that has the effect of heightening differences over commonalities.

This image of the hypocritical Gulf businessman-playboy had become cemented by the end of the 1970s, as a report on Saudi Arabia following the attacks on the mosque in Mecca attest. "The simultaneous verbal attacks voiced in Mecca and broadcast from Iran drew attention to the privileges enjoyed by the royal family and the more wayward activities of some Saudi princes, who have been branded in the foreign media as archetypal Arab voluptuaries and symbols of the hypocrisy pervading Saudi society" (*Times* [London] 1980).

However, the more on-the-ground, "You want to do business in the Gulf?" type of reporting emanating from the region in this period tended to highlight not Khashoggi's behavior but the general attributes of his primary occupation as the local agent. Many outside commentators found (and continue to find) this role both peculiar and infuriating. The duties of an agent—(usually) a national of the country one sought to do business in—varied slightly in each of Gulf states. In Bahrain and Kuwait, they both smoothed the way and secured land to allow new enterprises to open; in Saudi Arabia, they allowed foreign companies to bid on government contracts. In most Gulf states, they also had the exclusive right to import and market a company's products or services within a given territory. For these services, they received a fee or percentage of profits and were ideally supposed to be integrated into the ownership and ongoing management of the business as opposed to just receiving revenue. The initial emergence of the agent phenomenon shows (at least in part) a different value system at work. Instead of making arrangements based only on price and quality and letting the social chips fall where they may, the job of the agent in the Gulf was to make sure many different parties were happy about the coming economic transaction.

Even though reporters had (and have) a hard time coming to grips with the concept, according to Stephen Hertog agents are best understood as part of the generalized practice of "brokerage" by intermediaries in the Gulf. Hertog identifies five types of brokers: "gatekeepers," who filter information for the royal families; "paper pushers," who speed paperwork and grant exceptions; "contract brokers" (the classic agents), who get access to government contracts, exclusive import rights, and land for development; "labor traders," who deal in sponsorship rights for foreign residents; and "cover-up businessmen," who are the paper owners of many of the small businesses run by the Gulf's foreign residents—an act referred to as "concealment" (2010b, 302).

I return to the function of intermediaries again in chapter 6, but for now it is important to note how the emphasis placed on personal connection seemed to flummox English-language economic actors in the 1970s: "Agent selection is the most important and delicate process confronting business new to the Gulf. . . . Local reputations are widely known and the selection of an unknown or unqualified agent can have a detrimental effect on a company's chance of success. Companies should also be aware that it is difficult to get rid of an agent, once appointed. . . . Having said this, it seems that there is no machinery in existence to help companies to select a suitable agent. Only local contacts can advise if an agent is suitable" (Young 1978). The 1970s represent the infancy of distanciation (i.e., the viewing of markets from afar) as a key facet of transnational business life, but the notion that the Gulf could not be learned at a distance already marked it as a different type of impenetrable economy.

Most "doing business in the Gulf" articles in this era dwelt extensively on the concept of agents as if their employment were some sort of alien ritual, despite the fact that the occupation of "commercial agent" had existed for a long time in many parts of the world. Indeed, smaller companies without the resources to market their own products often utilized such commercial agents. Furthermore, the Gulf's version represented the formalization of a match-making practice that was common enough when dealing with new markets.

For their part, Gulf countries initially put this requirement for agents in place as a way for some nationals to share in the profits and business knowledge generated by the booming consumer economy, as opposed to just watching all of the money and know-how disappear abroad. The agent also helped foreign firms adjust to local expectations, even if the agent's service ultimately raised the price paid by government and consumers. Instead of the primacy of "markets," we have the centrality of negotiation and representation. True, the agent system was not a level playing field. Although there were a few rags-to-riches stories, the most successful agents were mostly either already well connected to ruling families or arose from established merchant families. But then again, inheriting an advantageous social position gives people a head start just about everywhere in the world. So, despite having a fairly clear reason for their existence (especially at first), agents were during this time rarely represented as anything but a nuisance.

But foreign firms ultimately saw these agents as a necessary nuisance because "the fact that there is no exchange control in the Gulf states and the local currencies are healthy and freely convertible, and no control of the remittance of profits, fees, salaries and equities, make [sic] the trading climate attractive enough to draw in companies who have not already done business in the area" (Young 1978). Or as another *Times* of London reporter put it, "But with local representation, backing from the British government, patience, a willingness to spend weeks rather than days shuttling between Jeddah and Riyadh, and working a long day the rewards can be immense" (Hobday 1975). Since the area was considered so very lucrative (thanks to what were actually a slew of pro-foreign investment policies mostly ignored by writing produced in the 1990s, which claimed that the Middle East was almost uniformly antiglobalization), it seems actors were willing to hold their nose and dive in. Thus, the Gulf was the attractive market that was not.

Indeed, the Gulf was attractive enough that new waves of foreigners continued to come. Although other Arabs (and eventually South and Southeast Asians) made up the majority of the foreign residents, the comfort level experienced by those from the United States and Europe was the primary concern of reporters from those places. Some reporters did accurately assess the reality of the situation: "There are few of the home comforts of any of the many nationalities living there which are not already available" (Fyfe 1976b). But, as chapter 7 discusses, the big exceptions were alcohol (in some places), a temperate summer climate, and the status of women—which make up most of the "few" home comforts this author alluded to. The lack of these features tended to animate many reporters' ire. Indeed, it was thought that in order to deal with some "difficult" conditions, the "right type of person" had to be found who could manage "to work in an area which, on the face of it, has little to offer apart from the opportunity to amass some capital" (Young 1978).

Another group of foreigners was often remarked upon as being conspicuous by their absence in the Gulf: tourists. Lack of tourism was seen as further indictment of a region that was thought to have "little to offer." During this time, it remained a landscape that did not appear "ready" to accommodate discerning Western visitors despite the fact that consumables were available in abundance. For example, one description of Oman's tourist capacity in the mid-1970s emphasized that "Oman remains out of reach to the aimless visitor, perpetuating the idea abroad that intrusion is actively discouraged by the Government. Misapprehension has it that Oman is determinedly shuttered against the tourist trade as it was to the world at large for a century before the present decade. The facts are otherwise. There is a more sensible reason . . . a country in a hurry to improve the lot of its citizens according to the accepted standards of modern development has no time to compete for the favors of tourists" (Ashworth 1976).

In some ways, it was actually a sign of power—and certainly of different priorities—that a developing country had primary concerns besides being a destination for tourists. That such a situation existed was, of course, a bit disconcerting for Western readers. But by the end of the decade, reporting seemed to indicate that the Gulf was becoming even less willing to provide a "comfortable landscape": "Not that any faction would do away with the amenities or standard of living, but a feeling is just discernible that the boutiques, nightclubs and projects for revolving restaurants may have reached the limit of what can comfortably be assimilated. A little nostalgia for a simpler life is in the air. . . . A reassertion of the traditional caution, perhaps spilling over into a re-reemergence of a certain natural Puritanism, may be on the way in, or at least a rethinking of the mania for all things Western" (Fyfe 1977).

But if these writers felt somewhat uncomfortable in the Gulf, perhaps equally disconcerting to them was the appearance of people from the Gulf in the writers' own heartland.

Since at least the 1950s, reporters have found it fascinating that the wealthy in the Gulf enjoy travel. Even Emir Abdullah III of Kuwait, otherwise described as modest, was noted to have spent "much of the year abroad." Princes and other wealthy Gulf citizens favored American hospitals, such as the Cleveland Clinic; some owned beachfront property in coastal Spain, Florida, or California; some bought estates in the English countryside. A big reason why pre–civil war Beirut and the surrounding areas enjoyed entrepôt status for the Gulf was that it was an enjoyable place for people with money to go to, especially during its comparatively temperate summers. As L. L. Wynn documents in her book *Pyramids and Nightclubs* (2010), once Beirut became too dangerous, much of this short-haul tourism shifted to Cairo. This phenomenon should not be surprising; international travel is what the very and moderately rich from many parts of the world have done since at least the nineteenth century. Yet in the case of the Gulf and people from the Gulf, travel abroad has been used as another indictment against its urban landscapes—that is, the region must be so uninteresting that people from there feel forced to take vacations elsewhere.

But nowhere that Gulf Arabs went in this period garnered them more attention in the English-language press than London (as opposed to the

Arabic-language press, which noticed them in Beirut and Cairo). "English is widely spoken (in Oman) and affection for England and the English remains strong," commented one writer. "London is the holiday city of choice and on the whole they seem to feel that we are a friendly enough race" (Fyfe 1976a).

In 1978, the *Times* published a lengthy article concerning the purchasing of London real estate by Gulf Arabs and Iranians, titled "The Special Properties That Make London So Much More Attractive Than Beirut" (Prest 1978). To its credit, the article itself was mostly nonalarmist and tried to dismiss "fears of a white robed invasion." It highlighted the growing presence of Arabs, in particular Gulf Arabs (to the tune of about twelve thousand homeowners), in the boroughs of Kensington, Chelsea, and Knightsbridge—that is, the heart of well-heeled London (which made this presence particularly visible). It noted how the earliest generation of Arabs to make home purchases were very highly placed royals and moguls who favored large townhomes, but after 1975 new millionaires from the region began buying flats for a variety of reasons such as the desire for a business base in the United Kingdom, a vacation home, investment returns, and a possible place of exile if domestic situations in the Gulf deteriorated. The author also argued that London had "a social atmosphere which is less inquisitive than that of Paris or New York," which was something privacy-oriented Gulf buyers—as well as Gulf tourists—appreciated.

However, the author also argued that Gulf Arab visitors were not the same as the business-savvy or well-cultured rich from elsewhere. "It was evident that some less scrupulous estate agents and lawyers were taking advantage of the newcomers' unfamiliarity with the city and its property market." The author also noted that some neighbors were upset that so much money was spent decorating and purchasing homes that were little lived in, arguing that "it is true that tastes can be fickle and apparently wasteful." So even though their wealth allowed Gulf Arabs to be in London and to be quite visible, it was clear they were still outsiders (just not as harmful as originally feared).

Another article that dealt with measuring the sophistication of newly rich Gulf Arabs concerned Saudis' increasing interest in the art world (or, perhaps, the ever-on-the-lookout-for-rich-individuals art world's increased interest in Saudis). The article noted that, despite several decades of wealth, collecting art started slowly in the kingdom: "It was a genuine clash of cultures. The old Islamic ban on representational art was allied to the natural suspicions of the newly-rich. The Saudis did not appreciate the dealers' need for speed in their affairs" (Mallalieu 1978). But now that Saudis had taken the plunge, the author actually came to their defense (at least somewhat): "All this has led some people to think that now that the Saudis are buying, they must be displaying poor and brash taste. Of course one can point to instances of this, but then no nation can boast of universal good taste, and it is natural that new buyers would make mistakes." He argued instead that although their "mistakes may appear gross," who are we to say "that a fresh viewpoint is of necessity wrong?" Plus, many dealers he talked to found that Saudis "generally have a keen eye for quality."

Again, this is another example where the author has little malicious intent (and is actually somewhat complimentary) but starts from the premise that Gulf Arabs are still mostly naïve in the circles of the ultrawealthy. In trying to explain that Saudi taste was not quite as bad as imagined (and if it was, they could be forgiven for it), he nevertheless left the impression they were unlike the other rich despite the fact that by the late 1970s the chances were decently high that the Gulf Arab elite who were now buying art in London had once studied in the United States or the United Kingdom (or at least had long exposure to these places from frequent travels). Such notions, however, served to maintain distance even when spatial access for the Other had increased.

But what began to mark Gulf Arabs as most culturally different—the main difference that sticks through the years—was the status of women. By the late 1970s, rejuvenated women's rights movements were nearly two decades old in the United Kingdom and the United States (built on a tradition established by pro-suffrage movements begun at least a century earlier), and the gap in women's workforce participation between those countries and the Gulf was starting to grow. This gap appeared in the media record as well—an increasing number of the reporters sent to cover the Gulf by Western newspapers were women.

The situation in Saudi Arabia, where restrictions on women's movement and participation in public life were more severe than in the rest of the Gulf, came to stand in for the situation of women in the Gulf (and perhaps the wider Middle East) in general. One common image used to demonstrate women's closed-off status despite a modern material culture was the curtained car. "Generally, Saudi women remain in the house or compound during the day. They are not encouraged to venture out, and if they do so they must be chaperoned. The car, however, with curtained and tasseled back windows remains, so to speak, part of the living room and allows the women to visit members of the family during the day without being exposed in the street. In the evening, with the whole family, they are able to tour the city" (de Brant 1976). This mixing of the height of modern engineering—the automobile—with what many authors considered the ancient and unchanging act of veiling proved irresistible to them. However, it was always read as a sign of continuing backwardness and victimhood rather than of women's ingenuity and agency in the face of limits.

But what brought Saudi women to the full attention of the United Kingdom and the United States was the controversy surrounding the airing of *Death of a Princess* in 1980, a docudrama concerning a journalist's attempt to uncover details of the story of the highly publicized execution of a young Saudi princess and her lover. Saudi officials, having been allowed to screen a preview of the program, made a public display of trying to keep it from being shown. But their efforts to censor the production were to no avail; in fact, the protests probably drove viewership numbers to higher than expected levels, especially given that it was to air on PBS in the United States. Apart from detailing the execution of a woman for adultery, the film also portrayed Saudi women as living frivolous lives and Saudi men as politically corrupt, hypocritical, and vindictive. As Edward Said (1997) notes, *Death of a Princess* was also perhaps the seminal representational moment that showed the gap between the Gulf's "economic capital and [its] cultural capital": the Gulf's money could not stop the film from being aired (despite powerful figures such as James Baker and Mobile Oil arguing in favor of censoring it and the threat of economic sanctions against Britain). Struggle as Saudi authorities did against it, they could not overcome the gap produced by market Orientalism.

Again, this is not say that, just because market Orientalism operates with respect to the Gulf, all criticism leveled at Gulf states is unwarranted.

Saudi Arabia did enforce restrictions on women's mobility in the 1970s at the same time women in other parts of the Gulf and the world were becoming more physically and economically mobile. As I am writing this chapter, it still does. In the era covered here, Saudi Arabia's judicial system executed people for a comparatively wide array of nonviolent offenses. Many Gulf polities attempted to tamp down on political dissent; many citizens chafed at the limited nature of formal representative government. Adnan Khashoggi was a real arms middleman who lived a very luxurious lifestyle and used money to try to buy his way into the orbit of famous people, whereas others who toiled in the Gulf came away with little to their name. Hotels were probably crowded, and service might have been slow by American East Coast standards. Some people in Gulf cities probably wished their buildings had more architectural distinction; others likely felt that in gaining much they had lost something of themselves.

But these ill examples of policy, feeling, and aesthetics (some more serious in nature than others) became the building blocks of the Gulf archetype because they fit the emerging structures of feeling about the Gulf's unsuccessful success. It is a classic case of Orientalist narrowing: take the complexity of the world and make it fit existing imaginations that maintain positional superiority. Most Gulf individuals who appeared in the newspapers of this period were either perfect examples of a negative type or the exception that proved the rule. Thus, men in the Gulf were labeled universally sinister and misogynist, and their money was thought to get them things that and into places where someone of their lowly cultural standing should not have or be. Women in the Gulf were viewed primarily as victims. This is not to say that unrigorous and unflattering understandings of other places did not circulate among Gulf Arabs, but the point of market Orientalism is who has the power to make their unrigorous ideas about Others the wider cultural economic norm.

Coda: The Era of Comeuppance, 1983–2001

Although the Gulf was by no means considered to have a "normal" cultural economy during the 1970s, it at least received begrudging acknowledgment of increased clout. In the 1980s and 1990s, however, many trends turned against the Gulf and caused further shifts in the structures of feeling that surrounded it.

One of those trends was the price of oil. It reached its twentieth-century peak (in both real and inflation-adjusted dollars) in 1980. It then began a gradual decline until 1985, when it fell off a cliff owing to Saudi Arabia's unwillingness to continue curtailing its output just to keep the price high for other producers (a group that included the Soviet Union)—a practice that had been causing Saudi Arabia to lose market share throughout the early 1980s. From a 1980 peak of $37 per barrel, oil fell to as low as $11 a barrel by 1986. It rose to $23 in 1990 and reached a low of $11 again in 1998, which, when adjusted for inflation, was less per barrel than the 1950 price. The economic children of high oil prices in the 1970s—quota cheating by OPEC members, new sources of supply in the North Sea and Alaska, and increased automobile fuel efficiency—all came of age by the 1980s.

With less money, governments of the bigger Gulf states began to run into structural problems. It was one thing to understand and prepare for the fact that oil might not stay at the 1980 peak price forever—Gulf polities generally (but not universally) seemed to have anticipated at least some decline. That the price would be all the way down to $11 per barrel in the 1990s, given oil's vital role in the world economy, was something most did not see coming.

The mid-1980s were tough on all of the Gulf oil producers. Most of the big development projects planned at the height of the boom came to completion during this time, just as incomes were shrinking. This left Gulf financial-sector entities in precarious positions owing to their exposure to these projects—a situation that necessitated personal and institutional bailouts. Petrodollar loans, originated by US and British banks (using OPEC money) and given en masse to developing states in Latin America and Asia, were being defaulted on as part of a global debt crisis in the early 1980s. Iran and Iraq were at war, making shipping in the Gulf more dangerous and those countries harder to export to. Many foreign residents (in particular those connected to the construction industry) returned home as work dried up and benefits accrued to them by Gulf states and employers became less generous owing to cost-cutting moves. This exodus further depressed Gulf economies.

By the 1990s, Saudi Arabia (because of its size), Bahrain, and Oman (owing to smaller oil resources) began to run regular deficits—not gigantic ones by world (or even US) standards, but remarkable for places that had been relatively flush just fifteen years earlier. High birth rates from the boom years hit the Saudi welfare state particularly hard as an ever-growing number of schools and jobs were needed for children and graduates across a large territory. Oil prices at such low levels strained to provide the needed stimulus to absorb job seekers.

Even some of the 1970s power brokers were knocked down a few pegs as the 1980s came to a close. Sheikh Yamani was pushed aside as oil minister in the early 1980s. Most of Adnan Khashoggi's many concerns were no longer able to pay their bills by the 1990s. But no place was hit harder than Kuwait, the once shining star of the Gulf. I discuss the case of Kuwait in more detail in chapter 9, but the most well-known of its problems during this era occurred when it was invaded by Iraq. As Said notes of this event,

> In 1991 it was as if an almost metaphysical intention to rout Iraq had sprang into being, not because Iraq's offense, though great, was cataclysmic, but because a small non-white country had disturbed or rankled a suddenly energized super-nation imbued with a fervor that could only be satisfied with compliance or subservience from "sheikhs," dictators, and camel-jockeys. . . . There seemed considerable but inexplicable enjoyment to be had in the prospect that at last "the Arabs" as represented by Sadaam, were going to get their comeuppance. Many scores would be settled against old enemies of the West: Palestinians, Arab Nationalism, and Islamic Civilization. (1993, 294–95)

Indeed, the entire era was defined by comeuppance. It was all over the headlines. In 1987, the *New York Times* ran a story titled "The Humbled Saudi Economy: Caution Now a Watchword" (Kilborn 1987). In 1996, a story ran on the front page of the *New York Times* with the banner "A Tutorial for Young Saudis on Ways to Toil for Money" (Jehl 1996). The 1980s may have been rough on the working classes in the United States and the United Kingdom, but these articles reveled in the idea that at least those formerly lucky Gulf Arabs were finally getting theirs, made humble, and forced to toil.

There was a brute materiality to all of the problems faced by the various Gulf states during this time. But nonetheless real is the fact that the Gulf's style of economic governance (setting a consumptive floor through infrastructure spending and extensive welfare provision) went out of fashion, badly. The 1980s was the decade of Reagan Thatcherism, where governments were being rolled back at a rapid rate. Indeed, the Reagan–Thatcher assault on welfarism was at least partially enabled by the era of high oil prices because it was stagflation in the 1970s that so strained Keynesian government machinery that possible alternatives grew more alluring (see T. Mitchell 2010). In fact, government rollback became the primary theme of IMF and World Bank structural adjustment policy, replacing capital-intensive projects that had been in vogue in earlier eras. Communism, a whole system based (at least theoretically) on the state caring for and employing its people, disappeared with the collapse of the Eastern Bloc and China's transformation into another type of economic beast. Not only did this collapse rob the Gulf of an economic measuring stick, but also not liking communism was something on which the Gulf rulers and NATO fully agreed.

Then the 1990s happened—during which success was measured by how much a country "opened up" to allow capital and people in and out rapidly. Although much reporting throughout the 1990s argued Gulf states were slow in opening up, thanks in part to Thomas Freidman's book *The Lexus and the Olive Tree* ([1999] 2000) the region came to be entrenched in imaginations as part of the "slow world" (as opposed to the fast world). Of course, on some levels this view is odd: because of foreign residents, Gulf societies were especially diverse and were easier for migrants to access than most places on earth. Once into a Gulf country, companies paid little taxes and were able to easily repatriate profits. But censorship (which led to a slow adoption of the Internet and then of higher-speed Internet), the limiting of women's opportunities in Saudi Arabia, sectors closed to foreign investment (such as oil and initially property ownership), and the agent system were strikes against the Gulf, given economic fashion. This antiglobal label combined with the established market Orientalist narratives about the Gulf being opaque, having unearned wealth, and being the home of religious fanaticism to create a perfect reputational storm.

The Gulf's perceived nose dive culminated with the attacks of September 11, 2001, enabled by Saudi citizen Osama bin Laden, with much of the suspected funding coming from Gulf residents and citizens and carried out by a group of attackers primarily from Saudi Arabia. Unsurprisingly, given views on the religion in the English-language media, Islam (which is, of course, a large and diverse religion that is not reducible to the actions of a few extremists) received the biggest chunk of the blame for the attacks. But next to Islam it was the cultural economy of the Gulf that sustained the most criticism. The basic argument went like this: because of high youth unemployment (and sometimes even the lack of gender mixing in public), young people in Saudi Arabia in particular but in the Gulf in general became disillusioned and depressed. This caused them to fall prey to drugs or radicalism, and Gulf states were often accused of turning a blind eye to these issues, at least in the case of radicalism.

So deviant was the cultural economy of the Gulf considered to be—with its supposed entrepreneurialism-crushing welfare states—that it was seen to produce terrorism. Never mind that bin Laden was from a wealthy, entrepreneurial family; that the Hamburg Cell that organized the attacks were for the most part not Gulf nationals and from "secular" families; that combat experience or training in Afghanistan (ironically sponsored in part by the United States) seemed to be the major factor that turned people toward violence; and that nineteen people carried out the attacks directly with the help of perhaps a few hundred others out of some 30 million or so Gulf residents. Do not misunderstand: many players in the attacks had ties to the Gulf, but the story of September 11 is far, far more complicated than "conservative Islam meets structural underemployment." Despite all of these objections, however, there remains a strong current in the US media in particular that if Gulf cultural economies would provide the proper incentives (as Beblawi [1987] argued in his work on the rentier state), then religious extremist violence would no longer be a big deal. This argument is the type of deflection onto Others that precludes a more in-depth self-examination of what the US foreign policy's role has been in shaping not so flattering imaginations of the United States within structures of feeling that circulate in the Middle East.

This deflection unfortunately connects to the all too prevalent idea that maybe all Arabs will understand is force. In a May 29, 2003, interview with Charlie Rose regarding why he supported the invasion of Iraq, Thomas Friedman of *The Lexus and the Olive Tree* fame offered the following explanation: "We needed to go over there, basically, and take out a very big stick right in the heart of that world and burst that bubble, and there was only one way to do it. What they needed to see was American boys and girls going house to house, from Basra to Baghdad, and basically saying, 'Which part of this sentence don't you understand?' You don't think, you know, we care about our open society, you think this bubble fantasy, we're just gonna to let it grow? Well, Suck. On. This" (Rose 2003).[1]

In sum, the Gulf economy went from being perceived as a machine that produces unscrupulous misogynist playboys in the 1970s to being perceived as one whose unglobalness produced terrorists by the 1990s. But as that economy moved from the heights of riches to the struggles of more limited funds, market Orientalism remained to separate the Gulf from cultural economic normalcy and create positional superiority.

Everything Old Is New Again

If the September 11, 2001, attacks were the nadir for the Gulf cultural economies' reputation in English-language media, within four short years these economies would be seen to be riding high again. Only the deck had been shuffled. In the 1970s, it was Saudi Arabia, Kuwait, and less-rich but supposedly well-planned Bahrain that garnered most of the attention. In the 2000s, one city-state began to rise rapidly up the cultural economic hierarchies: Dubai. Its combination of comparative lifestyle openness, corporate and transport free zones, and headline-grabbing projects made it by far the most prominent Gulf city apart from Mecca. Its ruler, Sheikh Mohammed bin Rashid al-Maktoum, became the most visible Gulf leader for his combination of perceived business acumen and

---

1. Hat tip to the blogger Atrios for keeping that interview alive in the popular memory.

flair for the dramatic. But formerly low-key players Abu Dhabi and Qatar (which, by 2005, had the region's most favorable population-to-resource-reserves ratios) soon began to follow a modified version of Dubai's path. Both actually moved ahead in terms of coverage when Dubai ran into the global financial crisis in 2008. That story is told in chapter 7. However, with the recent fall in oil prices, it would not be surprising to see some of the tropes from the "comeuppance era" deployed once again.

Although the protagonist states changed, the tropes remained the same. Dubai's ruler, Sheikh Mohammed (like his father, Sheikh Rashid), was praised for his merchantlike sensibility, an image he undoubtedly cultivated. Like Kuwait before it, Dubai was not considered to be a good place in and of itself. Indeed, problems with labor abuse and an unevenly applied legal system were often referred to as Dubai's "dark side." Instead, it was thought of as the best place "in the Gulf." In Dubai, Abu Dhabi, and Doha, the infrastructure was spoken of in the same anticipatory sense as what was being built in the 1970s, and dreams of limitless funds led to coverage of all sorts of spectacular (and sometimes unlikely) projects. Qatar and the word *insular* were paired together too many times to count. The fact that cars, watches, and yachts were conspicuously consumed still received attention. There was panic and derision when Gulf citizens or royals bought US assets or European football clubs. Some prophesied the coming of a new financial world order that would feature oil prices exceeding $300 a barrel. There were still calls for diversification of Gulf banking sectors.

I began research on the Gulf as a graduate student a little more than a decade ago, focusing mostly on what was happening in the then current cultural economic imagination surrounding Gulf landscapes. In doing the research for this book, I was surprised by just how much of what was being passed off as new insights on the Gulf in the past fifteen years resembled "insights" from the 1970s and even the 1940s. This is why I believe so firmly in the existence of market Orientalism: the separation and distinction work it carries out has been consistent across the decades, even as the particular details and places it attaches to shift. The Gulf is still thought of as a unified but Other region, full of merchants and opulent princes, living high within not fully mature, closed-off societies. In other words, the Gulf and its complexities are reduced to the role of the foil in a cautionary tale regarding what "our" economies are not supposed to be like. It offers both a market for expertise and a chance to enjoy righteous superiority. All of this cultural economic work to make the Gulf appear more than slightly off is certainly more about "us" than about "them." And the more I read about the Gulf, the more it reminds me of how the United States reacted to China's growth and to Japan's before it; how the US East Coast reacted to the growth of Texas; how Britain reacted to the early-twentieth-century industrial supergrowth of the United States; and on and on. For sure, market Orientalism has operated in the Gulf, but I could see its fingerprints elsewhere, too.

What this goes to show is that the Gulf and cultural economies more generally need to be thought about in new ways lest the same stories that enable the same power moves keep being told. The next three chapters strive to do that. I start by addressing what has proven to be a stubbornly persistent question: Why do the Gulf states, which seemingly have much in common, not work together more closely?

6

The Fantasy of the Postcolonial Regional Economy

The Case of the Gulf Cooperation Council

In May 2009, it looked as though the Gulf states were poised for a watershed moment. The Gulf Cooperation Council (GCC), which had been established in 1981, looked to be taking the next step toward greater integration. The finance ministers of the six GCC states—Kuwait, Saudi Arabia, Bahrain, Qatar, the UAE, and Oman—were meeting in Riyadh to decide on the location of a new Gulf central bank. The institution was to begin as a monetary council that harmonized policy in advance of the introduction of a common currency, the Khaleeji (meaning "of the Gulf"). As promoters noted, a Gulf economic union would have been the world's second-largest common-currency area by combined GDP (behind the Eurozone), with a 2009 combined nominal GDP of around $1 trillion (IMF 2013). By agreeing to meet, all six states seemed to indicate a belief that a common currency, policy coordination, and closer integration of their individual economies would be best for all. Their coming together was also seen as a validation of those who had been working to build the idea of a *khaleeji* identity distinct from but equally valued as other varieties of Arab identities.

Yet it was on the most material of questions—where the bank would be located—that the whole idea fell apart. Four of the states—Bahrain, Qatar, Saudi Arabia, and the UAE—wanted the bank located within their borders. In the UAE, it is likely that the rulers of both Dubai and Abu Dhabi wanted their cities to be considered, although it was later revealed that the UAE's official preference was for the bank to be located in Abu Dhabi. Each of these states could make an argument why it should host the institution. Saudi Arabia had the biggest economy. The UAE had the second-biggest economy and received the most business travelers. Qatar was the fastest growing. Bahrain already had a sizable banking sector and was home to the offices of the Accounting and Auditing Organization for Islamic Financial Institutions, which many people working in Islamic banking and finance cite as a key agenda-setting institution (Pollard and Samers 2011).

In the end, whereas Saudi Arabia, Bahrain, Kuwait, and Qatar agreed that the bank should be in Riyadh, the UAE and Oman (whose economy is tied to that of the UAE) did not agree and "postponed" any involvement in the currency. In November of that year, the governor of the UAE central bank released a statement saying that the UAE had withdrawn owing to "fundamental reservations" about a lack of time to test the effects of currency integration through the use of a precursor unit of account (similar to the European Currency Unit, which preceded the introduction of the Euro) (Reuters 2009). However, this stated reason was likely a case of assigning primary causality retroactively. In the immediate aftermath of the Riyadh meeting, none of the problems with the lack of a unit of account was mentioned; all of the international and Gulf-based reporting instead seemed to indicate that, from the UAE ministers' perspective, the other states' ministers had "decided to overrule the earlier formal undertaking made at GCC meetings in 2004, and went ahead with a new suggestion to locate the GCC Central Bank in Saudi Arabia" (*Gulf News* 2009) and that this was the reason for the UAE's and Oman's withdrawal.

Not surprisingly, longtime proponent of economic integration in general, the *Economist*, took the news badly. Upon reporting the stalemate, it declared that the "withdrawal raises serious questions about the Gulf governments' ability to overcome old political rifts for the sake of economic and financial integration" (2009). The author repeated that theme, noting that it would have been difficult to pull off a single currency because of "the problem of generating the political will to defend the central bank against national interests"—a statement that made eventual failure seem inevitable. Perhaps the ultimate condescension came when the article noted that "Abu Dhabi appears to have taken [it] rather personally" that the central bank would not be located there, before going on to declare that this case was "a reminder of how the region remains hostage to arbitrary decision-making from the top."

Here is a classic example of market Orientalism. According to the *Economist*, Gulf rulers cannot "overcome rifts" for the sake of what is "right," which in this case is financial integration. They "lack will," "take things personally," and are "arbitrary." Thus, they are immature, like children; only they have big piles of money. Also, they keep their true motivations opaque and impenetrable. As chapters 4 and 5 showed, this kind of description of the Gulf has been common for many years and productive of the creation of separation and enjoyment.

There are two interesting intellectual moments in this case, with implications beyond the Gulf. The first concerns the circumstances at hand: whether the lack of agreement was a "failure" to halt the progress of a GCC monetary union based on "national" interests. It provides a chance to think differently about the Gulf and its various situations as well as to consider what type of economic behavior might be obscured beneath the enjoyment of denunciation. The second moment involves looking at a wider issue: namely, "regionalism" as a fashion in economic thinking, a terrain on which "emerging markets" can be judged as succeeding and failing so that they can be slotted into cultural economic hierarchies. "Regional integration" is seen as something "mature" economies do. That the Gulf seemed to stumble at the finish line placed it (once again) under the sign of market Orientalism.

Most of this chapter focuses on an analysis of these two moments: this specific case of attempted regionalization and the case for regionalism more generally. However, it undertakes that analysis by borrowing from the diverse-economies literature, psychoanalysis, and consumption-centric (as opposed to production-centric) theories, which are not usually associated with the topic. By utilizing these perspectives, this chapter provides a different tool kit with which to examine the motivations for regionalization while also pointing to a way of thinking that goes beyond market Orientalism. It does not offer firm solutions, but it does suggest the need to look more widely for alternatives.

The first section applies the tropes surrounding market Orientalism highlighted in chapters 4 and 5 to examine the US and British media's treatment of the prospect of Gulf unity through the decades. It does so by focusing primarily on the major, actually existing instance of cooperation in the Gulf: the UAE, a federation whose prospects for success were initially met with great skepticism. The second section provides a critical reading of the concept of "regionalism" by drawing primarily on the frame of "fantasy" developed by Slavoj Žižek in his book *Parallax View* (2006). I chose Žižek's perspective because it provides an explanation for why regionalism gets insisted on in all circumstances, even in those where its benefit might be questionable at best. Armed with what was developed in these first two sections, the third section addresses the GCC case itself and makes the arguments that the lack of a more integrated GCC is not necessarily a failure and that the UAE's cities were right to worry about the materialities of the common currency. The fourth section then asks, "If not integration, then what?" It looks for possible answers by turning to another group of authors who are rarely consulted about issues of regionality: Jean Baudrillard, Georges Bataille, and J. K. Gibson-Graham. What they have in common are an emphasis on the need for (or perhaps the inevitability of) "waste" and more serious thought about the importance of distribution of wealth. Read together, they point toward ways Gulf regional economies might distribute better. I then conclude the chapter by summarizing its arguments and linking them back to both the market Orientalism concept and additional cases.

Gulf Unity and the United Arab Emirates

For all of the *Economist*'s talk of "old political rifts" besieging the Gulf, the truth is that the Gulf states have a half-century tradition of working together, even if imperfectly, when they feel that cooperating makes sense. Perhaps the most noteworthy area of cooperation before the GCC was the participation of the majority of its members in OPEC. Kuwait and Saudi Arabia were founding members, with Qatar and eventually the UAE joining later. Within OPEC, the Gulf states were on the same side of issues much of the time, aligned against larger states such as Libya and

Iran, which wanted even higher prices. The six Gulf states also participated in the Arab League and together (along with Iraq) entered into the Gulf Organization for Industrial Consulting in the mid-1970s. There was of course also talk, consultation, and cooperation among these states in more informal and bilateral ways. In his foreword to Rouhollah Ramazani and Joseph Kechichian's (1988) collection of GCC founding documents, Sheikh Sultan bin Mohamed al-Qasimi, the ruler of Sharjah and a scholar in his own right, dismissed the too prevalent notion that Arabs would never be able to work together and were particularly prone to war. He noted (quite correctly) that both the United Kingdom and the United States were stable states now despite having experienced civil wars and that "after many centuries of nearly continual warfare amongst themselves, the peoples of Europe . . . have entered into the first stages of a union" (1988, ix).

Although obvious if the name is examined, another major sign of cooperation in the Gulf is the United Arab Emirates. Now that it has existed for forty years, its status as a federation seems foregone and the country quite permanent. However, beginning as early as the 1950s most commentators considered the prospects for any kind of unity on the shores of the Gulf rather remote. For example, a 1959 article titled "Small States in Isolation" emphatically commented: "Britain cannot wave a magic wand to bring unity or equality to lands which have been so widely divided by geography and economics. If the dream of a united Arab world from Casablanca to the Straits of Oman were realized, then these small pieces would fit naturally into the jigsaw. Or if Saudi Arabia had the makings of a well conducted modern State there would be some local form of attraction. But without these openings each Gulf territory must for the time being plot its own future in more or less isolation" (*Times* [London] 1959b). Apparently, if Britain could not bring such entities together, they were doomed to be forever isolated because their "natural" parent state (Saudi Arabia) could not get its act together.

But that criticism is mild compared to that given a couple of years later in "A Quiver of Sheikhs" (*Economist* 1961b). The title implied that too many basically similar sheikhs were confined to a small area, a point that the article emphasized further when it declared that these rulers also lacked "much aptitude in getting together." The article praised Britain for the "brilliant diplomatic accomplishment" of keeping this "patchwork" of sheikhdoms together for more than half a century, initially to serve its interests in protecting shipping to India during colonialism and then later to regularize the supply of oil. The article went on to argue that "until recently the advantages of this cost in bringing profit to Britain far out-weighed the embarrassments it caused by its anomalous political charac-ter." Indeed, if the Gulf sheikdoms were not useful—and apparently a case study in British cleverness—the United Kingdom would have been rid of this "embarrassment" of a region.

How embarrassing did the author of this article consider the existence of these polities to be? "The rich ones are fabulously rich without the responsibilities that great inheritance should normally bring. Tiny princi-palities playing at independence . . . may charm the curio hunter in search of Victoriana. But they disturb rational thought by their unabashed feudal systems and general untidiness. It is no sin to be small; but it is dangerous to be so small and so emphatically outmoded."

As it turned out, however, the author did not fully believe that the sheikhs were actually all exactly the same as arrows in a quiver. The article noted that, besides the obvious gap in wealth between states with and without oil, there were also "geographical differences. The seafaring men of the coasts have practically nothing in common with the pastoral tribes of the interior." Given these parameters, Saudi Arabia should not exist. It contains the Hijaz, a region marked by its Red Sea coastline and more temperate highlands (which was previously loosely ruled by the ultradi-verse Ottoman Empire for hundreds of years); the Nejd, a desert plateau from which the al-Sauds originally hail; and al-Hasa, an oasis region in the northeastern part of the country.

"Quiver of Sheikhs" stands as by far the most colorful take on the topic of regional cooperation, but it expresses the general midcentury consensus that Gulf sheikhs were unlikely to get along owing to their tribal character. Thus, it was thought the Gulf would likely remain divided among king-doms so small that they "defy rationality." Here is an example of this view from a different article: "In Arabia frontiers are made to be disputed. It is a tradition of centuries, aggravated by the arrival of oil, because frontier disputes are now more than a matter of 'face'—they are big business as well. The area is an absurd complex of claims, which would be pressed more actively if British agreements with local rulers did not underwrite the territorial integrity of them all. The big powers in the area claim little powers, the little powers lesser ones. . . . The normal political process in the Middle East is likely to be violent" (*Times* [London] 1965b). Again, keep in mind that during the half-century prior to this article's publication, European states fought two mammothly destructive and "violent" wars over "an absurd complex of claims" along "disputed frontiers" within their own continent.

By 1965, however, change was in the air. Rumblings of what would become the UAE began to be heard around the same time Britain began looking for an exit strategy from the Gulf. The possibility of the withdraw of UK military support led to a meeting of the heads of the then Trucial States, along with those of Bahrain and Qatar. The effort was initially received with skepticism: "[The rulers] have met and discussed matters of common concern. They agreed to have a joint currency, and to coordinate development. What this cooperation might eventually mean in political terms remains necessarily uncertain. There is no place in the world harder to make tidy plans for than the Gulf, with its huge empty spaces and gigantic disparities of wealth and poverty" (*Times* [London] 1965a).

It became apparent by the late 1960s that Britain's Labour government was looking to pull back from some of the remnants of empire. Then UK defense secretary Dennis Healey was asked in an interview about the offer by Gulf sheikhs to pay for the British military's continued presence in the Gulf. Saying he did not want to transform the British military into mercenaries, he uttered his soon-to-be infamous phrase: he "didn't very much like the idea of becoming a white slaver for Arab Sheikhs."

Within a few short years, what many Western commentators thought unlikely to happen happened (for the most part). The two wealthiest members of the Trucial States—Abu Dhabi and Dubai—agreed to a union. The poorer states—Sharjah, Fujairah, Ajman, and Umm al Qawain (and Ras al Khaimah shortly thereafter)—joined as well. Well-developed Bahrain and Qatar, not physically connected to each other or to the Trucial States, decided (in the case of Bahrain based on pressure by Iran) to go it alone. In addition, the United States stepped into the vacuum created by the British: in some cases, it directly took over the leases on British bases.

Despite early dire predictions, the UAE came generally to be seen as a successful experiment in getting along. One assessment four years after its founding optimistically stated: "Until recently they counted for nothing: seven small feuding emirates scattered along a barren coastline in the back of beyond. . . . Today, having patched up their ancient quarrels, the United Arab Emirates have become in less than four years one of the richest and fastest developing nations anywhere, as well as one of the most generous" (Hopkirk 1975a). Or, as another author put it with less enthusiasm, "The UAE tends to attract the same kind of comment as the British broadcasting system: people are not quite sure how it works but they know that it does" (Hewson 1981). Some offhand remarks continued to be made about the patchwork of boundaries between the various emirates (as well with Oman), but in general—apart from a dispute among some of the rulers over the extent of federal powers and obligations in the late 1970s—the UAE began to stand as an example that Gulf states might be better off together than apart. The idea did not go away.

Regionalism as Economic Fashion and Postcolonial Fantasy

Region is an unusual imaginary because—unlike neighborhood, city, province, or state—its particular slot within common imaginations of nested hierarchies can vary. There are urban regions consisting of multiple cities and towns, subnational regions that are parts of larger states, and supranational regions consisting of multiple states. As foremost geographic scholar of the constructedness of regions, Anssi Paasi, notes, "While regional identity has been for a long time an important category in geographical research, its meanings are still vague. The phrase is an illustration of what Sayer labels 'chaotic conceptions,' i.e. abstractions that divide the indivisible and/or uncritically lump together unrelated elements" (2002, 138). To the extent that anything unites these very differently conceived spaces of the region, it is certainly not shared size. *I would argue that what these spaces have in common instead is a stance that their current organization is considered to be lacking*—perhaps in terms of rationality, perhaps in terms of fairness and "the common good" (Boltanski and Thévenot 2006). Promoting the idea of a region is to argue that the spatiality of the world might be better arranged. Of course, such rearrangements are always going to benefit someone, even if it is only those who craft new institutional architectures and thus get to enjoy the power to make something anew.

This view becomes apparent when examining different types of regions in turn. The idea of the urban region emerged because many scholars, planners, government officials, and citizens came to the conclusion that urban processes and materialities do not end at the boundaries of a city. These urban impacts spill over into other polities such as suburbs, sometimes into neighboring cities, and, depending on location, sometimes into adjoining counties, provinces, or even countries. The boundaries of these various polities come to be seen as barriers to forming integrated transportation networks, economic development schemes, and the like. Although I am not advocating against the utility of the urban regional approach, there is nonetheless an assertion of expertise in arguing for this approach—namely, that another, higher authority would manage things better through its superior vision.

The subnational region relates to "the lack" in a different way: advocacy for such a region argues that the nation-state fails to sufficiently acknowledge and care for a certain group of people that is also assumed to be in a certain territory. The current ordering of space is once again seen as insufficient: people attached to subnational regions are considered to be better able to care for themselves if given autonomy. Again, I am in no way denying the legitimacy or urgency of subnational groups' claims. However, the promotion of this type of region involves a critique of the current arrangement of space and the promotion of a different type of authoritative configuration, driven by different conceptualizations of what might be the common good.

Finally, there is the supranational region. Here, it becomes necessary to draw a distinction between two varieties: the "institutionalized" (to borrow a term from Paasi 1986) and the comparative. I do deal with comparative supranational regions later, but much of the focus of this chapter is on the institutionalized supranational region, which consists of a group of states (usually bordering each other or the same body of water) that have entered into some type of policy-coordination agreement. Sometimes these agreements involve political or security coordination; much of the time the basis for agreement is economic. The European Union (and its precursor, the European Economic Community); the North American Free Trade Agreement (NAFTA) among the United States, Canada, and Mexico; Mercosur (which groups states in South America), and the Association of Southeast Asia Nations (ASEAN) rank as the most well-known economic examples. However, even among these regional blocs, there is tremendous variation in terms of institutional thickness and volume of internal trade.

The impetus behind these institutionalized supranational regions is similar to that behind the urban region: they are driven by the idea that some processes are better addressed by a group of neighboring states acting together. For example, there exists a powerful notion that there are advantages to be had (in terms of attracting investment, achieving economies of scale, and increasing opportunities for citizens) in being party to a large internal market with a shared set of rules and, possibly, a single currency. The only way for smaller states to achieve this regional market is by linking their economies together.

These institutionalized regions are becoming increasingly central to economic imaginaries for a number of reasons. One, of course, is the overall massive (but not universal) failure since the 1950s of attempts to produce national economies through development policies (see Ferguson 1994 for a detailed account of the limits of the national approach and T. Mitchell 2002b for the connection between colonial rule and the creation of national economies). This time span also saw the general but not total inability of import-substitution industrialization policies to produce sustained manufacturing sectors. Unsurprisingly, these dual failures of nation-state-based policies lent support to those advocating for export-based approaches, allowing their view to come into fashion as a corrective. Furthermore, the advantages of large interactive markets came to be noticed in the tea leaves of economic examination. An institutionalized regional framework could plausibly be used to explain the collective success of the fifty American states (about as well as any theory can that ignores the importance of colonial hinterlands), and the European

Economic Community and European Union certainly increased Europe's (already high) levels of intraregional trade.

Chapter 3 highlighted how economic thinking is a terrain of distinction based on cycles of new ideas that critique and then overturn the old. In making this argument, I do not seek to diminish the impact that institutions, policy think tanks, and other well-funded actors with a stake in the global economy have in pushing the agenda away from national centrality. They not only shape opinions but make the rules that produce the "free-trade" phenomenon (T. Mitchell 2002b). However, in many important ways, a change in the structure of feeling deemed that institutionalized regionality's time had come. In all cycles of fashion, the new thought must replace the old, even if the new is not necessarily qualitatively better than the old (although it might very well be). As Gordon MacLeod and Martin Jones put it in their article "Renewing the Geography of Regions," "It is becoming something of a truism now to proclaim a resurgence of regions. Not least in that the conditions that are being formed through economic globalisation, the purported decline of the nation-state and, in the European Union, a stepwise integration of economic and political institutions appear to be providing certain regional spaces with a distinct competitive advantage. . . . Paralleling this has been a quite remarkable appeal to the regional scale by bourgeois interest groups, boosterist politicians, and business gurus" (2001, 669–70). Something had to come after national economies: thus, the focus has shifted to assemblages both bigger and smaller than the nation-state.

Yet, even though the economic space targeted by policy shifted from nation to region, the work such policies did on structures of feeling remained the same. The postcolonial periphery continued to be viewed in a less than flattering light under the sign of the regional economy, just as it had during the ascendency of the nation-state: a shadow or "not yet" version of the "baseline" standard, Europe and the United States. Thus, regionalness became another terrain on which market Orientalism could provide enjoyment by separating the good from the bad.

This is where the "comparative" supranational region comes into play. A comparative supranational region can consist of any group of states that border each other (although, as seen later in this chapter, this requirement does not appear to be hard and fast). It exists primarily to provide a means of comparison both between the states within the region as well as between the region and other regions beyond its borders. Unlike institutionalized regions, no place in the world (or at least nowhere that reports statistics) falls outside of a comparative supranational region. These comparative regions are the organizing categories for many United Nations, World Bank, IMF, and World Trade Organization directorates.

As Rick Fawn (2009) points out, a multitude of traits might theoretically be used to draw the lines between comparative supranational regions. In practice, however, these supranational comparative regions are the same "cultural regions" that appear in world regional geography textbooks. For example, the IMF website (at least the 2012 version) divides the world into "advanced economies" and "emerging and developing economies." Then, in producing a slightly discontinuous geography, it names the advanced economies as the Euro Area, the major advanced economies (United States, Canada, Japan, Australia), and the newly industrialized Asian economies. But once the focus shifts to the "emerging" category, contiguous culture regions take over. They include central and eastern Europe (much of which is actually in the European Union), the Commonwealth of Independent States, developing Asia, Latin America and the Caribbean, the Middle East, and sub-Saharan Africa.

Basically, what the IMF and countless other institutions do is naturalize culture regions (which are themselves problematic) as economic regions. These creations certainly are not climate regions, nor are they based on any particular economic similarity. The important point is that the world is totally covered by regions. Peter Gran bemoans this tendency to automatically "regionalize" everything based on shared boundaries, arguing that this area studies approach to economies can become "an obstacle for someone interested in political analysis. If, for example, one determines that Jordan is a 'tribal state,' would it not be more logical for a student of Jordan to compare Jordan to other tribal states, many of which are in Africa or Southeast Asia, than to follow the conventional political-economy methodology that plays a country like Jordan off against another Middle Eastern country, and one such as Egypt, which has a different type of society all together" (1990, 230).

If "comparative" supranational regions were treated like the flimsy constructs they are and simply used as shorthand to make conversations about economic difference easier, then they would not be a big deal. The problem is that these comparative regions are viewed as potential institutionalized regions, no matter what type of economic similarity or difference falls within their borders. After all, Europe the Culture Region managed to transform itself (over the course of several decades) into Europe the Institutionalized Region (i.e., the European Union). Similarly, North America the Culture Region became NAFTA (by adding a piece of Latin America). Thus, those postcolonial comparative regional economies that have yet to successfully institutionalize are marked as deficient, and all sorts of reports are and will be written about their need for more fully realized regional integration—albeit in a much more compressed time frame than Europe utilized. The thinking goes that if there is a North American economy and a European economy, there should be—if not now, then soon—a Latin American economy, an African economy, an East Asian economy, and, of course, a Middle Eastern economy.

That being said, imagining what the problems of postcolonial regional trade blocs might be is not a difficult task. From a political economy perspective, it is easy to see why a cluster of small, weak states (or even big states) that produce similar types of primary exports are likely to have trouble quickly creating the institutions and the diverse array of products necessary to nurture a robust regional trade area and its attendant economies of scale. But I also want to propose something that might be considered a cultural economy perspective on the issue: to see postcolonial regional economies as fantastical.

In what sense is the goal of institutionalized regions fantastical? Here, I am expanding on ideas formulated by Slavoj Žižek in his book *The Parallax View* (2006). For Žižek, desire (and thus fantasy) arises out of aspirations for, despite the impossibility of, fullness in some relationship or representational system. Fantastical categories emerge precisely because something is lacking. Such categories emerge either when an exhaustive list of traits cannot be established and a catchall residual arises to close the circle or because symbolic systems that aim for totality inevitably produce a glaring gap. Social scientists' schemas are littered with such fantastical categories: even many of the post-structuralists among us want beauty, consistency, and parallelism in our papers; we want to encompass our topic, as narrow or as wide as it may be.

For Žižek, the operation of fantastical categories is perhaps clearest in Marx's concept of the Asiatic mode of production. Whereas Edward Said (1994) sees Marx's treatment of Asia as in line with that of other colonial-era Europeans of the day, Žižek sees Marx's Asiatic mode of production as "a kind of negative container: the only true content of this concept is 'all modes of production that do not fit Marx's standard characterization of modes of production.' . . . [Thus,] while appearing to designate positive content, [it] merely reveals our ignorance" (2006, 39). Of course, as Said points out in his many critiques of Orientalism, it is no coincidence that this ignorance acting as fullness was projected onto the colonial world.

So how "fantastical" is a world of yet to be institutionalized comparative regions with a category called the "Middle East"? Examining trade is a good place to start. According to a pair of reports out of the World Bank's Middle East and North Africa (MENA) Division on the topic of Middle East regional integration (Akhtar and Rouis 2010; Rouis and Tabor 2012), 66 percent of trading in Europe was intraregional in 2007, compared to 25 percent of trade in Southeast Asia (a number that would be around 40 percent for all of developing East Asia). These reports put the share of intraregional trade within MENA to be around 8 percent. Per capita income certainly does not unite the region either, even among states that sit on the Arabian Peninsula—the gap between Yemen and Qatar is about as big as between any two countries in the world. Not all states have oil, and even among those who do the size of population and the size of reserves make huge differences. Some states in the Middle East have foreign resident populations exceeding 70 percent; others are heavily dependent on remittances from emigrants. Even Arabic as a lingua franca for services falters because two of the biggest states usually considered inside the region—Turkey and Iran—are not Arabic speaking. One gets the idea.

Ideally, an "aspiring" institutionalized supranational region comprises polities with some complementarity. For example, the countries in Europe and the states of the United States vary by climate type, size, and specialized sectors (and thus produce different types of products), but they are also institutionally similar enough and wealthy enough to make their integration relatively easy. Finding postcolonial areas with that type of well-matched diversity—and well-developed institutions—is difficult. In fact, the developing-world area with the largest amount of internal trade— East Asia—is a bit of a unique case. The reason eastern Asia has such high levels of internal trade compared to other developing-world regions has nothing to do with any similarity to Europe. This high level of trade is largely a result of the fact that China is located in eastern Asia (alongside other industrialized countries) and acts as a hub that takes in all varieties of raw materials and sends out finished products (Gruenwald and Hori 2008). That there is a strong trade relationship between China and its neighbors should not be a surprise because many states in the world have China as a top trading partner. As Jessie Poon (1997) argued nearly two decades ago, increased intraregional trading in a smaller number of bigger regions has not slowed "regional cosmopolitan"—that is, regions trading with other regions.

At this stage, it would be all too easy to get sucked into an endless debunking of the positive content of the postcolonial regional economy in the Middle East. Instead, let us return again to the idea of fantasy. To be sure, there is a fantasy concerning postcolonial regional economies—but this may not mean what you think it means. Calling the idea of a postcolonial regional economy a fantasy is not equivalent to saying it is false or that there is no such thing as a postcolonial regional economy. Nor does calling it a fantasy necessarily mean it also contains a focus on the sexual or exotic—although, as chapter 3 showed, in the case of imaginations about the Middle East, those characterizations are germane. Fantasy, in Žižek's figuring, does something more than escape reality: "fantasy mediates between the formal symbolic structure and the positivity of objects we encounter in reality. . . . To put it in somewhat simplified terms: fantasy does not mean that, when I desire a strawberry cake and cannot get it in reality, I fantasize about eating it; the problem is, rather, how do I know that I desire a strawberry cake in the first place? That is what fantasy tells me" (2006, 7). To put it yet another way, fantasy structures the hunger response so it attaches to a particular object, the strawberry cake. To the extent a fantasy is a mistake, it is a mistake in a certain direction.

The fantasy of postcolonial regional economies is a fantasy of complete schemas, of a world that is broadly and fully comparative, of something called a "global economy" that can be subdivided and made plain. As Michel Callon (1998a) and Timothy Mitchell (2002b) point out, any "economy" is always a reduction—a framing that excludes enough to allow exchange to occur. By its nature, economic activity produces a remainder, but the fantasy is the desire to forget these inevitable externalities, to remove all outsides to create a smooth, calculateable perfection. So in that sense terms such as *Middle East economy* and *Gulf economy* help fill in the gaps in the world economic picture between those spaces that are considered to have had "success" in the world economy, such as North America, Europe, and East Asia. But a postcolonial regional economy is also an aspirational figure, an empty signifier that promises a future wholeness. Within policy circles, states are told again and again that things will be better if only there were regional economic cooperation and that if they do not achieve this goal, they are somewhat "less." This becomes the case even if, as in the case of Qatar, success is obtained on other imagined economic grounds, such as GDP per capita rankings. This fantasy of economic equivalence—an anathema to diverse-economy perspectives—has become yet another terrain for sorting, ranking, and hierarchicalizing countries.

The GCC, an Untraditional Regional Success?

So far this chapter has demonstrated that, given the right set of circumstances, Gulf polities can indeed get along and work toward common ends. The UAE is a case in point. Yet the GCC stalled on the question of where to locate the central bank for a proposed monetary union. This "postponement" came in an overall climate where comparative regions—such as the Gulf—are supposed to become institutional regions lest they suffer the wrath of the *Economist* and its ilk. The reasons why the idea of regions became so charged include a change in fashion away from national economies and a form of fantastical thinking that posits that all of the world should be divided into institutionalized regions.

With that in mind, let us return to the specifics of the GCC case. Were the rulers of the UAE being obstinate when they did not agree to the central bank being located in Saudi Arabia, thus thwarting the Gulf's "inherent" regional potential? Was this objection especially hypocritical given that the emirates in the UAE already reap the benefits of being in a federation?

To begin with, there are some grounds to question whether a GCC common currency—the key reason for the creation of the central bank—would actually add to its regional potential or not. All of the GCC currencies, with the exception of the Kuwaiti dinar, are pegged to the US dollar. The Kuwaiti dinar is pegged to a basket of currencies. Thus, most of the currencies are already effectively interchangeable, even for retail customers, who can often shop with any GCC currency in other GCC states (at least within the big cities). As Giacomo Luciani put it recently, "Obviously, if all that is implied by launching a common currency is a transitioning from a rigid dollar peg for each individual currency, to a rigid dollar peg for the common currency, it will not amount to much of a change" (2011, 29). He speculates that perhaps some other plan might be afoot but also notes that the Gulf states benefit from the prestige and stability the dollar peg brings their currency and the fact that it allows the individual government budgets to absorb the impacts of currency fluctuation as opposed to the real wages of nationals.

Furthermore, the GCC already possesses a number of regional institutions from which all Gulf states benefit, at least in theory. There has been a shared GCC patent office since the 1990s. In 2008, the GCC Common Market was created, wherein GCC citizens can theoretically enjoy national privileges in other countries (such as right to work and an education), which would allow them to seek out the most promising opportunities. Although other policies have stalled—such as the customs union in 2003 and in 2008 aspects of the Common Market that would challenge the local business-agency system—it is easier than before to operate on a GCC scale. Some service-sector companies such as retailer and property manager Majid Al Futaim already operate in all GCC countries.

That being said, within the GCC only Bahrain and Oman have another GCC country (Saudi Arabia and the UAE, respectively) among their top-five trading partners (Eurostat IMF 2014). In both of these cases, the relationship exists because it is often less expensive to ship in large quantities to the bigger UAE and Saudi markets and to deliver goods by truck to the smaller markets in Bahrain and northern Oman as if they were peripheral cities. Oman also exports agricultural, livestock, and poultry products to the UAE. The Saudi–Bahrain connection is perhaps even closer because of the shared Abu Safah oil field (of which Bahrain gets 50 percent of the revenue) and a further allotment of Saudi crude that is sent to Bahrain for processing.

But for the most part the GCC consists of countries with sectoral specialties that more or less overlap. In fact, the 2010 World Bank report on economic integration in MENA, which largely supported the idea of the GCC (while de-emphasizing the currency union), contained the following assessment on the very first page of its GCC section: "Because GCC integration occurs against the backdrop of fairly similar circumstances in the member countries, the mechanisms and drivers of integration are somewhat different than in other regional blocs, where membership is more varied" (Akhtar and Rouis 2010, 1).

Indeed, a perception of a shared situation has been with the council since its founding. One must remember that when the GCC was announced in 1981, it was in many ways a reaction to the events of 1979. Egypt had made a separate peace with Israel, contra the Arab League's pro-unity ideals. The announcement of the creation of the GCC—which did not include neighboring Yemen or Iraq—was initially met with charges of its being a "rulers' club" or "extended royal family" (as noted in Ramazani and Kechichian 1988, xi), wherein the richest Arabs decided to abandon the project of Arab unity and close ranks. Indeed, the feeling that the Gulf states needed to look out for one another increased exponentially following the Iranian Revolution. It soon took on even greater urgency as Iran became embroiled in a war with Iraq that could potentially spill over to the Gulf states. Furthermore, citizens in the wider Middle East region had become very sensitive to allowing any foreign power into their region's affairs. Although not mentioned in the GCC's initial documents, most of the Gulf foreign ministers at the time talked about the need for shared, self-provisioned security to collectively deal with much larger threats. The economic issues are mentioned in the founding documents, but small-state security initially dominated the agenda. Thus, the GCC has always been about something slightly less economic than the European Union and other pure-trade agreements such as NAFTA.

The real benefit of a fully integrated GCC common market, let alone a common currency, would probably go disproportionately to those outside the region and to a subset of the currently well-connected individuals within it. It would probably (although not necessarily, given increased professionalization of the largest agent firms) make it easier for foreign firms to sell products in the Gulf if they have to deal with only one agent (or possibly no agent) across all the countries—something that the Common Market already might potentially allow.

In fact, the entire *Economist* article discussed at the beginning of this chapter has trouble coming up with any tangible, locally felt benefits that all Gulf countries would accrue by moving toward a single currency. It does, however, note that "many in the region's financial industry" argued that the introduction of the Khaleeji would "strengthen economic ties" and "help banks develop cross-border products and services" (*Economist* 2009). In other words, it would help banks and bankers, some of which are local, many of which are not.

That *Economist* article also suggests that a common currency would allow an unpegging from the dollar, which, as noted earlier, may not necessarily be in the GCC's interest. But Kuwait already allows its currency to float against an international basket of currencies to little real impact in its financial situation. Nothing is stopping all the others from agreeing to peg to the same basket while maintaining their own central banks to adjust the peg if local circumstances warrant. If they were truly interested in a power move (and the inherent risk such a move would entail), they might create a common, free-floating currency with no peg at all and price their oil and gas exports in it in an attempt to form a "currency region" (Cohen 1997), wherein neighboring Indian Ocean and Southwest Asian states would begin using the Gulf currency for international transactions. But no such thing has ever been mentioned.

In the end, the only argument the *Economist* comes up with is that the Gulf states should, as mentioned earlier, "overcome old political rifts for the sake of economic and financial integration." In other words, they should integrate for the sake of integrating because that is simply what one should do. This is the fantasy of completeness and the ritual of demonstrating fidelity to cycles of economic fashion.

But the *Economist's* is not the only view on integration. The World Bank report on MENA integration (Akhtar and Rouis 2010) does better, offering more specific areas where integration might benefit the Gulf—such as harmonization of immigration laws, multilateral coordination of aid to poorer areas within the GCC, and financial regulation policy. The report seems ambivalent at best about the lack of currency union. However, its final recommendation is for a "more empowered regional secretariat" informed by "technical support" that can overcome situations where "GCC countries compete with each other in sectors that might otherwise offer scope for regional initiatives" and decomplicate "the political economy of economic reform" in public-sector subsidies (Akhtar and Rouis 2010, 1, 22, 25). Thus, it wants a regional expert body to have a bird's-eye view to remove the Gulf's supposed inefficiencies caused by those "old political rifts" that the *Economist* mentions.

Here the World Bank is calling on the idea of region as critique of the current organization of space, in this case in the name of efficiency. It also seems as if one of the goals of the World Bank version of a more empowered regional secretariat is to produce even more regionalism. Furthermore, region-wide reform is also unlikely to succeed in accomplishing one of its primary goals—the creation of a fair market that is cleared of everyone but equally informed buyers and sellers (or perhaps policy makers) and in which only rational choices get made.

As Timothy Mitchell documents in the case of Egyptian "liberalization," efforts at market reform in the Gulf around a common market would most likely resemble a "multi-layered political readjustment of rents, subsidies and the control of resources" (2002b, 277). Such reforms would not magically disappear the well connected in Gulf society and the network of practices that sustain each country. Julia Elyachar shows this in her ethnographic research (again in Egypt), where an emergent focus on microlending, driven by international donors, did not erase existing power centers and ways of knowing within the country, but instead shifted their focus. Thus, one of the most powerful forces in Egyptian microlending was a career public-sector banker who created "communicative

channels, [through which] finance flowed—a kind of finance that was neither abstract nor flattening" (2012, 78) but based on reading people, past
experiences concerning who to trust, and buzz among economic-sector
communities. Indeed, reforms in Gulf would likely reshuffle the deck
in a similar manner based on who among the powerful and connected
manages to capture the opportunities opened up by new architectures.
Specific interventions the World Bank mentioned in its report—such as
coordinating labor and financial regulation—are likely to bring clarity and
actually help individuals; the benefits of deregulation, picking which territory gets which sectoral clusters, and market making are murkier.

I think that officials in Abu Dhabi, Dubai, and Oman were being
astute rather than contrary regarding the location of the central bank and
perhaps regarding the wider question of integration as well. For starters,
if the post-Greece Eurozone experience has shown anything, it is that
having your own currency might actually be a good thing in times of
trouble (especially if you have priorities separate from those of the biggest
economy in your currency union). And although I do think the location
of the central bank, not the lack of a unit of account, was the main reason
the UAE abandoned the currency, doing a trial run certainly seems like
a sound idea.

Furthermore, for the UAE, giving up its ability to make policy to
an institution dominated by a much larger Saudi neighbor *and* having
that neighbor host the symbolic head of that institution were apparently
too much. Banking is a key sector for most Gulf states: whichever state
received the bank would almost certainly gain an agglomeration advantage and pull personnel and foreign direct investment toward it and away
from other states. Such an advantage would mean a great deal to smaller
Bahrain (which already has a diversified banking sector) while not harm-
ing the remaining (larger) economies in the GCC, which banks would
still have to service.

It must not be discounted, however, that the relatively stable UAE and
Oman may not have wanted to get even closer to the other Gulf states.
They might have become wary of tying their fate more deeply to Bahrain,
with its internal strife. They could have conceivably felt the same about
Saudi Arabia, where there is a coming generational divide and at least the

possibility of royal-succession messiness. The UAE also has underlying tension with Qatar and its support of Islamist political parties—tensions that have come more to the fore since the Arab Spring protests.

Although the 1990s were full of talk about supranational regional integration (which obviously did not fully dissipate with time), the 2000s have very much been about the imaginations of interurban competition. Even without the kudos for "rationally" choosing the regional approach, are there more attractive urban markets within the Indian Ocean neighborhood than the markets of Dubai and Abu Dhabi (aside from maybe Doha and possibly Mumbai)? Dubai's ruling family has believed for decades that it has to out-compete other Gulf cities: with such a mindset, gifting a central bank to a rival seems out of character. Even if part of the promise of a currency union would be that UAE companies would have greater access to Saudi Arabian markets, those in the UAE know that access and actual ability to succeed, given the way Saudi economies are structured, are entirely separate things. The al-Sauds, for their part, must have seen the currency union as a way to rein in their rivals in the GCC. At the very least, both the Saudis and the Emiratis I have spoken to about the issue suspected this motivation for the Saudis' desire to move forward with a central bank in Riyadh.

Nor are the rulers of the UAE being hypocritical in rejecting one union while existing in another. The seven emirates, in fact, have much more varied conditions than the GCC as a whole. This makes their banding together more sensible. In the 1970s, Abu Dhabi had oceans of oil; Dubai had enough to develop rapidly if it pumped quickly; Sharjah had some; and the others basically had none. Those three oil producers also had many more people than the other emirates. By financially supporting the poorer and less-populous emirates (which, given their small sizes, was far from cost prohibitive), Abu Dhabi (and to a lesser extent Dubai) was able to buy peace and less threat of civil strife on their doorstep—something that the cases of insurgency in southern Oman and Yemen showed to be real possibilities. Dubai also gained access to additional markets for retailers and importers in its emirate, markets where they would not face well-funded competition and that were closer than Abu Dhabi. There were other advantages, too. Emirates on the Gulf coast could now move products directly into the Indian Ocean through Shar-jah and Fujairah's coastline if the Gulf ever became impassible to ships. Furthermore, the UAE can indeed get along with those outside the fed-eration when they see fit. For example, the UAE signed a tourist visa accord with Oman, making it easier for tourists to visit both states (and their different types of attractions) on a single trip; many Iranians also use Dubai as a business base.

Even though the conditions of the emirates varied more than the conditions among the Gulf states, the Gulf states themselves are far from identical (just as their citizens and residents display diversity among them-selves as well). Qatar and Abu Dhabi are now in the position that Kuwait and Saudi Arabia were in during the 1970s: they have so much oil and gas revenue compared to the size of their national population that they are more concerned about opening up more channels for distribution to keep the population happy and increasing their polities' prestige than about maximizing efficiency. For these places, economic speed bumps such as the agent/local ownership system for foreign businesses still serves a purpose. It is an indirect subsidy that funnels some foreign money that was coming into the country anyway toward citizens, only at the cost of occasionally being grumbled about in the business press—although in practice larger agent firms have become increasingly professionalized since the 1970s, making it hard for individuals to sponsor anything but the smallest of businesses (Hertog 2010b). Dubai firms, in contrast, would sup-port the implementation of a customs union and common market, which would allow its superior shipping operations to crowd out weaker competi-tors, but not if the market included a common value-added tax (i.e., sales tax) that was anything but nominal. Such a tax might decrease the price advantages that Dubai, as a luxury shopping destination, holds over much of Europe and other high-sales-tax regions.

Alternatively, Bahrain's rulers seem the most enthusiastic about the processes of integration because their country already benefits from Saudi Arabia's policy choices (more on this topic is included in chapter 7). More integration would also allow them to deflect some of the blame for local inequality onto higher levels of administration. Both Saudi Arabia and Bahrain could use the revenues from a value-added tax, and Saudi Arabian firms could potentially take advantage of their economies of scale to make inroads against similar but smaller firms in the other GCC states.

There are certainly benefits for most GCC countries in some aspects of integration, but each country would lose some of the support that keeps its economic ecosystem and regime afloat in the name of trying to pursue regional "efficiencies." The next section explores different ways to think about the situation in place of chastising the Gulf for letting "national interests" get in the way of regionalism.

If Not Integration?

With the argument that failing to move forward with a currency union might not be the worst thing for the Gulf (and the citation of several analysts who seem to agree) now on the table, the question that naturally arises is: If not integration, then what else?

First, a preface: By the time you read this book, there might already be a full GCC monetary union or some other more comprehensive movement toward integration. At the time of writing, the prospect seems remote, but if the bulk of postcolonial and post-structural theory teaches one thing, it is not to foreclose on the future through overconfident proclamations. Certainly, since the founding of the GCC, the idea that there might be a shared sense of being *khaleeji* has gained some acceptance (and governments and local media have certainly made great efforts to define national and regional distinctiveness). However, even if more integration happens and it turns out to be successful in the long term (i.e., after several decades of fits and starts), I do not think this outcome negates the applicability of anything I say to the present day.

A good first step in understanding the complexities of the Gulf's cultural economies is to avoid affixing labels to them because such labels often predefine and limit conclusions prior to any actual analysis (Marston, Jones, and Woodward 2005). This happens all too often, and it leads to the erasure of all information that falls outside well-established boundaries. For example, say one has predetermined that the Gulf is now neoliberal. But with large state sectors, comparatively few benefit cuts during recent decades, and a fair amount a difference from the regulatory system labeled "free trade," the Gulf is hardly neoliberal in the sense most scholars mean it (lest *neoliberalism* just becomes a synonym for an economy with some elements that are unjustly arranged). So if one forgoes the term *neoliberal* and instead asserts that the Gulf states are Keynesian or perhaps socialist welfare states, the problem simply shifts to new blind spots. Neither of those terms work fully because the Gulf states (in general) do not promote full equality or the democratic practice that those equality-centric policies are supposed to enable. Nor do the Gulf states resemble the state-aided market economies of East Asia, which also have heavy government involvement in the finance sector. Those East Asian economies (to the extent they even fit that model used to categorize them) relied on routinized industrial exports, as opposed to commodity export, to bring their initial prosperity. Although the label *rentier state* fits in many ways, it is hard to imagine it has that much meaning if it is used to describe both the kleptocracy that plagues gigantic, diverse Nigeria and the close-knit national economic ecosystem of Qatar. Yes, there are neoliberal processes, Keynesian processes, and of course rentier processes in these cultural economies, but identifying these processes is not the same thing as assigning definitive labels. Thus, an emphasis on process over labels is important if any progress on seeing past existing hierarchies is to be made. In fact, to the standard list of economic processes (mistakenly used as labels) listed earlier, I propose adding two more: waste and seduction.

"Waste" is a point of emphasis in the economic writings of early-twentieth-century philosopher Georges Bataille. Although he focused on a wide variety of topics during his career, in his conceptualization of the economy (Bataille [1949] 1988) he highlighted the pivotal role of overproduction. This approach puts him in opposition to many economists and political economists, who place competition under conditions of scarcity at the center of their theories (although it does put him close to David Harvey, who has for decades emphasized the impacts of crises of overaccumulation of capital).

Bataille's basic argument is that societies cannot be so rational as to accumulate and allocate capital perfectly. What will be produced is ultimately an "accursed share" that will be either "wasted" through people's consumption of it in pure enjoyment, luxury, or ritual sacrifice or

"creatively destroyed" in war and violence—a notion that echoes the conclusion to Harvey's final chapter in *Limits to Capital* (1982). For Bataille,
"waste" is not a bug in the economy's code; it is a feature. As Marcus Doel,
Bataille's biggest supporter in geography, argues, "For him [Bataille], the
most crucial problem that all societies face is not the miserly allocation of
scare resources, but rather how to deal with all of those resources—time,
effort, goods, people, energy and wealth—that are not required for mere
subsistence. This is a pressing problem in our affluent societies, not least
because the excess of resources over subsistence is astronomical" (2003,
220). Drawing on Marcel Mauss, Bataille argues that unlike many societies in the past, modern societies have resources "deliberately reserved for
growth." Thus, according to Doel, Bataille advances the notion that

> societies of growth are plagued by the social and environmental prob-
> lems that are caused by the hoarding of wealth: greed, envy, exploita-
> tion, pauperization, and so on. . . . So whereas everything in societies of
> consumption is geared towards the maintenance of social relationships,
> everything in societies of growth tends to be "relegated towards the
> level of things." Even people become considered as either instruments
> of growth (workers, labourers, managers) or impediments to growth
> (dependants, idlers, the unemployed). For Bataille, this instrumental
> mind-set is effectively an attempt to liquidate the social. (2003, 221)

A passage from Bataille himself further emphasizes the point made
here: "The excess energy (wealth) can be used for the growth of a system,
but if the system can no longer grow, or if the excess cannot be completely absorbed in its growth, it must necessarily be lost without profit;
it must be spent, willingly or not, gloriously or catastrophically" (1988,
21). Of course, Bataille would rather the former happen because through
"immodest" consumption "I reveal to my fellow beings that which I am
intimately" (58). Thus, for Bataille, consumption (especially shared in a
community) does the important work of social reproduction.

By taking seriously the key sociocultural role played by overproduction, Bataille's theories can speak to periods when Gulf cultural economies
were marked by abundance, not scarcity. His highlighting of situations

where "the excess cannot be completely absorbed" certainly describes Kuwait and Saudi Arabia of the 1970s. In an interview with *National Geographic* in 1980, Saudi oil minister Sheikh Yamani lamented just such a situation: "We lost seven billion dollars a year keeping Saudi crude at less than the world market price. And it would be in the national interest to keep the oil in the ground instead of [to] accumulate dollars that depreciate faster than we can investment them" (Azzi 1980, 297). Indeed, many of those accumulated petrodollars (which had become massive loans made by American banks to developing world states) were spectacularly wasted or disappeared in a global debt crisis in the early 1980s. Much of the Gulf's postoil history is about the rulers experimenting with ways to waste their money in the best manner possible (ideally for both current and future nationals, not just for themselves and their circle) through infrastructure spending, welfare provision, and subsidies for citizens. Make no mistake: in a time when inflation exceeded interest rates, there was no possible way to spend the 1970s windfalls perfectly. There had to be losses.

Regulations such as the requirement (mentioned in chapter 5) that foreign firms hire a local agent before doing business in the Gulf could function in a potentially productively wasteful manner, just like the civic methods of distribution listed earlier. Although not optimally cost efficient and undoubtedly beneficial to the well connected in the Gulf (such as the aforementioned Adnan Khashoggi, who counted many influential Saudi princes as childhood friends), the local-agent practice nonetheless stands as an attempt to prevent the complete liquidation of the social in favor of market structures. By having agents smooth introductions and ensure no hurt feelings on either side, Gulf policy prioritizes the feelings and people that are part of business as opposed to considering only the price of the transaction to be important. The stipulation that agents are supposed to be integrated into operations and not just collect a check attempts to force investment into being something more than the extraction of profit—a coproduction, more like a franchise arrangement.

This was especially key in the 1960s and 1970s, when the pool of people in the Gulf with international business experience was rather small—absent these regulations, these individuals might have been shut out of their own economies. Of course, actual agent arrangements often fall short of the ideals of sharing and good feelings—for example, the "concealment" type of business ownership (when a national owns a business in name but does none of the work) provides neither hands-on experience for the Gulf national nor any security for the foreign-resident operator (because it is easy to be booted from a business you do not own) (Hertog 2010b). Nonetheless, the existence of these requirements shows a willingness on the part of the Gulf states to "waste" money through formalized social processes (and we must admit that fraud in formalized channels is not absent from more democratic, market-device-centric economies sworn to ideas of efficiency). Furthermore, such arrangements are not hard and fast—taking a cue from Dubai's Jebel Ali Port, Internet City, and Media City, many Gulf states are considering "free zones" in select sectors (in particular ones that are otherwise reluctant to come to the Gulf), where no agent is required in order to operate. Saudi Arabia is in fact creating an entire new city near Jeddah, King Abdullah Economic City, where "free zone" rules will largely apply.

Such decisions not to put efficiency and lowest cost first in every possible instance are too often used as a means to position the Gulf as abnormal and inferior. However, as Max Horkheimer (1974) notes, a focus solely on price is not the "natural" state of affairs, but a produced one. For Horkheimer, the disruption caused by the transition to price centricity can be most clearly seen in the retail sphere, which even into the early twentieth century carried over with it many aspects of "honor" typical of the king–subject relationship (something that could said of many aspects of bourgeoisie society). Not the least of these aspects was the notion that customers were seen to receive "service," as in "servitude":

> The readiness to see in the other a potential buyer, the inclination to serve and please, were habitual throughout wide strata of society. . . . Neither friendliness nor expert knowledge, not even a favorable ratio between price and value, were enough to produce the all-important result. The businessman who traveled to meet a business friend abroad or welcomed him at his own place of business or in his own home, had to have good manners and a familiarity with other languages, countries, and ways. Anything that could pave the way to contacts with potential

buyers and win their good will fell within the businessman's purview. . . .
Even the man in the street experienced in the act of buying a little of his
own freedom and of respect for himself as subject. (1974, 140)

Horkheimer contrasts this regime of service with the type of subjectivity
enabled by department stores and mass media: the "self-service" customer.
For Horkheimer, this type of subjectivity means that "the personal relationship is being eliminated from the act of buying and selling. There is
no longer room for acts of courtesy to individuals, for the old bow to the
customer is being replaced by advertising" (1974, 141). This system not
only disciplines people into being subjects of the market but also places
pricing above all else. Or, to put it in the terminology used by Boltanksi
and Thévenot (2006), in retail you can see the transition away from a
"domestic" economy of value with its preference for manners, tradition, and hierarchy toward a "market" economy with its individualized
competition.

In contrast, through the agent system, with its forced sharing of revenues and engagement in negotiation and matchmaking, the Gulf attempts
to preserve some aspects of a system where streamlining is not everything.
In fact, the agent system in some ways resembles the currently emergent
"projective" (project-and-connection-based) economy of value, detailed in
Boltanski and Chiapello (2005), where the most respected actors are the
ones with the widest and most reliable networks of useful persons who can
come together to complete a project successfully (such as helping a foreign
firm enter a new market and find local partners).

A willingness to go beyond what people "logically" deserve from their
governments similarly can be seen operating in the continuation of many
of the Gulf state's individual subsidies (such as Kuwait's much maligned
electrical subsidies for citizens). Such polices are not optimally efficient in
a strictly logistical sense, and a store such as Walmart, for better or worse,
could hardly run itself on such a model that purposefully "wastes," given
its corporate priorities.

To be clear: there is no denying that much has been achieved in the
world through gains of efficiency. Every Gulf state has a sector or government department that runs on an efficiency model (oftentimes it is the

oil ministry). However, someone or some group almost always loses when "noncore" functions are eliminated for the sake of government streamlining. There are numerous cases where the social cost exceeds the gains made by efficiency. For Bataille, "consumption is the way in which separate beings communicate," and, if that communication becomes less common through market self-discipline, something of the social is lost. Thus, there are certainly more odious ways for governments to waste funds than to insist on involving nationals in economic activity through the agent system, as clunky and often unfair as that system may be.

If the Gulf became "more open" and streamlined via the higher power of a GCC directorate, large amounts of money would still flow through the region. Chances are, however, that even more of it would be "wasted" outside of the Gulf, likely by elites in New York and London. The Gulf states' ability to keep this money circulating internally—through agents, through comparatively generous subsidies and services (in most cases), and through a willingness to bankroll projects and government workers—helps shape the (sometimes inequitable) sociality of Gulf places. As authors such as Akhil Gupta (2005) and Steffen Hertog (2012b) argue, although people decry state distributions and the somewhat-related Gulf concept of *wasta* (i.e., making use of "who you know," a system of exchange just as likely to involve favors as actual money) as the enabling of "corruption" and deploy critiques of them as part of moralizing imaginations, most people tend to enjoy utilizing these techniques when doing so benefits them.

So although Dubai's property crash in 2008 shows the limits of how much could be invested internally—developers in Dubai committed to sinking so much capital into real estate that the capital completely ran out—the process of "waste" can also help explain why repetitious and so-called white elephant projects proliferate in the Gulf.

The presence of seemingly "wasteful" projects has always irked those who commentate on the Gulf—in this view, it stands as a sign of the rulers' cultural economic otherness. The World Bank report cited earlier (Akhtar and Rouis 2010) deemed the potential elimination of such projects as one of the best arguments in favor of greater regional policy coordination. Indeed, the dream of integration is to stop or to minimize this type of spending. Of course, such integration is unlikely to do so because, even though most of the Gulf lacks representative democracy, politics and competition will still exist. Plus, democracies have their own issues with spending on seemingly dubious and often replicated projects.

A sample of the criticism of "wasteful projects" can be found in a 1976 article in the *Times* of London. Published just a few years after the founding of the UAE, it shows that the creation of a higher authority provides no guarantee of being able to stop projects that some deem irrational. According to its author, "when money is no object there is a danger that the ability to differentiate between a good or a bad investment will be impaired" (M. Brown 1976). The article gives the example of Dubai's announcement of a plan to construct a large aluminum smelter complex, which was followed six months later by a report that Abu Dhabi was considering its own smelter. The reporter tried to make clear what he considered the illogic of the proposals: "Yet the two towns are less than 150 miles apart. Are they simply vying with one another for prestige projects? With Bahrain's smelter only a short way up the Gulf, does the UAE, a small country, really need its own smelter?"

Another article in the same period offered an example along the same lines: "Gestures of local pride or independence by some of the rulers have occasionally resulted in confrontation which noticeably stops short of armed conflict. Often, however, it is seen in absurd and wasteful duplication. Most serious has been the proliferation of seaport and airport developments. Sharjah opened one last year only 5 miles from the one in Dubai" (Weston 1978).[1]

1. Although I selected these quotations to demonstrate the point that a higher Gulf authority is unlikely to magically override local politics (despite reporters' great hopes), they also highlight a problem with such criticism: outside commentators do not always correctly pick which projects make sense or not. That aluminum smelter in Dubai, which belongs to DUBAL, has helped turn that company into one of the world's largest smelters. DUBAL smelters also generate electricity and desalinate 30 million gallons of seawater a day, meaning they perform an important public function for the city of Dubai. As for the "too many" airports comment: given the tremendous increase in air travel and shipment that has occurred since the 1970s, having multiple airports in growing urban regions is now considered fairly normal.

Although in some ways it might benefit the Gulf to have only one financial center (as opposed to six or seven)—in that such a city could be a potential rival to some of the larger world financial centers—most of the benefit would accrue only to the place with that center and, just as likely, mostly to those in that sector. Take the example of the United Kingdom: the growth of the City of London as a financial center since the 1980s has done very little to help other urban places in the country (in particular former industrial centers) and has driven up housing costs in London because of the financial sector's inflated salaries (Massey 2005). A similar situation exists in Manhattan, where Wall Street salaries have driven housing costs well beyond the means of all but the most affluent of households.

However, the presence of six or so Gulf banking centers does provide small but real benefits to some people in those cities by channeling some local revenues into building the infrastructure and some foreign revenues from those looking to latch onto flows of money. If foreign banks choose to have offices in six states instead of in two while trying to catch lightning in a bottle and find the "best" place, that is a transfer of wealth from the bank to multiple places in the Gulf. The same holds true for having twelve ports or fifteen airports or how many of whatever across the GCC. If executed moderately well, such projects can mix local money and foreign money (from renting offices, using facilities, paying for government-owned utilities, and putting foreign workers' earnings back in the economy), and get by. Foreign revenues do not need to be permanent in the sense that the firms stay forever (although it is a bonus if they do); Gulf states just require a steady stream of those willing to try. As long as there is money—and Abu Dhabi and Qatar seem the best situated in that regard—fortune seekers will come and do some wasting there, provided they are enabled.

Make no mistake, the execution of such projects can sometimes be poor, and money losses can be staggeringly real. Both the extreme oversupply of luxury residential and office condos during the Dubai property boom/crash and the long, slow money hemorrhage that is Bahrain's support of Gulf Air are examples of such loss. There is also a fair amount of fraud and theft that goes on in the Gulf (which is most definitely a byproduct of the "build anything worth trying" ethos), which hits foreign and local investors alike. However, there is a wide range of possible out-comes between optimally efficient and absolute disaster in both the Gulf and worldwide. Furthermore, in the Gulf the perception that something new is happening is perhaps as equally crucial as fostering sustained long-term success in every enterprise—after all, businesses fail at high rates everywhere.

The Gulf states have long demonstrated the ability and willingness to channel opportunities into niche sectors across their societies. Bah-rain—which, owing to its smaller oil reserves, does not have the luxury of building white elephant projects as other states do—relies on Saudi Arabia keeping its distinct cultural system in place so there are opportunities for the island kingdom in terms of leisure and housing. According to Hertog (2010a), even the Saudi bureaucracy is purposefully segmented internally into islands of efficiency (which deal with the most important export sec-tors and offer high salaries to the motivated), royal fiefdoms (that can be run efficiently but act as power and patronage centers for various branches of the royal family), and institutions of mass distribution (which are con-cerned primarily with employing the population).[2]

Is this optimally efficient? No, in fact it is wasteful, but I would argue it is somewhat productively so. Not everyone wants or is well suited to being dependent on a high-pressure job for their economic livelihood (even though it is beneficial for society that many people are). However, that does not make those who are not so inclined to hold pressure-cooker jobs less worthy of having access to a decent income. Nor does it necessar-ily mean such people are less dedicated or take less pride in what they do. The key is to figure out how to channel various revenue streams to take care of a wide variety of inclinations and social segments.

This potentially productive wastefulness is yet another reason why rep-etitious or seemingly wasteful projects make sense in the Gulf. Here, Jean

---

2. This was also my understanding of how Dubai's bureaucracy is structured. Exter-nally focused departments, such as Tourism and Commerce Marketing, are structured in an extremely "corporate" manner and have competitive hiring practices. Mostly internal services, such as the postal service or the drivers license bureau, are run at a much more leisurely pace.

Baudrillard proves useful. As the revolutionary spirit of the 1960s faded into the visible glamour and nihilism of the 1970s, Baudrillard became increasingly concerned that the "organic meaning" between signs and signifiers that he believed "primitive" societies once had was being lost, just as use value was replaced by exchange value in an earlier era. Baudrillard (1990) posited that in the place of a stable reference, all that was left driving society was "seduction"—which could also be read as charm, frivolity, irony, and challenge. If Baudrillard's rather uncritical ideas about the past, other cultures' ability to create abstraction, and the gendered nature of his use of the term *seduction* are put aside, there is something to be said about the appeal of the other than rational.

For Baudrillard, seduction is not about the deployment of power and panopticism to motivate others through structured coercion. Instead, it hinges on the potential in that which one cannot control. For Baudrillard, seduction is the sensing of possibility in something that is enticing but not fully understood. As he put it, "The secret is to know how to make use of death, in the absence of gaze, in the absence of gesture, in the absence of knowledge, or in the absence of meaning" (1990, 165). He also opposed seduction to the rationalists' focus on production, arguing that "production merely accumulates and is never diverted from its end . . . [but] an absence hollowed out at any point by the backfiring of any sign, the meaningless that is the sudden charm of seduction, is what waits, but without illusion, for production to reach its limits. . . . It is destiny" (166). In other words, maintaining the appearance of rationality requires great effort, but the seduction of looking for opportunities in meaninglessness will always lurk. As Doel (who is also Baudrillard's biggest supporter in geography) puts it,

> Baudrillard encountered seduction by way of production. While seduction diverts and leads astray, production "materializes by force what belongs to another order." In other words seduction removes something from the order of the visible, while production constructs everything in full view. So rather than situate production and seduction within the seemingly incongruous domains of industry and sexuality . . . Baudrillard situates them with respect to appearance and disappearance, and

specifically [with] the play—understood in a spatial sense—of appearances and disappearances. (2010, 187)

Seduction is thus similar to the type of potential Anna Tsing describes in "Inside the Economy of Appearances" (2001), which documents how Indonesia was continuously reimagined and "conjured" as a frontier of possibility for newly arriving waves of miners and investors, where the show of riches often trumped any ability to find them.

Seduction is a type of regional process the Gulf offers. As mentioned in chapter 3, one of the major aspects of market Orientalism is the supposed impenetrability of emerging markets. Although this misunderstanding can be used to cast emerging markets into otherness, it also seduces with the potential for opportunity. Thus, the perception of impenetrability can be repurposed as an asset. Dubai's rulers have been the masters of such repurposing (which I discuss further in chapter 7). In fact, what is remarkable about Dubai is that prior to the 2000s it was already known as a place where seeming white elephants such as the large convention center, container port, and free-trade zone were built—only to succeed!

My best anecdote of the seduction of Dubai comes from an interview I conducted with a sales representative for a German furniture manufacturer. When I asked why her company came to the emirate, her reply was that her head office really did not have a plan in place or a good idea of the preferences of the Dubai market. Nonetheless, they had set up a branch office in Dubai anyway because "something was happening." In this sense, Dubai was like a fire that created its own weather—convince enough people that there is money to be made, claim Dubai is by far the easiest place to make it, and enough people will come so that there is actual money to be made. In the 1970s, the price of oil provided all the advertising the Gulf needed. Perhaps going forward, what is needed is a sustainable stream of seductive (but nonfraudulent) opportunities in each place to convince potential workers and investors that where there is smoke, there is fire.

But perhaps, à la Baudrillard and Bataille, what the Gulf needs to do is worry a bit less about appeasing those who want it to produce or regionally coordinate more. In the case of the Gulf, the primary impetus for performing regionality (i.e., showing fidelity to the global economic consensus) potentially interferes with the very important function of "wasting" money on the population. As J. K. Gibson-Graham note, the entire development apparatus worldwide is focused on how to increase "exports" (really foreign moneys), and almost all possible advice is geared toward that goal:

> At the base of the development dream is faith in the incredible productive capacity of capitalist enterprise to generate wealth that can "float all boats," supporting higher standards of living and increased levels of well-being. What is rarely a part of this dream, however, is the mechanism by which these benefits will be distributed (let alone redistributed) to all *beyond* those who actively participate in capital investment or labor markets. . . . The ethical dimensions of surplus generation, its distribution and role in building society, are not up for discussion in mainstream development discourse. (2006, 178)

So much of the "advice" the Gulf receives is about how to create even more exports, when in reality these states already have (to varying degrees) at least a small amount of surplus to distribute. But advice on increasing production is usually all economic fashion has to give, so that is what the Gulf gets.

So it appears that the Gulf is not likely to perform regionality in ways the *Economist* hoped it would, at least any time soon. Perhaps that is for the best because that type of regionality is not without its potential problems—as evidenced by the recent turmoil that hit the European Union, which is the supposed model of best practice for the GCC. Gulf rulers will probably have to suffer more charges of "taking things personally" and being "hostage to arbitrary decision making" for failing to live up to the fantasy of a world seamlessly bundled into supposedly logical, spatially appropriate regional markets.

But simply enduring the scorn might be alright because, ultimately, the Gulf Cooperation Council is a different type of regional economic ecology with different processes. It is not one with huge volumes of

internal trade or one that is likely to focus on facilitating exactly the type
of fast-world/flat-world speed that Thomas Friedman advocates (even
though it has long offered tax-free repatriations of profit). It also does
not necessarily encourage specialization and realization of competitive
advantage across its territory as a whole. To better understand and move
beyond the various labels, we should draw on anti-Friedmans, such as
Bataille, Baudrillard, and Gibson-Graham, who point to different processes. I am not going to pound my fists on the table and say there is abso-
lutely no way more integration in the traditional sense would improve
livelihoods in the Gulf in the long term, but actual experience on the
ground studying Gulf economies makes me think that more integration
is hardly the automatic, quick winner some think it would be. More than
likely, it would primarily shift wealth among the already well-to-do.

This is not a policy book. I am not yet another foreign expert who
has policy advice for those in the Gulf about how it should be more like
"mature" economies. Furthermore, those in charge in the Gulf will ultimately do what they want in terms of policy based on their relationships
with various actors; it matters not to them what is said here. Nonetheless, I will emphasize this: Gulf economies are already more diverse than
nearly all the experts (and even some Gulf leaders) say they are. This is
true everywhere, of course—as long as you believe Gibson-Graham that
"important" economic activity includes not just "capitalist" production
but also various systems of surplus distribution and consumption (as well
as noncapitalist production and the commons).

Thus, in the Gulf, if one conceives of economic diversity as "diversity
of exports," then, of course, hydrocarbons by and large dominate in most
of the states. If hydrocarbons were magically to become irrelevant tomorrow, the Gulf states would indeed face a major dilemma. But if the Gulf
is viewed as a place where distribution and consumption of surplus matter
as much as nonoil exports, then there is real diversity. Most people do not
work in oil and gas; construction as well as retail and food service are by
far the most significant private-sector employers (although the majority of
workers in these areas are foreign). Construction is a symbiont that feeds
on the rest of the economy; if other sectors grow, then it grows. Retail
is not one uniform activity, but many (including wholesale, shipment,

advertising, sales agency, real estate, etc.). There is no harm in Gulf governments chasing biotech or medical tourism or green energy or any hot production sector that experts are convinced will be the next big thing in diversification, provided there are the funds to do it. But many places on earth are already chasing all those sectors.

In the Gulf and elsewhere, there is no one magic bullet to improve economic returns, even when comparatively huge funds are available to aid in the attempt. To continue the firearm metaphor, a shotgun approach is more appropriate. Dubai actually did this in the mid-2000s: it already had the Media City and Internet City free zones and tried to add not just biotechnology, medical tourism, and film production but also more obscure sectors such as publishing, warehousing, humanitarian logistics, gold, and motor sports. The big problems Dubai ran into were the oversupply of giant condos and hotels, the second Internet City in the middle of nowhere, multiple generic office zones, a second and third palm-tree-shaped island, all of which will likely get filled but followed too quickly on the heels of their predecessor projects. It is one thing for each Gulf city or sheikhdom to try projects similar to their neighbors because each is its own assemblage of relations, but it is another for each one to replicate its own projects too rapidly. A constant, regular drip of dispersed seductive opportunities seems more likely to produce steady results. Even though the Gulf is marked by structures of feelings produced by market Orientalism, many still find it intriguing. That in itself is a productive opportunity.

Although there are "standard" processes of integration in the Gulf already (far from the stereotype that Gulf Arabs are "naturally" unable to get along), including efforts to build a sense of regional distinctiveness, these processes take a back seat to regional processes of waste. In the case of the Gulf, there are many polities trying to find ways to make sure the "accursed share" that oil brings is enjoyed locally (and hopefully broadly), even if for Bahrain and Saudi Arabia that accursed share is comparatively smaller than it used to be. This enjoyment can occur even if the distribution mechanism repeats what is found nearby. To me, what is interesting about the Gulf is not how its cultural economies perform compared to the supposed norm, but that it is a place that has the potential to focus on livelihoods over standard measures of growth (and in select instances, it already does). In 2010, Kuwait set a modest minimum wage for all foreign, non-domestic, workers; Saudi Arabia is moving toward a similar policy and already has set one for domestic workers. Both have also negotiated bilaterally with labor-sending countries to secure higher wage floors for certain workers. Those are the types of policies I would personally be most interested in being shared and made more generous regionally.

In the end, the fact that every polity wants something different means there is a form of cooperation in the Gulf—*namely, benefiting from the unorthodoxy of others*. In some ways, that system—which can indeed be "slow" and far from transparent at times—also serves many (but certainly not everyone in all Gulf places) well because the Gulf always generates opportunities. Would a European Union–style system benefit the Gulf? Maybe in the long term, but no Gulf union would ever produce an economy identical to that of the United States or China or Europe, even if it followed all the supposedly best practices of those places. The circumstances are just too different. Indeed, such an assessment is probably true of most comparative regions that are supposed to transform into institutional regions—just because an idea worked in Europe does not mean it will work elsewhere in different circumstances.

Thus, there is quasi-cooperation in the Gulf, but it is very relational and, ironically, somewhat competitive. Especially since the early 2000s, many of the states there have been more proactive in trying to define themselves against each other and in staking out symbolic territory, all the while trying not to fall too far behind in any infrastructure category. Each plays off against the others, while not wanting any of the others to fail. This will not change just because they did not agree on the location for a central bank.

7

Heat and Booze

*Geopolitical Competition Meets
Cultural Economy in the Gulf*

Thus far, the idea of competition has remained largely in the background of this text, yet I would argue that it is at the heart of why market Orientalism matters. If economies are ranked and hierarchicalized, there will be winners and losers, and people and places will attempt to be among those counted as victors. As much as Gulf cultural economies are about distributing surplus internally, the pools of goodwill and investment from abroad are often quite shallow. Thus, there is also competition.

Chapters 4 and 5 traced the evolution of how the Gulf states and cities were compared to each other from the 1930s to the 1980s, oftentimes by how "merchantlike" they were said to be. Chapter 6 focused on the GCC's efforts to perform regionality in expected ways—efforts that were ultimately undermined (perhaps for the best) by the fact that even a group of similar, small, neighboring states can have competing (or at least differing) agendas. So, although competition has undoubtedly been a part of these previous chapters, this chapter places it front and center. It would be easy enough to stay within the comfortable analytical confines of geographic political economy to examine these competitive relationships—for example, by drawing on David Harvey (2005) or Neil Smith (2008)—this chapter meets the Gulf on its most common grounds of academic interpretation. This means venturing into the literatures that have been at the forefront of Gulf studies, literatures where competition and cooperation are analyzed most intensely: international relations and geopolitics.

Books by F. Gregory Gause (1994, 2010), Matteo Legrenzi (2011), and Kristian Ulrichsen (2011) make the argument that the Arab Gulf states behave geopolitically in traditional, expected, and rational ways given their status. Although each text has differing nuances and points of emphasis, the basic contours of their arguments are as follows: international relations and security for the GCC states are defined primarily by the gap between their tremendous economic and strategic importance and their small size, a gap that makes them potentially vulnerable. As Gause puts it, "The immutable effects of geography and demography— small populations, in some cases vulnerable borders, and valuable natural resources—combine with these domestic realities to create a Gulf diplomatic style. This style is characterized by reliance on policies of balance and maneuver to maintain security" (1994, 121).

As this statement shows, many commentators also believe domestic politics only add to the Gulf states' overall vulnerability because they are ultimately ruled by nonrepresentative monarchies (or, to use Anh Nga Longva's [2005] term, *ethnocracies*), while containing large numbers of foreign workers and sometimes major cleavages within the national population. In most texts, the Gulf state monarchies' geopolitical strategy centers on decreasing their vulnerability through a combination of strong international alliances, the flexibility to talk to those outside their main alliances, politically savvy domestic (and sometimes international) distribution of oil revenues, suppression of public, domestic dissent, and the assertion of national importance through increasing prestige or economic clout. This type of strategy, of course, sometimes requires attempts to outcompete neighboring states for resources and attention. These authors note that although oil wealth and large numbers of foreign residents make the Gulf somewhat unique, the Gulf exists in a pretty traditional, "realist"-flavored geopolitical world (i.e., one where states pursue their rational self-interests). Again, this is not a universal interpretation: for example, Arshin Adib-Moghaddam (2006) endeavors in his "cultural genealogy" of international politics in the Gulf to understand how competition (far from being a natural state of affairs) is constructed through norms and ideologies. Nevertheless, realism/neorealism remains the most common viewpoint to explain the Gulf's international context.

In calling this view "common," I by no means imply it is unimportant, unreal, or outdated. Vulnerability *is* a major concern for many actors in the Gulf. Although I do not agree that geography is destiny, a significant percentage of the world's oil does originate from the Gulf states, and (the much larger) geopolitical hot spots Iran and Iraq lie just to the north. As mentioned in the previous chapter, the GCC was initially as much about promoting security following a turbulent end to the 1970s as it was about economic integration. Plus, these countries are ultimately monarchies in a world where such governments are increasingly rare. How they deal with these geopolitical and diplomatic issues in what can seem like a hostile and anarchic world is a worthy topic. The dominance of international relations, security, and political economy in Gulf studies' publications reflects the importance of these topics to those residing in the region and those with interests in it.

The point of this chapter is not to say that the standard international relations takes on the Gulf are wrong. Nor is it to build a full "critical geopolitics" of the Gulf that expands on ideas such as Adib-Moghaddam's in order to take the standard international relations vision of the Gulf head on.[1] Instead, as the title of this chapter suggests, my argument is that geopolitical competition in the Gulf is in addition very much about things less grand in scope than nuclear armament, sweeping political philosophies, and secure oil supplies. I advocate instead for the importance of heat, booze, sports, and other such seemingly mundane things and practices. I do so because I believe those who shape geopolitical agendas—despite all the talk of rationality—are in the end fully embodied individuals, complete with unthought prejudices of routine and preference, who will inevitably favor spaces that make them feel comfortable. Such people care about power or money or both, of course, but that is not all the majority of them care about. These people also interact with many other embodied individuals within, near, and far from their polities who are less concerned

---

1. Although a wide-ranging critical geopolitical critique would be welcome for the alternative type of view it would bring, it is beyond the scope of what my research on cultural economy allows.

with the political and economic structures of competition. Thus, they are not immune to the structures of feeling that I have been documenting throughout this text.

What makes a good and important place in the Gulf—one that is seen as worthy of protection and inclusion in global political and security agendas—depends in part on the very type of cultural economy milieu that is the focus of this book. It is a milieu wherein actors in Gulf states are forced, in part owing to the work of market Orientalism on structures of feeling, to address (in ways other places are not) whether their territory meets expectations of what the "global standard" is thought to be. That they must do so is something that has consequences both at home and abroad for Gulf states. Chapters 4, 5, and 6 focused on how the region was imagined as having fallen short in such areas in the past. This chapter looks at more recent efforts to act around the confines of market Orientalism.

Thus, this chapter asks: What happens if we blend a critical cultural economy perspective with various visions of geopolitics? All but the staunchest political science purists already appreciate that geopolitics involves not just shows of military and economic might but also at the very least other types of linkages, such as those built through free zones and economic-promotion institutions. Furthermore, since the advent of constructionist perspectives in international relations—which hold that the categories that matter in geopolitical analysis are socially produced (as opposed to given or unchanging)—most scholars also acknowledge at least to some extent the impact of nonmaterialist factors. These factors include shared foreign-policy identity and constructed norms of statecraft (which sometimes even operate unconsciously). But what if the politics of making a congenial living environment (the elements of which, of course, are not universally agreed upon) is just as important as a congenial policy environment? Is it unreasonable to imagine that differing visions of how people should enjoy themselves matter geopolitically, even if these visions seem to be only on the periphery of statecraft? Taking these issues seriously can only enrich our understandings of competition in the Gulf.

But perhaps even more than impacting geopolitics, I feel this exercise can be fruitful for the cultural economy perspective. So much of the work done under the cultural economy banner, given its practice-centric leanings, is focused on spaces that are smaller in scope, such as neighbor-hoods, cities, and metropolitan regions. What international relations and critical geopolitics are particularly good at is locating and critiquing differ-ent viewpoints, especially the view of a global strategic space that standard geopolitics is famous for (and that cultural economy scholarship often lacks). What if all those practices we associate with cultural economies matter geopolitically, and what if geopolitical perspectives allow cultural economy some alternate views of wider spatial relations? Making use of these potentialities is the goal of this chapter, a goal that is also in keeping with the spirit of the book, which is to take the study of cultural economies into new realms.

This chapter argues that in attempting to move up the imagined international hierarchy of good places worthy of inclusion and security, Gulf states have to grab the attention of both state and private actors in ways that go way beyond merely keeping oil and gas flowing. Rightly or wrongly, they are forced to defend themselves against the perception of the Gulf as an Other type of cultural economy, which has resulted from processes of distinction that have opened a gap between the Gulf's wealth and its acceptance as part of the "norm."

Gulf polities are forced to field questions from empowered geopo-litical actors that include: Can you drink alcohol? Can women drive? Can women wear what they want? Can you eat pork? Is it too hot? The fact that those in Gulf places have to deal with these questions instead of being accepted on their own cultural economic terms demonstrates that status seeking and competition among polities involves more than supplies of military equipment, spatial strategy, projection of economic power, and protection of strategic resources. Indeed, the story of the geo-politics of the Gulf includes many things that matter to actual human-scale routines and preferences, involving axes of difference (such as gender and race) and the ways that (not always elite) bodies and culture are mutually coproduced, experienced, and imagined. In other words, this story brings cultural economy concerns about practice, aesthetics, and embodied hierarchies into geopolitical imaginings of competition and power. The next section of this chapter provides a brief overview of international relations and critical geopolitics theories where the links between competition in the cultural economic and geopolitical realms are already tentatively being made (such as feminist geopolitics, the everyday state, and popular geopolitics). However, the bulk of the chapter demonstrates how this interaction between cultural economic and geopolitical concerns plays out in three Gulf polities: Dubai, Bahrain, and Qatar.[2] In the case of Dubai, the focus is on the construction of the emirate as the region's preeminent meeting ground. The case of Bahrain demonstrates how international relations and internal politics for the island nation revolve in part around alcohol. Finally, the case of Qatar analyzes how gaining prestige through splashy events involves mediating the mundaneness of market Orientalism's embodied preferences. Through these case studies, this chapter demonstrates three mechanisms that have consequences for how the intersection of geopolitics and cultural economy are understood:

1. Emerging polities can gain geopolitical advantage by being perceived as having a comparably or relatively more comfortable cultural economy than neighboring polities.
2. Being comparably more comfortable is not a neutral, universal concept. There are hierarchies concerning what counts as properly comfortable—hierarchies that reflect cleavages of race, class, gender, and group membership.
3. There are both external and internal penalties for being seen as *too* accommodating.

After the case studies are discussed, the brief conclusion links back to the analysis of market Orientalism developed throughout this book.

2. I realize here that Dubai is a city-state within a federation, whereas Bahrain and Qatar are full, independent states. However, the experience of the past four decades, during which Dubai has continually pursued economic and urban policy meant to outshine Abu Dhabi, shows that it has much, much wider policy independence than would be typical of a city in the Gulf (see Davidson 2009b).

Geopolitical Inspirations

As is often the case with this book, this chapter highlights how looking closely at the situation of the Gulf reveals something previously underexamined in imaginations of how the world works. Thus, this section highlights inspirations from both the international relations scholarship on small states and the critical geopolitics canon that overlap with the cultural economy theories I outlined in chapters 2 and 3. All of these approaches, taken together, can shed a different kind of light on the broader contours of competition both inside and beyond the Gulf.

Let us begin with the literature on the international relations of small states because Bahrain, Qatar, Kuwait, the UAE, and Oman are often described as such. Even though Saudi Arabia is much larger than its GCC neighbors, Iran still has four times as many people, which makes Saudi Arabia far from large in the absolute sense. Barring a crisis, such small states typically do not garner much geopolitical attention. Indeed, before oil, the Gulf monarchies were once as peripheral to the region and the world political economy as places could be (Gause 1994). In many ways, the Gulf was (and still somewhat is) like the Caribbean, typified by what Jacqueline Anne Braveboy-Wagner (2008) has termed a geopolitical identity of "smallness," where the foreign-policy options of small states are somewhat limited by whatever particular interest larger superpowers happen to have in them because small states need assistance from these larger powers to ensure their security.

To counteract this smallness, the various GCC rulers have recently intensified their drive to shape their particular territory into the Gulf's most important or prestigious place. The key for places such as Qatar, Abu Dhabi, and Dubai (even when compared to Bahrain and Oman) is that their access to oil and gas revenues allows them opportunities to remake their imaginative geographies in orders of magnitude about which other small states can only dream (showing that smallness is neither natural nor absolute). Of course, different rulers, citizens, and residents in the Gulf possess a wide array of opinions concerning what is important and prestigious.

Nonetheless, actors in these states have shown a propensity toward participating in the discourses of "recognition, sovereignty and legitimacy"

(McConnell, Moreau, and Dittmer 2012, 805) that come with a territory that projects the trappings of international stateness. As Fiona McConnell, Terri Moreau, and Jason Dittmer note, such diplomatic maneuvers by nontraditional actors (which small monarchical city-states certainly qualify as) can be thought of as mimicry in Homi Bhabha's sense of the word—a participation that reinforces the authority and necessity of the diplomatic system but that also challenges it by pushing at its conceptual boundaries.

As of late, the Gulf polities have pushed increasingly hard to solidify their "stateness." Doha and Dubai have hosted major diplomatic conferences; Saudi Arabia has taken a lead position in the Arab League. These efforts are indicative of an attempt to be included in world conversations as the *peers* of much larger states, not just as wealthy, eccentric outsiders. What those in Gulf states want is a good "place in the world," as James Ferguson would put it. According to Ferguson, "'The World' in my usage, refers to a more encompassing categorical system within which countries and geographical regions have their 'places,' with a 'place' understood as both a location in space and a rank in a system of social categories (as in the expression 'knowing your place')" (2006, 6).

But one issue looms large in thwarting this attempt to "move up" while maintaining alliances: the problem of cultural economy. As Timothy Mitchell (2002a) and Robert Vitalis (2007) have noted, in the twentieth century the expansion of US military and capitalist power in the Gulf relied on conservative forces such as the Saudi religious police to control populations and to ensure that oil would continue to flow. However, although this tacit alliance between ruling families, certain varieties of conservative Islam, and the United States may have initially helped maintain security in some of the Gulf states, the situation seems to be changing. Works such as Michael Hardt and Antonio Negri's *Empire* (2000) and Susan Roberts, Anna Secor, and Matthew Sparke's article "Neoliberal Geopolitics" (2003) argue that the current geopolitical order has become deeply intertwined with the neoliberal order. As the map produced by Naval War College faculty member Thomas Barnett shows, there are many geopoliticians who think the Gulf is part of what Barnett calls the "nonintegrating gap" (cited in Roberts, Secor, and Sparke 2003, 890)—an imaginative geography of places not to be trusted geopolitically because they are seen as not being fully on the neoliberal, openness bandwagon. It is precisely the Gulf states' reputation (warranted or not) for economic unorthodoxy and cultural restrictiveness or otherness (which initially once helped them secure alliances through the promise of control) that makes their efforts to move up in rank fraught with difficulty. This situation is why ideas from critical geopolitics, despite not having focused extensively on the Gulf, are relevant to the Gulf. Although not seeking to ignore the authors who reinvigorated the field—such as John Agnew (1998), Simon Dalby (1991), Joanne Sharp (1996), and Gearoid O'Tuathail (1996)—I want to focus on three critical geopolitics subliteratures that have the most in common with cultural economy approaches: feminist geopolitics, theories of the everyday state, and popular geopolitics.

Jennifer Hyndman (2004) did a great deal of the work of consolidating the subfield of feminist geopolitics, arguing that a proper feminist geopolitics should not be a disengaged view from above like standard geopolitics (and some examples of critical geopolitics), but a passionate and partial yet grounded perspective, like that of Donna Haraway (1988), that highlights human-scale consequences. Furthermore, it should not be concerned just with the balance of military power but also with broader "human security" in all of its gendered, racialized, and class components. Although others, such as Jennifer Fluri (2009), have endorsed this shifting of scales as key to a feminist geopolitics, much recent work has foregrounded the role of embodiment (Nicley 2009) and emotion, especially fear (Pain 2009)—realms of inquiry that were unthinkable in earlier geopolitical imaginations. These perspectives connect well with both cultural economy and market Orientalism as I have outlined them in that feminist geopolitics shows how ideas around "culture," such as gender and race, in their material complexity and affective capacity intrude into supposedly unrelated, purified realms such as geopolitics.

Also of particular relevance are notions of the everyday state (Mountz 2004; Secor 2007), which hold that instead of seeing the state as a monolith with singular transparent interests, one should see it in its everyday diverse interactions and haunting presence. Authors such as James Sidaway (2009), in his walk through a Plymouth port, and Kathrin Hörschelmann (2008), in her studies of children's reactions to the Iraq War, note that geopolitics takes place in everyday landscapes and takes shape in the lives of those who are excluded from the standard geopolitical discourse. As in cultural economy, those with interests in chronicling the everyday state highlight how difference is manifested through the routines and small practices of wider networks of actors and institutions.

The final point of connection I want to make here is with popular geopolitics, which looks for geopolitics outside the standard repertoire of diplomatic actions, official government papers, "expert" books, and political science treatises. The term *popular geopolitics* was popularized in geography by Joanne Sharp's work on *Reader's Digest* (2000). It was picked up by other scholars, including Jason Dittmer (2005), who examines the role played by comic books in shaping geopolitical imaginaries, and François Debrix (2008), who examines tabloid journalism's impact on similar imaginaries. All of these authors' emphasis is on how geopolitics happens through the tools of soft power made available by popular media, which allow geopolitical discourses to mold and bend with the changing times. Within the wider Middle East region, the political scientist Waleed Hazbun (2008) has made a similar move in focusing on the political economy of tourism policy and how it helps shape international relations while enabling domestic authoritarianism. These authors' work on the impact of everyday representations on wider processes and positioning shares a spirit with my survey of reports on the Gulf in chapters 4 and 5.

But ultimately many of the points concerning everyday practice and preference raised by this chapter are similar to those made in one of the classics of feminist international relations theory, *Bananas, Beaches, and Bases: Making Feminist Sense of International Politics* by Cynthia Enloe (1989). Despite predating much of critical geopolitics, this book examines how the masculine practice of international politics and diplomacy has depended on a network of often unseen feminized bodies. Enloe shows how previously unnoted women drove demands for food products and colonial fashion, had "unmarked" diplomatic careers alongside diplomat husbands, and did the groundwork (and sometimes the sex work) that established an international tourism sector in the developing world.

Thus, taken together, the scholars in these three fields provided the intellectual inspiration for the embodied, cultural economic perspective on geopolitical competition that this chapter seeks to conjure—a perspective that looks past the usual suspects and focuses on more mundane but still politicized practices.

Dubai: Relatively Speaking

This section on Dubai is divided into two parts. The first part examines the history of attempts by Dubai's rulers to make their city comparably comfortable (see mechanism 1 listed earlier) and how this strategy of showing fidelity to the interests of those who are the trend setters of market Orientalism has been used to gain geopolitical advantage (mechanism 2). The second part examines the limits of this accommodation (mechanism 3) in terms of what happens when a place is seen as being too undefined by convention. It is important to present the Dubai case before the other two, Bahrain and Qatar, because so much of what decision makers in other Gulf states have done since 2000 has been an attempt to emulate or distinguish themselves from Dubai.

The Advantages of Being Comparatively Good

I was back in my office in Miami on the day the world's tallest building— which through years of planning had been called the "Burj Dubai"—was to be officially opened, January 4, 2010. Of course, this was big global news, as had been the openings of many of Dubai's profile-raising structures during the past ten years: the Atlantis Hotel, the Burj al Arab, and Ski Dubai. As it turned out, the biggest part of the story was that the newly opened building was not in fact to be called the "Burj Dubai" but had been renamed the "Burj Khalifa" in honor of Sheikh Khalifa bin Zayed al-Nahyan, the current ruler of Abu Dhabi and the president of the UAE. Abu Dhabi, of course, had bailed out Dubai in the wake of its financial crisis just a few months earlier. Multiple reports pointed to the name change as being made at the last minute—all the on-site and road network signage still read "Burj Dubai" on the day of the reveal (Kamin 2010).

Unsurprisingly, this change led to a period of wild speculation. Did Abu Dhabi's ruling family the al-Nahyans make Dubai's ruling family the al-Maktoums change the name just to show Dubai who was in charge? Or was the new name a momentary flourish of genuine gratitude from (or calculation by) Dubai's self-styled impresario, Sheikh Mohammed? No matter the reason, it was a major move for the publicity-conscious ruler to take his city's name out of the moniker of the world's tallest building.

I spoke with an academic colleague from the Gulf region that day. The first thing he asked me was if I had heard the news. I said yes, and we, too, played the speculation game. Then he said something I have always remembered: "Dubai is a very useful place. I hope this doesn't mean it is going away."

In this case, of course, "it" does not refer to the city of Dubai itself. Although in 2010 Dubai was down from peak population levels following its 2008 real estate crash, it was undoubtedly a much bigger city than its official population of just under one million in 2000. Planes still landed there, and ships still came. Nor had it lost its geopolitical importance. The United States still docked naval ships at the Jebel Ali Port and used its consulate there as a base from which to gather human intelligence about Iran. Despite initial headlines to the contrary—such as "Is This Bye Dubai?" (Spencer 2009)—Dubai had not become a ghost town, and the city did not go away (see Robin Bloch's [2010] excellent rundown of what actually happened contra what she calls the "good-bye Dubai" perspective). Even if all the announced projects did not get built, Dubai's stock of accommodations increased by at least 50 percent, an increase that was desperately needed given high rental prices. Both the Palm Jumeirah artificial island and the artificial Dubai Marina are occupied. There are two world-class water parks that run on desalinized water in addition to an indoor ski slope. There are multiple, successful free-trade zones. The world's tallest building, after some initial hiccups, is open for business. Dubai still has many issues surrounding transparency and fairness (and now maintenance of all these new structures), but the city did not completely perish.

However, the "it" to which my colleague referred is everything else Dubai stands for—the idea of Dubai, if you will. Although all those very material things—such as transshipments and air passengers—do matter very much, this other imaginative "it" has always equally mattered for Dubai, especially in its current era of high visibility. And it is also important to note that the "it" of Dubai varies tremendously depending on the positionality of the emirate's beholder.

According to my Gulf colleague, by "it" he meant Dubai's status as a meeting ground. To him (and to some of my other informants, including many Iranians), Dubai stands as the place you can go to gather openly with other like-minded people from the Gulf, no matter what happens to be on your mind. Immediately following the Dubai property crash, increased censorship of the local media's ability to report on the economy (thereafter loosened as the economic picture improved) brought Dubai's meeting-ground status into question (Davidson 2012).

But I have heard other definitions of the emirate's "it." For many of my Dubai-based Emirati friends and colleagues, whom I talked to in the wake of the Abu Dhabi bailout, "it" is their sense of independence from Abu Dhabi. This is true even of those who otherwise do not love how big and full of the world Dubai has become. Despite their ambivalence, they do not like the idea of any of the factions in Abu Dhabi being in charge. For many middle-class Indians, Dubai's "it" is the lack of complicating infrastructure and bureaucracy factors when it comes to doing business. Furthermore, for many people from many places (including those who "matter" geopolitically), Dubai is the most glamorous location in the wider region.

Thus, the "it" of Dubai is many things, but I would also argue that something connects all of these visions. These "its" are rarely ever Dubai's absolute superiority to all other places. Instead, they are almost always a reference to Dubai's *relative goodness*. What do I mean by this? I have met a few women and men who truly and whole-heartedly love Dubai and think it is the best place on earth (some are Emiratis, some grew up in Dubai, some are from elsewhere), just as there are people who truly love Tokyo, Paris, London, New York, or some other city. Generally, this love involves some combination of loving the "Gulf lifestyle" (whatever they feel it to be) and preferring Dubai to other Gulf cities because it has many of the same resources and opportunities as large cities elsewhere. If you are from South Asia or Central Asia, there are many people from your home country, and your home country is a short flight away (if you can afford it).

However, the people who think Dubai the best place on earth are the minority. Most people I have interacted with who have an overall positive or neutral view of Dubai (which would be most people I interviewed there, including some who have had a rough time in the emirate) see it as the best accessible alternative. For example, people will tell me they liked living in Beirut or Manchester or the Indian state of Kerala (whose beauty has been praised to me by dozens of Keralites, all of whom tell me I should visit). They explain how they like being with friends and family in Manila, feel nostalgic for the great arts and public transport of the Soviet Union, or (rather ominously) remember how great South Africa "used to be." Then they tell me why they cannot live in those places anymore and how they cannot get visas for popular destinations such as Canada and Australia (where permanent residence is more likely). They then say that Dubai is fine and that it gives them something (money or opportunity or proximity to family) they cannot get elsewhere. Yes, there is inequality in Dubai, they say; housing is expensive, and the days can get kind of "gray," where each plays out like the previous one (especially if they have few friends or family in the emirate), but they are glad they are not somewhere else in the Gulf. Therefore, in almost all cases, Dubai is relatively better or different in some way. "It has the most to do *in the Gulf*," and "*It's like India*, but it works." Its goodness is in reference to elsewhere but minus some of the harsher overtones of the "Kuwait is good for a Gulf state" rhetoric explored in chapters 4 and 5—more a side-by-side comparison than a hierarchicalization. This primarily comparative quality has been an underappreciated part of the Dubai story, which is so often focused on the spectacular.

Of course, the comparison and differentiation of places are hardly new concepts. Many cities attempt to stand out from their neighbors through policy and landscape differentiation. However, Dubai is quite often linked to one other city in particular, which is known for standing out in the least subtle way possible: Las Vegas.[3] In fact, when I asked the

3. For example, see the newspaper articles titled "Las Vegas vs. Dubai: Comparing Two World-Famous Tourist Destinations" (Clifford-Cruz 2011), "Dubai, Learning from Las Vegas (Benston 2007), and "Dubai's Vegas Game Plan" (Olson 2007).

highest-ranking Dubai government official I interviewed for this project if he had any questions for me, he queried: "What do you know about Las Vegas? It seems we are very similar." However, although many people draw comparisons between the two cities based on their shared reputation for high living and brash architecture, the real synergies lie in their respective relativistic strategies.

To put it simply, both cities are perceived as comparatively more permissive polities, dominated by economic actors who are aware of the uneven geographies of competition. Especially when a locational disadvantage is at play, doing what other places are already doing is rarely a pathway to success. Those in charge of Dubai and Las Vegas as well as major economic actors there know that they have to offer something that other places in their wider region are not offering. Their shared strategy involves producing big, one-of-a-kind structures: pyramid-shaped hotels, desert indoor ski slopes, and the like. Basically things that grab attention. But, truthfully, much of what happens in these cities that makes them comparatively attractive is less glamorous and much more mundane than their reputations would seem to predict.

That being said, there are indeed very glamorous parts of Dubai and Las Vegas. In fact, ever since Dubai World (one of the holding companies for the Dubai government's investments) bought a major stake in casino developer MGM Grand that helped fund the colossally expensive (and financially troubled) City Center project in Las Vegas, the ownership of some of these glamorous sites overlaps. Very rich people—as well as those enjoying a weekend pretending to be rich—can dispose of a great deal of money in either place by eating, shopping, and occupying hotel rooms. There is also a hedonistic aspect to both cities. They may not dominate "high-culture" circuits of art or theater (although they have made attempts to do so), but both have world-renowned nightclubs. Las Vegas has its strip clubs; in Dubai, many lower-end hotels basically function as large brothels. The biggest actual difference between the two is the presence of gambling (although one might say that gambling occurs in both because the real estate market in either city is akin to high-stakes wagering). So, yes, glamour and hedonism are very much a part of both places' relative novelty.

But they are only a part. Las Vegas and Dubai succeed just as much by being mildly different as by being truly exceptional. What strikes me when I walk around Las Vegas is not an overwhelming number of young, fit, wealthy partiers. Rather, it is the number of people who seem to fit within a typical cross section of American diversity, although perhaps a little older. Vegas may be known for its nightclubs, but it is also known for its buffets, a form of relative novelty in that you can eat everything you want. Although Las Vegas is the origin point of few top restaurants, it does offer accessible branches of many of the biggest names in fine dining—as does Dubai. Similarly, some people find it thrilling that the clubs, casinos, and restaurants are open late in Las Vegas; after 10:00 p.m., Dubai can seem like the liveliest place on earth compared to Muscat or especially Al Ain and Sohar.

Furthermore, one of the biggest attractions of Las Vegas is exactly the same as one of the biggest attractions of Dubai: Las Vegas is the most unionized city in America, meaning that those with little education or other opportunities still have a chance to earn a decent living there. Likewise, for many people from North and East Africa and from central, Southwest, South, and Southeast Asia, Dubai offers accessible opportunities that just do not exist elsewhere. It is not spectacularly better than home (sometimes it can turn out to be worse), but it provides a chance to make your way, and that is often enough.

For many, this is the "it" factor of Dubai I spoke of at the beginning of this section. It has little to do with the superlative structures, at least for those who live and work in the emirate. As one lifetime Dubai resident of mixed European and Latin American heritage put it when asked if he was excited about the opening of the new Dubai Mall complex (which is one of the largest in the world), "No, it's just going to be a really massive version of what we already have." His opinion was shared by many of my informants. As is the case in many frequently visited cities, the spectacular in Dubai is peripheral to most everyday residents (just as most Las Vegas residents spend scant time on the Strip, except for those who work there). The Dubai Mall added little in terms of lifestyle that people of means in Dubai did not already have in smaller commercial and public spaces. The "it" factor is that Dubai provides at least a little bit better option than other places do.

But the two cities have significant differences as well. Las Vegas has no worries about its geopolitical standing: Arizona is unlikely to invade, stage a coup, or launch missiles at it. Thus, the stakes are much higher for Dubai. Saudi Arabia and Abu Dhabi have much more oil and, like Kuwait before them, guarantees of support from important state actors. But what Dubai has is renown and a reputation for being a good-enough place to be in a world full of much less desirable locales. When foreign corporations are deciding on where to locate their Gulf headquarters, they almost always look to Dubai first.

An undeniably big part of Dubai's reputation for being comfortable enough among even the moderately well off is alcohol, although it seems an insignificant factor. Let me be clear: I am not in any way saying Dubai succeeds solely because it allows alcohol (as I have had some tell me); indeed, many in the emirate do not care about (or for) booze. But it is a major reason why Dubai is imagined as relatively more permissive than Doha, Kuwait City, and Muscat and much, much more permissive than Riyadh. Geographers have recently begun to pay more attention to the importance of alcohol while trying to get beyond the normal frames of violence, public health, and social disorder through which the topic is examined. As Mark Jayne, Gill Valentine, and Sarah Holloway explain the significance of alcohol,

> Whether you drink or not, alcohol, drinking and drunkenness are key features of everyday life as a "performative experience." . . . [They] are political, economic, social, cultural and spatial practices that are supported and nurtured not only at the level of vernacular experience but through political and policy discourses. . . . Multiple geographies of alcohol, drinking and drunkenness, constitute a unique ontological and epistemological terrain, with people actively engaging in practices that generate (often) unpredictable and complex emotions, embodied experiences and affective geographies. (2010, 541)

Although I would argue that in the Gulf alcohol is a less broadly considered key feature of "everyday" life than it is in Britain, it is still a major factor and needs to be examined in its contexts.

In Dubai, alcohol can be bought at fairly low prices at the official government duty-free store at the airport. It is also sold at a much higher cost in bars and restaurants located in hotels and social clubs as well as at liquor stores (usually tucked away on the back side of grocery stores), where purchases can be made with a (not too rigorously checked) pass the government issues to non-Muslim residents. It can also be bought more cheaply in some of the smaller emirates. In general, it is available in less-visible sorts of places or places that are predominantly thought to be spaces for foreigners.

For better or worse, the relative unavailability of alcohol in the Gulf is one of the primary ways the Gulf's cultural economic otherness is marked in places such as the United States and the United Kingdom. In fact, when trying to convince other Americans (including some academics) that Dubai is not the type of socially repressive, stifling place that all Gulf places are thought to be, I often resort to using the following line: "In Dubai, my wife, while wearing a T-shirt and jeans, is able to drive us to an Irish pub that serves both Guinness and ham potpies." In other words, to convince other Americans Dubai is OK and not so distant from what they know, I tell them they, whether man or woman, can eat, drink, and dress as they want, just like "normal." I am also not above (or proud about) saying that all of these features in part attracted me to Dubai as a research destination in the Gulf, which supplemented my very real intellectual interest in the relationship between culture and economy. But I do not represent everyone in the Gulf (or even in Dubai), and in the case of Bahrain we will meet others who feel decidedly differently about alcohol.

Alcohol availability or other such relative privileges are not a huge geopolitical difference in the sense that they are not a traditional asset like a giant seaport, airport, or oil terminal. For example, Saudi Arabia has only a tiny amount of such lifestyle privileges, but it still gets US military and intelligence support. However, all these privileges still matter. Allowing alcohol (let alone allowing women to drive) makes a place desirable to many actors; it is very much a part of business and government culture in a large number of the world's countries—largely because of the embodied experiences and affective geographies that Jayne, Valentine, and Holloway highlight. It is a part (but not the whole) of what makes Dubai an incredibly important outlet for all kinds of activities.

So what geopolitical and cultural economic functions does Dubai provide? It is a place for exiles and new postcolonial, post-Communist money to go abroad to shop and soak in the sun (or to find some more of that postcolonial and post-Communist money). Pakistan has held "home" cricket matches in the emirate when it is too dangerous for foreign teams to travel to Pakistan; Iranian rock bands play concerts there. It is a key node in the East African fabric trade (Mangieri 2008). It is a place where well-educated, former Soviet citizens can find work and meet to make deals; it also provides employment to Kerala's well-educated but underemployed population. It is the premier convention destination in the Gulf: it hosted a World Bank and IMF conference in 2003, and it hosts annual events such as the region's largest computer and property shows. It is without armed conflict. Unlike Saudi Arabia, there are visible Christian churches, Hindu temples, bars, and women drivers. Even though it has a population that is 70 percent male because of the large number of foreigners who work in construction, it has a hotline for women to call if they are being harassed—which, although hardly something that automatically eliminates harassment or changes attitudes, is at least an attempt to address potential problems. Yes, Dubai is also a city that has construction and domestic labor exploitation in the form of what Pardis Mahdavi (2011) calls "forced work" (sometimes to the point of death), crushing debt incurred to labor recruiters, an uneven justice system, high levels of nonrenewable-resource use, a lack of open politics, and very materialist things such as oil, transshipment, automobile traffic, and high rents. But it is all of the other things I mentioned in this paragraph, too.

Most of Dubai's neighbors share in its material assets: all GCC states have at least some oil or gas; most have massive airports (such as King Fahd International Airport in Saudi Arabia, which is currently the world's largest by square footage); and many have spectacular buildings. Some, such as Bahrain, at one point even had more liberal alcohol regulations (I clarify later the use of the past tense here). But none of these other places received a fraction of the coverage Dubai received during the first decade of the 2000s. Dubai was seen as doing something different, leading the way. It was trying to stand out from its neighbors by standing out less from the global geopolitical/geoeconomic/cultural economic consensus.

Saudi Arabia is bigger than the rest of the GCC combined and is the world's swing oil producer. It can somewhat afford the penalties that come with choosing a different cultural economic path (including the employment of a separate religious police force in addition to the main one), which some in the kingdom feel is required by virtue of being the keepers of Islam's holiest sites. But the recent profile-raising moves by Doha and Abu Dhabi show that they do not have the power to fully forge their own paths and expect everyone else to conform—they need and want to cultivate allies. To compete in broader geopolitical realms, they need to win in some cultural economic realms as Dubai has done (although they try to do so with different audiences). Even if much of the rest of the Gulf was never as restrictive as its reputation indicated, Dubai's promoters took care to proclaim that in most cases you (particularly if you were a Westerner or a wealthy person from anywhere) would not be prohibited from living as you choose, while implying that in neighboring states you would find no such guarantees. In other words, Dubai turned the feelings around market Orientalism against its neighbors and to its own benefit.

The Disadvantages of Being "Too Much"

In his widely influential if controversial book *The Rise of the Creative Class* (2002), Richard Florida draws attention to how cities in the United States that had initially developed as tourist destinations (such as Miami and Las Vegas) tend to suffer in other areas of economic and human development, especially in terms of attracting highly educated talent and starting up high-tech businesses. Some of this is obvious cause and effect: many tourism jobs are seasonal and low wage (and extremely procyclical); tourism can also push up food and land prices and cause externalities such as traffic. But Florida goes further than that in giving an explanation: he argues that places like Las Vegas and Miami have a hard time attracting creative businesses because they are seen as too tawdry, unintellectual, and somewhat unserious. Indeed, Miami has a well-documented brain drain, wherein many of its brightest young people move to Washington, DC, or New York City in search of more prestigious or higher-paying careers.

In some ways, Dubai has escaped the worst effects of a similar brain drain: the type of creative companies Florida likes plus tech stalwarts such as Microsoft and Samsung as well as a large number of media firms are located there, and it attracts plenty of skilled migrants. Also, Dubai was doing trade long before it was really in the tourism business. Nonetheless, as in other spots known for glamour and nightlife, the images of excitement and riches that play in Dubai's favor in some areas (especially in comparison to neighbors) are never far from charges of tackiness and seediness. From India, there is the propensity in films to locate gangsters or other types of sinister characters in Dubai. Some examples include actor Amitabh Bachchan's character "Don" in the movie *Boom* (2003), who lives in the Burj al Arab hotel, or the rich pedophile uncle in director Mira Nair's film *Monsoon Wedding* (2001).[4] From Russia, there are rumors of money laundering through all-cash real estate transactions in Dubai, which is a popular sun, sand, and shopping destination for former Soviets. Then there is Dubai's regionally (if not globally) well-known reputation for having an active sex industry.

Perhaps there is no more vivid example of the emirate's being on the wrong side of relative difference than when in the mid-2000s it was wondered in many of Dubai's English-language newspapers whether the city had become overrun with "chavs." The term *chav* is a controversial British derogatory slang term that emerged in the middle part of the first decade of the twenty-first century, directed mostly at the working class and nouveau riche who were envisioned as tending "to favor gaudy jewelry and expensive-but-tacky clothes with big logos and to behave in a way that others find coarse or obnoxious" (Lyall 2005). In other words, it represented the epitome of (mis)styling over substance—a mimicry of "proper" elite behavior. As Keith Hayward and Majir Nar (2006) argue, the term *chav*

---

4. This characterization probably derives from the fact that major Mumbai mafia don Dawood Ibrahim was based in Dubai in the 1990s and that one of his lieutenants, Sharad Shetty, was gunned down at Dubai's India Club in 2003.

is transference of the concept of the "underclass" from the realm of illegitimate production to the realm of illegitimate consumption. Needless to say, most developing (and developed) cities would try to avoid association with such a description—especially cities in the Gulf, which have long been charged with being too consumption-centric.

The first mention of a perceived "chav" presence in the emirate was noted in Dubai's weekly tabloid magazine 7 *Days* in 2005, which wondered, "Are you a Dubai Chav?"

> Chavs will buy their gear from any designer store but a special mention has to go out to the many clothes shops in Karama [the neighborhood where counterfeit goods are most readily available in Dubai] which offer classic Chav gear for very affordable prices. When it comes to accessories two things define a Dubai Chav. First, the latest mobile phone, complete with irritating ring tone, must surgically be attached to a Chav's hand. Second, even if it leaves a Chav with barely enough money to eat, they must own a souped up car with the required financially crippling monthly payment. (Khalid 2005)

Shortly after the article came out, I did an Internet search for "Dubai Chav" and found a guest's review of the Le Royal Meridien Beach Resort in Dubai, which she titled "Chav City!" According to the reviewer, the hotel left her young daughter wondering "why so many people had tattoos—and that was just the women!" She exclaimed that she had "never seen so much Burberry and Von Dutch in one place" and that another guest was "boasting for over an hour on his mobile phone about his dodgy business dealings—I think he owned his own building firm in London. You get the picture" (Langtonlady 2005). To prove that this association between Dubai and the chav concept cannot be dismissed as a localized phenomenon, I can point to an article titled "'Chav' Influx Drags Dubai down Market" in the *Times* of London in 2007, which argued that "mass market tourists are overwhelming the Emirate" and quoted one travel agent as saying that "Dubai is quite chavvy. Everyone has been there. It is overdeveloped and colonised by Premier League footballers. But even they are beginning to move on" (Chesshyhre 2007).

To be clear, I am not saying Dubai is empirically, verifiably "chavy." Nor I am advancing *chav* as a term of social scientific analysis or as anything other than a symptom of the production of distinction that emerged at a particular place and time. However, I bring it up because the word *chav* was a figure of discourse, a negative image of wealth floating in the media universe in the mid-2000s, at the same time that Dubai was ascending. And Dubai became linked with it. What this shows is that upstart Dubai was not perceived as always offering the right kind of fun to be enjoyed by the right type of people. In trying to displace market Orientalist imaginings of an austere and intolerant region, Dubai fell into another postcolonial trap—that of mimicry, of being obviously like but jiltingly "just off" the "real" thing. In other words, it was seen as inauthentically cosmopolitan and upscale—a return to the Adnan Khashoggi laughable playboy image of the 1970s.

For example, one cannot imagine another place in the Gulf (and perhaps only a handful of places in the world) having a monograph focused on it with a title similar to *Dubai Dreams: Inside the Kingdom of Bling* (Bradley 2010). This perception of Dubai, which the chav label personifies, in part led decision makers in Abu Dhabi (as well as in Doha) to focus on more prestigious projects such as the Louvre branch, the New York University branch, and Masdar City (Abu Dhabi's green, solar-powered development). Such projects promote the idea that Abu Dhabi represents a different type of Islamic modernity, which helps it stand apart from Dubai. Abu Dhabi's rulers sought to rise above the perceptions of its body-focused neighbor and to be an anti-Dubai. Some scholars agree: according to Christopher Davidson, Abu Dhabi, unlike its neighbor Dubai, is "far closer to being a real state" and does not try to "rely solely on the inward investments and vested interests of international business partners to keep it safe and functioning as a global hub" (2009a, 7).

Yet, despite the fact that many people (including a not small number of Emiratis) complain that Dubai has gone too far in the direction of bodily choice in its quest to achieve its geopolitical prominence, it is also always close to falling into the "too conservative or duplicitous Arab" trap that is part and parcel of market Orientalism. Basically, the latter image holds that Arabs, Gulf Arabs in particular, no matter how much they profit from the international capitalist system and the money, power, and pleasures it brings, always secretly hate it and the Westerners associated with it and that they hypocritically cannot wait to bring it down. This image, of course, is an update of the Orientalist image of the duplicitous Arab, who is contrasted to the supposedly always upright and forward European; only this time the Arab is wealthy instead of poor. The image can be trotted out even when there is no evidence to support it, as in the Dubai Ports World "scandal" in the United States described in chapter 1.

However, this image of an overly restrictive Arab who wants to take away privileged types of enjoyment can also be deployed when there is an unusual case, such as when Dubai's laws prohibiting cohabitation outside of marriage and public drunkenness are occasionally applied—especially if said laws happen to be applied to a British person (see Freeman 2008 and Garland 2009) as opposed to a Southeast Asian person. In reality, such arrests happen only a couple dozen times a year, usually after someone becomes belligerent with a police officer or a well-connected person. Although capricious arrests can and do happen (and arrested women rarely get the benefit of the doubt from authorities), most of the time these regulations are widely and totally ignored.

There are also instances (not frequent but more so since 2008) when both Emiratis and foreigners have been jailed for something they post on the Internet (and even for satirical videos). Such actions are always treated as the "exception that proves the rule" that Arabs are hypocrites, that the emirate has a "dark" side hidden by its glittering towers and clubs, and that Arabs are "backward." But to write that such arrests represent a unique dark side is to believe that no one in the United States or Britain (especially those who are marked by race or class) is ever arrested, searched, or jailed on a flimsy premise, especially after upsetting a police officer. Such actions are inexcusable wherever they happen, but they are not unheard of even in far more democratic places than Dubai.

Again, what the use of this image of the "too conservative or duplicitous Arab" shows is that relative comfort is not a straightforward geopolitical prospect for Dubai, even though going in that direction earlier than its neighbors has paid dividends for the emirate. It can have alcohol restrictions hardly more extensive than some US states and counties, it can be much more permissive than its larger Saudi and Iranian neighbors, but that often is not enough and sometimes is just too much. But most of all, the situation of Dubai shows that these relative perceptions of mundane embodied materiality matter in the calculus of reckoning within the structures of feeling that market Orientalism produces. Dubai's undoubted geopolitical and geoeconomic importance (for good or ill) was not built on military strength or on having the most oil—it was built on perceptions of comparative ease and comfort. Threats to those perceptions are real threats to Dubai.

Bahrain, Alcohol, and Unequal Privileges

The previous section detailed how Dubai's rulers developed a strategy of making the city relatively comfortable for certain types of lifestyles and how that strategy increased Dubai's geopolitical and geoeconomic visibility. Whereas that discussion concluded by examining some of the consequences of Dubai's developing a "too open" lifestyle, this section on Bahrain puts opposition to such accommodation front and center. Again, what I want to show is that in geopolitics some visions of what constitutes a comfortable lifestyle count more than others (mechanism 2) and that there can be very real opposition if such choices are made, especially if it involves shifting the location of those choices elsewhere (mechanism 3). Whereas in Dubai geopolitics may be in the background of its cultural economic goals, in Bahrain the geopolitical implications of its cultural economies are crystal clear.

Since the Arab Spring of 2011, Bahrain has been experiencing a three-year-long protest movement against the ruling family that has drawn the bulk of its support from Bahraini Shia communities. The recent protests are built on decades of political contestation between those Shia (as well as some Sunni) communities and the royal family, who are Sunni.

To be clear: the reasons behind the more recent uprising have very little to do with religious doctrinal differences between the Sunni and Shia and much more to do with forms of structural inequality built around that sectoral divide: the neglect of the infrastructure of Shia villages, failed promises of wider availability of state-provided housing, the cutting off of villagers' sea access in order to build luxury housing, higher levels of unemployment in Shia villages, the relatively high salaries of (and sometimes offers of citizenship for) foreign Sunnis who make up the police force, the gerrymandering of districts for the lower house of its Assembly that leaves the Shia underrepresented, the unelected upper house's right to veto the lower house's decisions, and detention of activists in general but of Shia activists in particular. Justin Gengler (2013) also argues that for the past decade a faction of the ruling family has advocated treating the Shia as a "security" problem as opposed to a political one. For Gengler, the resulting policies also lie near the heart of recent problems.

My informants who were nationals of other Gulf countries had various opinions about who to blame for the unrest in Bahrain—some blamed Iran and problems within the Shia community; others pointed to massive, purposeful inequality. Reports in Gulf media tended toward the blame Iran position. However, there is a consensus that the situation there is bad. Although the Saudi state has had a similarly checkered relationship with its own Shia minority, the other Sunni-led monarchies in the Gulf do a better job of sharing (their mostly larger) rents with their domestic Shia minorities (Kamrava 2012b). In fact, when one of my Dubai informants found out I was going to Bahrain, he gave the following pessimistic assessment, which many others share: "Why would you want to go there? That's a bad place. Things are so unfair there. I had to go there for a wedding of a friend, and just seeing the differences, I was uncomfortable the whole time. It's not good."

During the height of the protests in 2011, when the Pearl Roundabout in the Bahrainian capital Manama was occupied, troops were deployed under the banner of the GCC's Peninsula Shield Force to quell the uprisings. The majority of the troops were sent by Saudi Arabia, which is connected to Bahrain by a twenty-six-mile causeway, and the rest by the UAE. In May 2012, the rulers of Saudi Arabia and Bahrain even came out in favor of exploring the potential for bringing Bahrain into economic and military union with Saudi Arabia.

Again, it is easy to point to standard geopolitical scripts to understand why Saudi Arabia is so concerned about Bahrain and its Shia. For starters, the al-Sauds are wary of any potential growth in Iran's power in the region and fear that a Shia-led Bahrain might ally itself with Iran, putting a Saudi rival twenty-six miles off its coast. Such a switch of allegiance might also jeopardize the ability of Saudi Arabia's key ally, the United States, to host its Fifth Naval Fleet headquarters in Bahrain, which is key to both US dominance in the Gulf and its protection of Saudi Arabia. The al-Sauds may also want to keep the Shia in Bahrain from getting control because their success might inspire insurrection among Saudi Arabia's own Shia minority, who are concentrated in its main oil-producing region. There is also the less-sectarian notion that Saudi Arabia's monarchs want to limit democracy generally in its neighboring monarchies lest a precedent be set. All of these concerns are undoubtedly factors for various figures within the Saudi state because Saudi ministers and diplomats are fully immersed and trained in a discursive world that values traditional (read as "realist") geopolitical strategy. But these standard geopolitical ideas are not the whole story.

What is also at stake is exactly what I described as the confluence of cultural economies (especially the regional ecosystem of economic waste discussed in chapter 6) and embodied geopolitics. Saudi Arabia is known for having some of the strictest personal-conduct laws on the planet, including a ban on showing most types of movies in public, a ban on the sale of alcohol, and a lack of an easily attainable tourist visa. Some of these laws are also blatantly gendered, such as not letting women drive and requiring all women (regardless of nationality) to veil. But given easy mobility out of Saudi Arabia by air and even by land, these restricted practices are not unobtainable for those in the kingdom if they travel (or can travel to the right places in the kingdom). Indeed, many Saudis (those who can afford to do so and can get away from their jobs) spend the hot summer months in Europe, Lebanon, Malaysia, and the United States. They also travel to Egypt en masse with family and friends as tourists to broaden the type of social and nightlife experiences they can have together (Wynn 2007).

But much of what Saudi Arabia prohibits is accessible in nearby Bahrain. It is just a few hours' drive from greater Riyadh (and even closer to the oil fields), thanks to the King Fahd Causeway. Although truck trade is a key use of the bridge, leisure is undoubtedly the other, as witnessed by the famous Thursday and Friday night lines that form on the causeway.

According to the Causeway Authority, some 17 million passengers use the causeway every year; the Bahrain Economic Development Board also notes that 79 percent of Bahrain's tourists arrive there via the causeway (2014, 123). This traffic occurs despite Bahrain's population of only 1.3 million people.

Some of this traffic is bound for family-friendly attractions such as malls, movie theaters, and water parks, and some of it also consists of people who work in the Saudi oil fields but choose to have their families live in Bahrain. A portion of it, however, used to be in search of alcohol. Unlike almost anywhere else in the rest of the Gulf (including Dubai), even restaurants not located in hotels were able to serve alcohol in Bahrain. However, it was not these restaurants or the nightclubs and bars at the newer five-star properties that were at the center of the contentious issues.

The source of this tension was a series of nightclubs in nonchain, three-star or less hotels along Manama's Exhibition Road. Some of them are nationality-specific clubs for groups such as Filipinos; some are hangouts for particular groups, such as American sports fans stationed at the navy installation in the nearby Juffair neighborhood. However, some of these clubs and hotels, although not all, are also known as "open-secret" congregation points for sex workers, like many similar hotels in Dubai. As one Bahraini lawmaker who led the crusade against the nightclubs noted in a *Gulf Daily News* article, "Prostitution is obvious even to the blind and what are the Interior, and Culture and Information ministries doing? The problem is that hotels are owned by VIPs in the country and police and tourism inspectors turn a blind eye most of the time to what's going on" (al A'ali 2010).

This is not merely a Bahraini domestic issue: Saudi Arabia counts on Bahrain to act as one of its de facto vice zones. Of course, polities all over the world make such decisions to externalize or limit what some consider to be unsavory activities to certain districts or a limited number of establishments or both. This option is often considered better than letting a black market thrive. For example, when gambling was first expanded in the United States in the 1990s, it was initially confined to undocked riverboats, so it was literally not in the fabric of the town where the casino was located. What Saudi Arabia does is a similar but more extreme version of the policy found in much of the rest of the Gulf: it says that alcohol is OK for foreigners but not for nationals. When alcohol is allowed in the Gulf, it is often restricted to spaces meant for foreigners—such as hotels or social clubs (or foreign compounds such as US military bases)—that can serve as sort of internal externalized spaces. Even though regulations frown on it, in practice Gulf nationals are able to enter such spaces if they want.

Saudi Arabia chooses not to have any such spaces internally, arguing that it cannot because it is home to the holiest sites of Islam. Although until the early 1950s non-Muslim foreigners in Saudi Arabia were allowed to have alcohol in their homes, after a series of incidents involving a handful of Abdulaziz's sons who had drunk alcohol at foreigners' residences—including the murder of a British vice consul—a complete ban was decreed (*Time* 1952).[5]

Thus, Saudi Arabia fully externalizes such spaces. The existence of the causeway shows that a given percentage of almost every society, even highly controlled ones such as Saudi Arabia, will seek to push at the boundaries of personal-conduct restrictions. In fact, one measure of the causeway's key role is that the al-Sauds are considering the construction of a new bridge in the sparsely populated northwestern region of the country. It would cross the Gulf of Aqaba to connect to the Sinai Peninsula in Egypt. Besides carrying cargo, this causeway would also take advantage of Egypt's greater opportunities for public socialization and nightlife as well as the Sinai's beaches—only furthering the type of tourism that L. L. Wynn (2007) describes in her text.

On Bahrain's end, the presence of (mostly male) weekend tourists is an important economic factor. In 2010, right before the Arab Spring, travel and tourism accounted for just more than 25 percent of both employment and GDP for Bahrain, joining banking, construction, aluminum

---

5. Kuwait has a similar alcohol ban. Its ban was passed by the National Assembly in the mid-1960s and cited public health, road safety, control of the trade by a British firm (Gray and Mackenzie), and religion as reasons for the prohibition (*Time* 1965). At the time, alcohol could be purchased in Basra, Iraq, which was only a couple of hours away by car—although, obviously, that option has been unavailable since the beginning of the Iran–Iraq War.

smelting, and logistics among the most important nonpetroleum sectors (Bahrain Economic Development Board 2014, 123). Tourism is all the more critical because Bahrain has rapidly depleting oil reserves and possesses only small amounts of natural gas. As mentioned in chapter 6, its biggest chunk of oil money comes from two fields: one jointly owned with Saudi Arabia and another that is fully owned by Saudi Arabia but whose oil is gifted to Bahrain for refining, which in itself is another sign of Bahrain's importance to Saudi Arabia. The island nation also gains money from the United States for hosting its Fifth Fleet headquarters. Otherwise, Bahrain suffers many of the same economy-of-scale problems other small island nations face. Thus, it has turned to the things small island nations can do to get foreign currency: tourism and offshore banking.

Bahrain, however, does not have large stretches of wide sandy beach or world-class shopping as Dubai does, nor does it have Cairo's or Beirut's star power as an Arabic-language media hub, nor does it have the money to build a wide array of mammoth attention-grabbing structures.[6] In many ways, it is like Reno, Nevada, and countless Indian reservations in the United States, left to grapple with the choice of whether to be more permissive than its neighbors. This comparative lack of restrictions and availability of familiar things for well-to-do foreign residents undoubtedly helps with both the offshore banking and US Navy base. Indeed, the navy base publishes a guide called *Camel Crossings* for newly stationed personnel that says as much (Fleet and Family Support Center 2011). As an earlier version of the guide noted, "There are lots of familiar restaurants, including fast food. Lots deliver," and "I could get most everything I need except for Martha White Cornmeal mix."

So although comfort is important for foreign residents of Bahrain, it is permissiveness, especially concerning alcohol, that is the key for the weekend breakers. Bahrain's hotels are owned or sponsored mostly by the

---

6. The Bahrain government did spend large amounts of money (currently around US$150 million a year, but once as high as $500 million) to prop up Gulf Air. Gulf Air was formerly co-owned by multiple small Gulf states and headquartered in Bahrain. Now, however, Qatar and Abu Dhabi have their own airlines, and so Gulf Air has an aging fleet and higher costs than competitors. Thus the subsidies.

elite of the island, who are mostly Sunni. According to official estimates, whereas some two thousand Bahrainis work in hotels—composing around 20 percent of the hotel workforce (Bahrain Economic Development Board 2014, 128)—the staff of the nightclubs and bars are almost entirely foreign residents. In other words, although lucrative for the island, the bar trade does little to directly address Bahrain's national inequality problem. Like Wynn's (2007) example of Saudi tourism to Egypt, where Saudis are not nearly as wild or as decadent as Egyptians popularly imagine them to be, Saudis (and foreigners who reside in Saudi Arabia) visiting Bahrain are also not universally boorish. Nonetheless, the presence of alcohol had been a rallying cry for protest on the island on several occasions prior to 2011. In 2004, a group of Shia youth attacked a series of brothels and alcohol dispensaries operating illegally out of private homes as well as a French restaurant that served alcohol and was owned by an Iranian.

The politics of alcohol came to a head in 2009 when a second-tier "men's" website, AskMen.com, published a list titled "Top 10: Sin Cities" (Voyer 2009), in which, miraculously, Manama came in at number eight. In so doing, it beat out much more famous and larger Dubai to join Amsterdam and Pattaya, Thailand, in the rankings. "Welcome to the party oasis of the Middle East," the article's author hailed.

> Connected by a causeway to nearby Saudi Arabia, Manama is a popular spot for Saudis to kick back from their country's restrictive laws. Here they can get hammered, go clubbing, mingle with the opposite sex, and if they're really daring, they can pick up prostitutes—a practice that's illegal but widely available. . . . For many Saudi males this proximity to an open culture is irresistible and many jam the causeway and fill flights to the city every weekend. Do *you* want to see what happens when Saudis cut loose and leave the rules behind? You may need to get in line.

Despite having all the appearance of being quickly thrown together by a freelancer, the list became a rallying point for all kinds of opposition to the status quo once word of its existence spread in Bahrain.

Why would a list on a second-tier website cause such an uproar? Of course, there is precedence for minor media productions—such as the

Danish cartoons of the Prophet and *The Innocence of Muslims* film—being turned into major focal points for discontent in the wider region. But this is different. The vice list was not a broad insult against Islam; many in Bahrain (not just Shia Islamists) saw it as a sad reflection of their national situation. Many Bahrainis—in particular those who did not work in the bars, did not profit from them, and did not set foot in them—did not like what their island was seen to have become. The list provided something around which their frustrations could coalesce. As one legislator from the lower house of its parliament put it when discussing the list, "I'm sorry to say, but Bahrain has become the brothel of the Gulf, and our people are very upset about it. It's not only the drinking that we oppose, but also what it drags with it: prostitution, corruption, drugs and people-trafficking" (quoted in Trofimov 2010).

Both the Sunni and Shia Islamist parties threatened to push for a ban on alcohol, using the list as proof that the world now knew of Bahrain's previously regionalized secret. First, they targeted all hotels rated three or less stars for an alcohol ban, covering primarily the nonchain, nonluxury hotels where sex workers were most apparent. By the end of 2009, a ban did go into effect for one- and two-star hotels, although some of these hotels were later able to upgrade to three stars. Then in 2010 the lower house voted for a total ban on the sale of alcohol in Bahrain and on government-owned Gulf Air flights. This ban was eventually overturned by the upper house, which instead put in a restriction that only non-Muslims could be served (or serve) alcohol—a rule that also exists in Dubai but is very rarely enforced. Although the Islamists argued that Bahrain should focus on being a "family-friendly" tourism destination, the upper house decided that the direct (and perhaps the indirect in the form of foreign investment) knockoff from the ban would be too intense. Local domestic fortunes and embodied geopolitical standing were at stake.

This issue is not just about "the sleaze," as one government minister described the situation on Exhibition Road (showing that even some of those connected to the government are not terribly fond of the situation there). Many of my Bahraini informants (regardless of sect or class) feel bullied by their richer, bigger Saudi neighbor, and it is the fact that Saudis are the ones coming to Bahrain that upsets them. The fear of Saudi Arabia was only amplified when Saudi Arabia sent troops to stop the Arab Spring protests at the Pearl Roundabout. The ills surrounding alcohol tourism also play into the Sunni–Shia narrative—it is felt that the presence of this type of tourism is one more humiliation that the Sunni elite (if not all Sunnis) are heaping on the Shia majority. This argument over alcohol was one of the last major legislative spats between the government and the Shia community before the Arab Spring.

Even following the protests, the issue did not go away. During the summer of 2014, citing the flouting of a wide variety of regulations, the Culture Ministry accepted that the ban on alcohol and entertainment would be extended to three-star hotels effective immediately (what legislators originally proposed). Although the owners of the hotels (including one member of the wider al-Khalifa family) argued that many of them would have to shut down owing to the abrupt policy change (showing that the bars made more money than the hotel portion of the business), at a meeting with owners the Culture Ministry offered assistance to help the affected properties "upgrade their status" to four stars (A. al-Omari 2014). These bans will essentially clear the lower reaches of the ecosystem—that is, the hotels more likely to be frequented by various Asian communities—and move the "entertainment" industry upmarket.

Again, I am not asserting that standard geopolitical scripts about balance of power in the Gulf are unimportant in the case of Bahrain. Instead, I argue that differences in expectations about embodied cultural economy practices—in this case between expectations of those who want (or privately want) alcohol and those who find it poison to their society—matter, too. Although comparative alcohol policy is not as big a factor outside of the Gulf region, alcohol is not so different from the trades in cocaine, opium, and other recreational drugs or the phenomenon of sex tourism, which are also embodied in their affects and dispersed in their geography. Permissiveness has its potential benefits, but it also has its costs. Even though permissiveness is very far from the one and only cause of tension in Bahrain, it is very much part of the constellation of divisions that shape various actors' geopolitical reactions to the structures of feeling around Bahrain.

Qatar, Hosting the World Cup for the Arab World?

The final case study in this chapter returns to the ideas that there are hierarchies to what makes a good and comfortable place and that these hierarchies affect geopolitical standing (mechanism 2). In particular, it focuses on realms of geopolitics outside direct state-to-state relations by examining how Qatar's rulers and those associated with them have had to address expectations of what makes a worthy place while gaining the favor of one of the world's highest profile organizations: the International Federation of Association Football (FIFA).

In recent years, Qatar's rulers have become increasingly focused on raising their state's international visibility (Kamrava 2013). This was not always the case: until the mid-1990s Qatar was one of the lowest-profile GCC countries, noted mostly for a few early efforts to stand out for refined architecture. A number of my Dubai-based informants, who had lived or done brief project-based stints in Qatar, used the same word to describe it: *boring*. This idea that Doha's landscape does not provide the same level of excitement as Dubai is widely felt in the UAE. As one Dubai government official put it in an interview I conducted in 2005, "Yes, I am familiar with the projects there. But that is what we were doing five or ten years ago. We are so far ahead, they will not catch up." Such characterizations come from a certain perspective, of course. It is not surprising that people living in Dubai prefer Dubai. For their part, my Qatari informants generally like living in Doha, often because "it is calmer than Dubai." However, it was clear that in the very earliest years of the new millennium, in many quarters Qatar was not imagined as having that same "it" factor as Dubai.

It is true that Qatar does not have a world-renown equivalent of the Burj al Arab (the world's tallest hotel) or the Burj Khalifa (the world's tallest building) or malls and airports as big as those in Dubai. It does have less-ambitious versions of these things, but its efforts have been directed toward other areas. In international economic arenas, Qatar is well known as a host for major conferences, including the semidubious privilege of having been the meeting site for the beginning of the seemingly never-ending Doha Round of World Trade Organization negotiations. Within the region, its prominence increased with the formation of al-Jazeera television news network in 1996. In light of the Arab Spring, Qataris have taken an increasingly prominent role in highlighting (and in the case of Syria and Egypt supplying) the popular uprisings that occurred outside of the Gulf. When Saudi Arabia's rulers asked the United States to withdraw most of its troops from the country in the 1990s, it was Qatar that built al Uedid Air Force Base, which served as the US headquarters for its operations in Iraq. Taking a page out of Dubai's Emirates Airline playbook, the profile and size of Qatar Airways have also increased greatly over the past decade. Air competition not withstanding, the emphasis of Qatar's ruling family, the al-Thanis, has been very different than that of Dubai's rulers. Although almost everything Dubai's rulers have attempted has a commercial or lifestyle connection, Qatar's rulers have focused more intently on geopolitical prestige.

Nothing, however, could have more of an effect in terms of garnering international attention (for better or worse) than the events of 2010, when Qatar was granted the right to host the 2022 FIFA World Cup—the culmination of a decade of groundwork during which Qatar did all the things a prospective host should. It successfully hosted a smaller major sporting event, the 2006 Asian Games, and became active in FIFA's charity work. However, even in light of this major triumph, Qatar could not escape questions of lifestyle and market Orientalism in its quest to succeed on both commercial and geopolitical grounds.

The English-language media was stunned by the choice.[7] Some of this reaction was undoubtedly the result of "home-team" bias in that the United States and Australia were also bidding for the same World Cup, and England lost to Russia for the right to host the 2018 Cup on that same day. However, much of it also drew on pools of condemnation formed by market Orientalism. English-language football blogs immediately lit up with proclamations that Qatar could only have had bought or stolen the World Cup, notions that many newspaper columnists quickly echoed. For example, *New York Daily News* columnist Flip Bondy, who had actually

---

7. For a nice rundown of various headlines, see Reuters 2010.

been to Qatar, argued, "The ball has been flicked away from our ready-to-go NFL stadiums, to a land that nobody should want to visit" (2010). From the Rupert Murdoch–owned Australian website *The Punch*, columnist David Pentherby posted the following comments, nearly all of which were conjecture at the time (with the exception of his mention of aid to developing nations, which is a common practice among bidding nations): "The rumour at the time was that as many as 14 members of FIFA's all-powerful 24-strong executive committee were being offered direct payments by Qatar of up to US$10 million. In addition, Qatar was writing blank cheques for the world's football federations for any projects they wanted, in the order of US$60–70 million. A reporter on one German newspaper wrote on Twitter last week that he had established a paper trail showing that four members accepted payments of US$5 million, but the full story has not yet eventuated" (2010). While subsequent investigations have alleged that any given FIFA bidding process is likely to have involved the solicitation of bribes, usually very specific allegations of fraud require at least some form of well-vetted proof before publication.

Accusations of impropriety eventually found their way into mainstream news sections following a leaked email from FIFA general secretary Jérôme Valcke in which he off-handedly said Qatar "bought" the World Cup (Hughes 2011). Charges of fraud have percolated ever since, including allegations about Qatari officials considering (but not actually sponsoring) a dinner organized by the son of a Nigerian FIFA official (O. Gibson 2012) and in the summer of 2014 a report in the *Times* of London (Calvert and Blake 2014) that was based on a cache of emails provided by a whistleblower, which allege, among other things, payments and gifts from Qatari businessman and former FIFA Executive Committee member Mohammed bin Hammamm to several African football officials as well as to a FIFA vice president. Although only a few of these officials had votes that would award the World Cup, all of them could vote on bin Hammamm's possible election to the FIFA presidency. The legitimacy of some of this cache was later called into question by the publicly released portion of the FIFA-commissioned report on the 2018/2022 bidding process (Eckert 2014), which alleged that some of the material provided by this whistleblower had very likely been altered to fit that person's story or in some cases outright falsified (although the evidence of this alteration has not been made available for public review by FIFA).

Given the structures of feeling surrounding the Gulf, for some there could be no possible explanation besides outright fraud for Qatar's winning the World Cup. Other outlets, although stopping short of accusations of impropriety, nonetheless bemoaned the lack of "a level playing field" because the "Sheikhs' unlimited resources" were thought to trump "worthier" bids. Such statements were made despite the fact that Australia, for example, spent a staggering $46 million on its bid and the United States provided a guaranteed ticket-sales windfall for FIFA that none of the other bidders could match. Of course, the United States has its own history of bribery to win major sporting events, such as the 1996 Atlanta Summer Olympics and the 2002 Salt Lake City Winter Olympics (Molotosky 1999). Thus, here again we see the market Orientalist dynamic: Gulf Arabs are thought to succeed only because of superior monetary resources, which they wield in suspicious ways, whereas places such as the United States are thought to win on merit alone. As it would turn out, suspicious activity surrounded the entire bidding process for the 2018/2022 World Cups (and other FIFA events), much of it driven by FIFA's own Executive Committee, and the majority of bidding delegations participated in it.

Although on the surface a country as small as Qatar seems like a break with tradition in terms of who hosts major sporting events, the reasoning behind the choice is not too difficult to determine.[8] The path to Qatar hosting in 2022 begins with 2010 FIFA World Cup. That event was considered a sort of locational triumph in that it was hosted by South Africa, which—during coverage of the event—metonymically stood in for all of Africa (portrayed as a magically more-united landmass than any other). The triumph, of course, was that neither of the two most watched sporting events—the Summer Olympics and the FIFA World Cup—had ever been hosted on that continent. In choosing South Africa to host, FIFA continued a recent pattern of alternating between rewarding football heartlands

---

8. For an example of a media report that presents FIFA's choice as reasonable given the context, see "Russia and Qatar Expand Soccer's Global Footprint" (Longman 2010).

and pushing the game into new markets—a sort of expand-and-hold approach to the game's geopolitics of representation.

With 2014 already slated for Brazil, the task in 2011 was to pick the hosts of the 2018 and 2022 World Cups. With Europe virtually assured of hosting the 2018 World Cup,[9] the rest of the world (minus South America) was left to fight it out for 2022. This left four FIFA regions: Africa, North America, Asia, and Oceania. The member nations of Oceania (excluding Australia, which had decided to switch to the Asian region to offer more stern tests for its qualifying teams) and Africa (unlikely to win because it hosted in 2010) did not submit bids. The only bids thus came from North America and Asia—specifically the United States, Australia, Japan, South Korea, and Qatar.

For hosting the World Cup, very materialist and realist factors such as size of market and infrastructure across multiple urban areas (or capability to construct that infrastructure) have historically been important. At the same time, FIFA has also shown a willingness to push the game into new regions and markets for reasons as equally symbolic as economic. South Africa, as the wealthiest large market in sub-Saharan Africa, fit both of these criteria. It had also previously hosted the Cricket and Rugby World Cup tournaments successfully. It is believed that China, following its generally well-run Summer Olympics, will likely get to host the World Cup whenever it chooses to bid owing to that same combination of new territory and market size.

English-language pundits from early on had (unsurprisingly) deemed the United States and Australia as the frontrunners for 2022. The United States had existing stadium infrastructure thanks to the National Football League, college football, and Major League Soccer, with at least seventy-five stadiums having a capacity that exceeds sixty thousand persons and eleven having a capacity of more than ninety thousand. No other country

9. As mentioned later in this chapter, the World Cup and professional football are structured so that Europe is the dominant zone, and two World Cups would have passed since that region had hosted the 2006 tournament in Germany. According to the investigation into the 2018/2022 World Cup bidding (Eckert 2014), an informal agreement was in effect where all federations agreed Europe would host every third tournament.

comes close. Experience had also shown that a US World Cup would be an almost guaranteed financial success in terms of ticket sales because even the 1994 tournament hosted there had drawn huge numbers at a time when the sport was less popular in the United States than it is today. Australia, although a much smaller country than the United States in terms of population, also possessed the necessary sporting infrastructure across multiple cities thanks to rugby and Australian Rules Football. In addition, Australia had never hosted the World Cup (nor had any South Pacific country), so new ground would be broken. It shares one time zone with the key emerging market China and is not too many zones from India, a factor that would improve viewership in those places. It is also considered a desirable destination for travelers and has a good hosting reputation based on the 2000 Sydney Olympic Games as well as other major sporting events. Japan and South Korea were considered some-what long shots because they had served as World Cup cohosts in 2002. Both of these East Asian countries, like the other bidders, are larger than Qatar and have more in-place infrastructure. Indeed, FIFA's Technical Evaluation Committee, which examines the feasibility of all of the host bids, identified Qatar's as the only "high-risk" bid, giving the small size of Qatar's domestic market and its extremely limited existing sporting infra-structure as reasons for its decision.

However, none of these places except Qatar represented the oppor-tunity to break entirely new sporting ground by bringing the World Cup to a region that has a multitude of football fans but had yet to host the sport's most important event. As James M. Dorsey (2012) has argued, soc-cer fandom has been one of the few available venues for publicly venting frustration at the status quo in wide swaths of the Middle East, making it more than just an amusing pastime. But of all the countries in the region, why tiny Qatar? The answer mostly concerns the fact that the Middle East has no equivalent of South Africa, which possesses an overwhelm-ingly more ideal combination of market size, financial resources, and visitor infrastructure than any other possible location in its region. For example, the most populous country that is often considered a part of the Middle East is Turkey. It does have a long football history and is a top-twenty world economy. But in the world of FIFA, it (like Israel) qualifies in Europe, and it would have had to compete for the 2018 cup. Iran is also a big country with multiple large cities and World Cup appearances, but sanctions and internal policies make its hosting any time soon extremely unlikely. Countries with past football success, such as Egypt, Algeria, Morocco, and Tunisia, although connected through shared language and some institutions with other Arabic-speaking countries, qualify for FIFA competitions in Africa (and they all would also have considerable infrastructure and funding issues). Iraq, Yemen, and Syria were out owing to internal conflict. Jordan, which gets a large number of tourists, is simply too poor.

This leaves the Gulf states, the rich periphery of the region. Saudi Arabia has participated in the World Cup four times and certainly has the money and a large enough internal market to host, but it has shown little interest not just in hosting but in letting nonpilgrimage tourists in general into the country. Although the UAE would seem in some ways a better choice than Qatar—its population is three-times larger, and it has multiple significant cities and more infrastructure for visitors in place—it did not bid either.

A bid did come from Qatar, which would seem to have a number of strikes against it. For example, it has only one significant city: Doha. All recent World Cups (unlike the Olympics) have taken place across a country in multiple venues in multiples cities, lasting for one month (as opposed to the Olympics' two weeks). Visitors to these events often make it a double vacation: see the tournament and the country. In South Africa, many visitors combined spectating with safaris or historical tourism based on the struggle against apartheid. Unless a plethora of permanent attractions appear in Doha, the necessary hotel capacity there will have to be (1) greatly expanded and then instantly converted to apartments and condos in the style of an Olympic Athletes Village and/or (2) provided through docked cruise ships, which happened when small-market Jacksonville, Florida, hosted the NFL's Super Bowl to very few good reviews. Indeed, Qatar noted in its bid that some of the proposed stadiums are going to be "temporary," with plans to ship them to developing countries after the tournament—a neat but expensive plan, both in terms of shipping cost and site preparation at the destination.

More culturally tinged imaginations also worked against Qatar in the English language press. The restrictive gender policies in Saudi Arabia and Iran were mentioned in the run-up to the vote—even though none of the strictest prohibitions actually exist in Qatar (mainly those same restrictions found in Dubai regarding public display of affection and cohabitation). However, as the case of Dubai shows, the actual lack of restrictions has never stopped people from thinking otherwise. Nonetheless, Qatar was very skillful in how it bid. The idea of temporary stadiums was a smart touch, since most FIFA states are not wealthy. In addition, Qatar highlighted the advantages of a compact bid: namely, that supporters would not have to get on planes to follow their team as it advances through multiple rounds (as they would in the United States). An additional bonus is that the reduced travel would also decrease the tournament's environmental footprint (at least compared to a hypothetical country much bigger than Qatar but with a similar hot climate). Furthermore, unlike other governments suffering from the Great Recession, Qatar certainly has the money to build the stadiums, even if many of them never get used again. Although Qatar's committee occasionally utilized language that implied hosting would increase long-term economic production, it was refreshing that the committee understood that the tournament did not have to make money to be considered a success. Qatar could truly make the World Cup a spectacular form of Bataille's "waste"—something to be enjoyed with no other productive expectation.

The most-cited line from Qatar's bid presentation, however, concerns the geographic argument I noted earlier. It came from the emir's wife, Sheikha Mozah bint Nasser al-Missned: "I would like to ask you a question, When . . . when do you think is the right time for the World Cup to come to our region?" It is quite possible this factor swayed the vote. However, despite all the detail I provided that supports an argument for why Qatar can be seen as a "logical" choice, every indication is that those who voted spent little time dwelling on specifics and technical details. According to the report based on the FIFA investigation into possible fraud in the selection process, "It appears that, despite the 'core' relationship to the bid's merits, few [Executive Committee] members reviewed the [bid] books" (Eckert 2014, 10). In other words, the majority of the people who decided the fate of the World Cup ignored all the technical information and lines of argument each country had spent many years and millions of dollars preparing. The FIFA Executive Committee members instead behaved like many humans tend to do when faced with a reading assignment—they blew it off. To anyone who has ever participated in a book club or taught, this should not come as a shock.

Whatever the actual thought process was within the FIFA Executive Committee, what the English-language press focused on was much clearer. Although the dress code for women got some mention in the run-up to the vote, and the fact that Qatar is a small country with little football success was dwelled upon, these factors did not drive conversation. Furthermore, the plight of construction labor *initially* received scant attention, although Qatar shares (and perhaps exceeds) the other Gulf states' fairly abysmal record of treating construction laborers inhumanely. It was only following an Amnesty International report in 2012 that the issue became a staple of the "why Qatar shouldn't host" discourse. (Unfortunately, Qatar's rulers have yet to seize the opportunity the attention has provided to enact reform.) Instead, the two factors that garnered the most attention were heat and alcohol. The fact that these were the points of emphasis shows the ways that market Orientalism and embodied cultural economy intersect with the desire for geopolitical prestige.

Let us start with heat. Qatar has daytime temperatures of around 75°F in the winter months, but temperatures that often top 110°F in the summer, when the World Cup is traditionally played. Humidity during the summer can also exceed 90 percent. The fact that the World Cup takes place in the summertime reflects Europe's traditional dominance in FIFA the institution: most elite football professionals play for European clubs (regardless of the country in which they were born). These clubs take breaks only during the summer (in part to accommodate the playing of international football). Holding the event any time of year other than June and July would require a severe disruption in a multi-billion-Euro European business from the loss of games played if European leagues suspended play during the Cup or from the unavailability of star players and lost spectatorship owing to competition from the World Cup if play were not suspended. The Gulf is already set off from global cultural economy time rhythms by virtue of having a Friday–Saturday weekend. The temperate Northern Hemisphere dominance of the sports calendar works against the Gulf as well.

This is not all overblown, colonizeresque fretting about environments different than one's own—although the comment that Qatar is a place "no one should want to visit" is exactly that type of fretting. There is a nonimagined risk of heat stroke and certainly general discomfort for players and fans alike. That the risk is severe is evidenced by the fact that Gulf countries have a ban on construction work during the afternoon hours in the summertime, which is one of the few labor provisions generally enforced with any vigor. As someone who has spent time in the Gulf in midsummer, I can confirm that nighttime offers no respite because the humidity remains high and sweat does not instantly evaporate as it does in the daytime.

This was a real problem for Qatar's bid. FIFA president Sepp Blatter has hinted that the 2022 tournament may eventually be moved to a month when Qatar has more moderate temperatures, which certainly has to be the host's (yet unstated) preference. However, this change could potentially decimate ratings in the US market. A move to the winter would conflict with college and professional American football and thus reduce the significant amount of money FIFA would receive from the Fox Broadcasting Company, which purchased the right to broadcast the 2022 World Cup. But of even greater economic consequence, such a move would, as noted, immensely disrupt key European football leagues, and perhaps FIFA would have to offer some sort of compensation to the federations there as well as to other impacted leagues around the world.

A calendar shift was not (nor likely allowed to be) part of the plan set out in Qatar's official bid. Instead, it was forced to peddle in technological solutions to the heat issue. The delegation's World Cup plan proposed to air-condition all of the event's open-top stadiums using a new type of cooling system powered entirely by solar panels. One British environmental columnist showed his extreme skepticism (while deploying an Orientalist metaphor), declaring that the idea was "a mad Ozymandian desert folly" equivalent to "leaving all the lights and heating appliances blazing away in a house, and claiming to be green because there is a wind turbine on the roof" (Blacker 2010). A second aspect of the cooling plan calls for a fleet of remote-controlled, artificial clouds—or, to be more specific, giant, carbon-fiber, helium-filled, floating shields that would track the movement of the sun and keep the stadiums in constant shade. However, neither of these solutions will be able to cool the entire city of Doha, which is ultimately where visitors will have to spend most of their time.

The second embodied cultural economic and geopolitical issue, however, has nothing to do with players' or fans' health. If the issue were eliminated, an athletically successful tournament could still be held. That issue is the sale of alcohol, which is currently limited in Qatar to hotels, restaurants in a few special zones, and a select number of social clubs. Certainly, under current laws it would not be permitted in stadiums or plazas or other venues where it has been featured in other World Cups. Qatar has so far pledged that it will be allowed at least in stadiums and "public areas."

It turns out alcohol is not just theoretically a big deal for FIFA: it was a major sticking point with the host country in the run-up to the 2014 World Cup in Brazil (Vickery 2012). In an effort to stop fan violence in the early 2000s, the Brazilian government banned the sale of alcohol in stadiums used by its domestic league and national football teams. Brazil considered the policy a success in that violence began to decrease. However, FIFA insisted that alcohol must be sold in the stadiums during the World Cup and asked for the ban to be overturned for the duration of the tournament. Although alcohol is certainly a part of enjoying football in some countries (but not in all, including many countries in the Middle East), of more concern for FIFA is its official beer sponsor, Budweiser/In-Bev. FIFA's insistence that alcohol be sold in stadiums during the World Cup reflects a kind of broad power that is increasingly being given to major sponsors at such events. For example, McDonald's purchased the exclusive rights to manage all food concessions within Olympic venues at the Beijing Games despite the fact that many items on its menu run counter to the health ideals of elite athleticism. It is no longer enough for corporations that their logos are seen at events; their products must be there, too.

FIFA's insistence on in-stadium imbibing is (as the Bahrain and Dubai cases have shown) just the latest foray into the Gulf's dealings with alcohol. The wrinkle here is not whether alcohol will be available at the matches themselves (again, Qatar has assured FIFA it will be) but whether it will be available during all the times that people are not at the games. A big part of the visitor experience of the month-long World Cup has been roaming around and enjoying the cities and surrounding regions because there is often only one match per city per day. It is extremely debatable whether alcohol is a fundamental part of the in-stadium experience, but there will be hundreds of thousands of visitors spending weeks in Qatar, many of whom will be looking for things to do in a city with only a few days' worth of attractions. It is hard to imagine alcohol not being a big part of how many visitors, especially those from outside the region, would like to be able to pass that time (however rightly or wrongly). In fact, English Premier League chairperson Dave Richards, while venting about a Qatar World Cup, made clear just how important alcohol would be when he declared that beer is "part of our [sporting] heritage, part of our tradition" and that "if you don't do something about it you're starting to bury your head in the sand a bit" (quoted in Doherty 2012). Although it would be nice to think that it is possible for visitors to reduce alcohol consumption out of respect for the norms of the society they are touring, everything I have said about market Orientalism thus far suggests that this expectation is unrealistic. Alcohol availability is more than likely going to serve as a terrain of cultural economic distinction regardless of whatever policy Qatar eventually settles on.

Alcohol aside, the strain placed on Doha's leisure infrastructure by the sheer volume of visitors will be immense. This will be true even if a large percentage of tickets are bought by citizens of the GCC states, who may fly or drive in only for matches of interest. The situation may be alleviated somewhat if some extraregional visitors also choose to stay outside of Qatar and fly in for match days: perhaps in leisure-rich Dubai or somewhere in India (most of which is well connected to the Gulf by air). In the end, part of the solution will likely be that a fleet of cruise ships will dock in Doha for the duration of the tournament. This plan will help with the accommodation crunch, and the ships will almost certainly be allowed to serve alcohol and host nightclubs (because they are not in "national" space), but the use of such a fleet will create a resort effect, which is very different from the city-hopping experience a World Cup usually provides. So although there will be many free-time challenges for visitors to the World Cup in Doha, whether they indulge in alcohol or not, it is important to note that only booze has received much international attention.

This discussion links back to one of the main points raised by the Dubai and Bahrain cases: that certain embodied factors such as heat, alcohol, fitting in, and boredom matter as terrains of distinction in multiple geopolitical realms (including the geopolitics of cultural spectacles). Again, I am not saying that they are the only factors that matter—far from it. FIFA the institution (if not its Executive Committee) is in many ways bluntly "realist," putting self-preservation first. It only picks places it thinks are at least somewhat capable of putting on the tournament in a way that ensures revenues for FIFA. Yet FIFA, with a majority of its members hailing from the Global South, also cares for matters of representation and identity—as international relations constructivists would note. It actively seeks to bring its geopolitical spectacle to new realms to reinforce football's identity as a "global game," which is why the World Cup was in the United States in 1994, in Japan and South Korea in 2002, and in South Africa in 2010. As the vote for the 2018/2022 Cups showed, in line with a cultural economy perspective, sometimes FIFA does things "just because" or perhaps based on loyalties of Executive Committee members—indeed, such "imperfect rationality" is normal, not odd. It would be more unusual if this type of rationality *had not* been applied in the bidding process.

In the end, the Middle East loves football and has never hosted the World Cup. For this reason alone, Qatar did not "steal" the World Cup, since it is not "owned" by Global North fans alone. As the FIFA report put it, "The perception, for example, according to which a FIFA World Cup vote must have been 'bought' if the host selected is not the one that has been generally considered a favorite (a position that is quite common in the media), is mere speculation and far from anything a judicial body like the FIFA ethics committee is allowed to accept as proof" (Eckert 2014, 41).

Did it help that Qatar funded projects that provided aid and that its bid committee served as the title sponsor for the Confederation of African Football conference? Of course it did because many African football federations (and governments generally) are not overflowing with revenue.

Plus, with a number of Arabic-speaking countries in FIFA's Africa region, it is not a stretch to imagine Qatar would have carried some votes from Africa anyway. Furthermore, Africa had only four votes out of the twelve it took to win the final round, so Qatar needed broader support. And given the generally low opinion of US foreign policy in many corners of the world, is it all that shocking that the United States lost a popularity contest? It may turn out that Qatar did buy votes, but it is also possible that it did not have to.

Plus, as I briefly mentioned earlier in this section, during this World Cup bidding process Qatar was not alone in promising to improve poorer states' (especially those that had Executive Committee members) sporting facilities or in having citizens interact in suspicious ways with FIFA Executive Committee members. According to Hans-Joachim Eckert (2014), despite lack of subpoena power, the investigation into the bidding process uncovered that Australia worked to "conceal" its attempt to gain favor with one Executive Committee member, implied it would provide development money to the Oceania Federation if it voted for Australia, and transferred money to the Caribbean/North American Federation (some of which likely ended up in the personal account of that federation's then president, Jack Warner); England's bid team found work for an acquaintance of Jack Warner, let a junior national team from Warner's native Trinidad train in England on England's tab, paid for a gala hosted by Warner's federation, and promised development assistance to the Oceania Federation in exchange for votes; and South Korea promised to create a $777 million Global Football Fund if it were allowed to host. Unfortunately, such actions seem to be the "norm" for FIFA bidding processes.

For Qatar's part, besides the aforementioned payments by bin Hammamm (which went primarily to officials who voted on his presidential candidacy but not on Qatar's hosting bid) and the sponsoring of the African Football Conference (which was not illegal under FIFA bylaws), Eckert's report also noted the presence in Qatar of the Aspire Academy (a global youth football-training ground). Although not "formally" connected to the bid, the academy did make space for promising young players from many Executive Committee members' countries.

Almost all of the remaining bidding nations also had more minor suspicious behaviors. To be clear—when all is said and done, it is still quite possible that Qataris other than bin Hammamm might also be brought up on FIFA ethics charges or face legal action. But the way the bidding for the World Cup was scripted in the English-language media made it seem like a pure process had been corrupted by Qatar (and Russian) oil money. If FIFA's imperfect report shows nothing else, it makes clear that the process was hardly tainted by Qatar's and Russia's supposedly bad behavior alone—the majority of bidders were critiqued in serious ways. And asking for payments and favors seemed to be driven by FIFA's own Executive Committee, who, unlike the bidding nations, were under no obligations to report their finances and interactions during the bidding period—although this point does not in any way excuse any fraudulent behavior by any of the bidders. FIFA's own report claims that the oft-mentioned Jack Warner "demonstrated an expectation that bidding teams would react favorably and seek to curry favor with a voting member of the FIFA Executive Committee" (Eckert 2014, 22). It seems likely others on the Executive Committee held that same opinion, which is why the 2026 World Cup will be awarded by the wider FIFA Congress instead of solely by the Executive Committee.

In the end, Qatar's case was as good as that of any other state in the Middle East, and FIFA has shown repeatedly that geography really does matter to it. In fact, geographical representation matters so much that FIFA sacrificed hosting the tournament in a large market with an already-existing tourist infrastructure and a hospitable summer climate in order to reward a key region. Bringing the World Cup to a new region is something FIFA has won plaudits for in the past, and at least some members of its Executive Committee probably thought it would again in this case. Even though Qatar is not universally beloved (or necessarily disliked) in the Middle East, general opinion there seems excited that the wider region is finally being recognized by a major sporting body.

However, no World Cup has been held in a summer climate like Qatar's; no World Cup has been held in a country as small as Qatar; and, for the past few decades, no place where the World Cup has been held has

254 • *Market Orientalism*

led some people to question whether football's biggest festival would even be "festive" in the ways they expect. No choice of host has faced so many questions of whether it is deserving or not as Qatar's selection has. Put simply, no other World Cup host has been so marked by market Orientalism as Qatar. Hosts are normally queried about whether they will be able to supply the stadiums in time and fill them with people. Both Brazil and South Africa faced such questions—Qatar has not, despite its small size. The questions it has dealt with have concerned the embodied nature of market Orientalism, wherein Qatar is thought to have all the infrastructure of a globalized place but not—as one of the reporters quoted in chapter 4 argued—"the spirit" of one. This "spirit" dwells in the structure of feeling, having to do with affects such as enjoyment and comfort. It is an image that is only being fed by Qatar's slowness to improve the too-often deadly conditions its laborers are facing. Thus, putting representatives first, FIFA and Qatar risked upsetting the waters of cultural economic hierarchy. What is perhaps most telling is that, although FIFA was willing to bend on physical discomfort to achieve representational goals (and fail to notice labor issues until after the fact), it made clear that the nonavailability of alcohol in stadiums would have been a step too far.

In sympathy with almost all of the critical geopolitics authors cited in this chapter, it is safe to say that the world inhabited by Dubai, Bahrain, and Qatar is, as James Ferguson (2006) describes, one of hierarchy and ranking on wide and narrow politicized grounds, where countries find and scramble to improve their place. After a brief flash of notoriety in the mid-1970s, the Gulf states and their people remained somewhat outside imaginings of international and diplomatic prominence, just as they did in imaginings of economic prominence despite their obvious strategic importance. It was not lack of money that kept them in these outward places where smaller states often dwell; rather, it was a combination of their status as previously unknown entities and their violation, whether perceived or real, of norms of what have come to be international embodiment standards. These states did not aggressively court the presence of foreigners as leisure tourists until Dubai began to make a concerted effort to build attractions in the 1990s. These polities and "their people" seemingly (if not actually or only partly) frowned on rituals of courtship, on the consumption of alcohol, and on women enjoying equal rights as men. Furthermore, their wealth was seen as an "accident," given what poor, inhospitable, hot places they were thought to be. To move up, these states undoubtedly had to participate vigorously in the usual military, domestic, and diplomatic realms of geopolitics, but they also had to address the realm of everyday practice and cultural economy.

Bahrain found a continued outlet to Saudi funds and protection via causeway alcohol tourism, but at the cost of increased domestic strife. Dubai's stature rose because it was perceived as being friendly to embodied activity in an unfriendly neighborhood, which left it trying to walk the tightrope between being fashionable and being flamboyant. Qatar gained possibly the most viewed event on the planet despite the challenges of being "boring" and hot. Although Saudi Arabia will always be bigger and have more oil, I venture to say that Doha and Dubai have gained more widespread visibility than any city in Saudi Arabia, apart from Mecca and Medina, in the competition that includes prestige and recognition. Both have calculated that being interesting to multiple embodied, hierarchically positioned actors will in the end get them further than having hosted World Bank and World Trade Organization talks ever did. However, making such calculations is the easy part—bringing them to fruition is much harder.

Importantly for the purposes of this book, these case studies show that if you begin to add embodied geopolitics to cultural economy, you get access to new views and terrains of interstate competition. Indeed, the Gulf and the pervasive climate of market Orientalism in which it is viewed should be seen as an invitation for scholars of international politics to follow the mantra of looking "down" into complexity instead of "up" into the "romanticism" of familiar views of how the geopolitical world works (Law 2004). And for scholars of cultural economy, recognition of imagined hierarchies and wider processes certainly has the potential to raise the stakes of the intellectual enterprise.

8

The Gulf's Diverse Urban Cultural Economies

By now, it should be clear that Gulf cities and states, both individually and collectively, disturb "normal" cultural economic categorization. They are imagined as rich but "tribal," advanced but conservative, small yet high profile, seemingly capitalist yet seemingly socialist, similar yet fractious. Thus, they are often labeled as lesser copies, mimicking (and sometimes seemingly mocking) but never equaling the best practices. This makes them seem to be in need of guidance, advice, and paternalism. Their cities are described as ugly, stifling, without soul, and not worth visiting. Gulf states are often said to have "dark sides" that contrast with how much their infrastructure shines. They are thought to spoil those who are from there and crush all but a few elites who come to work there. Through all of these imaginations, market Orientalism transforms the Gulf into a measuring stick against which to define "normal" and a place for some to righteously oppose. If nothing else, all of these views of the Gulf show that structures of feeling—thoughts about soul, mimicry, darkness, being spoilt—very much influence how hierarchies of economic value are imagined, where people, money, and intentions go or do not go. Even if the effects of the structures of feeling around economic activity are most baldly displayed in the Gulf, they register everywhere.

However, as the previous chapter showed, such imaginations and feelings are not fully static—even when it comes to the Gulf. Dubai's rulers attempted to position their emirate as the permissive Other within what many considered to be an Other region. Qatar's rulers pushed strongly to elevate the Gulf brand among key regional and geopolitical audiences.

Bahrain's rulers have tried to find niches within the larger Gulf ecosystem for things such as alcohol and American bases, but perhaps at the cost of adding to social turmoil.

Despite (and sometimes because of) its ill reputation in some corners of the globe, the Gulf is frequently viewed as a place of possibility—both as a place for potential investment and as a place full of potential investors. For some cities, the Gulf also provides urban models to emulate. Indeed, one of the effects of market Orientalism, to use that classic Marxist formulation and apply it to diverse economies, is that it "hides" all the work done in the Gulf to distribute surplus. The benefits and costs of these distributions (which some might just dismiss as externalities or waste) flow not just to elites but also to citizens and foreign residents, tourists, business travelers, and investors as well. When petrodollars are earned by Gulf oil companies, they do not completely disappear into dividends within investment portfolios—they are distributed and redistributed throughout the globe, even if they get built into the infrastructure of Gulf cities (because these cities are generally hyperconnected to other places). But such movements are hard to see because market Orientalism shifts the focus to what the Gulf does not export enough of to be considered "correctly" diversified (industrial products, advanced producer services, and the like) and to what is consumed by extreme examples taken as type. Thus, much of what happens in Gulf cultural economic ecosystems remains just out of view; as a result, the work and impacts of distribution do not get the attention that they should.

How people in the Gulf maneuver within and beyond these structures of feeling is worthy of attention (and was at the heart of previous chapter). But yet much of what goes on in the Gulf is more than those hierarchies in which places find themselves. Much of what I learned, heard, and witnessed in the Gulf falls into this category—far from untouched by market Orientalism but not dominated by it either. Gulf landscapes and the people who work in, travel through, and inhabit them are not just pawns in this imaginative geography I have described. Sure, they shape market Orientalism and are impacted by it, but not in every instance, just as they shape and are shaped by neoliberal, social, rentier, and other processes, but also not in every instance. In this chapter, I focus on people in the

Gulf, their spaces, and the cultural economic values and diversity they comprise. I do so for a number of reasons.

First, I feel that presenting what I have witnessed has value in its own right, as John-David Dewsbury (2003) and other scholars have claimed. Second, if widely spread cultural economic imaginations such as market Orientalism are ever going to be disrupted, one has to make visible those practices it has obscured. In particular, J. K. Gibson-Graham (2006) would have us focus not just on production but also on consumption and distribution as well as the values that underpin them. Admittedly, what follows is (mostly) not a tale of the type of community economic practices that Gibson-Graham highlight and try to support. Indeed, some examples in this chapter, such as the nationality-based wage system, are hardly uplifting.

With the goal of showing diverse economic practice and values, this chapter takes the form of a series of vignettes rather than a single narrative. The five vignettes presented here concern (A) the appeal of Gulf cities, (B) the segmented wage system, (C) malls and retail, (D) the growing Chinese presence in the Gulf, and (E) the practices of Ramadan. All of them signify important moments in the Gulf's cultural economies but have only a bit to do with the usual suspects, which are oil and whatever sectors the Gulf states are said not to have.

In these vignettes, I focus on the place in the Gulf where I have spent the most time: Dubai. So keep in mind: what I present here is somewhat particular to life in that emirate. Saudi Arabia, for example, relies more heavily on the mega-foreign-resident compound and has a much larger domestic population spread over a wider territory (not to mention a more expansive set of personal-conduct laws), all of which produce different cultural economic practices. The results I describe are also undoubtedly somewhat particular to me.[1] That I was able to observe and talk to the people I did has to do with my interests, my background, the ways I appear

---

1. If you want another author's take on a related set of topics concerning the everyday in Dubai (although more from a built-environment perspective), Yasser Elsheshtawy's book *Dubai: Behind an Urban Spectacle* (2010) is a good read.

to others, my likes and dislikes, among many other factors I cannot begin to perceive or guess at. To be clear, from the research on which the preceding chapters were based, I feel I know quite well what market Orientalism looks like; this chapter is my effort (partial, as it should be) to present practices that glance off market Orientalism. Let me begin with one idea that does not get highlighted enough—at least in the United States: the Gulf can be an appealing place.

Vignette A: Why the Gulf Works

I begin with a moment from one of the in-depth interviews I conducted with Dubai residents. The informant was a retail worker from the Philippines, and the topic was how life in Dubai compared to life in her home city. I eventually came to a standard question I asked all my noncitizen, long-form interview subjects: "Is there anything from home you can't get here?" Only this time I added a clause at the end: " . . . like is there some type of food?" This question caused her to laugh quite loudly, which briefly took me aback. Then she replied, "Are you joking? Here, the grocery stores have all types of vegetables, all the time. I can always get all the food I want here; the shelves are always full." As a comparatively privileged person who has spent my life where the shelves are nearly always full, this is not a perspective that jumped immediately to my mind: namely, that volume and quality can trump having specific items. I do not mean to imply here that in the Philippines all working-class people are so poor they cannot afford food or that Pinoy food is at all hard to find in Dubai. Instead, the point is that the urban and economic infrastructures in major Gulf cities are fairly dependable.[2]

From my research in Dubai, I found that what primarily impresses many middle- and working-class residents from "developing" countries

---

2. Some smaller cities and settlements in the Gulf face periodic (and sometimes chronic) issues with power supply, water/sewage systems, and housing quality. Sharjah is good example, which grows quickly but lacks the petrodollar-funding stream to which Dubai has access. Many Shia villages in Bahrain suffer similar issues.

is *not* that the emirate's landscape offers freedom from prohibitions that would inhibit dressing and eating or drinking how they please. Although these residents do appreciate this lack of restrictions to varying degrees, the freedoms I was told were most often appreciated included freedom from occurrences such as periodic shortages of quality produce in grocery stores, freedom from brownouts, freedom from petty crime, freedom from having to pay frequent bribes to officials, and freedom from dealing with street crime (although, unfortunately, foreigners who do manual or domestic labor in the emirate do not always experience these same freedoms). Although some employers in Dubai are rotten, only traffic, high rents, sometimes spotty visa rules enforcement, and overly expensive telecommunications can fully be put at the foot of authorities. Time and again I heard from business-minded Indian informants living in Dubai that it was very much like India, only "everything works" (or that Dubai is a model of what India could become). A lack of alcohol or pork grates on some people in places where it is prohibited, but the basic if imperfect functionality of Gulf cities is what keeps impressing their residents. For many (but not all) residents from the "developing" world, the Gulf stands as a counterpoint to the many infrastructure problems that plague their home territories.

Cities are achievements, and many commentators who quickly decry this or that Gulf megaproject as irrational folly fail to note how comparatively well Gulf cities function on a basic-infrastructure level. Distributing surplus in order to create space for people to live and work is an important economic activity, not just largesse. The discourse in the United States in particular has recently undervalued basic infrastructure (something that was once considered critically important across the political spectrum even twenty years ago). This lowered value is demonstrated by the fact that countless roads, bridges, and sewer systems in the United States are in need of repair or replacement yet go without funds year after year. The amazing work these infrastructures do tends to get noticed only when they break. Nigel Thrift is similarly puzzled by this recent trend of not appreciating infrastructures: "I believe that on many dimensions the contemporary Western city is more robust than it has ever been and I want to explain why. But I am also sure that the inhabitants of Western cities often think the opposite" (2005, 133). Although media images of catastrophe drape

cities in what Thrift calls a "sense of misanthropy" about their functionality, he also notes that infrastructures of urban repair and maintenance
"work on the structure of anticipation, producing a comforting sense of
regularity and a corresponding (and probably amplified historically) sense
of annoyance when things do not play out exactly as it is intended that
they should. In a sense, speed has produced a new landscape of anticipation" (137).

Chapter 4 showed how this lack of wonder was not always the case:
commentators in the 1960s were initially amazed at how "developed"
infrastructures in the supposedly "medieval" Gulf became. Indeed, the
infrastructure there is highly functional, but the Gulf is more than what
cement and rebar have wrought. There are beautiful mountains in many
Gulf states, and the coastal places without mountains tend to have sandy
beaches (which are generally popular across class and nationality when
made accessible) or coves for diving or both. In addition, people in the
United States are somewhat spoiled by the fact that they can move to Florida, Texas, Arizona, or southern California if a lack of sunshine bothers
them; countries such as the United Kingdom, Canada, Germany, and
Russia offer few to no equivalent internal options. Many Gulf nationals
(and other people throughout the world) love the desert. In other words,
from many perspectives oil is not the only gift earth bestowed on the Gulf.
People have recognized this for a long time, having lived in the area for
millennia and producing significant archaeological records at places such
as Dilmun in Bahrain and Mada'in Saleh in Saudi Arabia even before the
coming of Islam. And of course, for the one billion Muslims worldwide,
there could hardly be places of greater spiritual significance than the holy
cities of Mecca and Medina, whose management is a colossal, complex
task. Perhaps those who think about economies might regain some of
that sense of wonder (minus the racist overtones) about both natural and
human-made infrastructures—or at least pay more attention to them, as
Stephen Graham and Simon Marvin do in *Splintering Urbanism* (2001).

As chapter 7 argued, one of the "it" factors of Dubai is its status as a
meeting ground for business and common causes—Dubai's beaches, sand
dunes, hotels, roads, restaurants, airports, water-desalinization plants,
and the like make those meetings possible. Thus, Dubai's infrastructure,

besides being a project for citizens, makes cultural economies in that neighborhood of the world work in ways that are hard to put a monetary value on. When I noted in the introduction to this chapter that even money sunk into Gulf cities circulates more widely, I meant it in exactly this sense.

So, yes, these economies do produce (sometimes striking) inequalities, and such inequalities *must* be documented and functionally understood.[3] Furthermore, city maintenance and repair in the Gulf rely on large numbers of generally low-paid foreign residents as well as the massive burning of fossil fuels, just as social reproduction relies on an army of domestic workers from other parts of Asia. However, despite the unfairness, it must also be remembered that many people come to the Gulf because they want to be in a place where there is a thickness of amenities and dependable infrastructures.

Vignette B: Foreigners and the Cultural Economy of Gulf Wages

Even in my current home base of Miami (the US city with the highest percentage of foreign-born citizens), I often get shocked looks during class meetings or public lectures when I note that upward of 90 percent of Dubai's population consists of noncitizen, foreign residents[4] (indeed, by some insider estimates, Indians make up 50 percent of the population). Such reactions are repeated when I note that Dubai is at least 70 percent male, largely because of the enormous number of construction workers. The rest of the Gulf outside the UAE and Qatar does not quite reach such numbers. Riyadh and Muscat, for example, sit at only around 40 percent foreign population (officially). Even numbers such as Muscat's and

3. For example, Mehran Kamrava and Zahra Babar's edited collection *Migrant Labor in the Persian Gulf* (2012) does an excellent job of documenting not only the unfairness but also the appeal.

4. Throughout this book, I have tried for the most part to follow Attiya Ahmad's (2012) plea to refer to foreigners in the Gulf as "residents" (as opposed to "expats," "bachelors," or "guest workers") to emphasize that their impact on the Gulf goes beyond their work and that their lives are also more than that same work.

Riyadh's are comparatively high, of course, but none is without precedent. Gold Rush California (and many resource boomtowns before and since) had a similar male-skewed gender imbalance. Similarly, many export-processing zone factories employ disproportionately female workforces that come from other places within whatever country they happen to be located.

Now, of course, one might imagine that the diversity of Gulf places would be celebrated, as such diversity is in Miami, London, Singapore, New York, and Vancouver. The Gulf might be proclaimed a vibrant mosaic that renews the cosmopolitanism of old Ottoman Istanbul, where diverse cultures come together to pursue their own faiths under the benevolent eye of a Muslim monarch. Food lovers would flock there, scouring working-class cafés for new fusion treats born of Indian cooks and a Filipino front of house.

But by this point in this book about market Orientalism, it is obvious such a celebration is not likely to happen (and, as highlighted later in this chapter, most Gulf states' stance toward certain segments of their diverse populations does not help matters). The large foreign-resident population is instead one of the primary ways Gulf economies are marked as Other. So to the list of the oppositions that started this chapter, let me add one more: the Gulf is diverse but seemingly closed. Yet adding to the list of representations is not the main goal here; understanding what is unique or typical about Gulf cultural economies is.

There are a number of qualitative differences in how foreign residents are treated in places such as the United States, Canada, the United Kingdom, and the Gulf (just as there are differences among the United States, Canada, and the United Kingdom as well as among Gulf countries). For example, in the 1980s Miami's boosters slowly began to embrace the city's Latin-ness, which has ever since been promoted as one of its major attractions. Gulf states do not promote their large South Asian populations in a similar manner (although, as the next section describes, several are starting to embrace China more). The closest to such promotion I have seen is literature from Dubai Ports and Dubailand noting their proximity to South Asian markets. Although certainly the United Kingdom, the United States, Canada, and Singapore all have very real issues of equity in terms of which migrants are allowed in (and the capriciousness of the deportation process), none have the *kafala* system of employee sponsorship, where the employer (or perhaps a sponsor who has contracted the worker out) controls a worker's visa (and often his or her passport), which means the employer can prevent the worker from finding a new job or leaving the country. Even though many of the most potentially abusive aspects of the *kafala* system have been outlawed in most GCC states, some practices associated with it—such as passport holding and wage withholding—continue among some employers in a climate of too lax enforcement. Low-wage workers are particularly affected. The networked labor-recruitment process that links South Asia and the Gulf also tends to leave migrants and their families in deep and sometimes inescapable debt (Osella and Osella 2012), which can be exacerbated when a contracting sponsor insists on keeping a portion of the worker's salary. In countries such as the United States, undocumented workers tend to face the worst conditions; in much of the Gulf, even proper documentation is no assurance of rights protection.

More positively, the Gulf does not put quotas on foreign residents from particular countries (although entry rules are laxer for workers from certain favored countries, mostly those with a higher GDP per capita). Almost anyone who can find an employer or sponsor in the Gulf can legally work in the Gulf. That being said, Gulf states are also much more likely (even if it happens sporadically) than other destinations to deport foreigners for political, critical, or even satirical speech. For example, Syed Ali, the sociologist author of *Dubai: Gilded Cage* (2010), was told to leave the UAE because of his research.

Another way that the Gulf stands out from other major in-migrant destinations is its wage system. A general rule of thumb is that a foreigner in the Gulf is supposed to make more than he or she would make at home—some people receive substantial raises, and others see their home salary matched but effectively get more take-home pay because there are no income or value-added taxes. This has been true since the 1970s, barring periods of rapid inflation in cost of living. According to Alan Richards and John Waterbury, "during the late 1970's an unskilled rural Egyptian could earn *thirty times* more money working at a Saudi construction site than working on an Egyptian farm. Jordanian engineers could double or triple their incomes by going to Kuwait" (1990, 390, emphasis in the original). Before the 2000s, covering all accommodation costs for employees was not unusual; the skyrocketing costs in the past decade, however, have made it less commonplace outside of the highest and lowest tiers of foreign residents.

That migrants get paid more than they do in their home is not unusual—in fact, it is expected. However, this increase in pay does not lead to anything close to a prevailing wage for any given job category in the Gulf. This is unusual. In the Gulf, two people doing the same job will make very different amounts depending on how much a job pays in their country of origin. According to anthropologist Karen Leonard, in the UAE "Arabs of Lebanese, Palestinian, and Syrian origin command the highest wages and salaries, Egyptians and Sudanese receive half as much, and South and Southeast Asians receive one third as much. Among laborers, Indians reportedly ranked above Pakistanis, who ranked above Bangladeshis and Chinese" (2005, 679).

The emergence of a prevailing wage is hindered because employers in the UAE and other Gulf countries recruit most of their workers from abroad (offering them a salary that is high by their domestic standards) or have labor recruiters do it for them. For example, although the practice is changing, all but the most sought-after categories of workers previously required a "no objection certificate" (NOC) from their current employer to switch jobs within the UAE (UAE Ministry of Labor 2008). If an employer refused to issue an NOC (or, in current iterations, if the person has switched jobs too many times), the passport was stamped with a six-month "ban" during which time the person could not obtain another job in the country. Even though NOCs have been waived for many more job categories (often after a set period of time) in recent years, once a person is in the Gulf, it is still harder than usual to chase higher wages by job switching. For those on the lower end of the wage scale, switching can be impossible without venturing into the informal sector (Mahdavi 2011). In addition, higher-skilled workers are fairly likely to land their next job outside the region as opposed to finding another one in the Gulf. Thus, wages are somewhat depressed by raises occurring through emigration.

The result is that Indians often get paid less for the same job than their European or even Filipina counterparts (if the job is in food service)—something nearly all of my Indian informants confirmed when asked.[5] Similarly, eastern Europeans get paid less than western Europeans and Americans. For example, one of my informants, who was originally from eastern Europe, told me he probably made $20,000 more per year because he applied for his current job using his recently earned New Zealand passport instead of the one from his home country. Although with somewhat less rigidity and uniformity, the gendered wage system of each country is also reproduced (but it depends on the job category). As one of my colleagues put it, "It is like they reproduce the entire international wage hierarchy within a single city." Instead of putting international wage disparities out of sight and out of mind, the Gulf makes them visible and proximate.

This cruise-ship-style wage system is something nearly all my informants were aware of, but surprisingly some actually endorsed it (although generally those nearer the top of the wage hierarchy). In many ways, work practices have become a terrain of distinction among different nationalities in the Gulf, and talking about the work habits of Others becomes a way various residents in the Gulf argue for their own value. Almost everyone I spoke to in Gulf, regardless of background, explained to me—without being prompted—that their national group consists of the hardest-working, most indispensable people in the Gulf.[6] Furthermore, people almost universally feel that their group is slighted by other groups, whom they view as approaching work or going to the mall or standing in line or driving in a completely wrongheaded way. This feeling of being slighted explains why many of my informants from South and Southeast Asia,

---

5. While I was attending a networking event, a group of Indians who worked in the shipping industry emphatically emphasized to me that Indians get paid less. The words "we are treated like shit" were used more than once.

6. Interestingly enough, Americans were the most hesitant to be vocally judgmental about other groups in Dubai (save perhaps having feelings about the UAE nationals). This silence probably does not mean that Americans are free of prejudice; it is more likely that growing up in the racially charged United States has taught them not to appear racially insensitive while being interviewed.

when I inquired if they had any questions for me, asked if I knew anything about how to get a Canadian visa. Although Canada is harder to get into than the UAE, if you manage to get there, you are treated more or less the same as everyone else and can access the same set of state resources.

What is interesting is the multiple directions in which this "nationalized thinking" moves. For example, one of my British informants who worked as an engineer told me—in a display of barely hidden colonial sensibility—that the Brits "certainly deserve[]" to earn higher salaries than everyone else because they have superior training and "[know] how to get things done," especially compared to Indians, who are "cattle." Among many eastern Europeans, there is a feeling that the British and local Arabs are overpaid, boorish, and lazy despite having the run of the town. But many eastern Europeans also hold the belief that their Soviet-era education is superior to that of Indians, who, according to one informant, are "always protecting each other from doing work" and "always hir[ing] more Indians." Indians, as mentioned earlier, are not unaware of what other groups think of them but believe they are in fact the hardest workers and that other groups are lazy and overpaid. Filipinos feel largely the same way about themselves. Alternatively, several Iranians told me that Dubai is successful only because their homeland does not function normally and is trapped under sanctions. As one Iranian informant put it, "If Iran became free, our money [in Dubai] would disappear, and Dubai would disappear."

Group membership (be it according to ethnicity, religion, or nation/subnation) is often something that defines economic opportunity around the globe. Indeed, most places have a dominant economic group and one or more marginalized groups that may or may not be numerically dominant. The Gulf is much more fragmented, and group dominance often varies by the individual workplace.

Although there are some very real differences from other large receivers of migrants, in other ways the Gulf is very typical. Each national group's belief that it is important or underappreciated or both is most likely one of those ways. Highly skilled migrants have a very different experience than working-class migrants just about everywhere in the world. Migrants from some countries get treated better than others: in Miami, Cubans generally get to stay if they have merely manage to set foot on dry land, whereas Haitians can potentially get sent back if they are caught without a visa. Although the United States does not have many formalized migrant labor camps in large cities, as the Gulf does, they are common enough in agricultural areas. Some argue that foreigners come to the Gulf only for higher salaries and that this reason for its high foreign-born population should be held against the region, as if it is a factor nowhere else. Plus, despite the large number of laborers and domestic servants who have little chance of getting ahead, there are also both wildly and moderately successful migrants in the Gulf. Some of these people are indeed European or Arab, but many are South Asian, Iranian, Central Asian, East African, and Southeast Asian. Despite occasional images to the contrary, not all South Asians in the Gulf are abused, even if many face real prejudices and some are actually abused.

All of this is not to say, "Oh, everywhere is equally bad." Nor is it an attempt to excuse the very real issues of fairness that exist in Gulf migration. But the story one hears about the Gulf is overwhelmingly the story of a managerial elite (largely of Gulf national and European extraction) living grossly high off the pain of laboring masses. The elite do live well, and the laborers do toil, but the middle- and working-class residents of the Gulf (many of whom are Gulf nationals) get much less attention. It often seems the Gulf is the only region in the world chastised for benefiting from a "brain gain" of skilled and motivated foreign workers. This is another case of the Gulf economies being viewed as a "bad copy" of other wealthy economies instead of as the unique collections of good and bad activities that they are. Even though wealthy economies are supposed to gain dynamism from welcoming foreigners, the way the Gulf states do the same thing is considered to be tainted by the original sin of their oil money or of Oriental despotism or of some other trope that "proves" why the Gulf should not be recognized at all for doing something that successful economies do. Thus, the Gulf is once again "familiar but not quite right," and market Orientalism has again reared its head.

But pointing out the work of market Orientalism in yet another arena is not this chapter's primary goal. Understanding the diversity of Gulf economies is. People and the distribution of the money they make is one of the major global economic flows involving the Gulf, and the actual trajectories of those distributions is far messier than the generalization that "high fliers take most of it, the poor are left with nothing." Staffing in the Gulf is a balancing act of wage rates, skills, and workforce cohesion, all judged according to a hierarchy of valued nationalities. All of this together creates systems of inequity but also chances for the negotiation of worth.

Again, it is the easy path to imagine the Gulf as "oil out, money in" and leave it at that. However, how and why that money circulates are incredibly complex, providing opportunities within the various tiers of migrants to provide niche services. For example, the wholesale districts and Dhow ports on and near Dubai Creek (also known as "the Creek") are vivid places where one can see the more minor cultural economic flows involving the Gulf. Although those would make an excellent study, I instead examine diversity in one of the region's most visible but often derided sectors: retail.

Vignette C: Malls, Hotels, and Retail Diversity

Although retail is a dominant sector in terms of employment both in the Gulf and in the wider world, nowhere in the Indian Ocean region is more associated with this sector than Dubai. Just what is the extent of its retail sector? During the height of its boom, the Dubai Chamber of Commerce produced the book *1000 Numbers & Reasons Why Dubai* (Kassar 2006). The book noted that in 2006 there were 250 malls in the Middle East, 40 of them in Dubai. That number has only grown since then. Many of the largest ones throughout the Gulf (and wider region) are associated with the powerful mall developer Majid al Futtaim, which is based in Dubai. The same Chamber of Commerce publication bragged that in 2005 Dubai's malls received 79 million visitors; in 2007, Dubai topped 2 million square meters of mall "gross leasable area" (*Middle East Economic Digest* 2006). By comparison, Abu Dhabi had 500,000 square meters of mall in 2007, and the Mall of America, the largest mall in the United States, covers 390,000 square meters. One of Dubai's major civic cultural events is the annual Dubai Shopping Festival, the heart of which is an emirate-wide series of mall-based sales and raffles (which include prizes such as luxury SUVs and piles of gold bars). It received 4 million visitors in

2012. This yearly event combines with Dubai's traditional strength in gold sales and showpiece hotels as well as with a lack of sales tax (and strategic use of the image of "Arab riches") to place Dubai among the world's leading shopping destinations, despite being much smaller than competing destinations like Tokyo, London, or New York.

Although these statistics are somewhat startling, they do not fully convey how important malls have become to the Gulf. In Dubai in particular, malls are utilized by nearly all types of people who reside in the emirate, even laborers and household staff. In fact, laborers often use part of their weekly afternoon off to put on their best clothes and go to the mall or at least to whatever big-box hypermarket anchors the mall (see fig. 4). Thus, malls (especially a few of the larger ones) are the primary site where social proximity occurs in the emirate. If you work for government ministries, most of your colleagues are UAE nationals (or from somewhere else in the

4. Laborers walking on a Friday afternoon, going from their trailer park labor camp near Jebel Ali to Ibn Battuta Mall in Dubai, 2007. Photograph by the author.

Gulf). If you work in the private sector, each type of work site tends to have predominant nationality or regional populations. The malls—above all French big-box discount retailer Carrefour—are where all groups bump into each other. Thus, shopping malls are key sites to witness the Gulf's amazing cultural economic diversity in one place. These same malls also display some measure of diversity among themselves. However, they have not always been a part of the Gulf's postoil era.

Dubai before Malls

It was not until 1992 that Dubai's first mall opened. This seems relatively late, given that Dubai already had around five hundred thousand people and its megaport, first skyscraper, and convention center had opened at least ten years earlier. In markets such as the United States, indoor malls were already yielding ground to big-box retailers located in cheaper-to-construct strip malls. The honor of being Dubai's first mall goes to MaGrudy's Shopping Mall on Jumeirah Beach Road, which is located in an area largely populated by Europeans (MaGrudy's 2006). However, MaGrudy's was only a small plaza; the first truly large mall was Deira City Centre, which opened in 1996.

Before the mall boom of the 1990s, Dubai in many ways was like the other oil sheikhdoms on the Gulf—albeit with a greater density of some amenities such as parks, beaches, bars, churches, and grass golf courses. People tended to live in very segregated neighborhoods, much like they did in neighboring states (Khalaf 2006). In Dubai, Indians lived in Karama, Iranians in Satwa, Western families in villas in Jumeirah near the beach, single Westerners in the Golden Sands area near the bars, Emirati in peripheral areas where the government provided land and there was enough room to build large villas. The royal family was farther inland in Zabeel. These patterns persist somewhat to this day, although new developments and time have scrambled the clarity of the ground order.

Social clubs, business councils, and clubs for various large employers (such as Dubal Aluminum) were the center of various foreign-resident social scenes, as were the nationality-based primary and secondary schools. Although there were some transnational social institutions, such as the golf clubs, they were only for the elites. Those outside the labor camps shopped in grocery stores such as Spinneys (dating from 1800s British Egypt) and Lulu Hypermarket and went to souks or shopping districts in Bur Dubai (for electronics and cloth) or to the Karama Souk (which had a little of everything, including counterfeit items). What all these districts had in common was that small shops or local chains dominated.

As the previous chapter indicated, hotels also had a lofty position in the pantheon of premall social life—in particular the string of hotels along Bank Street. Again, only hotels rated three stars or higher and social clubs (such as the Dubai Exiles Rugby Club or India Club) could hold liquor licenses in Dubai. A side effect of this was that in Dubai almost every bar and upscale restaurant was hidden from street view, accessible only from the hotel lobby. This made visible, walkable bar, art, and café districts almost nonexistent until a few master-planned developments such as the Walk at Jumeirah Beach Residences brought the concept to Dubai. Even in 1999, *Culture Shock! The United Arab Emirates*, an English-language guide for new UAE residents aimed primarily at Europeans, warned that Dubai is a "small town" and that you can easily "get a reputation" if you behave badly at key hotel bars (Crocetti 1999, 47). Hotel restaurants are still important in Dubai's upscale dining scene and for watching sports, but hotels are now much more dispersed throughout the emirate, often attached to malls or situated in the far-flung new residential developments.

Before the mall boom, for residents—especially laborers—who could not pay for such luxury (or even the nationality-based social clubs), the inexpensive entertainment options were parks, mosques, bus stations, the retail zones in some of the more permanent labor camps, the promenade along Dubai Creek, a series of cricket and soccer pitches, and the large, single-screen theaters that showed primarily Bollywood movies. Other possibilities included dinner at a communal table in the cheap-and-cheerful South Asian joints—such as the Karachi Darbar chain of restaurants—that served good food at comparatively low prices (and also usually had family rooms upstairs). Furthermore, Dubai had wide swathes of underdeveloped or fairly undeveloped Gulf-front beaches where anyone who could reach them could camp out and barbeque.

That being said, Dubai before malls was perhaps more encouraging of commercial diversity than it is today. Nothing has emerged in any Dubai shopping mall to equal the cheeky brilliance of the restaurant named "TGI Thursday's" (so named for the fact that Dubai's weekend starts on Thursday night). It was in the vicinity of Bank Street that many of these quirkier businesses thrived before the mall-based international chains came to dominate the emirate's retail sector (see figs. 5 and 6). But such businesses could be found in other areas, too. Dubai had a number of districts dedicated to the wholesale and retail of an often startling narrow range of items. On Plant Street in Satwa, shops sold plants and pet birds. On the other side of the Creek in Deira was the car-parts district, including one entire block dedicated to the sale of automobile seat covers. In fact, this landscape littered with these bars and businesses helped cement Dubai as the anything-goes "merchant" playground in the eyes of the international media.

In 2006, there were 250,000 businesses registered in the UAE—the majority of them in Dubai (Kassar 2006), *which means there was one business for every seventeen residents of the country at that time.* For comparison, the US rate is around one establishment for every forty-three residents; only the major metropolitan areas of Miami and New York best the UAE's national rate. In the past, these small companies (many involved in re-export) were the bread and butter of the emirate's cultural economic landscape; now they take a back seat to attracting the big global players as well as media and tech firms, ranging from major conglomerates to startups. In other words, Dubai has been chasing the "right" kinds of "economic diversification" (admittedly, with some success) to the detriment of its already-existing diverse economies (and the nationals involved in sponsorship of these businesses, who are shut out of the new economic zones).

However, possibly the most niche Dubai small business I encountered was al Meher Recording music shop (fig. 6), whose operator—a Pakistani and lifelong Dubai resident—stocks primarily American crooner, cowboy music as well as Christmas albums from the late 1940s through the 1970s. The shop has a particular focus on Jim Reeves, who was one of the most internationally popular singers in that genre (Ghosh 2013). In

5. Mr. Shoekran shoe maker and repair shop near Bank Street, Dubai, 2005. The name "Shoekran" is a play on the Arabic word for "thank you," *shukran*. Photograph by the author.

the late 1990s and early 2000s, al Meher was written up in the *Khaleej Times, Gulf News, Time Out! Dubai, Emirates Evening Post,* and *Gulf Today* (the owner handed me photocopies of the articles—sans dates—when I came into the store and asked him some questions) as part of the celebration of this "unusual" emirate. Now, as the owner confirmed, the crowds who discovered his shop during a night out at the nearby hotels thinned as the city expanded and new nightlife options near the Burj al Arab emerged. A shop with his extremely select offerings (in the increasingly niche business of selling recorded music) could never afford rent in any of the malls (complete with their air-conditioned thoroughfares and ample parking), which dominate newer sections of Dubai and to which most of the emirate's even moderately well-heeled shoppers have fled. The type of landscape that can be found around Bank Street, much of it

6. Al Meher Recording, a Pakistani-resident-owned record store in Bur Dubai that specializes in country, jazz, and crooners from the 1940s through the 1970s, 2005. Photograph by the author.

scarcely three decades old, is no longer a top priority for the emirate (or for most places in the world, quite frankly).

Malls are *the* entities that led the charge away from Dubai's traditional heart on the Creek and out to its farthest reaches. The changes they wrought are many. Although the destroying of "downtown" retail by malls is a common phenomenon in many parts of the world, in Dubai it also left small re-exporters (who also did a little retail) a thinner slice of Dubai's consumer pie. Shop workers (as opposed to owners) might be paid slightly better in chain stores than in one-off shops, but it was the middle-income group of owners who were squeezed out by this switch. Yet the malls also created a more generalized consumer space with a more diverse clientele than most premall stores used to attract. It is to those malls that the next section turns.

Dubai after Malls

As I write, there are seven large shopping malls in Dubai, each with 150 shops or more—Deira City Centre and Festival City in Deira; BurJuman and Wafi City in Bur Dubai; Mall of the Emirates and Ibn Battuta Mall near Jebel Ali; and the Dubai Mall at the base of the Burj Khalifa. Ibn Battuta (fig. 7) is of particular note because it is elaborately decorated, with each section of the mall themed to resemble architecture from each different country that fourteenth-century explorer Ibn Battuta encountered on his journeys. Several other smaller plazas stand out. Lamcy Plaza (styled more like some shopping malls in India, where there are no walls between stores), Mercato (the Venice-themed mall), and the shops under Emirates Towers (very high-end luxury shops) are all in Bur Dubai. Souk Medinat Jumeirah (which is built to resemble a traditional Middle Eastern souk but with air-conditioning and no-haggle prices) and the Walk at Jumeirah Beach Residences (which is a resort-style shopping promenade) are near the Palm Jumeirah. In addition, thirty smaller malls can be found in many of Dubai's neighborhoods, and the major souks (textile, gold, spice, electronics) stretch along the Creek. In fact, most of these smaller indoor malls serve the function a strip-mall cluster would in the United States—to provide an array of frequently consumed goods in a location close to consumers.

Despite Dubai's glittering reputation, most people living there are not extraordinarily wealthy. Even though it is a city associated with excess, two retailers are by far the busiest: Carrefour, the French equivalent of Walmart (see fig. 8), and IKEA, whose Dubai store is the company's largest and most profitable branch in the Middle East (and possibly the most profitable store of any kind in the entire Middle East; Donnelly 2006;

7. The Starbucks at Persia Court in Ibn Battuta Mall, Dubai, 2007. Photograph by the author.

Middle East Economic Digest 2006). IKEA's success makes sense: in a city with a rapidly increasing population and proliferating amount of accommodation as well as a large number of people who believe they will be staying there only a few years and do not want to invest too much in furniture, IKEA's low prices and decent quality fit the bill.

What is striking about visiting IKEA and Carrefour is the mix of people one sees in them compared to the people who patronize more upscale malls such as the architecturally stunning BurJuman (see fig. 9), where

8. A multicultural, packed Carrefour store at the Mall of the Emirates, Dubai, 2005. Photograph by the author.

locals, Arabs, and Europeans tend to dominate and where the occasional Bollywood luminary can be spotted. BurJuman is dominated by luxury brands and anchored by a Saks Fifth Avenue, with only a small food court and no grocery or general-merchandise store—a lack that adds to its "luxury" air.[7] In Carrefour and IKEA, Filipinas and Indians shop alongside Arabs and Europeans. These big-box stores are among the few places in Dubai where the mingling of diverse groups actually happens. As much

7. Despite being one of Dubai's most dated malls and being in an unfashionable, traffic-jammed district of the city, BurJuman underwent a major expansion and renovation in the early 2000s. As it turned out, the Dubai Metro selected a location abutting BurJuman as the primary transfer station for the entire network—which makes one suspect that the owners of BurJuman knew this would happen well before the rest of the public and before it underwent that costly renovation and expansion.

9. BurJuman, an upscale mall in Bur Dubai, 2005. Photograph by the author.

as Dubai's rulers want to be known for upmarket brands such as Armani (who designed the hotel at the Burj Khalifa), Carrefour is in many ways Dubai's emblematic store.

Besides the big boxes, what one finds in the largest malls is primarily a mix of European and American midprice to luxury chain stores, dotted with a smaller number of one-off stores and outlets of local and regional chains. However, most of the major malls (following a practice established by the original Deira City Center) also have a corner dedicated to stores specializing in *abayas* (the black robes Gulf national women wear) and dishdashas (the mostly white robes Gulf national men wear). Usually the "national dress corridor" is outside of the main areas of foot traffic, often on a high floor, probably to provide national customers with privacy and to accommodate the lower margins on shops with a more limited clientele base (which is somewhat made up for by the fact that much of what they sell is quite expensive).

Although the main malls can be sites of mixing, the most striking example of a lack of mixing can be found in Karama, which is traditionally a South Asian neighborhood that has recently seen an influx of Filipinos. Along one of the major streets there are two small malls side by side (see figs. 10 and 11). The first one, the Karama Centre, has an almost exclusively Indian clientele and shops geared toward Indian consumers (for example, it has sari and bangle shops) as well as the usual (by Dubai standards) computer shop and cell phone shop. The other, the al-Attar Centre, has an almost exclusively Filipino clientele and contains a pool hall and a popular Filipino restaurant.

That images of South Asians are absent from any particular mall is not surprising. Just as South Asians are sometimes (though far from always) erased from the face of prominent companies in the emirate, they also get marginalized within the consumer space. Multiple South Asian retail chains are present within the cityscape of Dubai, such as sweets maker

10. Karama Centre, a shopping mall geared toward a South Asian clientele, 2005. Photograph by the author.

11. Al-Attar Centre, next door to Karama Centre but geared toward a Filipino clientele, 2005. Photograph by the author.

Bikanervala, as well as local chains such as Chicken Tikka Inn and hundreds of one-off shops and restaurants. In the mall-based (as opposed to neighborhood) retail spaces of Dubai, South Asian shops and advertisements are far less prominent. Of the largest shopping malls in Dubai I visited during my 2005 visit—Mall of the Emirates, Deira City Centre, Ibn Battuta Mall, Wafi City, and BurJuman—only Ibn Battuta mall had a pair of stores that sold South Asian fashions. *That means only two stores out of more than one thousand in Dubai at the time sold South Asian fashions in a city that is at least half South Asian.* By contrast, about forty stores in those malls sold *abaya*s. Granted, South Asian men outside of construction generally wear "Western" dress, and South Asian women vary clothing by workplace and individual preference. For South Asian women's fashion, it is also unlikely the prices offered in Dubai's malls would beat those available on the nearby subcontinent (or even in Bur Dubai's shops). Still, the gap in numbers is unexpectedly large.

South and Southeast Asians also figure very little in the advertising for government-backed projects such as condo developments and the annual Shopping Festival. In my time in Dubai, except for one banner featuring the renowned Indian actor Amitabh Bachchan that hung on the al Ghurair City mall and a billboard featuring Aishwarya Rai, I do not remember seeing any other billboard or large advertisement in which an identifiably South Asian person was featured prominently (although I can think of a handful where they appeared in mixed-group shots)—despite the fact that South Asians make up the majority of those on the road. These billboards, of which there are hundreds, promote everything from real estate and shopping malls to soft drinks and cell phones yet feature few South Asians, despite the fact that, in the case of cell phones, 95 percent of UAE residents own one (*Gulf News* 2005), which means most South Asians own one.

The lack of a visual presence of Dubai's majority group likely has multiple causes. One explanation is that the South Asian community has genuinely different shopping habits. Despite the recent growth of malls, until 2011 India had very strict retail regulation that protected smaller merchants by limiting foreign investment in retail. Thus, anyone from India has more familiarity with visiting one-off shops than someone who grew up where large chains dominate. However, another explanation undoubtedly has to do with the values that underlie the nationality-based wage system. Whatever the job category is, South Asian labor in Dubai lies at the low end of the pay scale. So although there are plenty of well-off and moderately well-off South Asians in Dubai, they are not the "aspirational" figure in any income tier owing to the structures of feeling concerning the value of South Asian labor—UAE nationals and Europeans are. Advertising tends to be nothing if not "aspirational."

Certainly, Dubai-as-idea is also about aspiration, and its high-end, architecturally stunning malls are a part of that. But most malls in Dubai are more than places to spend large amounts of money—they are diverse public spaces (to the extent there are such things in Dubai) and spaces of economic transition that are far from identical to one another. They are also places of wide selection and even bargains. Just as in other countries, there are many uses for malls (Goss 1999) in the Gulf, perhaps more so because the relative lack of big-box strip-mall plazas forces people to bump into each other when traveling between stores. Malls are often dismissed as the height of sameness, and their prevalence in the Gulf is usually seen as one more strike against the region's vibrancy. The stores may repeat themselves, but if one looks closely, one can see that the malls display as much complexity as the Gulf wage system.

But one "mall" is so relatively different from the others that it bears mentioning in its own section because it shows the evolving diversity of Gulf economies: Dragon Mart.

Vignette D: Dubai's Chinatown?

Dragon Mart (see fig. 12) is located in International City, a freehold development located on the road to the Oman border and built by Nakheel, which is backed by the Dubai government. The mixed residential and retail zone was meant eventually to house sixty thousand people. International City's design concept seems to have involved blocks of nearly identical, balconied, four- to five-story apartment buildings, surrounded by parking lots—the only differentiation being that the apartment buildings in each "cluster" of the development are painted a unique color and utilize slightly different trim to signify nations such as England, Russia, India, and Spain. It was by far the most affordably priced development in Dubai in the mid-2000s; one-bedroom apartments can be purchased for $100,000 in today's (2013) market.

Besides mild trim and color differentiation, what primarily makes International City "international" is the presence of Dragon Mart. It was envisioned as a semipermanent trade show where Chinese factories could set up booths for the purpose of meeting importers from around the world while doing some direct-to-consumer retail. The idea was to use the cachet of Dubai's landscape to build deeper links to China, which is the emirate's number-one source of imports, especially those items Dubai later re-exports (Emirates News Agency 2008). Or as then Nakheel chairman Sultan Ahmad Bin Sulayem described it, "The Dragon Mart is Nakheel's acknowledgment of China's influence in international trade and commerce and will create a space for traders and entrepreneurs from

12. Dragon Mart during opening week, 2005. Photograph by the author.

the mainland to offer their services to the lucrative Middle East markets" (quoted in *Gulf News* 2004). Dragon Mart was meant to provide a beachhead in Dubai for Chinese business networks, which had previously lacked an extensive presence in the emirate—or at least that was what it was supposed to do. Instead, it became something rather different.

One of the ways Dragon Mart is different from other malls is who staffs it. Although Filipinas are most studied in this region for their role in care giving (see Brochmann 1993; Moors 2003; Silvey 2004), during the time I did my research in Dubai their presence was obvious in other areas of the service sector—notably internationally brand fast-food chains, all but the most expensive restaurants, hotels, and malls. Indeed, the sound of a bored-looking Filipina saying, "Hello, sir," as I walked past a customer-less mall store was a common Dubai occurrence. In contrast, at Dragon Mart all the workers I spoke to were from China.

This mall's material structure stands out as well. The Dragon Mart building is a 1.2-kilometer-long series of hangars, shaped like the winding body of a dragon. A single aisle runs its entire length, flanked on either side by at least six rows of white, roughly twenty-by-twenty-foot cubicles, with sections of larger cubicles near exits. Each booth is allegedly connected to one factory—some are distinguished by their names, such as "Rambo Domination Import & Export Company," and others by their mix of products, such as the store Shanghai Forever, which sells artificial turf, bicycle parts, and bowling pins.

However, the most striking thing about Dragon Mart when I visited it shortly after its opening to nonwholesalers in March 2005 was that it was mostly empty (fig. 13)—empty of customers, empty of employees, empty of cubicle content (especially after the first half-kilometer). In those early days, I remember seeing lines of freshly arrived Chinese workers at the management office who had been recruited in China and given visas to work specifically at Dragon Mart. The only problem was there was not much to do. I did see a few home furnishing/fixture companies and a few construction equipment manufacturers striking deals, but by and large the place was devoid of customers. The Chinese workers I talked to were generally frustrated, not knowing what or even if they could sell to retail customers. Many had few connections in Dubai (given that the city had a relatively small Chinese community), and bus service to Dragon Mart was infrequent, leaving them trapped in the desert. The workers mostly just wandered around the building.

In fall 2005, things at Dragon Mart were beginning to shake out. Even more booths were empty; some were abandoned with their wares inside and eviction notices on the door. Many booths had some wares but no clerks—only a phone number on the door. I wondered if the whole thing was going to go under in spite of the fanfare with which it had opened. Like the Aramis project Bruno Latour (1996) studied, the chains of translation did not appear strong enough to sustain Dragon Mart—not enough importers wanted to sift through the mountains of mismatched products of unknown brand, and many stands were too idiosyncratic to sustain retail. Building a landscape meant to connect China and Dubai's traders is one thing; sustaining it is something different. Indeed, the mammoth overbuild of Dragon Mart turned out to have been a sign of things to come for the emirate's real-estate sector.

13. Empty stores two-thirds of a kilometer into Dragon Mart, 2005. Photograph by the author.

Fast-forward to May 2007: The situation actually seemed to be looking up. Admittedly, more of the stands in the now obviously oversize building were closed, but the ones that remained open seemed more alive (and clustered together). Several firms expanded to control multiple booths, so there was some hope of economies of scale. More lanterns had been hung from the ceiling, and lights had been draped from signs—the whole place looked less sterile and more lived in. Dragon Mart also seemed to have found its niche—as a home base for the sale of cheap toys and various counterfeit products. Many shops sold replica versions of iPods, and customers seemed to come—not in huge numbers—but they came nonetheless. This fact was confirmed by the *Gulf News*, which noted "a raid on a stall in Dragon Mart yielded 4,500 fake Casio watches and 4,500 pieces of assorted brands of USB flash drives and memory sticks" (Hilotin 2007). When I came back in 2009, the situation remained similarly positive, with the addition of a new section dedicated to wholesale furniture meant to outfit offices, hotels, and multiple condo units—which was a smart move given the amount of construction happening in the Gulf. A wall had been built to close off access to the empty back half of the structure. Although the product mix was slightly different, it reminded me of the Karama Souk, an "Old Dubai" institution—only with East Asians instead of South Asians as the staff and an emphasis on knock-off electronics and toys over watches and purses. (See fig. 14.)

But more than what was being sold, I noticed that the Chinese workers were conversing with each other, setting up folding chairs outside their shops. Some other people just seemed to be there hanging out. The whole thing appeared much less grim than when it first opened. Whatever the original intention might have been, Dragon Mart had undoubtedly become Dubai's Chinatown. The lamp posts around the parking lot were covered in fliers adorned in Chinese characters; if you looked at balconies on nearby buildings, you saw laundry drying. Many of those original

14. More settled in at Dragon Mart in the summer of 2009. Photograph by the author.

workers who did not go home had filtered into Dubai's economy—for example, during my 2007 and 2009 trips, my apartment was visited many times by door-to-door Chinese salespeople, mostly hawking pirated DVDs.

These workers' grassroots efforts to establish a foothold were paralleled by UAE and Dubai government initiatives. For major infrastructure projects in Dubai, Chinese construction firms that import Chinese labor are becoming an increasingly common choice. Dubai's ruler, Sheikh Mohammed, has established an executive training program exchange, which brings promising Chinese MBAs to the Gulf to get more familiar with business there and sends Gulf MBAs to China. Spots are reserved for Chinese students at New York University Abu Dhabi, and several new Chinese-language academies are situated within the UAE educational system. Despite the official push, path making for the new Chinese community has not been straightforward. For example, when Dragon Mart workers tried to celebrate the Year of the Pig, they were forbidden from naming or depicting pigs so as not to cause offense (Issa 2007).

Although one wonders how much money is in bootleg DVD and unbranded toy sales, in just a few years a group of people had established a foothold (albeit precariously) in this city. They created a Chinatown in a generic apartment suburb out of an automobile-plant-size failed import center. Indeed, Nakheel recently announced it was "expanding" Dragon Mart—only this time, it will be a neighborhood-level mall with a Geant hypermarket, the usual chain restaurants, a few retail chains from China, and a section (in the original spirit of Dragon Mart) selling bridal and wedding supplies directly from Chinese manufacturers. In other words, it will have mostly stores that help the Chinese population live more comfortably in the emirate.

Dragon Mart's transformation says a great deal about homemaking in Gulf landscapes. But it also says a great deal about cultural economic hierarchies: only with China can one imagine a sort of permanent trade exhibition being dreamed up (and prioritized over existing East African and South Asian re-exporters that were already entrenched in older parts of the emirate). But success comes only with strong networks, which China did not have in the Gulf (especially since many Chinese manufacturers produce components and the Gulf manufactures very little). For all the talk of Chinese success in the global economy, Chinese nationals found themselves struggling to fit into the slightly differently imagined hierarchies of the Gulf, where other Asian communities are much more firmly established. This gap is not likely to be a permanent obstacle—especially considering that Dragon Mart was just the first of many efforts by the UAE government to promote a connection to China.

What is also admirable about Dragon Mart (and International City) is that it is the first new district of Dubai that isn't either high end or a labor camp. The model that justified building a thousand twenty-by-twenty-foot stores in a series of hangars seems hard to conjure in hindsight, but it ended up creating a big space and an opportunity for Chinese immigrants to make something happen. It is the sandbox of free play compared to the more regimented free zones Dubai attempted in sectors such as media production, publishing, gold, health care, and the like. It is unlikely to produce any single economy-shifting company or product, but it does provide small opportunities for people to make a living—the exact type of diverse economies that flourished in Dubai prior to the 1990s and that the emirate should encourage more. The opportunity presented by Dragon Mart is something that at least has the potential (but not the inevitability) of being a good thing. And whereas an indoor ski slope is in keeping with the "it" of Dubai mentioned in the previous chapter, Dragon Mart—though far less spectacular—demonstrates some of the too often obscured pluckiness of an urban population that created a district dedicated to the sale of automobile seat covers.

Vignette E: Ramadan

During the Holy Month of Ramadan, when Muslims who are physically able should fast from sunup to sundown, the rhythms of the Gulf's cultural economies change. In Saudi Arabia, all nonessential government services practically shut down for the whole month; in Oman, bars close down. Even in the UAE, nonretail and food-service working hours are reduced to six hours per day. This shortening of the workday theoretically includes laborers (but not household workers), regardless of whether the person is a Muslim or not.

During my stays in Dubai, because I was a non-Muslim without family in the emirate, life seeming "less hectic" was my primary experience of Ramadan. Yet English-language newspapers and guidebooks so prepare their readers for what are promised to be overwhelming changes during Ramadan that it is easy to for non-Muslims to develop a siege mentality in anticipation. Even the normally fairly sane expat-centric magazine *Time Out Dubai* foretold a major event when I was there in 2005, where every move made in public during daylight hours would be fraught with the potential to cause major offense. According to *Time Out Dubai*, the following actions are among those that should be refrained from for the duration of Ramadan: "Don't smoke, drink, chew gum or eat in public in the hours between sunrise and sunset. It's not only seen as offensive but could get you a warning or even a short spell in jail for any flagrant flouting of the rules. This goes for any place which is open to the public gaze, including your car, the beach and your garden if it is open to the roadside" (Madsen 2005, 10). The article also warned residents not to dance, sing, "play loud music," or "swear." Despite this lengthy list (of which I quoted only half), an article sharing the same page noted that "in the U.A.E., Ramadan is not quite so evident as in some areas" (Montague 2005). Lonely Planet's guide to Dubai offered a similar list, noting that "it is unlikely you will be arrested for breaking these rules, as you would be in Saudi Arabia" (Callan 2000, 60).

Now some of this is reader education (i.e., asking people in *extremely* detailed ways not to draw unnecessary attention to themselves and cause a distraction during what many consider to be a sacred time). It is likely that authorities attempt to distribute these rules widely and ask publications to share them every year with the admirable goal of helping everyone get along. But the execution of educational efforts creates the perception of a bunker mentality and promotes the idea that Ramadan is a time of unusual denials and difference. Or, to put it another way, the impression struck among the uninitiated is that Ramadan turns Dubai into something a little more like what the rest of the Gulf is thought to be—extremely somber.

Perhaps the authorities were less strict in 2005 than previously, but Ramadan really did not transform Dubai into an enforced-hunger police state as the articles intimated, which no one who has ever lived in Muslim-majority place would find at all surprising. For sure, routines change, but non-Muslims are hardly made unwelcome, and the government forces no one to fast (although many non-Muslims choose to do so at least once during the month). Many people have more time off than before, despite the monetary cost. By the UAE central bank's estimate, the six-hour work-day enforced during Ramadan (which is two hours shorter than the "official" UAE workday) cost the UAE nearly $90 billion in lost productivity in 2004 (Rahman 2005b). Even Saudi Arabia recently moved its week-end from Thursday–Friday to Friday–Saturday to keep in better contact with transnational business—showing that money matters are increasingly trumping established religious routines in the Gulf. Yet Dubai continues to observe Ramadan by letting everyone off work early—a bit of wasting that is broadly (as opposed to narrowly) shared.

There is debate about the merits of this policy. Some segments of Dubai's Muslim population (both local and foreign) would be quite upset if government regulation of holiday hours were to disappear. Others feel Ramadan has been made too easy. In 2005, *Gulf News* ran an excellent article, "Officials Differ over Ramadan Rules" (al Nowais 2005), in which officials at the UAE Ministry of Labour—which decrees Ramadan work-ing hours—openly disagreed with each other on the record about whether the reduced workday during Ramadan was a good thing. One official argued that the law was fine as is, saying, "Seven or eight hours of work is too much. Even if they are in air-conditioned offices people are still fast-ing." Another official argued that "Ramadan is not a time to slack off and be lazy. . . . People hardly do any work[,] using the excuse that they are fast-ing." He went on: "It is not discrimination if hours are reduced for Mus-lims only."[8] One of my Lebanese Muslim informants who had previously worked in the United States agreed with the notion that the reduced hours were bad not because productivity was reduced but because the shorter

---

8. Reducing the number of hours worked only for Muslims during Ramadan will likely never happen because if only Muslims were to be given time off, some companies would simply stop hiring Muslims in order to maintain productivity.

workday "takes away some of the struggle. Part of Ramadan is sacrifice and feeling accomplished for having committed to the fast. If you get to sleep half the time it is light, then it does not mean so much."

Many non-Muslims have also become attached to what the Dubai media refer to as "the festive season." The time off in the afternoons (and lack of late working nights) is appreciated. On the first night of Ramadan, my flatmates and I shared the Iftar meal (that breaks the fast), despite only one of us being Muslim. Another of my eastern European informants had been fasting during Ramadan since she arrived in Dubai in 2004 to "feel clean." *Gulf News* documents similar reactions from a variety of non-Muslims on an annual basis. One Indian Hindu noted that when his family had seen "the wonders fasting does for [Muslims], both for their body and their character, we realized fasting is about more than mere abstinence from food." Alternatively, they quoted a British woman as saying, "I think it's a nice month. It is something to respect and it's a very sociable month. Through business we do Iftar with clients and I usually go with friends—it's just a nice thing to do" (*Gulf News* 2007).

Landscapes of Ramadan in Dubai are far different from the repressive images some outsiders may have of Muslim societies. Generally, they function on the following principle: if someone is going to break the fast, as long as he or she does it out of sight, it is out of mind. Thus, street-visible vending machines are turned off during Ramadan (including those that sell inexpensive bottles of water, which is a hardship for some), but convenience stores are open. Similarly, restaurants cannot have people visibly dining in them from sunup until sundown. However, most nonchain restaurants—predominantly Indian and Chinese—offer special take-away box lunches during Ramadan, which people of many different nationalities purchase (see fig. 15). McDonald's utilizes the same system—food can be ordered but not eaten there. Contrary to the policy of some other Gulf countries, the grocery stores in Dubai (at least the major ones such as Spinneys) remain open even during the daylight hours. So unless a worksite expressly forbids eating (or food is not provided, as inevitably happens to some laborers and domestic servants)—food and drink are accessible. By slightly modifying the rules of the landscape, consumption is allowed to continue—the Muslim landscape is visible, the slightly hidden landscape

15. Man walking with a carryout lunch purchased during Ramadan in Karama, Dubai, 2005. Photograph by the author.

is where non-Muslims can do (mostly) as they please. It is the application of the hotel ideal to the country as whole.

Two sites at extreme ends of the economic spectrum demonstrate how Ramadan is practiced through the landscape in Dubai. The first is the Internet City and Media City complex. This is how lunch works there: at the CNN building, which is one of the most easily accessible buildings in the complex since it is situated on the centerpiece lake, there are a couple of restaurants and a coffee shop. The bagel shop as well as the little Italian restaurant next door put big black tarps over their entrances and draw the blinds down on their windows. These restaurants are completely hidden from casual glances; you would have to really, really try to see people eating. Farther into the development, at the big Internet City food court—where there is Subway sandwich shop, a Chinese buffet-service restaurant, and several take-away counters—wooden screens are put up between the lobby of the building and the food court, which partly obstructs the view (see fig. 16). Because there is nowhere near enough indoor seating available for everyone, people eat at the tables in the patio area in the back of the building—visible to those who happen to be walking by but not exposed to the vast majority of the development. However, in a distant building with only a few restaurants on the edge of the Internet City (where you would probably go only if you had to, unlike in the case of the more centrally located buildings), there are no screens or blinds or tarps covering up the restaurants, and people can just walk in and eat in full view. In other words, as with so much else in Dubai (such as bars in

16. Partially screened food court in Dubai's Internet City during Ramadan, 2005. Photograph by the author.

hotels), the less visible the space, the less that is prohibited. Accommodation and visibility are often inversely proportional.

Even people without the means to order takeout from restaurants or enjoy meals at Internet City food courts are able to eat if they choose to do so. At this other end of the economic spectrum is the bus station, where those who work in smaller establishments have to go to get home. Even though its inexpensive cafeteria is closed, little stands selling baked and fried goods and water are allowed to be open, provided they are nominally hidden behind a tarp (see fig. 17). Also, people can go to the interior courtyard of the bus station and eat and drink. Although they are not totally invisible there, the space suffices to hide them enough.

But that is during the day. When the sun goes down, consumption returns to the open. Car accidents go up by 50 percent during Ramadan,

17. Tables marginally hidden by tarps, where merchants are selling samosas and other fried goods at the Bur Dubai Bus Station during Ramadan, 2005. Photograph by the author.

mostly owing to low blood sugar and hurried drivers (al Theeb 2005). These accidents occur in bunches mostly around 2:00 p.m., when people return from work, and then right after sundown, when people are rushing to get to a restaurant. As in many Muslim majority countries, hotels offer stupendously lavish dinner buffets during Ramadan: the offerings at most international-class properties cost upward of $80 per person, feature various Arabic, Indian, and Western cuisines, and include the opportunity to smoke a flavored tobacco *sheesha* (water pipe) in a lounge area. The big, established South Asian restaurants also convert to supersize buffets, with nearly every regional dish available plus a huge dessert table—but with a more modest price tag of about $20 for adults and $10 for children. Almost everyone at these buffets is dressed up and spends hours socializing in large groups. Nationals (and others) also set up Iftar tents—sometimes out in the desert, sometimes on vacant lots—to enjoy breaking the fast with family and friends.

Even more accessible is the food provided by the Indian Muslim Association of Dubai (see fig. 18). Every night of Ramadan in mosques, parks, and bus stations across Dubai, the association provides a free meal to anyone who wants one (although in practice it is overwhelmingly men who take the meals), whether Muslim or not. Meals are provided in both sit-down and take-away forms. Some stands even provide vegetarian meals for Hindus. This service—which feeds up to five thousand people—is actually one of the most brilliant things done for laborers in Dubai—making the landscape communal in ways it rarely is. It is also part of wider trans–Indian Ocean charity and patronage networks that involve some of India's more successful Gulf migrants (Osella and Osella 2009).

As mentioned previously, the malls also have Ramadan sales and late closing times, with shops open until midnight and food served until two or three in the morning—something that represents a bit of novelty for patrons and long, late shifts for workers. The malls also have big displays set up for Ramadan (see fig. 19). Most depict "traditional" camp life, although BurJuman once had a giant, rotating copy of the Quran in one of its atria.

That being said, objections to the consumption-centered landscapes that emerge during Ramadan have been raised. A significant segment of

18. Iftar at the bus station in Bur Dubai, where meat *briyani* (spiced rice) is being served during Ramadan, 2005. Photograph by the author.

the population dislikes the overcommercialization of Ramadan (just as similar segments of other religions dislike the commercialization of their particular religion's holidays), feeling that shopping sprees and hundred-dollar buffets distract from the spiritual reflection the month is supposed to encourage. The *Gulf News* runs a piece on the topic almost every year. One of these pieces quoted a cleric from Fujairah, who worried about the overindulgence that has come to be associated with the holiday: "When the human body is weighed down with food and material objects the soul will likewise be tied down and empty, but when the body is bare and light so will the soul be, and that's how people should approach Ramadan" (Ali 2007). In another article, a prayer leader from Al Ain worried about all the food wasted during Ramadan, suggesting that "many people wrongly consider Ramadan a festive season. Such an attitude means they have lost the real concept behind the month. They should not waste their time in idle talk, watching television, and getting involved in activities that are

19. Desert camp scene on display to celebrate Ramadan in Wafi City Mall, Dubai, 2005. Photograph by the author.

part of non-Muslim traditions and celebrations" (quoted in Kazmi 2006). But then again there is a significant camp that enjoys what is on offer and participates in Bataille's process of spectacular social wasting—malls see a 22 percent increase in business over the month before Ramadan, and gold and diamond sales jump 30 percent (Rahman 2005a).

Of course, this happens in many Muslim-majority countries, especially in urban areas. Ramadan at night is a festive time of visiting family and enjoying food and sweets. But the festiveness of Ramadan rarely breaks into the imagined geographies held by outsiders. Fasting as denial takes precedence in those external imaginaries, which misses the fact that Islamic holidays are like most religious holidays and so combine the sacred and contemplative with the familial and enjoyable.

But speaking to the point of this book, Ramadan demonstrates the multiple configurations of Dubai's cultural economic landscapes. There is charity from fellow migrants and time off for many. Many non-Muslims (both rich and poor) can find spaces to eat if they choose not to fast, even if some of these spaces are quite makeshift. There are differing ideas about how much consumption should go with the holiday, and a great deal of Ramadan- and Eid-themed shopping takes place. As mentioned in the opening of this chapter, all of the productions that surround Ramadan (and those that surround wages, malls, and reliable infrastructure) are tangential to the story of Dubai as rentier oil state or Dubai as transshipment capital. But these productions are happening in the emirate, and they involve nearly all of those who live there. So why are these processes of enjoyment, sharing, and waste excluded from Dubai's cultural economic story?

The first seven chapters of the book were spent outlining the terrain wrought by market Orientalism—the process through which Gulf economies came to be imagined as the bad version of "normal" markets within structures of feeling while providing opportunities for profit and chances to feel superior. This chapter managed to highlight yet more ways the Gulf is positioned outside of orthodoxy: it has diversity that is supposedly met with closedness; it has holidays that are supposedly about having less instead of more. But this chapter also moved beyond these oppositions to show a few of the complexities of the Gulf's diverse economies that are reducible neither to standard political economy nor to the work of market Orientalism.

My intention has not been to praise the Gulf and declare it trouble free. For example, similarly qualified people should not be paid differently for the same job in the same place because of where they are from (or because of their gender). No one should be forced to work; theft should not happen. Furthermore, Gulf countries could do more to highlight their extremely real human diversity and to facilitate less-splashy types of economic diversity. But that human diversity is there, and so is that economic diversity, and both are part of the story. There are places in the Gulf, such as the box-store Carrefour, that reproduce very globally common consumption patterns but produce new relations in cities such as Dubai; other initiatives such as Dragon Mart are emergent (if not terribly lucrative).

People generally get paid more in Dubai than they do at home, and many enjoy the benefits of a well-maintained infrastructure. If we are ever to get past the routine binary condemnations and the forms of distinction they enable, we must be willing to see beyond the usual economic suspects.

I made the case in this chapter that in the future places like the Gulf can and should be thought of differently. However, as it turns out, even the Gulf's future is all too often scripted as likely to produce a steady stream of more of the same.

9

Gulf Futures

About a decade ago, chronicler of the urban condition Mike Davis turned his attention to Dubai. Davis's essay "Sinister Paradise: Does the Road to the Future End in Dubai?" (2005) was both beautifully worded and for a few years probably the most widely circulated work on Dubai or any Gulf city by someone widely read in academia (for example, it was forwarded to me at least a half-dozen times). It is a breathlessly written thirteen paragraphs. In it, he highlighted many aspects of what would come to be known as the "Dubai model"—the marketing of the emirate, its many free zones and low taxes, its hodgepodge of architecture, its quest to collect the biggest of everything, and the abuse of labor that occurs there. But if others were calling Dubai a model, Davis considered it an ill one, referring to it as "not just a hybrid but a chimera: the offspring of the lascivious coupling of the cyclopean fantasies."

However, for all its brilliant wordplay, Davis's article remained a rehash of good and bad hype about Dubai and the Gulf. It was a polemic (albeit from a true and much appreciated polemic master) that (1) looked at Dubai out of context (not fully appreciating why it built big to get the world's attention), (2) occasionally reinforced Orientalist stereotypes (refer-ring to the Burj Dubai as the "Tower of Babel"), and (3) too easily mapped Dubai as the fantasy of neoliberalism come true, which either relies on a loose definition of neoliberalism or severely underestimates the enormous, long-term presence of the al-Maktoum-led state in the economy and the delivery of welfare (which predated neoliberalism). Davis, like most com-mentators, highlighted all of Dubai's extremes but passed over its banal-ity—proposing that labor camps disturbed the image of a city "without slums or poverty" and thus brushing aside the hundreds of thousands of working-class and middle-class people there.

That Davis painted Dubai in broad brushstrokes is not why I give his essay attention here; countless others have done that as well. More to the point, much as he did with Los Angeles in his book *City of Quartz: Excavating the Future in Los Angeles* (1990), he also used Dubai as vehicle to critique trajectories in wider urban political economy. In other words, Dubai provided him a chance to talk about the future of cities, which Davis views as increasingly dystopian. In his essay on Dubai, Davis answered his titular question by deciding that, yes, the road to the future does indeed end in the emirate and that it will be lined with both seven-star hotels for the global economy's "pampered mercenaries" and labor camps for the serf majority. For Davis, this future will not be something totally new but instead a resurrection of a horrible, Gilded Age past. In looking for a paradigmatic example for future trends in a newly high-profile city, Davis was far from the first to attempt such a maneuver. Thus, in using Dubai as an example, he carried on a long tradition of utilizing the upending of cultural economic hierarchy as a chance to prognosticate about a day of reckoning (for either "our" place or "theirs").

This final chapter summarizes some of the key ideas from this book, but it also focuses on how structures of feeling concerning "the future" stand as one of the primary terrains through which market Orientalism produces positional superiority in the present.

In an odd way, Davis actually had a sunny outlook on the Gulf's prospects compared to the outlook of many commentators who write about Gulf futures. He did not see the Dubai model as an aberration that is doomed to fail due to its unorthodoxy, as so many have. In fact, Davis proposed that Dubai's successful horribleness will eventually enslave us all! Over the years, others have felt the same way. As noted in chapter 5, there was a brief time in the 1970s when the Gulf was thought to contain smooth operators. Gulf leaders were viewed as possessing an oil weapon and having built up enough postcolonial resentment to use it. People from the Gulf were thought to be buying all the nice real estate in London along with all the fancy paintings. Certainly, the tone varies among those bullish on the Gulf's prospects: some feel the Gulf is sinister; others anxiously settle on the idea that Gulf rulers will be odd but OK overlords. Some more thoughtful observers, such as Yasser Elsheshtawy (2010), think the Gulf's impact as a model is primarily on the wider Middle East as opposed to on the entire globe.

But ultimately the idea that the Gulf is on a path to permanent preeminence is nearly always short-lived. Several statements from other writers show how the tide turned concerning Dubai's prospects over the course of sixteen months starting in mid-2008:

> But as the deepening bite of the credit crisis spreads from Wall Street and takes a global toll—torpedoing once-buoyant markets from Shanghai to Stockholm—the Gate [the centerpiece of Dubai Financial Centre] has recently become an even more powerful beacon for a swarm of deal makers looking to stake their claim in one of the world's last remaining bull markets. (Thomas 2008)

> For a few hours, the glitz and the glamour, the red carpet and, above all, the astonishing fireworks disguised the reality that is dawning over Dubai—but only for those few hours. Not even the £13.5 million extravaganza that launched the £1 billion Atlantis Resort could hide the fact that Dubai's property boom, which has fuelled double-digit growth for five years, is showing signs of turning to bust. (Verma 2008)

> With the benefit of hindsight—and you didn't need much—there were plenty of other signs back then that Dubai was building a financial mirage in the desert. . . . It's a pretty good bet that a city with an average temperature of 90 degrees and an indoor ski slope is probably living a little too large. . . . They were the places most likely to write a quick billion-dollar check; their eagerness should have also been a tip-off. (Sorkin 2009)

Although the progression of quotes does a nice job of demonstrating the changing tide of opinion that Dubai weathered, so to do the titles of the articles they came from: "Boom Times Take Root in Dubai" (Thomas 2008), "First Came a Boom, Then Fireworks, but Is Dubai's Property Market in Trouble" (Verma 2008), and, finally, "A Financial Mirage in the

Desert" (Sorkin 2009). So even as late as the summer of 2008 (a full four months after the disintegration of Bear Stearns alerted the world that all might not be alright in the realms of banking and real estate), one article was proclaiming that the Dubai boom was here to stay. Smart, architecturally interesting megaprojects such as the Gate were still in the works in Dubai, which the article deemed as having a "welcoming social" climate and a "serious" economy based on finance and trade. Then four months later, some doubt—Dubai was no longer bold but "glitzy" and *might* be headed toward a bust. Then one year later Dubai's flaws leaped off the desert plane to heights that exceeded even the world's tallest building. Dubai was no longer just friendly and fun; it was trivial. It promised too much; it aimed too high. It even built a ski slope in the desert. Beyond that, as the last reporter claimed, *New York Times* readers should have known that "project Dubai" was always already doomed to fail.

As Robin Bloch put it in her thorough overview of Dubai's financial trouble, the collapse of the real estate market in Dubai was met with "a mixture of shock and *schadenfreude*" (2010). Her excellent article goes into the details of Dubai's economic intangibles and explains why the wider political economic currents that led to the bubble should not have left people shocked, but my focus in this book has instead been on the schadenfreude. This feeling that Dubai had received its comeuppance, which—although not universally shared—was experienced not just by English-language reporters but also by some in Dubai and in other parts of the Arabic-speaking world (notably Beirut and Cairo, the region's long-established cultural economic capitals). This idea of the future, wherein the Gulf will finally be made to pay for being a successful contradiction, does work in the structures of feeling that maintain positional superiority. By turning to the terrain of the future, a shift is performed wherein present circumstances no longer matter and almost any argument can be put forth because the future has not yet happened. As the phenomenon of the permanent media punditry class demonstrates, there tend to be few consequences for making consistently wrong prognostications—and those few do not include the loss of one's outlet for making the wrong prognostications.

Dubai's reputational collapse—from future star to inevitable victim of economic law—is hardly unique in the annals of postoil Gulf history. One or another place in the Gulf at one time or another is said to be poised to radically upend cultural economic hierarchies. But the majority of the time the future is held to be a day of reckoning for the region. Unsurprisingly, this narrative of inevitable blowback was established fairly early on. The article "Riches Changing Saudi Life," already highlighted in chapter 4, intoned in the late 1950s: "The feudal and religious dynamic of the old desert kingdom, in fact, is no match for the commerce and technology of the twentieth century. . . . In Jeddah, where there is still history to contend with, one has the impression amid the ugly mixture of raw novelty and crumbling age of witnessing a spiritual as well as a material holocaust" (*Times* [London] 1958).

Thus, *as early as the 1950s* Saudi Arabia and its seemingly peculiar ways were going to be swept away by "commerce and technology": a "holocaust" for its entire way of life was said to be nearing. Although Saudi Arabia changed a great deal over the decades, that often predicted radical cataclysm never came. But the repeated lack of a cataclysm is apparently no reason to stop making predictions of a future one, as a selection concerning Saudi Arabia from the 2002 *Economist* "Survey of the Gulf" demonstrates. Keep in mind this article was written some forty-three years after the *Times* piece: "With the [Saudi] government's budget chronically in the red even without such extra outlays, and the post-September oil-price slump adding further urgency, the only hope is to open up the economy, fast. 'The country is at a critical juncture,' says the manager of a regional investment fund. 'It can coast along without radical changes for only one or two years, maximum.' . . . To one degree or another, all the Gulf states suffer similar problems" (Rodenbeck 2002). More than four decades had passed, and the story had barely changed (even if the level of vitriol was reduced). Saudi Arabia is never to be allowed off the edge of oblivion. The idea that Saudi Arabia has been a thoroughly contemporary, fairly stable state that enforces extremely conservative social policies—rather than a living anachronism soon to drown in its unorthodoxy—rarely gets as much attention.

This 2002 article discussing the imminent collapse of Saudi Arabia's cultural economy within "one or two years" was followed by the biggest run-up in oil prices since the 1970s. The run-up allowed Saudi Arabia to begin to build again, along much the same model as before (some money for high-profile, internationally focused sectors, some for royal patronage, and some for mass employment). In fact, Bahrain—which that same article praised for "diversifying" into niches outside of oil—was the Gulf state most destabilized by the Arab Spring. To be fair, the *Economist* survey raised quite a few valid points. For example, it noted that Saudi Arabia has the expense of covering a much bigger territory with many more people, which is in part the reason why it is less rich per capita than its smaller neighbors. It also mentioned that the added political weight of an influential clergy and the large and diverse royal family make policy changes slower to conjure for the kingdom. However, despite briefly seeing Saudi Arabia in context, the article fell again into old tropes—that the whole system will be crushed by modernity (or postmodernity or globalization) and that problems across the Gulf are deep down all the same.

But they are not the same, nor are they unchanging, and even the media record reflects this variety. As earlier chapters showed, the late 1960s was a time that Saudi Arabia was the "sick man" of the Gulf, a status it returned to by the early 2000s. But the 1980s through the mid-1990s were particularly bad for Kuwait. Remember, it was Kuwait, from almost the first moment oil was extracted, that was deemed the best of the Gulf bunch. This view set it up for a fall. This fall began in 1982 with the collapse of the Souk al-Manakh, which was an extremely loosely regulated but highly capitalized unofficial stock market located in Kuwait City. Its implosion led to a front-page *Washington Post* headline that read "The Eagles of the Gulf Have Crashed" (Ottoway 1982). Much subsequent ink was devoted to how "shadowy" the market was, how it was the result of a lack of "normal" private-investment opportunity in Kuwait, how many average Kuwaiti citizens liked to "gamble" in the market, and how the market was housed on the site of a former camel market (which was taken as a clear sign of the Kuwaitis' lack of modernity). By comparison, blame for the 2007 Great Recession in the United States—which also certainly involved "shadowy" markets and gambling—was displaced onto "bankers" or "Wall Street" or poor mortgage borrowers rather than attributed to failings by "Americans" and "Main Street." In the United States, the economic structure and those higher up in that structure get the blame (but rarely the punishment), but in the Gulf the failure is considered a collective one.

Although the effects of the 1982 collapse were massive—it took the Kuwait government many years and many billions of dinars to unwind—it was just the first hurdle Kuwaitis had to jump. The Iran–Iraq War raged next to Kuwait for much of the 1980s, severely limiting shipping at the same time that oil prices were falling. Articles with titles such as "The Persian Gulf Rediscovers Belt-Tightening" began to emerge, which noted that Kuwait was running deficits and that the Souk al-Manakh fallout was "politically embarrassing" (Paul Lewis 1986). Then Iraq actually invaded Kuwait, scattering the foreigners who once felt compelled to use Kuwait City as their base for wheeling and dealing in the Gulf. The Iraqis also left behind lasting environmental damage as oil wells were burned and oil was sent flowing into the Gulf. As Edward Said points out in *Culture and Imperialism*, "Even if one grants that Kuwaitis were unpopular (does one have to be popular not to be exterminated?) and even if Iraq claimed to champion Palestine in standing up to Israel and the United States, surely the very idea that nation should be obliterated along the way is a murderous proposition" (1993, 299).

The aftermath of the Iraq invasion also brought a change of tone in how Kuwait was treated. Coverage of the mid-1980s crash was pretty much a precursor of the cheering that accompanied Dubai's more recent real estate bust in its moralizing and denouncing of those who try to fly too high above their station. But in the wake of the Iraqi occupation, the idea of the Kuwait "malaise" emerged. The first article I found in English that raised the concept was from 1991 in the *New York Times*, titled "A Year Later, Kuwait Sinks into Malaise" (Hedges 1991). The particulars of the concept are there in full in this first instance. There is the obligatory description of how the signs of wealth and consumption have returned after the invasion. Here is what the author chose to go with: "The supermarkets are stocked with fresh fruit, bottles of Perrier and choice cuts of beef. The car dealerships are packed with new GM Buicks, Chrysler Jeeps and Japanese Isuzus. Clean water runs from the taps, and new air-conditioners hum inside the lavish villas to ward off the furnace-like summer

heat. The highways are clear, telephones work, and traffic signals function. But . . ." (suspension points added).

When it came to Kuwait after the Iraqi invasion, there was always
a "but. . . ." Fear was usually mentioned: early on, it was of Sadaam or
environmental pollution; over time, it drifted to Iran. However, the real
cause of the malaise was always something along the lines of what then
National Assembly opposition leader Mubarak al-Adwani was quoted as
saying: "Over the long term we realized that we are faced with an even
deeper problem, and that is the philosophical basis on which this whole
country is built" (Hedges 1991). This problem was usually described as
"lack of direction."

This idea of malaise stuck throughout the subsequent two decades.
In 1995, the *New York Times* sent the author of the previous piece back to
Kuwait on the third anniversary of its liberation from Iraq. He continued
with his previous themes: "But the glitter and affluence mask a country
that has lost faith in itself, lives in fear of a resurgent Iraq and sees a future
darkened by forces beyond its control," and so bad is the situation that
many "young Kuwaitis see their futures in the United States" (Hedges
1994). Jump ahead to 2008: the discourse of Kuwaiti malaise had become
so pervasive that Kuwaiti-based political scientist and *Gulf News* columnist Abdullah al Shayji wrote two pieces on the subject: "The False Malaise of Kuwaiti Politics" (2008a) and "Not Much Has Changed" (2008b).
In the latter, he argued: "Over the past 50 years, Kuwait has been a proto-
type for what happen[s] to a tiny entity which has mastered how to harness
its oil wealth and survive in a hostile environment and put to great use its
oil wealth to benefit its own little population and share it through mega
development projects with the less fortunate countries and peoples." He
also noted that, although Kuwaiti democracy works in fits and starts and is
slowed by internal divisions and interference from the royal family, it still
strives and debates—which, as I see it, is hardly "malaise."

Of course, very few people outside the region read the *Gulf News*,
and other major periodicals have invested a great deal in that storyline of
a Gulf that does things wrong. Thus, there exists a string of malaise headlines up to the present, including "Bid to Address National Malaise" (Peel
and Hall 2012) in the *Times* of London and "Rich but Backward: Politics,

Oil Poison Kuwait Economy" (Westhall and Sleiman 2012) from Reuters, whose focus is summed up in the following claims: "Kuwait's malaise runs deeper than politics, however; its heavy dependence on oil seems to have crippled other parts of the economy. Oil accounts for over 90 percent of state budget revenues, a high level even by Gulf standards. But Kuwait's oil wealth is so big that it has prospered while ignoring the private sector. This limits the immediate pressure for it to develop a business-friendly environment." In the eras covered in chapters 4 (1932–72) and 5 (1973–82), Kuwaitis were thought to be the best "natural" businessmen in the Gulf; their portrayal nowadays would lead one to believe the ruling family has known nothing about business.

This is the discursive fate to which Kuwait is condemned. I have zero doubt that many Kuwaitis do feel that the country is in a malaise because people in many countries feel their country is in a malaise. Feeling that the structures of society are poorly or unfairly arranged to the point of hindering progress is a normal feeling. Kuwait's infrastructure is more established and thus older than the rest of the Gulf's; it is unsurprising that it looks less shiny and needs more repair than Dubai's or Doha's. Most likely, none of the complaints that the various Kuwaiti citizens quoted in these articles make are false or trumped up. And yet al Shayji is correct: Kuwait is also a success by many measures and certainly came out of the early 1990s in much better shape than Iraq. But these articles are not really about Kuwait: they are about enjoying the wrongness of the Gulf.

The situation is thus: one of the central features of market Orientalism is that at some point the Gulf states (or all upstart places, for that matter) have to pay for their immaturity, cultural difference, and impenetrability, which have so turned structures of feeling against them. They are supposed to be made to pay in a Barthesian cultural economic pro-wrestling match. But as the "Rich but Backward" article noted at one point, "Oil wealth means Kuwait can carry on for years" (Westhall and Sleiman 2012). Kuwait had a horrific economic flare-out when the Souk al-Manakh collapsed, thereby disappearing many people's personal savings (as well as the money banks had loaned to them, which led to a government bailout); its Assembly has disbanded and reformed multiple times. Kuwait has been invaded, burned, and occupied by a neighboring state. *But* it still remains one of the world's wealthiest states, with a mostly functioning infrastructure and a comparatively generous provision of services to its citizens. It has also elected women legislators without having to utilize a quota—which seems impossible in many imaginations of the region. Kuwait has its problems, but sixty years in, it is still there. Despite low oil prices recently, its "postoil future" is not in immediate sight.

Because Kuwait will not help fulfill its imagined role by collapsing and seemingly cannot be made to pay in full, its success has to be qualified. Yes, all the articles note, Kuwait is materially fine (because no one can deny that), *but in the end that does not matter.* It is under this thing called a malaise, wherein anything it has counts for nothing. It no longer gets to have a future or to evolve—Kuwait has been labeled the malaise state of the Gulf despite its long-term success in distributing surplus to segments of its national population. Thus, its successes will always be qualified, and its mature complexities will always be a sign of its shortcomings. It is thus that the basic separation between "our" economies and "theirs" produced by market Orientalism remains undisturbed.

So What of Gulf Futures?

In some ways, this book is an odd endeavor in that I end up advocating for a more nuanced examination of the cultural economic product of a group of six states, all of which are ruled by hereditary monarchies, five of which are quite small, and one of which does not allow women to drive. Yet this book is not meant to be a broad defense of what goes on in the Gulf states—that is neither my position nor my intention. I would not write such a book about anywhere even if I feel that many places are only partially understood and experience very real struggles when structures of feeling turn against them. Apart from purposefully partial survey efforts in chapters 6, 7, and 8, this book is also not meant to be taken as a comprehensive survey of what the Gulf's cultural economy "really" looks like.

What this book *does* provide is a critique of market Orientalism, which is not just an imagination that afflicts the Gulf but a widespread process through which the world divides economically good from economically bad. As Edward Said notes in his original critique of Orientalism, the primary goal of Orientalism was not to create new and better knowledge about the Orient—it was about creating separation and positional superiority and about the enjoyment of the potential for power. Thus, positive knowledge alone cannot displace Orientalism—and by extension market Orientalism. Echoing Barthes, Said notes how "underlying all the different units of Orientalist discourse . . . is a set of representative figures or tropes. These figures are to the actual Orient as stylized costumes are to characters in a play" that serves "to characterize the Orient as alien and to incorporate it schematically on a theatrical stage whose audience, manager, and actors are for Europe, and only for Europe" (1994, 71–72).

The dramatic script of the Gulf was locked in early on: the Gulf did not earn and has not earned its wealth, and someday the universe or karma or the invisible hand will make it pay because "we" are on the side of right and "they" are not. Different characters came and went over the years: one state was always the hermit, another was said to spend lavishly while seemingly lying about, and yet another was the wily merchant with moments of relative triumph—most of them like but still different from the global business norm. New acts keep getting added to the play because the foretold day of complete reckoning never seems to come. But through it all belief in an ultimate resolution—that the Gulf will pay—remains undisturbed.

So to review: Chapter 1 opened with the tale of a billboard that rotated between Hope and Chastity, establishing the tension between seemingly having the riches to accomplish anything and being seen as overly focused on purity. But as the Dubai Ports World story showed, trying to negotiate those perceptions is not easy. The first chapter also introduced the notion that much of the work that market Orientalism does in creating separation and positional superiority occurs within structures of feeling. Chapter 2 situated this work as an intervention into the field of cultural economy to provide focus and a theory that can travel across topics. Chapter 3 began by emphasizing the importance of cultural economic hierarchy in producing positional superiority and sought to understand the process by drawing on scholars such as Bourdieu and Barthes as well as on perspectives such as postcolonialism and psychoanalysis. It then looked at how market Orientalism works on the structures of feeling that influence imagination of cultural economic hierarchy. For the sake of clarity, I list here once more the four aspects of market Orientalism. First is the notion that assumptions about emerging markets reflect centuries of thought and practice about how to deal with the spaces and practices of Others. Second is the idea that the world can be transparently divided into identifiable and practicable fields of economic action, known as regional markets. Third is the notion that markets such as the Gulf display a lack of full contemporaneous modernity and thus maturity. Fourth and finally is the concept of impenetrability. All of these notions work together to produce opportunities to script established cultural economies as having the upper hand—sometimes for the purpose of pursing profit or control, sometimes only for the sake of enjoying superiority.

Chapters 4, 5, 6, and 7 brought the imagination of market Orientalism to the Gulf's past and present. Chapter 4 focused on the imaginations that emerged surrounding the Gulf in the first few decades after the discovery of oil. This era saw the initial formation of assumptions about what the Gulf's new wealth might mean. It also witnessed the first pronouncements (most of which were disapproving) concerning how states and economies were being built in the Gulf. These pronouncements focused mostly on how the culture remained "medieval" and potentially dominateable and how impenetrable the royal families were even while the infrastructure became modern. It also introduced the character of the Gulf male consumer, the big spender who supposedly kept his white dishdasha clean by avoiding physical work—the opposite of how mature male cultural economic subjects are supposed to behave. The 1970s boom era, covered in chapter 5, saw the emergence of new refinements to these imaginations. The first painted the Gulf as a new type of impenetrable state: the shadowy, sinister (but more capable) possessor of the oil weapon. Yet it also showed Gulf cities as less than fully mature and without soul despite their material abundance; they became reassuring examples of unsuccessful success. Finally, this era also rounded out the cast of Gulf characters with the repressed Gulf woman, the jet-setting Gulf playboy, and the usually hard-working foreign residents.

Chapters 6 and 7 focused on more contemporary and specific issues. Chapter 6 questioned the idea that the Gulf should be considered a "traditional" regional market and wondered whether it had really "failed" by not establishing a common currency. In place of that idea, it sought to view the Gulf as a regional economy with differential and often inefficient opportunities. It also noted that postcolonial regional economies are in general fantastical in that they are a dream of complete and comparable schemas. Chapter 7 looked at recent efforts by Gulf states to increase their broadly defined geopolitical prestige while maneuvering within the confines of market Orientalism. It was an effort to show that embodied ideals like those of market Orientalism also matter in geopolitical competition. Dubai and Bahrain were shown to seek niches in part based on the idea of openness to things such as alcohol, which cost each in different ways. Doha competed in the more staid realms of diplomacy and event hosting but also ran into problems of acceptance on embodied grounds.

But in chapter 8 the focused shifted. Although that chapter highlighted some additional ways in which the Gulf is marked as a cultural economic Other, it also tried to do something else. Namely, it sought to present positive knowledge about the diverse cultural economic processes of the Gulf and the people who make them in order to highlight some of what market Orientalism obscures.

In the end, market Orientalism is not just about the Gulf. It is about how so much writing and thinking about economic activity fall into the same familiar scripts, looking for characters to perform the roles in the reassuring story everybody already knows. So often the heroes and villains are predetermined, divided from each other by older ways of separating us and them. That is why I was drawn to the cultural economy movement initially—it seemed to open up the study of economic activity to a whole new set of ideas and terrains rarely utilized before. It could make more of what people do to shape their livelihoods count. This is what the book has endeavored to do—to show that market Orientalism is real, persistent, and impactful but then also to gesture toward some other ways to view economic activity. Without the critique, any noting of practices other than those sanctioned by market Orientalism tends to fall on deaf ears, but without some looking beyond the confines of market Orientalism we are stuck forever reimagining the same stories. I do not want that to be the future for the Gulf's—or any other place's—cultural economies.

Works Cited

Index

Works Cited

Al A'ali, Mohammed. 2010. "'Sex Tourists' Alert on Vice." *Gulf Daily News*, June 22.

Adib-Moghaddam, Arshin. 2006. *The International Politics of the Persian Gulf: A Cultural Genealogy*. London: Taylor & Francis.

Adorno, Theodor W. [1947] 2006. *Philosophy of New Music*. Edited by Robert Hullot-Kentor. Minneapolis: Univ. of Minnesota Press.

Agamben, Giorgio. 1998. *Homo Sacer: Sovereign Power and Bare Life*. Stanford, CA: Stanford Univ. Press.

———. 2005. *State of Exception*. Chicago: Univ. of Chicago Press.

Agnew, John A. 1998. *Geopolitics: Re-visioning World Politics*. London: Routledge.

Ahmad, Attiya. 2012. "Beyond Labor: Foreign Residents in the Gulf States." In *Migrant Labor in the Persian Gulf*, edited by Kamran Mehrava and Zahra Babar, 21–40. New York: Columbia Univ. Press.

Akhtar, Shamshad, and Mustapha Rouis. 2010. *Economic Integration in MENA: The GCC, the Maghreb, and the Mashreq*. Washington, DC: World Bank.

Alatas, Syed Hussein. 1977. *The Myth of the Lazy Native: A Study of the Image of the Malays, Filipinos, and Javanese from the 16th to the 20th Century and Its Function in the Ideology of Colonial Capitalism*. London: F. Cass.

Ali, Fuad. 2007. "'Greatest Peril' of Ramadan Is 'Overindulgence.'" *Gulf News*, Sept. 21.

Ali, Syed. 2010. *Dubai: Gilded Cage*. New Haven, CT: Yale Univ. Press.

Althusser, Louis. 1969. *For Marx*. New York: Penguin.

Amin, Ash, and Nigel Thrift, eds. 2004. *The Blackwell Cultural Economy Reader*. Malden, MA: Blackwell.

———. 2007. "Cultural-Economy and Cities." *Progress in Human Geography* 31, no. 2: 143–61.

Anheier, Helmut K., and Yudhishthir Raj Isar, eds. 2008. *Cultures and Globalization: The Cultural Economy*. London: Sage.

Arendt, Hannah. 1968. *Imperialism: Part Two of the Origins of Totalitarianism*. New York: Houghton Mifflin Harcourt.

Ashworth, Norma. 1976. "Too Busy for Tourists." *Times* (London), Nov. 18.

Azzi, Robert. 1980. "Saudi Arabia: The Kingdom and Its Power." *National Geographic*, Sept., 286–333.

Bahrain Economic Development Board. 2014. *Kingdom of Bahrain Economic Yearbook 2013*. Manama: Bahrain Economic Development Board.

Baily, Michael. 1977. "The Great Freight Race." *Times* (London), Oct. 28.

Barber, Benjamin R. 1996. *Jihad vs. McWorld*. New York: Times Books.

Barnes, Trevor J., and Eric Sheppard. 2010. "'Nothing Includes Everything': Towards Engaged Pluralism in Anglophone Economic Geography." *Progress in Human Geography* 34, no. 2: 193–214.

Barthes, Roland. 1972. *Mythologies*. Paris: Farrar, Straus and Giroux.

Bataille, Georges. (1949) 1988. *The Accursed Share: An Essay on General Economy*. New York: Zone Books.

Baudrillard, Jean. 1975. *The Mirror of Production*. St. Louis: Telos Press.

———. 1990. *Seduction*. New York: St. Martin's Press.

Beblawi, Hazem. 1987. "The Rentier State in the Arab World." *Arab Studies Quarterly* 9, no. 4: 383–98.

———. 1990. "The Rentier State in the Arab World." In *The Arab State*, edited by Hazem Beblawi and Giacomo Luciani, 85–98. London: Routledge.

Beblawi, Hazem, and Giacomo Luciani, eds. 1987. *The Rentier State*. London: Croom Helm.

———. 1990. *The Arab State*. London: Routledge.

Belgrave, James H. D. 1966. "Birth of a New Middle Class." *Times* (London), Dec. 30.

Benjamin, Walter. [1936] 1988. "The Work of Art in the Age of Mechanical Reproduction." In *Illuminations*, edited by Hannah Arendt, translated by Harry Zohn, 217–52. New York: Schocken Books.

Benston, Liz. 2007. "Dubai Learning from Las Vegas." *ScrippsNews*, Nov. 9.

Bhabha, Homi K. 1994. *The Location of Culture*. London: Routledge.

Blacker, Terence. 2010. "A Triumph of Human Hubris: The Qatar World Cup Is the Global Equivalent of Leaving All the Lights On." *Independent*, Dec. 7.

Blake, David. 1977. "Equipped to Cope with Comfort." *Times* (London), Feb. 18.

Bloch, Robin. 2010. "Dubai's Long Goodbye." *International Journal of Urban and Regional Research* 34, no. 4: 943–51.

Boltanski, Luc, and Eve Chiapello. 2005. *The New Spirit of Capitalism.* Translated by Gregory Elliot. London: Verso Books.

Boltanski, Luc, and Laurent Thévenot. 2006. *On Justification: Economies of Worth.* Princeton, NJ: Princeton Univ. Press.

Bondy, Flip. 2010. "In Awarding 2022 World Cup to Qatar over America, FIFA Shows It's Either Stupid or Corrupt, or Both." *New York Daily News*, Dec. 3.

Bourdieu, Pierre. 1984. *Distinction: A Social Critique of the Judgment of Taste.* Translated by Richard Nice. Cambridge, MA: Harvard Univ. Press.

Bozarslan, Hamit. 2012. "Revisiting the Middle East's 1979." *Economy and Society* 41, no. 4: 558–67.

Bradley, Nicholas. 2010. *Dubai Dreams: Inside the Kingdom of Bling.* London: Nicholas Brealey.

Braveboy-Wagner, Jacqueline Anne. 2008. *Small States in Global Affairs: The Foreign Policies of the Caribbean Community (CARICOM).* New York: Palgrave Macmillan.

Brochmann, Grete. 1993. *Middle East Avenue: Female Migration from Sri Lanka to the Gulf.* Boulder, CO: Westview Press.

Brown, Kenneth. 1978. "What £25,000m Can Do for a Fishing Village." *Times* (London), Oct. 19.

Brown, Malcom. 1976. "Serious Inflation despite Immense Prosperity." *Times* (London), Mar. 31.

Bunnell, Tim. 2002. "Kampung Rules: Landscape and the Contested Government of Urban(e) Malayness." *Urban Studies* 39, no. 9: 1685–701.

———. 2013. "Antecedent Cities and Inter-referencing Effects: Learning from and Extending beyond Critiques of Neoliberalisation." *Urban Studies* 50, no. S1: 1–18.

Callan, Lou. 2000. *Dubai.* 1st ed. Melbourne: Lonely Planet.

Callon, Michel. 1998a. "An Essay on Framing and Overflowing: Economic Externalities Revisited by Sociology." *Sociological Review* 46, no. S1: 244–69.

———. 1998b. *The Laws of the Markets.* Oxford: Sociological Review; Malden, MA: Blackwell.

Callon, Michel, Cécile Méadel, and Vololona Rabeharisoa. 2002. "The Economy of Qualities." *Economy and Society* 31, no. 2: 194–217.

Callon, Michel, and Vololona Rabeharisoa. 2003. "Research in the Wild and the Shaping of New Social Identities." *Technology in Society* 25, no. 2: 193–204.

Calvert, Jonathan, and Heidi Blake. 2014. "Plot to Buy the World Cup: Huge Email Cache Reveals Secrets of Qatar's Shock Victory." *Times* (London), June 1.

Caminada, Jerome. 1978a. "Further Education Abroad Ingredient of Success." *Times* (London), June 12.

———. 1978b. "Government Is a Multipurpose Cash Dispenser." *Times* (London), June 12.

Carmical, J. H. 1951. "Mideast Oil a Vital Factor in World Economy." *New York Times*, Nov. 18.

Chessyhre, Tom. 2007. "'Chav' Influx Drags Dubai Down Market." *Times* (London), Sept. 15.

Chow, Rey. 2002. *The Protestant Ethic and the Spirit of Capitalism*. New York: Columbia Univ. Press.

Clifford-Cruz, Rebecca. 2011. "Las Vegas vs. Dubai: Comparing Two World-Famous Tourist Destinations." *Las Vegas Sun*, Dec. 23.

Cohen, Benjamin J. 1997. "The Political Economy of Currency Regions." In *The Political Economy of Regionalism*, edited by Edward Mansfield and Helen Milner, 50–76. New York: Columbia Univ. Press.

Cook, Ian, and Michelle Harrison. 2003. "Crossover Food: Re-materializing Postcolonial Geographies." *Transactions of the Institute of British Geographers* 28, no. 3: 296–317.

Cooper, Frederick, and Ann Laura Stoler. 1997. *Tensions of Empire: Colonial Cultures in a Bourgeois World*. Berkeley: Univ. of California Press.

Cosgrove, Denis E. 1984. *Social Formation and Symbolic Landscape*. London: Croom Helm.

Crew, Bob. 1976. "Luxury Class for Camp Beds and Pubs with No Beer." *Times* (London), Sept. 24.

Crocetti, Gina L. 1999. *Culture Shock! The United Arab Emirates*. Portland, OR: Graphic Arts Center.

Cronon, William. 1991. *Nature's Metropolis: Chicago and the Great West*. New York: Norton.

Dalby, Simon. 1991. "Critical Geopolitics: Difference, Discourse, and Dissent." *Environment & Planning D: Society & Space* 9, no. 3: 261–83.

Daniels, Stephen. 1989. "Marxism, Culture, and the Duplicity of Landscape." In *New Models in Geography*, edited by Richard Peet and Nigel Thrift, 23–35. London: Unwin-Hyman.

DarkSyde. 2006. "A Toxic Deal in the Making." *Daily Kos*, Feb. 28. At http://www.dailykos.com/story/2006/02/27/190403/-A-Toxic-Deal-in-the-Making.

Daragahi, Borzou. 2015. "Recording Claims to Show Egypt Leaders' Disdain for Gulf Donors." *Financial Times*, Feb. 8.

Davidson, Christopher M. 2009a. *Abu Dhabi: Oil and Beyond*. New York: Columbia Univ. Press.

———. 2009b. *Dubai: The Vulnerability of Success*. New York: Columbia Univ. Press.

———. 2012. "The Dubai Model: Diversification and Slowdown." In *The Political Economy of the Persian Gulf*, edited by Mehran Kamrava, 195–220. New York: Columbia Univ. Press.

Davis, Anthony. 1976. "Mixed Architecture Marks Modern Face of City." *Times* (London), Sept. 3.

Davis, Mike. 1990. *City of Quartz: Excavating the Future in Los Angeles*. London: Verso.

———. 2005. "Sinister Paradise: Does the Road to the Future End in Dubai?" *TomDispatch*, July 14. At http://www.tomdispatch.com/post/5807/mike_davis _on_a_paradise_built_on_oil.

De Brant, Peter. 1976. "Big Changes at Port of Entry for Holy City." *Times* (London), Sept. 23.

Debrix, François. 2008. *Tabloid Terror: War, Culture, and Geopolitics*. London: Routledge.

De Soto, Hernando. 2000. *The Mystery of Capital: Why Capitalism Triumphs in the West and Fails Everywhere Else*. New York: Basic Books.

Dewsbury, John-David. 2003. "Witnessing Space: 'Knowledge without Contemplation.'" *Environment & Planning A* 35, no. 11: 1907–32.

Dickens, Kate. 1999. *Serve Them Right: A Practical Guide to Multicultural Customer Care*. Dubai: Motivate.

Dittmer, Jason. 2005. "Captain America's Empire: Reflections on Identity, Popular Culture, and Post-9/11 Geopolitics." *Annals of the Association of American Geographers* 95, no. 3: 626–43.

Doel, Marcus. 2003. "Introduction to Part 5: Theory." In *The Consumption Reader*, edited by David B. Clarke, Marcus Doel, and Kate M. L. Housiaux, 219–26. New York: Routledge.

———. 2010. "Seduction." In *The Baudrillard Dictionary*, edited by Richard. G. Smith, 186–87. Edinburgh: Edinburgh Univ. Press.

Doherty, Regan. 2012. "Premier League Chairman Criticises FIFA over World Cup." *Reuters*, Mar. 14.

Donnelly, Peter. 2006. "Shops in City Centre Witness Decrease in Sales." *Khaleej Times*, Jan. 24.

Dorsey, James M. 2012. "Pitched Battles: The Role of Ultra Soccer Fans in the Arab Spring." *Mobilization: An International Quarterly* 17, no. 4: 411–18.

Du Gay, Paul, and Michael Pryke, eds. 2002. *Cultural Economy: Cultural Analysis and Commercial Life, Culture, Representation, and Identities*. London: Sage.

Duncan, James S. 1980. "The Superorganic in American Cultural Geography." *Annals of the Association of American Geographers* 70, no. 2: 181–98.

Eckert, Hans-Joachim. 2014. *Statement of the Chair of the Adjunctery Chamber of the FIFA Ethics Committee on the Report on the Inquiry into the 2018/2022 FIFA World Cup Bidding Process Prepared by the Investigatory Chamber of the FIFA Ethics Committee*. Zurich: Fédération Internationale de Football Association.

Economist. 1950. "The Koweit's Millions." Feb. 18.

———. 1961a. "The Awakening Saudis." June 10.

———. 1961b. "A Quiver of Sheikhs." July 15.

———. 1966. "Middle East Oil: Higher Stakes." Nov. 26.

———. 2009. "Finance and Economics: Disunited Arab Emirates; Monetary Union in the Gulf." May 21.

Elsheshtawy, Yasser. 2010. *Dubai: Behind an Urban Spectacle*. London: Routledge.

Elyachar, Julia. 2005. *Markets of Dispossession: NGOs, Economic Development, and the State in Cairo*. Chapel Hill, NC: Duke Univ. Press.

———. 2012. "Before (and after) Neoliberalism: Tacit Knowledge, Secrets of the Trade, and the Public Sector in Egypt." *Cultural Anthropology* 27, no. 1: 76–96.

Emirates News Agency. 2008. "Mohammad: Gulf–China Talks Could Lead to Free Zone." *Gulf News*, Apr. 4.

Enloe, Cynthia H. 1989. *Bananas, Beaches, and Bases: Making Feminist Sense of International Politics*. London: Pandora.

Entwistle, Joanne, and Don Slater. 2013. Reassembling the Cultural. *Journal of Cultural Economy* 7, no. 2: 161–77.

Escobar, Arturo. 1995. *Encountering Development: The Making and Unmaking of the Third World*. Princeton, NJ: Princeton Univ. Press.

———. 2008. *Territories of Difference: Place, Movements, Life*, Redes. Durham, NC: Duke Univ. Press.

Eurostat (International Monetary Fund). 2014. *Bahrain—Trade with World; Oman—Trade with World*. Brussels: European Union Directorate General for Trade.

Al-Fahim, Mohammed. 1998. *From Rags to Riches: A Story of Abu Dhabi*. London: I. B. Tauris.

Fanon, Frantz. 1967. *Black Skin, White Masks*. New York: Grove Press.

Fawn, Rick. 2009. "'Regions' and Their Study: Wherefrom, What for, and Where to?" *Review of International Studies* 35, no. S1: 5–34.

Fenelon, K. G. 1974. "Expanding Economy Will Bolster Region's Importance." *Times* (London), May 23.

Ferguson, James. 1994. *The Anti-politics Machine: "Development," Depoliticization, and Bureaucratic Power in Lesotho*. Minneapolis: Minnesota Univ. Press.

———. 1998. *Expectations of Modernity: Myths and Meanings of Urban Life on the Zambian Copperbelt*. Berkeley: Univ. of California Press.

———. 2006. *Global Shadows: Africa in the Neoliberal World Order*. Durham, NC: Duke Univ. Press.

Field, Peter. 1978. "Altruism Overlaid by Other Considerations." *Times* (London), Apr. 10.

Fisk, Robert. 1980. "Sanctions Fail to Depress the Iranian Economy." *Times* (London), July 11.

Fiske, John. 1992. "Audiencing: A Cultural Studies Approach to Watching Television." *Poetics* 21, no. 4: 345–59.

Fleet and Family Support Center, Navy Region Southwest Asia, NSA Bahrain. 2011. *Camel Crossings: A Newcomers Guide to Bahrain*. Manama: NSA Bahrain.

Florida, Richard L. 2002. *The Rise of the Creative Class and How It's Transforming Work, Leisure, Community, and Everyday Life*. New York: Basic Books.

Fluri, Jennifer L. 2009. "Geopolitics of Gender and Violence 'from Below.'" *Political Geography* 28, no. 4: 259–65.

Freeman, Colin. 2008. "Britons Party on in Dubai despite Arrest of Woman for Alleged Sex on the Beach." *Daily Telegraph*, July 12.

Friedman, Thomas L. [1999] 2000. *The Lexus and the Olive Tree*. New York: Anchor Books.

Fuccaro, Nelida. 2009. *Histories of City and State in the Persian Gulf: Manama since 1800*. Cambridge: Cambridge Univ. Press.

Fyfe, Ann. 1976a. "Hatred of Communism Abounds amid Improved Lifestyle." *Times* (London), Nov. 18.

———. 1976b. "Military Merger Next Big Hurdle." *Times* (London), Mar. 31.

———. 1977. "Shaikh's Reelection Brings a New Normality." *Times* (London), June 21.

———. 1981. "Still Suffering from Booming Economy." *Times* (London), Dec. 9.

Gaffney, Frank J., Jr. 2006. "Peril in Port." *New York Sun*, Feb. 15.

Gardner, Andrew. 2010. *City of Strangers: Gulf Migration and the Indian Community in Bahrain*. Ithaca, NY: ILR Press.

Garland, Ian. 2009. "'It's All a Blur': £100k-per-Year British Woman Accused of Having Sex in a Dubai Taxi Reveals She Went on a 10 Hour Drinking Marathon before Arrest." *Daily Mail*, May 27.

Gause, F. Gregory. 1994. *Oil Monarchies: Domestic and Security Challenges in the Arab Gulf States*. New York: Council on Foreign Relations Press.

———. 2010. *The International Relations of the Persian Gulf*. Cambridge: Cambridge Univ. Press.

Gengler, Justin J. 2013. "Royal Factionalism, the Khawalid, and the Securitization of 'the Shia Problem' in Bahrain." *Journal of Arabian Studies* 3, no. 1: 53–79.

Gertler, Meric S. 2005. "Tacit Knowledge and the Economic Geography of Context, or the Undefinable Tacitness of Being (There)." *Journal of Economic Geography* 3, no. 1: 75–99.

Ghosh, Palash. 2013. "Not Elvis, Sinatra, nor Beatles: Jim Reeves Is the Biggest Western Singer in South India and Sri Lanka." *International Business Times*, Sept. 4.

Gibson, Chris. 2012. "Cultural Economy: Achievements, Divergences, Future Prospects." *Geographical Research* 50, no. 3: 282–92.

Gibson, Chris, and Lily Kong. 2005. "Cultural Economy: A Critical Review." *Progress in Human Geography* 29, no. 5: 541–61.

Gibson, Owen. 2012. "FIFA to Investigate New Allegations over Qatar 2022 World Cup Bid." *Guardian*, Nov. 18.

Gibson-Graham, J. K. 1996. *The End of Capitalism (as We Knew It): A Feminist Critique of Political Economy*. Cambridge, MA: Blackwell.

———. 2006. *A Postcapitalist Politics*. Minneapolis: Univ. of Minnesota Press.

Goss, J. 1999. "Once-upon-a-Time in the Commodity World: An Unofficial Guide to Mall of America." *Annals of the Association of American Geographers* 89, no. 1: 45–75.

Graham, Stephen, and Simon Marvin. 2001. *Splintering Urbanism: Networked Infrastructures, Technological Mobilities, and the Urban Condition*. New York: Routledge.

Grainge, Alan. 1980. "The 'Smart Operators' of the Gulf." *Times* (London), June 6.

Gran, Peter. 1990. "Studies of Anglo-American Political Economy: Democracy, Orientalism, and the Left." In *Theory, Politics, and the Arab World: Critical Responses*, edited by Hisham Sharabi, 228–54. New York: Routledge.

Granovetter, Mark S. 1985. "Economic Action and Social Structure: The Problem of Embeddedness." *American Journal of Sociology* 91, no. 3: 481–510.

Gregory, Derek. 1995. "Imaginative Geographies." *Progress in Human Geography* 19, no. 4: 447–85.

————. 2004. *The Colonial Present: Afghanistan, Iraq, and Palestine*. London: Blackwell.

Gregson, Nicky, and Louise Crewe. 1998. "Dusting Down Second Hand Rose; Gendered Identities and the World of Second-Hand Goods in the Space of the Car Boot Sale." *Gender, Place & Culture: A Journal of Feminist Geography* 5, no. 1: 77–100.

Gruenwald, Paul, and Masahiro Hori. 2008. *Intra-regional Trade Key to Asia's Export Boom*. Tokyo: Regional Office for Asia and the Pacific, International Monetary Fund.

Gulf News. 2004. "Dragon Mart to House Massive Collection of Chinese Products." Nov. 2.

————. 2005. "95% UAE Residents Own Mobile Phones." Aug. 6.

————. 2007. "Ramadan Is a Shift from Routine." Sept. 8.

————. 2009. "UAE Withdrawal from Monetary Union Is Justified" (editorial). May 21.

Gupta, Akhil. 2005. "Narratives of Corruption: Anthropological and Fictional Accounts of the Indian State." *Ethnography* 6, no. 1: 5–34.

Hall, Sarah, Jonathan V. Beaverstock, James R. Faulconbridge, and Andrew Hewitson. 2009. "Exploring Cultural Economies of Internationalization: The Role of 'Iconic Individuals' and 'Brand Leaders' in the Globalization of Headhunting." *Global Networks* 9, no. 3: 399–419.

Hall, Stuart. 1992. "The West and the Rest: Discourse and Power." In *The Formations of Modernity*, edited by Stuart Hall and Bram Gieben, 275–332. London: Polity.

Hanieh, Adam. 2011. *Capitalism and Class in the Gulf Arab States*. New York: Palgrave Macmillan.

Haraway, Donna. 1988. "Situated Knowledges: The Science Question in Feminism and the Privilege of Partial Perspective." *Feminist Studies* 14, no. 3: 575–99.

Hardt, Michael, and Antonio Negri. 2000. *Empire*. Cambridge, MA: Harvard Univ. Press.

———. 2005. *Multitude: War and Democracy in the Age of Empire*. New York: Penguin Books.

———. 2009. *Commonwealth*. Cambridge, MA: Belknap Press of Harvard Univ. Press.

Hargrove, Charles. 1974. "Man Whose Innovations Shook the Money Temple." *Times* (London), Feb. 14.

Harris, Derek. 1977. "Boom Points to a Return to Buying British." *Times* (London), July 12.

Harvey, David. 1982. *The Limits to Capital*. Chicago: Univ. of Chicago Press.

———. 2003. *The New Imperialism*. New York: Oxford Univ. Press.

———. 2005. *A Brief History of Neoliberalism*. New York: Oxford Univ. Press.

———. 2012. "History versus Theory: A Commentary on Marx's Method in *Capital*." *Historical Materialism* 20, no. 2: 3–38.

Hayward, Keith, and Majid Yar. 2006. "The 'Chav' Phenomenon: Consumption, Media, and the Construction of a New Underclass." *Crime, Media, Culture* 2, no. 1: 9–28.

Hazbun, Waleed. 2008. *Beaches, Ruins, Resorts: The Politics of Tourism in the Arab World*. Minneapolis: Univ. of Minnesota Press.

Hedges, Chris. 1991. "A Year Later, Kuwait Sinks into Malaise." *New York Times*, Aug. 2.

———. 1994. "Three Years after Gulf War, Sense of Siege Grips Kuwait." *New York Times*, Oct. 8.

Herbert, Nicholas. 1969. "Federation May Ease the Pains of Affluence." *Times* (London), June 10.

Hertog, Steffen. 2010a. *Princes, Brokers, and Bureaucrats: Oil and the State in Saudi Arabia*. Ithaca, NY: Cornell Univ. Press.

———. 2010b. "The Sociology of the Gulf Rentier Systems: Societies of Intermediaries." *Comparative Studies in Society and History* 52, no. 2: 282–318.

Hewson, David. 1981. "The Economy: A New Emphasis on Planning." *Times* (London), Feb. 23.

Hilotin, Jay B. 2007. "Facing the Rising Tide of Counterfeits." *Gulf News*, Mar. 8.

Hirst, Nicholas. 1979. "Has Shaikh Yamani Saved OPEC and the West?" *Times* (London), Dec. 22.

Hobday, Peter. 1975. "Patience and Partnership the Key to Opening a Market." *Times* (London), Sept. 15.

Hopkirk, Peter. 1974. "Richest State Seeks More Than Oil." *Times* (London), May 23.

———. 1975a. "From Rags to Riches for the Seven Shaikhdoms." *Times* (London), June 19.

———. 1975b. "Kuwait: The Unassuming Face of Capitalism." *Times* (London), Feb. 25.

Horkheimer, Max. 1974. *Critique of Instrumental Reason: Lectures and Essays since the End of World War II.* New York: Seabury Press.

Horkheimer, Max, and Theodor W. Adorno. [1944] 1986. *Dialectic of Enlightenment.* 2nd ed. London: Verso.

Hörschelmann, Kathrin. 2008. "Youth and the Geopolitics of Risk after 11 September 2001." In *Fear: Critical Geopolitics and Everyday Life,* edited by Rachel Pain and Susan J. Smith, 139–56. Aldershot, UK: Ashgate.

Howarth, David. 1967. "King Who Knows the West." *Times* (London), May 9.

Hughes, Rob. 2011. "FIFA Official Hinted Qatar 'Bought' World Cup." *New York Times,* May 30.

Hyndman, Jennifer. 2004. "Mind the Gap: Bridging Feminist and Political Geography through Geopolitics." *Political Geography* 23, no. 3: 307–22.

International Monetary Fund (IMF). 2013. *Economic Prospects and Policy Challenges for GCC Countries.* Riyadh: IMF.

Issa, Wafa. 2007. "Chinese Drop Key New Year Figure." *Gulf News,* Feb. 24.

Jackson, Peter. 2000. *Commercial Cultures: Economies, Practices, Spaces, Leisure, Consumption, and Culture.* Oxford: Berg.

Jayne, Mark, Gill Valentine, and Sarah L. Holloway. 2010. "Emotional, Embodied, and Affective Geographies of Alcohol, Drinking, and Drunkenness." *Transactions of the Institute of British Geographers* 35, no. 4: 540–54.

Jehl, Douglas. 1996. "A Tutorial for Young Saudis on Ways to Toil for Money." *New York Times,* Nov. 21.

Kamin, Brad. 2010. "The Burj Dubai–Burj Khalifa Name Change: Better Change Those T-shirts and Caps in the Gift Shop—and a Whole Lot More." *Chicago Tribune,* Jan. 4.

Kamrava, Mehran, ed. 2012a. *The Political Economy of the Persian Gulf.* New York: Columbia Univ. Press.

———. 2012b. "The Political Economy of Rentierism in the Persian Gulf." In *The Political Economy of the Persian Gulf*, edited by Mehran Kamrava, 39–68. New York: Columbia Univ. Press.

———. 2013. *Qatar: Small State, Big Politics*. Ithaca, NY: Cornell Univ. Press.

Kamrava, Mehran, and Zahra Babar, eds. 2012. *Migrant Labor in the Persian Gulf.* New York: Columbia Univ. Press.

Kanna, Ahmed. 2011. *Dubai, the City as Corporation*. Minneapolis: Univ. of Minnesota Press.

Kassar, Khaled, ed. 2006. *1000 Numbers & Reasons Why Dubai*. Beirut: BISC-Beirut.

Kazmi, Aftab. 2006. "Stop Wasting Food during Ramadan, Urge Scholars." *Gulf News*, Oct. 11.

Kessler, Ronald. 1986. *The Richest Man in the World: The Story of Adnan Khashoggi*. New York: Warner Books.

Khalaf, Sulayman. 2006. "The Evolution of the Gulf City Type, Oil, and Globalization." In *Globalization and the Gulf*, edited by J. W. Fox, Nada Mourtada-Sabbah, and Mohammed Al-Mutawa, 244–65. Oxford: Routledge.

Khalid, Ali. 2005. "Are You a Dubai Chav?" *7 Days*, Aug. 3.

Kilborn, Peter T. 1987. "The Humbled Saudi Economy: Caution Now a Watchword." *New York Times*, Feb. 12.

Kingsbury, Paul. 2005. "Jamaican Tourism and the Politics of Enjoyment." *Geoforum* 36, no. 1: 113–22.

———. 2007. "The Extimacy of Space." *Social & Cultural Geography* 8, no. 2: 235–58.

———. 2011. "The World Cup and the National Thing on Commercial Drive, Vancouver." *Environment & Planning D: Society & Space* 29, no. 4: 716–37.

Kinzer, Stephen. 2003. *All the Shah's Men: An American Coup and the Roots of Middle East Terror*. Hoboken, NJ: Wiley.

Koch, Natalie. 2010. "The Monumental and the Miniature: Imagining Modernity in Astana." *Social & Cultural Geography* 11, no. 8: 769–87.

Langtonlady. 2005. "Chav City." *Tripadvisor*, Oct. 5. At http://www.tripadvisor.com/ShowUserReviews-g295424-d301584-r3994696-Le_Royal_Meridien_Beach_Resort_Spa-Dubai_Emirate_of_Dubai.html.

Latour, Bruno. 1996. *Aramis, or Love of Technology*. Translated by Catherine Porter. Cambridge, MA: Harvard Univ. Press.

Law, John. 2004. "And if the Global Were Small and Noncoherent? Method, Complexity, and the Baroque." *Environment and Planning D: Society and Space* 22, no. 1: 13–26.

Legrenzi, Matteo. 2011. *The GCC and the International Relations of the Gulf: Diplomacy, Security, and Economic Coordination in a Changing Middle East*. London: I. B. Tauris.

Leonard, Karen. 2005. "South Asians in the Indian Ocean World: Language, Policing, and Gender Practices in Kuwait and the United Arab Emirates." *Comparative Studies of South Asia, Africa, and the Middle East* 25, no. 3: 677–86.

Lewis, Paul. 1986. "The Persian Gulf Rediscovers Belt-Tightening." *New York Times*, June 1.

Lewis, Peirce. 1979. "Axioms for Reading the Landscape: Some Guides to the American Scene." In *The Interpretation of Ordinary Landscapes: Geographical Essays*, edited by Donald Meinig, 174–82. New York: Oxford Univ. Press.

Licklider, Roy E. 1988. *Political Power and the Arab Oil Weapon: The Experience of Five Industrial Nations*. Berkeley: Univ. of California Press.

Lien, Marianne E. 1997. *Marketing and Modernity*. London: Bloomsbury Academic.

Longman, Jere. 2010. "Russia and Qatar Expand Soccer's Global Footprint." *New York Times*, Dec. 2.

Longva, Anh Nga. 2005. "Neither Autocracy nor Democracy but Ethnocracy: Citizens, Expatriates, and the Socio-political Regime in Kuwait." In *Monarchies and Nations—Globalisation and Identity in the Arab States of the Gulf*, edited by Paul Dresch and James Piscatori, 114–35. London: I. B. Tauris.

Luciani, Giacomo. 2011. "The Political Economy of Monetary Integration and Exchange Rate Regime in the GCC." In *Shifting Geo-economic Power of the Gulf: Oil, Finance, and Institutions*, edited by Matteo Legrenzi and Bessma Momani, 23–38. London: Ashgate.

Lury, Celia. 2011. *Consumer Culture*. 2nd ed. New Brunswick, NJ: Rutgers Univ. Press.

Lyall, Sarah. 2005. "At Wit's End, a Town Dithers over Its Millionaire Pest." *New York Times*, Sept. 30.

MacKenzie, Donald A., Fabian Muniesa, and Lucia Siu, eds. 2007. *Do Economists Make Markets? On the Performativity of Economics*. Princeton, NJ: Princeton Univ. Press.

MacLeod, Gordon, and Martin Jones. 2001. "Renewing the Geography of Regions." *Environment and Planning D: Society and Space* 19, no. 6: 669–95.

Madsen, Michelle. 2005. "Ramadan Dos and Don'ts." *Time Out Dubai*, Sept. 29.

MaGrudy's. 2006. "About MaGrudy's." At http://www.magrudy.com/about.php. Accessed Apr. 5, 2008.

Mahdavi, Pardis. 2011. *Gridlock: Labor, Migration, and Human Trafficking in Dubai.* Palo Alto, CA: Stanford Univ. Press.

Mahdavy, Hossein. 1970. "The Pattern and Problems of Economic Development in Rentier States: The Case of Iran." In *Studies in the Economic History of the Middle East,* edited by M. A. Cook, 428–67. Oxford: Oxford Univ. Press.

Makdisi, Ussama. 2002. "Ottoman Orientalism." *American Historical Review* 107, no. 3: 768–96.

Malkin, Michelle. 2006. "STOP THE PORTS SELLOUT." *Michelle Malkin,* Feb. 16. At http://michellemalkin.com/2006/02/16/stop-the-port-sellout/.

Mallalieu, Huon. 1978. "Nostalgia for Desert Scenes Parallels British Love of Landscapes." *Times* (London), Oct. 30.

Mangieri, Tina. 2008. "African Cloth, Export Production, and Secondhand Clothing in Kenya." In *Moving Frontier: The Changing Geography of Production in Labour Intensive Industries,* edited by Lois Labrianidis, 301–18. London: Ashgate.

Marcuse, Herbert. 1955. *Eros and Civilization: A Philosophical Inquiry into Freud.* Boston: Beacon Press.

———. 1964. *One Dimensional Man: Studies in the Ideology of Advanced Industrial Society.* Boston: Beacon Press.

Marlowe, John. 1966. "Oil Riches Bring Worry as Well as Welfare." *Times* (London), Dec. 30.

Marston, Sallie, John Paul Jones III, and Keith Woodward. 2005. "Human Geography without Scale." *Transactions of the Institute of British Geographers* 30, no. 4: 416–32.

Martin, Paul. 1977. "Saudi Arabia: Oil Is Mightier Than the Sword in the Modern Arab World." *Times* (London), Feb. 14.

Marx, Karl. [1939] 1973. *Grundrisse: Foundations of the Critique of Political Economy.* New York: Random House.

Massey, Doreen B. 2005. *For Space.* London: Sage.

Maull, Hanns. 1975. *Oil and Influence: The Oil Weapon Examined.* London: International Institute for Strategic Studies.

Mauss, Marcel. [1925] 1990. *The Gift: The Form and Reason for Exchange in Archaic Societies.* Translated by W. D. Halls. New York: Norton.

McClintock, Anne. 1995. *Imperial Leather: Race, Gender, and Sexuality in the Colonial Contest.* New York: Routledge.

McConnell, Fiona, Terri Moreau, and Jason Dittmer. 2012. "Mimicking State Diplomacy: The Legitimizing Strategies of Unofficial Diplomacies." *Geoforum* 43, no. 4: 804–14.

McDowell, Linda. 1997. *Capital Culture: Gender at Work in the City.* Oxford: Blackwell.

———. 2001. "Men, Management, and Multiple Masculinities in Organisations." *Geoforum* 32, no. 4: 181–98.

McFarlane, Colin. 2010. "The Comparative City: Knowledge, Learning, Urbanism." *International Journal of Urban and Regional Research* 34, no. 4: 725–42.

McRobbie, Angela. 2002. "From Hollaway to Hollywood: Happiness at Work in the New Cultural Economy." In *Cultural Economy: Cultural Analysis and Commercial Life,* edited by Paul du Gay and Michael Pryke, 97–114. London: Sage.

Mernissi, Fatima. 1987. *Beyond the Veil: Male–Female Dynamics in Modern Muslim Society.* Bloomington: Indiana Univ. Press.

Middle East Economic Digest. 2006. "The Mall the Merrier: The UAE's Real Estate Boom Continues to Feed Consumer Appetite." Apr. 7.

Miller, Daniel. 1998. *A Theory of Shopping.* Ithaca, NY: Cornell Univ. Press.

Mills, Amy. 2006. "Boundaries of the Nation in the Space of the Urban: Landscape and Social Memory in Istanbul." *Cultural Geographies* 13, no. 3: 367–94.

Mitchell, Don. 1995. "There's No Such Thing as Culture: Towards a Reconceptualization of the Idea of Culture in Geography." *Transactions of the Institute of British Geographers* 20:102–16.

———. 1996. *The Lie of the Land: Migrant Workers and the California Landscape.* Minneapolis: Univ. of Minnesota Press.

———. 2000. *Cultural Geography: A Critical Introduction.* Malden, MA: Blackwell.

Mitchell, Timothy. 1988. *Colonising Egypt.* Cambridge: Cambridge Univ. Press.

———. 2002a. "McJihad: Islam in the US Global Order." *Social Text* 20, no. 4: 1–18.

———. 2002b. *Rule of Experts: Egypt, Techno-politics, Modernity.* Berkeley: Univ. of California Press.

———. 2005. "The Work of Economics: How a Discipline Makes Its World." *European Journal of Sociology* 46, no. 2: 297–320.

———. 2007. "The Properties of Markets." In *Do Economists Make Markets?* edited by Donald A. MacKenzie, Fabian Muniesa, and Lucia Siu, 244–75. Princeton, NJ: Princeton Univ. Press.

———. 2010. "The Resources of Economics: Making the 1973 Oil Crisis." *Journal of Cultural Economy* 3, no. 2: 189–204.

Molotosky, Irvin. 1999. "Olympics Corruption Investigated." *New York Times,* Oct. 15.

Montague, James. 2005. "From Dawn 'til Dusk." *Time Out Dubai,* Sept. 29.

Moors, Annelies. 2003. "Migrant Domestic Workers: Debating Transnationalism, Identity Politics, and Family Relations: A Review Essay." *Comparative Studies in Society and History* 45, no. 3: 386–94.

Morison, Ian. 1972. "Curing a Financial Xenophobia." *Times* (London), Feb. 25.

Morris, Jan. 1959. "The Sheikh of Araby Rides a Cadillac." *New York Times,* Aug. 16.

Moser, Sarah. 2012. "Circulating Visions of 'High Islam': The Adoption of Fantasy Middle Eastern Architecture in Constructing Malaysian National Identity." *Urban Studies* 49, no. 13: 2913–35.

Mountz, Alison. 2004. "Embodying the Nation-State: Canada's Response to Human Smuggling." *Political Geography* 23, no. 3: 323–45.

Nayak, Meghana V., and Christopher Malone. 2009. "American Orientalism and American Exceptionalism: A Critical Rethinking of US Hegemony." *International Studies Review* 11, no. 2: 253–76.

Negus, Keith. 2002. "Identities and Industries: The Cultural Formation of Aesthetic Economies." In *Cultural Economy: Cultural Analysis and Commercial Life,* edited by Pauk Du Gay and Michael Pryke, 115–31. London: Sage.

Nevarez, Leonard. 2003. *New Money, Nice Town: How Capital Works in the New Urban Economy.* New York: Routledge.

New York Times. 1961. "Storm over the Arab World: Aspects of Kuwait." July 9.

———. 1964. "Saudis Preparing Projects to Remake Face of the Nation." Jan. 10.

Nicley, Erinn P. 2009. "Placing Blame or Blaming Place? Embodiment, Place, and Materiality in Critical Geopolitics." *Political Geography* 28, no. 1: 19–22.

Al Nowais, Shireena. 2005. "Officials Differ over Ramadan Rules." *Gulf News,* Oct. 30.

Olson, Parmy. 2007. "Dubai's Vegas Game Plan." *Forbes,* Aug. 22.

Al-Omari, Ahmed. 2014. "Alcohol Ban to Stay." *Gulf Daily News,* July 15.

Al-Omari, Jehad. 2003. *The Arab Way: How to Work More Effectively with Arab Cultures*. Oxford: How to Books.

Osella, Caroline, and Filippo Osella. 2012. "Migration, Networks, and Connectedness across the Indian Ocean." In *Migrant Labor in the Persian Gulf*, edited by Mehran Kamrava and Zahra Babar, 105–36. New York: Columbia Univ. Press.

Osella, Filippo, and Caroline Osella. 2009. "Muslim Entrepreneurs in Public Life between India and the Gulf: Making Good and Doing Good." *Journal of the Royal Anthropological Institute* 15 Supplement no. 1: S202–S221.

Ottoway, David. 1982. "The Eagles of the Gulf Have Crashed." *Washington Post*, Nov. 24.

O'Tuathail, Gearoid. 1996. *Critical Geopolitics: The Politics of Writing Global Space*. Minneapolis: Univ. of Minnesota Press.

Paasi, Anssi. 1986. "The Institutionalization of Regions: A Theoretical Framework for Understanding the Emergence of Regions and the Constitution of Regional Identity." *Fennia: International Journal of Geography* 164, no. 1: 105–46.

———. 2002. "Bounded Spaces in the Mobile World: Deconstructing 'Regional Identity.'" *Tijdschrift voor Economische en Sociale Geografie* 93, no. 2: 137–48.

Pace, Eric. 1976a. "A New Middle East Boom." *New York Times*, Apr. 25.

———. 1976b. "Saudis Having Second Thoughts about Their Oil-Boom Growth." *New York Times*, Apr. 22.

Pain, Rachel. 2009. "Globalized Fear? Towards an Emotional Geopolitics." *Progress in Human Geography* 33, no. 4: 466–86.

Peck, Jamie. 2002. "Political Economies of Scale: Fast Policy, Interscalar Relations, and Neoliberal Workfare." *Economic Geography* 78, no. 3: 331–60.

Peck, Jamie, and Adam Tickell. 2002. "Neoliberalizing Space." *Antipode* 34, no. 3: 380–405.

Peel, Michael, and Camilla Hall. 2012. "Bid to Address National Malaise." *Financial Times*, Apr. 16.

Penberthy, David. 2010. "No Level Playing Field in Qatar's 2022 World Cup." *The Punch*, Dec. 3.

Pike, Andy, ed. 2011. *Brands and Branding Geographies*. Northampton, MA: Edward Elgar.

Pollard, Jane, Cheryl McEwen, and Alex Hughes, eds. 2011. *Postcolonial Economies*. London: Zed Books.

Pollard, Jane, and Michael Samers. 2011. "Governing Islamic Finance: Territory, Agency, and the Making of Cosmopolitan Financial Geographies." *Annals of the Association of American Geographers* 103, no. 3: 710–26.

Poon, Jessie P. 1997. "The Cosmopolitanization of Trade Regions: Global Trends and Implications, 1965–1990." *Economic Geography* 73, no. 4: 390–404.

Porter, Michael E. 1998. "Clusters and the New Economics of Competition." *Harvard Business Review*, Nov.–Dec., 77–90.

Prahalad, C. K. 2005. *The Fortune at the Bottom of the Pyramid: Eradicating Poverty through Profits: Enabling Dignity and Choice through Markets.* Upper Saddle River, NJ: Wharton School Publications.

Pratt, Andy C., and Paul Jeffcutt. 2009. *Creativity, Innovation, and the Cultural Economy.* London: Routledge.

Prest, Michael. 1978. "The Special Properties That Make London so Much More Attractive Than Beirut." *Times* (London), May 8.

Pryke, Michael, and Roger Lee. 1995. "Place Your Bets: Towards an Understanding of Globalisation, Socio-financial Engineering, and Competition within a Financial Centre." *Urban Studies* 32, no. 2: 329–44.

Putnam, John. 1975. "The Arab World, Inc.: Who Are Those Oil-Rich Arabs, and What Are They Doing with All That Money?" *National Geographic*, Oct., 494–533.

Al-Qasimi, Sheikh Sultan bin Mohamed. 1988. Foreword to *The Gulf Cooperation Council: Record and Analysis*, by Rouhollah K. Ramazani and Joseph A. Kechichian, ix–x. Charlottesville, VA: Univ. of Virginia Press.

Rahman, Saifur. 2005a. "Ramadan Retail Sales Top Dh1b." *Gulf News*, Nov. 2.

———. 2005b. "Reduced Timings Cost UAE Dear." *Gulf News*, Oct. 14.

Ramazani, Rouhollah K., and Joseph A. Kechichian. 1988. *The Gulf Cooperation Council: Record and Analysis.* Charlottesville: Univ. of Virginia Press.

Rendel, A. M. 1969. "Defense Force Problems Solved?" *Times* (London), June 10.

Resnick, Stephen A., and Richard D. Wolff. 1987. *Knowledge and Class: A Marxian Critique of Political Economy.* Chicago: Univ. of Chicago Press.

Reuters. 2009. "UAE Withdrew from Monetary Union for 'Fundamental Reasons.'" *Arabian Business*, Nov. 23.

———. 2010. "Soccer Newspaper Reaction to World Cup Decision." Dec. 3.

Richards, Alan, and John Waterbury. 1990. *A Political Economy of the Middle East: State, Class, and Economic Development.* Boulder, CO: Westview Press.

Roberts, Susan, Anna Secor, and Matthew Sparke. 2003. "Neoliberal Geopolitics." *Antipode* 35, no. 5: 886–97.

Rodenbeck, Max. 2002. "Time Travellers." In "Survey of the Gulf," special section, *Economist*, Mar. 21.

———. 2005. "Unloved in Arabia." *New York Review of Books*, Oct. 21.

Roeber, Joe. 1971. "Building a Future on Oil and Money." *Times* (London), Feb. 25.

Rose, Charlie. 2003. Interview with Thomas Friedman. *Charlie Rose*, PBS, May 29.

Rose, Gillian. 1993. *Feminism and Geography: The Limits of Geographical Knowledge*. Minneapolis: Univ. of Minnesota Press.

Rose, Mitch. 2006. "Gathering 'Dreams of Presence': A Project for the Cultural Landscape." *Environment & Planning D: Society & Space* 24, no. 4: 537–54.

Rostow, Walter W. 1960. *The Stages of Economic Growth: A Non-Communist Manifesto*. Cambridge: Cambridge Univ. Press.

Rothman, Hal. 2002. *Neon Metropolis: How Las Vegas Started the Twenty-First Century*. New York: Routledge.

Rouis, Mustapha, and Steven R. Tabor. 2012. *Regional Economic Integration in the Middle East and North Africa: Beyond Trade Reform*. Washington, DC: World Bank.

Roy, Ananya, and Aihwa Ong. 2011. *Worlding Cities: Asian Experiments and the Art of Being Global*. New York: Wiley.

Said, Edward W. 1993. *Culture and Imperialism*. New York: Vintage Books.

———. 1994. *Orientalism*. Rev. ed. New York: Vintage Books.

———. 1997. *Covering Islam: How the Media and the Experts Determine How We See the Rest of the World*. Rev. ed. New York: Vintage Books.

Sayer, Andrew. 2005. *The Moral Significance of Class*. Cambridge: Cambridge Univ. Press.

Schein, Richard. 1997. "The Place of Landscape: A Conceptual Framework for Interpreting an American Scene." *Annals of the Association of American Geographers* 87, no. 4: 660–80.

Schmidt, Dana Adams. 1959. "Saudis Struggle with Modern Era: They Fear Ridicule of Their Efforts to Adapt Ancient Society to 20th Century." *New York Times*, Dec. 30.

———. 1968. "Oil Revenue Spurs Modernization in Saudi Arabia." *New York Times*, Mar. 13.

Scott, Allen John. 2000. *The Cultural Economy of Cities: Essays on the Geography of Image-Producing Industries.* London: Sage.

Secor, Anna. 2007. "Between Longing and Despair: State, Space, and Subjectivity in Turkey." *Environment & Planning D: Society & Space* 25, no. 1: 33–52.

Semmerling, Tim Jon. 2006. *"Evil" Arabs in American Popular Film: Orientalist Fear.* Austin: Univ. of Texas Press.

Shaheen, Jack G. 2001. *Reel Bad Arabs: How Hollywood Vilifies a People.* New York: Olive Branch Press.

Sharabi, Hisham. 1990. "The Scholarly Point of View: Politics, Perspective, and Paradigm." In *Theory, Politics, and the Arab World,* edited by Hisham Sharabi, 1–51. New York: Routledge.

Sharp, Joanne P. 1996. "Hegemony, Popular Culture, and Geopolitics: The *Reader's Digest* and the Construction of Danger." *Political Geography* 15, nos. 6–7: 557–70.

———. 2000. *Condensing the Cold War:* Reader's Digest *and American Identity.* Minneapolis: Univ. of Minnesota Press.

Al Shayji, Abdullah. 2008a. "The False Malaise of Kuwaiti Politics." *Gulf News,* Feb. 25.

———. 2008b. "Not Much Has Changed." *Gulf News,* May 26.

Shechter, Relli. 2009. "From *Effendi* to *Infitāhī*? Consumerism and Its Malcontents in the Emergence of Egyptian Market Society." *British Journal of Middle Eastern Studies* 36, no. 1: 21–35.

Sidaway, James Derrick. 2009. "Shadows on the Path: Negotiating Geopolitics on an Urban Section of Britain's South West Coast Path." *Environment and Planning D: Society and Space* 27, no. 6: 1091–116.

Sidaway, James Derrick, and Michael Pryke. 2000. "The Strange Geographies of 'Emerging Markets.'" *Transactions of the Institute of British Geographers* 25, no. 2: 187–201.

Silvey, Rachel. 2004. "Transnational Domestication: Indonesian Domestic Workers in Saudi Arabia." *Political Geography* 23, no. 3: 245–64.

Simmel, Georg. 1997. *Simmel on Culture: Selected Writings.* London: Sage.

Sklair, Leslie. 2001. *The Transnational Capitalist Class.* Oxford: Blackwell.

Smith, Benjamin. 2010. "Scared by, of, in, and for Dubai." *Social & Cultural Geography* 11, no. 3: 263–83.

———. 2011. "Engineering New Geographies with the Burj Dubai." In *Engineering Earth,* edited by Stan D. Brunn, 955–66. Dordrecht, Netherlands: Springer.

Smith, Neil. 2008. *Uneven Development: Nature, Capital, and the Production of Space*. Athens: Univ. of Georgia Press.

Smylitopoulos, Christina. 2008. "Rewritten and Reused: Imaging the Nabob through 'Upstart Iconography.'" *Eighteenth-Century Life* 32, no. 2: 39–59.

Sorkin, Andrew Ross. 2009. "A Financial Mirage in the Desert." *New York Times*, Oct. 9.

Spencer, Richard. 2009. "Is This Bye-Bye Dubai?" *Telegraph*, Nov. 27.

Spivak, Gayatri Chakravorty. 1996. *The Spivak Reader: Selected Works of Gayatri Chakravorty Spivak*. New York: Routledge.

Sultan, Atef. 1980. "Biggest Donors to the Third World." *Times* (London), Mar. 11.

Sulzberger, C. L. 1946. "US Oil Towns Dot Saudi Arabian Soil." *New York Times*, Nov. 28.

Sunlight Foundation. 2014. *Foreign Influence Explorer: 2013 Lobbying Totals*. Washington, DC: Sunlight Foundation. At http://foreign.influenceexplorer.com/lobby-location2013.

Al Theeb, Alia. 2005. "Police Blame Sharp Rise in Crashes on Reckless Driving during Ramadan." *Gulf News*, Oct. 10.

Thomas, Landon, Jr. 2008. "Boom Times Take Root in Dubai." *New York Times*, July 18.

Thrift, Nigel J. 2001. "'It's the Romance, Not the Finance, That Makes the Business Worth Pursuing': Disclosing a New Market Culture." *Economy and Society* 30, no. 4: 412–32.

———. 2005. "But Malice Aforethought: Cities and the Natural History of Hatred." *Transactions of the Institute of British Geographers* 30, no. 1: 133–50.

———. 2011. "Lifeworld Inc. and What to Do about It." *Environment and Planning D: Society and Space* 29, no. 1: 5–26.

Time. 1952. "Dry Desert." Dec. 22.

———. 1965. "Oil, Oil Everywhere, but Not a Drop to Drink." Jan. 22.

Times (London). 1955. "Oil Exploration Spreads across Arabia." June 29.

———. 1958. "Riches Changing Saudi Life." May 13.

———. 1959a. "Oil Riches Smooth Troubled Waters of Kuwait." June 6.

———. 1959b. "Small States in Isolation." Feb. 26.

———. 1961. "Will Kuwait Garden Be Lovely Long?" May 18.

———. 1964. "A Wilderness without Charm." June 29.

———. 1965a. "Room for Reason" (editorial). July 14.

———. 1965b. "Smoothing the Flow of Oil." Oct. 13.

————. 1971a. "Consolidation of a Conservative State among Its Radical Neighbors." Nov. 29.

————. 1971b. "A Small Country Moulded by a Hard-Headed, Individual, and Adaptable People." Feb. 25.

————. 1974. "Bahrain: Pioneer's Great Leap Forward." Jan. 28.

————. 1977. "Focus on the Emirates: Banking." June 21.

————. 1978. "Success Based on Foreign Links." Oct. 30.

————. 1979. "The Voice of the Saudi Past" (editorial). Nov. 29.

————. 1980. "Saudi Arabia." Dec. 9.

Trofimov, Yaroslav. 2010. "Upon Sober Reflection, Bahrain Reconsiders the Wages of Sin: Island Reliant upon Debauched Visits from Thirsty Saudis Looks to Clean Up." *Wall Street Journal*, June 9.

Tsing, Anna Lowenhaupt. 2001. "Inside the Economy of Appearances." In *Globalization*, edited by Arjun Appadurai, 155–88. Durham, NC: Duke Univ. Press.

Ulrichsen, Kristian. 2011. *Insecure Gulf: The End of Certainty and the Transition to the Post-oil Era*. London: Hurst.

United Arab Emirates (UAE) Ministry of Labor. 2008. *Instructions for Foreign Laborers*. Abu Dhabi: UAE Ministry of Labor.

United Nations Development Program. 2002. *Arab Human Development Report 2002: Creating Opportunities for Future Generations*. New York: United Nations Publications.

————. 2003. *Arab Human Development Report 2003: Building a Knowledge Society*. New York: United Nations Publications.

————. 2004. *Arab Human Devleopment Report 2004: Freedom and Good Governance*. New York: United Nations Publications.

————. 2005. *Arab Human Development Report 2005: Empowerment of Arab Women*. New York: United Nations Publications.

VandeHei, Jim, and Jonathan Weisman. 2006. "Republicans Split with Bush on Ports: White House Vows to Brief Lawmakers on Deal with Firm Run by Arab State." *Washington Post*, Feb. 23.

Veblen, Thorstein. [1899] 1994. *The Theory of the Leisure Class*. New York: Penguin Books.

Verma, Sonia. 2008. "First Came a Boom, Then Fireworks, but Is Dubai's Property Market in Trouble?" *Times* (London), Nov. 24.

Vickery, Tim. 2012. "Beer 'Must Be Sold' at Brazil World Cup, Says FIFA." *BBC News*, Jan. 19. At http://www.bbc.co.uk/news/world-latin-america-16624823.

Vinodrai, Tara. 2006. "Reproducing Toronto's Design Ecology: Career Paths, Intermediaries, and Local Labor Markets." *Economic Geography* 82, no. 3: 237–63.

Virilio, Paul. 2002. *Ground Zero.* New York: Verso.

Vitalis, Robert. 2007. *America's Kingdom: Mythmaking on the Saudi Oil Frontier.* Stanford, CA: Stanford Univ. Press.

Voyer, Marc. 2009. "Top Ten: Sin Cities." *AskMen*, Aug. 13. At http://www.askmen.com/top_10/travel/top-10-sin-cities.html.

Wall, Michael. 1970. "A Jump of Centuries: A Survey of the Arabian Peninsula." *Economist*, June 6.

Wall Street Journal. 2006. "Ports of Politics: How to Sound Like a Hawk without Being One" (editorial). Feb. 22.

Weber, Max. 1930. *The Protestant Ethic and the Spirit of Capitalism.* Translated by Talcott Parsons. London: Allen and Unwin.

Westhall, Slyvia, and Mirna Sleiman. 2012. "Rich but Backward: Politics, Oil Poison Kuwait Economy." Reuters, Nov. 14.

Weston, Geoffrey. 1977. "Life without a Heart." *Times* (London), Oct. 21.

———. 1978. "Federation Makes Progress despite Internal Rivalries." *Times* (London), Apr. 24.

Whelan, John. 1980a. "Revenue Depends on Western Buyers, Eastern Workers." *Times* (London), May 9.

———. 1980b. "When the Well Runs Dry." *Times* (London), May 23.

Williams, Jeremy. 1998. *Don't They Know It's Friday? Cross-Cultural Considerations for Business and Life in the Gulf.* Dubai: Motivate.

Williams, Raymond. 1973. *The Country and the City.* New York: Oxford Univ. Press.

———. 1977. *Marxism and Literature.* Oxford: Oxford Univ. Press.

Wilson, Rodney. 1976. "Shortage of Manpower Hinders Progress." *Times* (London), Sept. 23.

———. 1977. "Designers Freed from Cost Shackles." *Times* (London), Oct. 21.

Wright, Melissa W. 2001. "Asian Spies, American Motors, and Speculations on the Space–Time of Value." *Environment and Planning A* 33, no. 12: 2175–88.

———. 2006. *Disposable Women and Other Myths of Global Capitalism.* New York: Routledge.

Wylie, John. 2005. "A Single Day's Walking: Narrating Self and Landscape on the South West Coast Path." *Transactions of the Institute of British Geographers* 30, no. 2: 234–47.

Wynn, L. L. 2007. *Pyramids & Nightclubs: A Travel Ethnography of Arab and Western Imaginations of Egypt, from King Tut and a Colony of Atlantis to Rumors of Sex Orgies, Urban Legends about a Marauding Prince, and Blonde Belly Dancers.* Austin: Univ. of Texas Press.

Young, David. 1978. "Services in the Arab World: The Serious Business of Briefing for Business." *Times* (London), May 8.

Zein-Elabdin, Eiman O. 2011. "Postcolonial Theory and Economics: Orthodox and Heterodox." In *Postcolonial Economies,* edited by Jane Pollard, Cheryl McEwen, and Alex Hughes, 37–62. London: Zed Books.

Žižek, Slavoj. 1999. *The Žižek Reader.* Edited by Elizabeth Wright and Edmund Wright. Malden, MA: Blackwell.

———. 2006. *The Parallax View.* Cambridge, MA: MIT Press.

Zukin, Sharon. 1991. *Landscapes of Power: From Detroit to Disney World.* Berkeley: Univ. of California Press.

Index

Benjamin Smith is an assistant professor of geography in the Department of Global and Sociocultural Studies at Florida International University, where he is also a member of the Middle East Studies Center. He earned an MA and PhD in geography from the University of Kentucky and a BSJ from Ohio University. He lives in Miami with his wife and daughter.